# Lecture Notes in Artificial Intelligence 4363

Edited by J. G. Carbonell and J. Siekmann

Subseries of Lecture Notes in Computer Science

## FoLLI Publications on Logic, Language and Information

Balder D. ten Cate  Henk W. Zeevat (Eds.)

# Logic, Language, and Computation

6th International Tbilisi Symposium
on Logic, Language, and Computation,
TbiLLC 2005
Batumi, Georgia, September 12-16, 2005
Revised Selected Papers

 Springer

Series Editors

Jaime G. Carbonell, Carnegie Mellon University, Pittsburgh, PA, USA
Jörg Siekmann, University of Saarland, Saarbrücken, Germany

Volume Editors

Balder D. ten Cate
Universiteit van Amsterdam
Instituut voor Informatica
Kruislaan 403, 1098 SJ Amsterdam, The Netherlands
E-mail: balder.tencate@uva.nl

Henk W. Zeevat
Universiteit van Amsterdam
Faculteit der Geesteswetenschappen, ILLC
Nieuwe Doelenstraat 15, 1012 CP Amsterdam, The Netherlands
E-mail: H.W.Zeevat@uva.nl

Library of Congress Control Number: Applied for

CR Subject Classification (1998): I.2, F.4.1

LNCS Sublibrary: SL 7 – Artificial Intelligence

ISSN        0302-9743
ISBN-10     3-540-75143-2 Springer Berlin Heidelberg New York
ISBN-13     978-3-540-75143-4 Springer Berlin Heidelberg New York

Springer is a part of Springer Science+Business Media

springer.com

© Springer-Verlag Berlin Heidelberg 2007
Printed in Germany

Typesetting: Camera-ready by author, data conversion by Scientific Publishing Services, Chennai, India
Printed on acid-free paper        SPIN: 12162659        06/3180        5 4 3 2 1 0

# Preface

This volume presents a selection of papers presented in Batumi on the occasion of the Sixth International Tbilisi Symposium on Logic, Language and Information, jointly organized by the Centre for Language, Logic and Speech (CLLS) in Tbilisi, the Georgian Academy of Sciences, and the Institute for Logic, Language and Computation (ILLC) in Amsterdam. The conference and the volume are representative of the aims of the organizing institutes: to promote the integrated study of logic, information and language. While the conference is open to contributions to any of the three fields, it hopes to promote cross-fertilization by achieving stronger awareness of developments in the other fields, and of work which embraces more than one field or belongs to the interface between fields.

The topics and brief characterizations of the contributions in this volume bear witness to these aims.

*Modal Logic.* Giovanna D'Agostino provides a survey of recent results on bisimulation quantifiers in modal logic, and their connection to uniform interpolation.

*Modal Logic.* Be Birchall makes new contributions to our algebraic understanding of modal logic. She considers a generalization of Boolean algebras with operators called distributive modal algebras, and characterizes simplicity and subdirect irreducibility for these algebras.

*Linguistics and Typology.* Rusudan Asatiani presents an overview of different devices for foregrounding in Georgian. The discussion includes patient foregrounding in the ergative tenses Aorist and Perfect and agent foregrounding in the present tense, active passive alternation, intonation, word order variation, syntactic devices and particles, the latter two in combination with intonation.

*Formal Pragmatics.* Maria Aloni applies ideas deriving from formal pragmatics and optimality theory to the analysis of expressions of ignorance, indifference or free choice like German *irgendein* or Italian *qualunque* and especially disjunction. The implicatures of ignorance and indifference result as implicatures in bidirectionally optimal context utterance pairs.

*Linguistics and Formal Pragmatics.* Kata Balogh investigates the use of *only* in Hungarian (*csak*). Hungarian offers the special problem that there is a syntactic focus position, which means exhaustivity. Since exhaustivity is normally taken to be the meaning of *only*, *csak* appears to be superfluous. The paper proposes a distinction between the exhaustivity operator, interpreting syntactically and intonationaly expressed focus and a different operator for *only*.

*Semantics and Pragmatics.* Peter Bosch motivates a proposal for a different conception of the way the lexicon helps to determine the propositional content of utterances. In this proposal, important aspects of the concepts are left unspecified, so that there is no proposition expressed by purely compositional means.

Interaction between the context and the conceptual system contributes the extra information that is needed to obtain a proposition. The proposal is contrasted with lexical semantics and the pragmatic enrichment view.

*Linguistic, Typology, Semantics and Pragmatics.*    Alastair Butler and Mark Donahue investigate the expression of argument dependencies in Tukang Besi (Indonesia). They show that a simple model based on the lambda calculus and the assumption that case markers and pragmatic markers determine abstraction variables is able to explain a wide range of properties of Tukang Besi, including restrictions on scope and placement of adverbials.

*Linguistics and Typology.*    George Chikoidze discusses the possibilities of explaining the verb actant relations in Georgian by means of the action chain metaphor due to Langacre. Georgian is compared in this respect with Russian and it is shown that where the expression of verb-actants in Russian is limited to case, in Georgian it involves a combination of two morphological markers, one appearing on the verb and one on the argument.

*Linguistics, Semantics and Learnability.*    Nina Gierasimczuk studies natural language quantifiers from a computational viewpoint. She considers the complexity of evaluating sentences containing such quantifiers, as well the learnability of their semantics.

*Linguistics and Typology.*    Michael Götze, Stavros Skopeteas, Torsten Roloff and Ruben Stoel present a database for the collection of cross-linguistic production data gathered by uniform data collection methods. The database has features both of a monolingual corpus and of a typological database and contains an extensive user interface supporting exploration of the data.

*Linguistics and Typology.*    Scott Grimm offers an optimality-theoretic explanation of case attraction in classical Greek. He uses a hierarchical analysis of case using a feature-based agentivity lattice loosely derived from Dowty's work on proto-agentivity. The analysis captures both the regularities and the frequencies that are found in classical Greek.

*Information and Artificial Intelligence.*    Frans Groen, Matthijs Spaan, Jelle Kok and Gregor Pavlin give an overview of techniques used in real-world multi-agent systems for information sharing, coordination and planning.

*Linguistics and Typology.*    Barbara Partee and Vladimir Borschev discuss the potential of a type-shifting approach to the Russian genitive of negation, in which the genitive NP is of type property and in which the case shift is an expression of argument demotion. They present arguments for and against this view and end up with expressing doubt at whether the approach is sufficiently fine-grained to capture all the semantic properties associated with the shift.

*Formal Pragmatics and Typology.*    Kjell Johan Sæbø addresses the question of why only factive propositional attitude verbs take indirect questions as complements and why there are restrictions on this possibility for the emotional attitudes. The solution proposed uses optimality theoretic pragmatics and Gricean informativity and is based on a careful analysis of the presuppositions of factive and superfactive verbs.

*Linguistics, Semantics and Typology.*    Reut Tsarfaty gives an analysis of the effect on the aspectual semantics of verbs of verbal binyanim that are traditionally analyzed as merely expressing changes in the thematic structure of the verb. She shows that the event calculus approach is able to describe both thematic structure and aspectual class in a unified way and can so directly express the aspectual effects of the binyanim.

*Logic and Linguistics.*    Jan van Eijck develops a natural logic for dealing with monotonicity inferences. It is then shown how this logic can be applied to the analysis of syllogistic reasoning. For this second topic, it is also necessary to address the doctrine of distributivity.

*Linguistics, Semantics and Typology.*    Henk Verkuyl applies the idea of Te Winkel of analyzing tense systems by a series of binary oppositions (instead of the Reichenbachian ternary system) to the Georgian tense system. In Georgian linguistics, the screeves (the verbal morphology) clearly involves much more than just tense and aspectual information and it is debated whether the category of tense applies at all to Georgian. The paper aims to give not only a description of Georgian tense but also tries to explain why it is what it is.

*Logic.*    Igor Zaslavsky studies the decidability of theories in Lukasiewicz's three-valued first-order logic. In particular, he shows how this can be reduced to the problem of decidability for classical (two-valued) first-order theories.

*Linguistics, Semantics and Typology.*    Hedde Zeijlstra develops a view of functional features in which they do not belong to universal grammar but are derived from semantic features and acquired in L1 learning. The argument is underpinned by an analysis of negative concord in which it can be seen as a special case of agreement and by a typological and historical argument: there are no $NEG^0$ markers without negative concord and changes in the syntactic status of NEG-markers can lead to negative concord.

We want to thank the anonymous reviewers for their help in the preparation of this volume, as well as Johan van Benthem, Paul Dekker, Anne Troelstra and Albert Visser for their support in obtaining funding for the conference.

July 2007                                                            Balder ten Cate
                                                                     Henk Zeevat

# Organization

*Sixth International Tbilisi Symposium on Language, Logic and Computation*
*Batumi, September 12–16, 2005*

## Organization

Centre for Language, Logic and Speech at the Tbilisi State University
Georgian Academy of Sciences,
Institute for Logic, Language and Computation of the University of Amsterdam

### Organizing Committee

Loredana Afanasiev
Rusudan Asatiani
Kata Balogh
Nick Bezhanishvili
Balder ten Cate
George Chikoidze
Paul Dekker (Chair)
Leo Esakia
David Gabelaia
Dick de Jongh
Kakhi Sakhltkhutsishvili
Henk Zeevat

### Local Organization

Rusudan Asatiani
Nani Chanishvili
George Chikoidze (Chair)
Marina Ivanishvili
Nino Javashvili
Theimuraz Khurodze
Liana Lortkipanidze
Khimuri Rukhaia
Nana Shengelaja

## Program Committee

Kata Balogh (University of Amsterdam)
Nick Bezhanishvili (University of Amsterdam)
Igor Boguslavsky (Russian Academy of Sciences)
Balder ten Cate (University of Amsterdam)
Nani Chanishvili (Tbilisi State University)
George Chikoidze (Georgian Academy of Sciences, Co-chair)
Paul Dekker (University of Amsterdam)
Leo Esakia (Tbilisi State University)
Claire Gardent (CNRS, Nancy)
Frans Groen (University of Amsterdam)
Wilfrid Hodges (Queen Mary, London)
Dick de Jongh (University of Amsterdam, Co-chair)
Manfred Krifka (Humboldt-Universität, Berlin)

Barbara Partee (University of Massachusetts)
Kakhi Sakhltkhutsishvili (Utrecht University)
Remko Scha (University of Amsterdam)
Carl Vogel (Trinity College Dublin)
Andrei Voronkov (University of Manchester)
Henk Zeevat (University of Amsterdam)
Ede Zimmermann (J.W. Goethe Universität Frankfurt)

## Tutorials

Caroline Fery (Universität Potsdam, *Language*)
Yde Venema (University of Amsterdam, *Logic*)
Aravind Joshi (University of Pennsylvania, *Computation*)

## Invited Lectures

Giovanna D'Agostino (University of Udine)
Matthias Baaz (University of Technology, Vienna)
Leo Esakia (Georgian Academy of Sciences)
Frans Groen (University of Amsterdam)
Robin Hirsch (Computer Science, University College London)
Igor Melcuk (Montreal University)
Barbara Partee and Vladimir Borschev (University of Massachusetts)
Henk Verkuyl (Utrecht University)
Michael Zakharyashev (Department of Computer Science, King's College)
Ede Zimmermann (J. W. Goethe Universität Frankfurt)

# Table of Contents

# Expressing Ignorance or Indifference
## Modal Implicatures in Bi-directional OT

Maria Aloni*

ILLC/University of Amsterdam
M.D.Aloni@uva.nl

**Abstract.** The article presents a formal analysis in the framework of bi-directional optimality theory of the free choice, ignorance and indifference implicatures conveyed by the use of indefinite expressions or disjunctions. Ignorance is expressed by standard means of epistemic logic. To express indifference we use Groenendijk and Stokhof's question meanings. To derive implicature, Grice's conversational maxims, and an additional principle expressing preferences for minimal models, are formulated as violable constraints used to select optimal candidates out of a set of alternative sentence-context pairs. The implicatures of an utterance of $\phi$ are then defined as the sentences which are entailed by any optimal context for $\phi$ (but not by $\phi$ itself). Entailment is defined in a version of update semantics where contextual updates are derived by competition among contexts. Free choice and other modal implicatures of disjunctions and indefinites will follow, but also scalar implicatures and exhaustification.

**Keywords:** free choice indefinites, disjunction, implicatures, bi-directional optimality theory.

## 1 Modal Implications of Indefinites and Disjunction

The article proposes a formal analysis of the ignorance, indifference and free choice effects conveyed by the use of disjunctions or indefinite pronouns. As an illustration consider the German prefixed indefiniteness marker *irgend* in examples (1) from Haspelmath, (2) from Kratzer and Shimoyama (2002) and (3) from Kratzer (2005):[1]

(1) a. *Irgend jemand* hat angerufen. (# – Wer war es?)
    'Someone (I don't know/care who) has called. (# – Who was it?)'

---

* Thanks to Katrin Schulz and Robert van Rooij for their inspiring work. I would also like to thank Paul Egre, Benjamin Spector, and the other participants to the PALMYR workshop for their insightful comments. Finally, I am also very grateful to two anonymous reviewers for their extremely valuable suggestions. This research has been financially supported by the NWO (Netherlands Organisation for Scientific Research).

[1] For ignorance effects see also, for example, the *to*-series in Russian (Haspelmath, 1997), for indifference and free choice readings the Italian *uno qualsiasi* (Chierchia, 2004).

B.D. ten Cate and H.W. Zeevat (Eds.): TbiLLC 2005, LNAI 4363, pp. 1–20, 2007.
© Springer-Verlag Berlin Heidelberg 2007

b. Jemand hat angerufen. (– Wer war es?)
'Someone has called. (– Who was it?)'

(2) Mary musste *irgendeinen* Mann heiraten.
'Mary had to marry irgend-one man'.
 a. There is some man Mary had to marry, the speaker doesn't know or care who it was.                                    (ignorance or indifference)
 b. Mary had to marry a man, any man was a permitted marriage option for her.                                                    (free choice)

(3) *Irgendein* Kind kann sprechen.
'Irgend-one child can talk'.

 a. Some particular child is able/allowed to talk - the speaker doesn't know or care about which one.              (ignorance or indifference)
 b. Some child or other is permitted to talk - any child is a permitted option. (free choice)

In (1), by using *irgend*, the speaker conveys that she doesn't know or care about who called. So it is odd for the hearer to ask who it was. Examples (2) and (3) are ambiguous between a specific reading (2-3a), conveying an ignorance or indifference meaning, and a non-specific reading (2-3b), conveying a free choice effect.

Disjunction gives rise to similar effects as shown in the following examples:

(4)  a. Ron is a movie star or a politician.          (ignorance or indifference)
     b. Have you ever kissed a Russian or an American?          (indifference)

(5) Ron must go to Tbilisi or Batumi.
     a. The speaker doesn't know which of the two.                    (ignorance)
     b. Ron may go to Tbilisi and may go to Batumi.               (free choice)

(6) Ron may go to Tbilisi or Batumi.
     a. The speaker doesn't know which of the two.                    (ignorance)
     b. Ron may go to Tbilisi and may go to Batumi.               (free choice)

Following Kratzer and Shimoyama (2002), Schulz (2004) and Alonso-Ovalle (2005), I assume that ignorance, indifference and free choice effects are not part of the meaning of the *irgend*-indefinites or disjunction, rather they have the status of an implicature. An indication that this is indeed so comes from the fact that these effects disappear in the scope of downward entailing contexts (cf. Gazdar 1979):

(7)  a. Ron isn't a movie star or a politician.
     b. Niemand musste *irgend jemand* einladen.
        'Noone had to invite anyone'

If modal effects were part of the meaning of the sentence, (7a) could be true in a situation where Ron is a movie star or a politician and the speaker knows or cares about which of the two. And (7b) 'could be true in a situation where people had to invite a particular person, hence weren't given any options. This is clearly not so.' [Kratzer and Shimoyama (2002), p.14]

Ignorance implicatures have received a lot of attention in the literature (e.g. Gazdar 1979, Sauerland 2004). Free choice effects have also been largely discussed (e.g. Kratzer and Shimoyama 2002 and Schulz 2004). None of these approaches, however, is completely satisfactory. The problematic case is the one illustrated in (3b) and (6b), involving the free choice interpretation of an indefinite or a disjunction in the scope of a possibility operator. While free choice inferences of necessity statements (examples (2b) and (5b)) can be easily explained, free choice inference of possibility statements always require *ad hoc* solutions (cf. Fox 2006 for a recent overview). One of the goals of this article is to explain the behavior of indefinites or disjunction under possibility by standard Gricean pragmatics without *ad hoc* moves. On my proposal, Gricean reasonings will be recasted in the formal framework of bidirectional optimality theory. The advantage of such formalization is that it gives us a perspicuous account, for each implicature, of the principles and the complexity of the reasoning required for its derivation. Grice's conversational maxims, and an additional principle expressing preferences for minimal models (cf. Schulz and van Rooij 2004, 2006), are formulated as violable constraints used to select optimal candidates out of a set of alternative sentence-context pairs. The implicatures of an utterance of $\phi$ are then defined as the sentences which are entailed by any optimal context for $\phi$ (but not by $\phi$ itself). Scalar implicatures and exhaustivity inferences (cf. Spector, 2003) will follow, but also the modal implicatures of indefinites and disjunctions including the somehow non standard indifference implicatures.

The rest of the article is structured as follows. The next section reviews a number of previous analyses and motivates the present account. Section 3 presents a BiOT analysis of implicatures. Section 4 shows how ignorance, indifference and free choice implicatures follow from such an analysis, but also scalar implicatures and exhaustification. Section 5 draws conclusions and describes some further lines of research.

## 2   Modal Implications as Conversational Implicatures

Conversational implicatures are inferences which arise from interplay of basic semantic content and general principles of social interaction. The key ideas about implicatures have been proposed by Grice who identified four of such principles.

(8) QUANTITY (i) Make your contribution as informative as is required for the current purposes of the exchange; (ii) Do not make your contribution more informative than is required.
QUALITY Make your contribution one that is true.
MANNER Be brief and orderly.
RELATION Be relevant.

In what follows we will see whether modal implications of indefinites and disjunctions, in particular when they occur under a possibility operator, can be derived from the assumption that speakers satisfy these maxims.

In the present analysis, ignorance and indifference implications follow from the following intuitive reasoning where the first QUANTITY submaxim plays a crucial role. For ease of exposition we restrict ourselves to the case of disjunction (existential sentences can be seen as generalized disjunctions).

(9)  a. The speaker S said 'A or B', rather than the more informative 'A'. Why?
    b. Suppose 'A' were relevant to the current purposes of the exchange, and S had the information that A. Then S should have said so.  [QUANTITY]
    c. Therefore,
        (i) Either 'A' is irrelevant;                                  (indifference)
        (ii) Or S has no evidence that 'A' holds.                      (ignorance)
    d. Parallel reasoning for 'B'.

Indifference readings of 'A or B' arise in situations where it doesn't matter which of the two disjuncts hold. In case it matters, ignorance readings arise. The speaker knows that 'A or B' is true but has no evidence that 'A' holds or 'B' holds. Therefore, both options are epistemically possible.

Free choice effects of necessity statements follow by the same reasoning under the assumption that the speaker is maximally informed about the specific modality involved (cf. Zimmermann 2001).

(10)  a. S said '$\Box$(A or B)', rather than the more informative '$\Box$A'. Why?
     b. Suppose '$\Box$A' were relevant to the current purposes of the exchange, and S had the information that $\Box$A. Then S should have said so.
     c. Therefore,
         (i) Either '$\Box$A' is irrelevant;                            (indifference)
         (ii) Or S has no evidence that '$\Box$A' holds.                (ignorance)
     d. Parallel reasoning for '$\Box$B'.

If both '$\Box$A' and '$\Box$B' are relevant, we can conclude that the speaker does not know $\Box$A and does not know $\Box$B. Under the assumption that the speaker is *maximally informed* we can conclude that '$\Box A$' and '$\Box B$' are both false. This fact, in combination with the original sentence, implies the free choice implication '$\Diamond A$ and $\Diamond B$'.

In what follows, I will formalize these Gricean reasonings in the framework of bi-directional optimality theory. The main motivation for assuming such a framework concerns the free choice implications of possibility statements as in the following example.

(11) John may go to Tbilisi or Batumi. $\Rightarrow$ John may go to Tbilisi and John may go to Batumi.

We would like to derive from $\Diamond(A \vee B)$ the conjunction $\Diamond A \wedge \Diamond B$. It is easy to see, however, that if we apply the reasoning illustrated above, assuming as alternatives to $\Diamond(A \vee B)$ the natural candidates $\Diamond A$ and $\Diamond B$, we do not obtain the desired free choice effects.

(12)  a.  $\Diamond(A \lor B)$                                                        (sentence)
 b.  $\Diamond A, \Diamond B$                                                     (alternatives)
 c.  $\# \neg \Diamond A, \neg \Diamond B$                                (quantity implicature)

A different, but less natural choice of alternatives would give us better results. Schulz (2004) and Aloni & van Rooij (2004), for example, assume the following compositionally defined set of syntactic alternatives for a given sentence:

(13)  a.  $\text{Alt}(A \lor B) = \{A, B\}$ closed under Boolean operators
 b.  $\text{Alt}(\Box \phi) = \{\Box \psi \mid \psi \in \text{Alt}(\phi)\}$
 c.  $\text{Alt}(\Diamond \phi) = \{\Box \psi \mid \psi \in \text{Alt}(\phi)\}$

The behavior of disjunction under possibility is then captured as follows, where, roughly, quantity implicatures are obtained by negating the alternatives of the sentence.

(14)  a.  $\Diamond(A \lor B)$                                                        (sentence)
 b.  $\Box A, \Box B, \Box \neg A, \Box \neg B$                          (alternatives)
 c.  $\Diamond \neg A, \Diamond \neg B, \Diamond A, \Diamond B$    (quantity implicature)

Note, however, that this analysis requires for $\Diamond$ an *ad hoc* move (necessity statements as alternatives, rather than possibility ones), which is hard to justify.

Another interesting option are the 'exhaustive' alternatives that Kratzer and Shimoyama (2002) seem to assume (see Chierchia, 2004 for an explicit proposal). Let us first have a look at the intuitive reasoning behind Kratzer and Shimoyama's account (henceforth K&S). Speaker said $\Diamond(A \lor B)$, rather than $\Diamond A$. Why? The reason cannot be that speaker had no evidence for $\Diamond A$ (this is exactly what we want to derive, that speaker *had* evidence for $\Diamond A$). As alternative reason, K&S propose what they call the *avoidance of a false exhaustivity inference*. If speaker had said $\Diamond A$, by exhaustivity inference I would have concluded $\neg \Diamond B$. If speaker had said $\Diamond B$, by exhaustivity inference I would have concluded $\neg \Diamond A$. Since speaker did not use the shorter alternative forms, I can conclude that speaker did hold both $A$ and $B$ as possible.

Chierchia (2004) in his formalization of K&S reasoning assumes as alternative for modal disjunctions the following 'exhaustive' sentences:

(15)  a.  $\text{Alt}(\Box(A \lor B)) = \{\Box A \land \neg \Box B, \Box B \land \neg \Box A\}$
 b.  $\text{Alt}(\Diamond(A \lor B)) = \{\Diamond A \land \neg \Diamond B, \Diamond B \land \neg \Diamond A\}$

As the following shows this choice of alternatives gives us the right results for the possibility case, where again implicatures are obtained by negating stronger alternatives:

(16)  a.  $\Diamond(A \lor B)$                                                        (sentence)
 b.  $\Diamond A \land \neg \Diamond B, \Diamond B \land \neg \Diamond A$    (alternatives)
 c.  $\Diamond A \rightarrow \Diamond B, \Diamond B \rightarrow \Diamond A$    (implicatures)
 d.  $\Diamond A$ and $\Diamond B$                                     (follows from a and c)

But first of all, these 'exhaustive' alternatives cannot be defined compositionally, so it remains somehow unexplained, where they originate. Secondly, this proposal does not generalize to the case of plain disjunction. If $\text{Alt}(A \vee B) = \{A \wedge \neg B, B \wedge \neg A\}$, then $A \vee B$ would implicate $A \wedge B$.[2] Furthermore, once we assume stronger 'exhaustive' alternatives which are then negated for Gricean reasons, it is hard to explain why 'exaclty 3' (3 and not 4 or 5,...) should not count as alternative to '3', or exclusive 'or' should not count as alternative to inclusive 'or'. The question that arises for this proposal is why exhaustive alternatives should play a role in the free choice case, but not in the scalar one.

My analysis of free choice implicature incorporates many important insights from Schulz (2004) and Aloni and van Rooij (2004). On the other hand, it can also be seen as a formalization of K&S anti-exhaustivity reasoning. It differs from K&S and Chierchia's accounts, however, in many essential aspects. For example, K&S and Chierchia's derivations only work for those examples where the indefinite or disjunction occurs under a modal. To account for free choice or ignorance implicatures of episodic sentences, like $A \vee B$, they need to assume the presence of a covert modal operator. My account, like Schulz (2004) and Aloni and van Rooij (2004), solves this problem by being explicit about the epistemic nature of the implicatures involved. Implicatures will have a modal nature (usually of the form 'speaker believes/doesn't believe...'), the original sentences do not need to.

The most important aspect of my proposal, however, is that contrary to all previous analyses of free choice implicatures, no notion of an alternative for a given sentence needs to be defined. Rather, as usual in optimality theory, each sentence will be taken to compete with every other sentence in the language. The set of *relevant* alternatives for a particular sentence will be automatically 'selected' by the constraints. In particular, for $\Diamond(A \vee B)$, the natural alternative forms $\Diamond A$ and $\Diamond B$ will play an essential role, and not the 'exhaustive' forms $\Diamond A \wedge \neg \Diamond B$ and $\Diamond B \wedge \neg \Diamond A$. The latter alternatives will be ruled out by my manner constraint that will also be responsible for ruling out 'exactly n' as alternative for 'n'. The reason why the alternatives $\Diamond A$ and $\Diamond B$ will be good enough to derive free choice reading is that, in my formalization, they automatically obtain an exhaustive interpretation. Exhaustive interpretations are indeed selected by the minimal model principle, unless they are ruled out (blocked) by the existence of a better alternative form. This is precisely what happens for $\Diamond(A \vee B)$. It doesn't

---

[2] Chierchia would partially disagree with this criticism. According to him, 'exhaustive' alternatives do also play a role in existential episodic sentences and are used to account for universal readings of free choice items in subtrigged constructions like *John kissed any women with a red cup.* His analysis, however, presupposes an essential difference between implicatures of existential sentences and disjunctions, the latter indeed never receives such universal interpretation. In my analysis instead implicatures of disjunction and existential sentences will be explained by the same mechanism. As for the universal meaning of subtrigged sentences, somewhere else (see Aloni, 2006) I have proposed an alternative account that also uses exhaustification, but not at the sentential level, to create sets of mutually exclusive propositions, but at the DP level to create maximal sets of individuals.

obtain an exhaustive interpretation (e.g. only A is possible) because such content could have been expressed by another form (e.g. $\Diamond A$) in a more perspicuous way. Here is the intuitive reasoning involved in the case of disjunction under possibility, according to my solution:

(17)  a.  Speaker said $\Diamond(A \vee B)$
     b.  Could it be that $A$ is not possible? No, otherwise the speaker would have used $\Diamond B$;
     c.  Could it be that $B$ is not possible? No, otherwise the speaker would have used $\Diamond A$.
     d.  Therefore, we can conclude that $A$ is possible and that $B$ is possible.

This kind of reasoning involving competition and blocking between different forms for different contents, has been perspicuously formalized in the framework of bi-directional optimality theory (henceforth BiOT).

## 3    Conversational Implicature in BiOT

In optimality theory (Prince and Smolensky, 1993/2004), ranked constraints are used to select a set of optimal candidates from a larger set of candidates. In the present analysis, the constraints are the Gricean maxims (appropriately formulated) and the minimal model principle. The competing candidates will be form-content pairs, but interpreted in a way that departs from previous work on OT semantics (Hendriks and de Hoop, 2001, Blutner, 2000): the form component will be identified with a sentence or better its logical form (determining its semantic interpretation); whereas the content part will be a context (determining the pragmatic interpretation of the sentence). Intuitively, if a sentence-context pair $(\phi, C)$ is optimal, a speaker in C can use $\phi$ with a minimal violation of the constraints.

Optimal pairs are defined by Blutner and Jäger's notion of weak optimality (see Blutner, 2000):

(18)  A candidate ⟨FORM, CONTENT⟩ is *weakly optimal* iff there are no other better *weakly optimal* pairs ⟨FORM′, CONTENT⟩ or ⟨FORM, CONTENT′⟩.

As standard in OT, a candidate $\alpha$ is at least as good as $\alpha'$ iff $\alpha$'s constraint violations are no more severe than $\alpha'$'s, where single violations of a higher ranked constraint override in severity multiple violations of lower ranked constraints. In the following subsections I give a precise definition of the competing candidates and of the adopted constraints.

### 3.1    Sentences and Contexts

Let $W$ be a set of worlds and $V$ a valuation function which assigns in each world a truth value to each propositional letter. Then a context $C$ is a pair $\langle Q, s \rangle$ where $Q$ is an issue (an equivalence relation over $W$) and $s$ is a state (a subset of $W$). States represent what the speaker believes. Issues represent what the speaker cares about (cf. Groenendijk, 1999). For example, a speaker in $\langle W, W^2 \rangle$ knows and cares about nothing, a speaker in $\langle W, \{(w, v) \in W^2 \mid w = v\} \rangle$ knows nothing and cares about everything, and finally a speaker in $\langle \{w\}, W^2 \rangle$ knows everything and cares about nothing. Intuitively, if two worlds are related by $Q$, then their differences are irrelevant to the speaker. So indifference wrt $p$ can be represented by an equivalence relation connecting $p$-worlds with not $p$-worlds.

We will say that a context $\langle Q, s \rangle$ entails $\heartsuit ? \phi$ to be read as 'I care whether $\phi$' iff $Q$ entails $? \phi$ according to the standard Groenendijk and Stokhof's notion of entailment between questions (see Groenendijk and Stokhof, 1984); and, as standard in update semantics, a context $\langle Q, s \rangle$ entails $\Diamond / \Box \phi$, to be read epistemically, iff $s$ is consistent with/entails $\phi$ (see Veltman, 1996). Here are more detailed definitions of these notions in terms of an update semantics. The language under consideration is that of modal propositional logic with the addition of the sentential operator '$\heartsuit ?$'.

**Definition 1.** [Updates]

- $C[p] = C'$ iff $s_{C'} = \{w \in s_C \mid V(p)(w) = 1\}$ & $Q_{C'} = Q_C$
- $C[\neg \phi] = C'$ iff $s_{C'} = s_C \setminus s_{C[\phi]}$ & $Q_{C'} = Q_C$
- $C[\phi \wedge \psi] = C[\phi][\psi]$
- $C[\Box \phi] = \begin{cases} C & \text{if } C[\phi] = C \\ \langle \emptyset, Q_C \rangle & \text{otherwise} \end{cases}$
- $C[\heartsuit ? \phi] = \begin{cases} C & \text{if } C[? \phi] = C \\ \langle \emptyset, Q_C \rangle & \text{otherwise} \end{cases}$

where $C[? \phi] = C'$ iff $s_{C'} = s_C$ & $Q_{C'} = \{(w, v) \in Q_C \mid \langle \{w\}, Q_C \rangle[\phi] = \langle \{w\}, Q_C \rangle$ iff $\langle \{v\}, Q_C \rangle[\phi] = \langle \{w\}, Q_C \rangle\}$

Disjunction, implication and possibility are defined as standard in terms of conjunctions, negation and necessity. Entailment is defined as follows.

**Definition 2.** [Entailment] $C \models \phi$ iff $C[\phi] = C$

All clauses in definition 1 are standard in update semantics, except that for $\heartsuit ? \phi$. Sentence $\heartsuit ? \phi$ is, like $\Box \phi$, a test returning either the original context (if updating with $? \phi$ does not bring anything new) or the absurd state (otherwise). An update with $? \phi$ can only modify the issue parameter. In most cases the output issue is the intersection between the input issue and the partition assigned to $? \phi$ by Groenendijk and Stokhof's standard theory of questions. So, for example, $[? \phi] = [? \neg \phi]$, and, therefore, $\heartsuit ? \phi$ iff $\heartsuit ? \neg \phi$. The only difference with the standard partition theory concerns the epistemic cases $? \Box / \Diamond \phi$. On the present account, $[? \phi] = [? \Box / \Diamond \phi]$. Therefore, we obtain that whenever $\heartsuit ? \phi$ holds $\heartsuit ? \Box / \Diamond \phi$ holds as well. Finally note that $\heartsuit ?$ can be iterated, but its iteration yields a tautology. $\heartsuit ? \heartsuit ? \phi$ is true in any context. The intuition is that disregarding whether you care or not whether $\phi$, you always care whether you care whether $\phi$.

## 3.2   Ranked Constraints

*Gricean Constraints* On the present account, Grice's maxims are formulated as properties of sentence-context pairs $\langle \phi, C \rangle$, and are ordered, according to their relative degree of violability:

(19) QUALITY, RELATION > MANNER > QUANTITY

QUANTITY formalizes only the first submaxim of Grice's original principle. The second submaxim is covered by RELATION.

**Definition 3.** [Gricean Constraints]

QUALITY: $C \models \Box \phi$
RELATION: $C \models \heartsuit? \phi$
MANNER: Avoid sentential operators (negations and modals).
QUANTITY: If $\phi \models \psi$ and $\psi \not\models \phi$, then $\phi \prec \psi$.

For a candidate $\langle \phi, C \rangle$, QUALITY holds iff the context $C$ entails the sentence $\phi$; RELATION holds iff $C$ entails $?\phi$.

MANNER penalizes negative or modal candidates. This formalization of Grice's maxim is somehow stipulative. The empirical motivation is to block unwelcome alternatives like (i) $A \wedge \neg B$ for $A$, (ii) $(A \vee B) \wedge \neg (A \wedge B)$ for $(A \vee B)$, and (iii) $\Diamond A \wedge \Diamond B$ for $\Diamond (A \vee B)$, without blocking, for example, $\neg (A \vee B)$ for $\neg A$ or $\neg B$.

QUANTITY expresses a preference for stronger sentences, where strength is defined in terms of entailment. It assigns gradient violations (cf. the Nuclear Harmony Constraint of Prince and Smolensky 1993/2004, section 2.2.): $\alpha \prec \beta$ means that $\alpha$ incurs a lesser violation than $\beta$.[3]

*The minimal model principle.* At the level of information processing, language comprehension can be thought as construction of an internal model for a piece of discourse. These models contain representations of the individuals mentioned in the discourse, their properties and relations. Two standard assumptions in AI are that (i) world knowledge plays a role in the constructions of these models, and (ii) these models are **minimal** in the following sense: they are constructed by making only those sentences true which have to be true (cf. closed-world reasoning largely used in planning, and McCarthy's predicate circumscription).

The idea that I am trying to formalize here is that implicatures are entailments of internal representations of possible speaker's states i.e. sets of these internal models. The minimality assumption (ii) will be used to explain the classical scalar implicatures and exhaustivity inferences (see Schulz and van Rooij 2004, 2006 for similar accounts)

(20) Ron is a movie star or a politician. $\Rightarrow$ not both        (scalar implicature)

(21) Q: Who signed the petition?  A: Ann $\Rightarrow$ nobody else   (exhaustification)

---

[3] This formulation has been suggested to me by an anonymous reviewer who is gratefully acknowledged.

Assumption (i) that world knowledge plays a role in the constructions of these internal states could be used as a starting point to explain the so called I-implicatures (or R-implicatures in Horn, 1984).

(22)  a. John had a drink. ⇒ John had an alcoholic drink.     (I-implicatures)
    b. John has a secretary. ⇒ John has a female secretary.
    c. John was able to solve the problem. ⇒ John solved the problem.

If language comprehension is obtained via construction of internal representations, it seems natural to assume that in processing these sentences people would more easily come up with models where a stereotypical interpretation obtains rather than a non-stereotypical one.

To formalize the minimality constraint, I will define an ordering $\leq_Q$ between worlds with respect to an issue $Q$ (cf. Schulz and van Rooij 2006):

**Definition 4.** [Minimal worlds] $v \leq_Q v'$ iff $\forall p$ s.t. $Q \models ?p : v \models p \Rightarrow v' \models p$

Minimal worlds are worlds which satisfy the least number of relevant atomic sentences. As an illustration, let us assume $A$ and $B$ as the unique two atoms under consideration. We are considering then only four worlds: $w_\emptyset, w_A, w_B, w_{AB}$, where each world is indexed with the atomic propositions holding in it. Suppose $A$ and $B$ are both relevant wrt $Q$. Then $\leq_Q$ would determine the following ordering:

$$w_\emptyset \leq_Q w_A, \ w_B \leq_Q w_{AB}$$

In terms of $\leq_Q$ I define now an ordering between states and contexts (note that here my definitions are different from those in Schulz and van Rooij 2006).

**Definition 5.**

1. $s \leq_Q s'$ iff $\forall v \in s : \exists v' \in s' : v \leq_Q v'$
2. $C \leq C'$ iff $Q_C = Q_{C'}$ & $s_C \leq_{Q_C} s_{C'}$
3. $C < C'$ iff $C \leq C'$ & $C' \not\leq C$

States are ordered wrt the relevant atoms they hold as possible. Again, assuming that $A$ and $B$ are the unique atoms under discussion and that they are both relevant with respect to $Q$, then $\leq_Q$ orders the possible states as follows, where $\{w_\emptyset\}$ is the minimal state, and any set containing $w_{AB}$ is maximal.

$$
\begin{array}{cccc}
\{w_\emptyset\} < \{w_A\} & < \{w_A, w_B\} & < \{w_{AB}\} \\
\{w_\emptyset, w_A\} & \{w_\emptyset, w_A, w_B\} & \{w_\emptyset, w_{AB}\} \\
\{w_B\} & & \cdots \\
\{w_\emptyset, w_B\} &
\end{array}
$$

Contexts with the same issue are ordered wrt the minimality of their states. Contexts with different issues are incomparable.

The minimal model principle expresses a preference for minimal contexts. Like quantity, it assigns gradient violations. If $C < C'$, then $C$ incurs a lesser violation than $C'$.

**Definition 6.** [Minimal model principle] If $C < C'$, then $C \prec C'$.

For reasons that will become clear, the minimal model principle is taken as the lowest constraint:

(23) QUALITY, RELATION > MANNER > QUANTITY > MINIMAL MODELS

To sum up, we have presented five constraints formalized as properties of sentence-context pairs. The Gricean constraints can be thought as speaker's constraints, in particular manner and quantity that determine an ordering between possible forms. The minimal model principle, instead, which compares alternative states is typically a hearer constraint. Interestingly the latter is taken to be the lowest principle. These constraints select for each sentence $\phi$ a set of optimal contexts. The implicatures of $\phi$ can then be defined as what must hold in all these optimal contexts.

*Implicatures.* Let $opt(\phi)$ be the set of contexts $C$ such that $(\phi, C)$ is optimal. The implicatures of $\phi$ are defined as follows.

**Definition 7.** [Implicatures] $\phi$ implicates $\psi$, $\phi \mathrel{|\!\approx} \psi$ iff $\forall C : C \in opt(\phi)$: $C \models \psi$ & $\phi \not\models \psi$

To my knowledge, the idea of defining implicatures in terms of entailment of contexts has been introduced by Schulz (2004), and then has been used in a number of papers by Schulz and van Rooij. It is reminiscent of treatments of presuppositions. For example, in the standard satisfaction theory, the presupposition of $\phi$ is defined as what is entailed in any context in which $\phi$ can be felicitously uttered. On the present account, however, the two issues of deriving implicatures from context and of determining the felicitous contexts for an utterance are treated as independent. The defended OT analysis only accounts for the former.

## 4    Applications

### 4.1    Exhaustivity Inferences

The first result we will present concerns the exhaustification of positive answers. Let $A$ and $B$ be different atomic sentences. Then we predict that $A$ implicates not $B$, if $B$ is relevant.

(24) $A \mathrel{|\!\approx} \heartsuit?B \rightarrow \neg B$

This result captures the obvious fact that exhaustivity implicatures depend on the question under discussion which determines what are the relevant alternatives. Consider the answer 'Anna signed the petition' as a reply to the following two questions. Only in the first case the answer receives an exhaustive interpretation.

(25) Q: Who signed the petition?  A: Anna $\Rightarrow$ not Bill
    Q': Did Ann sign the petition?  A: Yes $\not\Rightarrow$ not Bill

To illustrate how (24) obtains, let us assume again that $A$ and $B$ are the unique atoms under consideration, and so $w_\emptyset, w_A, w_B, w_{AB}$ the unique worlds. By $[w, w', ...]$, I will denote the state consisting of the worlds $w$, $w'$,....

If $B$ is relevant, then $[w_A]$ is the only optimal state for $A$. Any other stronger form true in $[w_A]$, notably $A \wedge \neg B$, is ruled out by manner. Any other state satisfying $A$ is ruled out either by MMP, which requires states to be minimal (e.g. $[w_A, w_{AB}]$); or by quantity, if there is a stronger optimal sentence holding in the state (e.g. $A \wedge B$ in $[w_{AB}]$).[4]

Consider now the case in which $B$ is irrelevant. In this case any state entailing $A$ is optimal for the sentence: state $[w_A]$, but also states $[w_A, w_{AB}]$, and $[w_{AB}]$. State $[w_A, w_{AB}]$ is optimal because being $B$ irrelevant it does not play a role in ordering the states for MMP. State $[w_{AB}]$ because it cannot be ruled out by the irrelevant $(A \wedge B)$. Therefore, in this case, no conclusion can be drawn about the truth value of $B$.

The previous discussion is illustrated by the following tableau. By $\mathbf{Q}_{(?\phi)?\psi}$ I denote the partition expressed by (the conjunction of $?\phi$ and) $?\psi$. As usual in OT, '$\Rightarrow$' indicates an optimal candidate, '!*' a crucial constraint violation.

| | | QUAL, REL | MAN | QUAN | MMP |
|---|---|---|---|---|---|
| | $A$ - $\langle \mathbf{Q}_{?B}, [w_A] \rangle$ | !* | | * | |
| | $A$ - $\langle \mathbf{Q}_{?A}, [w_B] \rangle$ | !* | | * | |
| $\Rightarrow$ | $A$ - $\langle \mathbf{Q}_{?A?B}, [w_A] \rangle$ | | | * | * |
| | $(A \wedge \neg B)$ - $\langle \mathbf{Q}_{?A?B}, [w_A] \rangle$ | | !* | | * |
| | $A$ - $\langle \mathbf{Q}_{?A?B}, [w_A, w_{AB}] \rangle$ | | | * | !*** |
| | $A$ - $\langle \mathbf{Q}_{?A?B}, [w_{AB}] \rangle$ | | | !* | *** |
| $\Rightarrow$ | $(A \wedge B)$ - $\langle \mathbf{Q}_{?A?B}, [w_{AB}] \rangle$ | | | | *** |
| $\Rightarrow$ | $A$ - $\langle \mathbf{Q}_{?A}, [w_A] \rangle$ | | | * | * |
| $\Rightarrow$ | $A$ - $(\mathbf{Q}_{?A}, [w_A, w_{AB}] \rangle$ | | | * | * |
| $\Rightarrow$ | $A$ - $\langle \mathbf{Q}_{?A}, [w_{AB}] \rangle$ | | | * | * |
| | $(A \wedge B)$ - $\langle \mathbf{Q}_{?A}, [w_{AB}] \rangle$ | !* | | | * |

We turn now to the case of a negative sentence $\neg A$. Let us just consider the case in which both $A$ and $B$ are relevant. Interestingly, no exhaustive implicature arise in this case.

(26) $\neg A \not\models_{?A?B} \Diamond B \wedge \Diamond \neg B$

Assuming that both $A$ and $B$ are relevant, the only optimal state for $\neg A$ is $[w_\emptyset, w_B]$. The alternative states $[w_B]$ and $[w_\emptyset]$ are blocked by the optimal forms $B$ and $\neg(A \vee B)$ respectively. The former form is preferred by manner, the latter by quantity.

---

[4] Sentence $A \wedge B$ does not violate manner, because it does not involve negation. Note, however, that this is not essential for the final result. If $A \wedge B$ had violated manner, $[w_{AB}]$ would have been ruled out for $A$ by MMP, rather than by quantity.

| | | QUAL, REL | MAN | QUAN | MMP |
|---|---|---|---|---|---|
| ⇒ | $\neg A$ - $\langle \mathbf{Q}_{?A?B}, [w_B, w_\emptyset]\rangle$ | | * | * | * |
| | $\neg A$ - $\langle \mathbf{Q}_{?A?B}, [w_\emptyset]\rangle$ | | * | !* | |
| ⇒ | $\neg(A \vee B)$ - $\langle \mathbf{Q}_{?A?B}, [w_\emptyset]\rangle$ | | * | | |
| | $\neg A$ - $\langle \mathbf{Q}_{?A?B}, [w_B]\rangle$ | | !* | * | * |
| ⇒ | $B$ - $\langle \mathbf{Q}_{?A?B}, [w_B]\rangle$ | | | * | * |

These predictions seem to be sustained by the facts. Compare the following two answers to question Q.

(27) Q. Who signed the petition?
    A. Maria ⇒ nobody else signed the petition
    B. Not John ⇒ I don't know about anybody else

The first positive answer receives an exhaustive interpretation, no relevant alternative individuals signed the petition. The negative answer does not have this implicature, as predicted by the present account. A proper analysis of the effect of negation on exhaustification requires, however, further empirical investigation.

Let us now consider the epistemic modal cases. Again we will consider only the interesting case in which both $A$ and $B$ are relevant. We start with $\Box A$.

(28) $\Box A \mathrel{\not\approx}_{?A?B} \neg\Box B$

Assuming that both $A$ and $B$ are relevant, the unique optimal state for $\Box A$ is $[w_A, w_{AB}]$. The alternative relevant states $[w_A]$ and $[w_{AB}]$ are blocked by the non modal (and therefore preferred by manner) optimal forms $A$ and $A \wedge B$ respectively. Thus, $\Box A$ implicates that $\neg\Box B$, but not that $\neg B$. This fact captures the intuition that adding 'I know' in an answer blocks an exhaustive interpretation.

(29) Q. Who signed the petition?
    C. I know that Maria signed ⇒ I don't know about anybody else

Let us now turn to the case of possibility. Assuming that both $A$ and $B$ are relevant, the unique optimal state for $\Diamond A$ is $[w_A, w_\emptyset]$. Indeed, the alternative state $[w_A]$ is blocked by the optimal form $A$, and any other state either does not satify the sentence (e.g. $[w_\emptyset]$) or contains $w_B$, and therefore will be ruled out by the MMP, if not by quantity. The optimal state $[w_A, w_\emptyset]$ entails that $A$ is not necessary, and that $B$ is not possible.

(30) $\Diamond A \mathrel{\not\approx}_{?A?B} \neg\Box A, \neg\Diamond B$

Note that $[w_A, w_\emptyset]$ is also optimal for $\neg B$. The two forms are incomparable by quantity, and violate manner in the same way. In this system they are predicted, correctly, to have the same implicatures.

The following tableau summarizes these results:

|  |  | QUAL, REL | MAN | QUAN | MMP |
|---|---|---|---|---|---|
| $\Rightarrow$ | $A - \langle \mathbf{Q}_{?A?B}, [w_A]\rangle$ |  |  | * | * |
|  | $\Box A - \langle \mathbf{Q}_{?A?B}, [w_A]\rangle$ |  | !* |  | * |
|  | $\Diamond A - \langle \mathbf{Q}_{?A?B}, [w_A]\rangle$ |  | !* | * | * |
| $\Rightarrow$ | $(A \wedge B) - \langle \mathbf{Q}_{?A?B}, [w_{AB}]\rangle$ |  |  |  | *** |
|  | $\Box A - \langle \mathbf{Q}_{?A?B}, [w_{AB}]\rangle$ |  | !* |  | *** |
|  | $\Diamond A - \langle \mathbf{Q}_{?A?B}, [w_{AB}]\rangle$ |  | !* | * | *** |
| $\Rightarrow$ | $\Box A - \langle \mathbf{Q}_{?A?B}, [w_A, w_{AB}]\rangle$ |  | * |  | *** |
|  | $\Diamond A - \langle \mathbf{Q}_{?A?B}, [w_A, w_{AB}]\rangle$ |  | * | !* | *** |
| $\Rightarrow$ | $\Diamond A - \langle \mathbf{Q}_{?A?B}, [w_\emptyset, w_A]\rangle$ |  | * | * | * |
|  | $\Diamond A - \langle \mathbf{Q}_{?A?B}, [w_\emptyset, w_A, w_B]\rangle$ |  | * | * | !** |

To summarize our predictions on exhaustification: if both $A$ and $B$ are relevant, $A$ implicates $\neg B$, $\Box A$ implicates $\neg \Box B$, and $\Diamond A$ implicates $\neg \Diamond B$. The latter result will play a crucial role in my explanation of the emergence of free choice inferences for $\Diamond(A \vee B)$, as we will see in the next subsection.

## 4.2   Modal and Scalar Implicatures of Disjunction

The BiOT analysis presented in the previous section makes the following predictions.

(31)   a. $\phi_1 \vee \phi_2 \not\approx \neg\Box\phi_i \vee \neg\heartsuit?\phi_i$ $\qquad\qquad\qquad\qquad \forall i \in \{1, 2\}$
    b. $\Box(\phi_1 \vee \phi_2) \not\approx \neg\Box\phi_i \vee \neg\heartsuit?\phi_i$
    c. $\Diamond(\phi_1 \vee \phi_2) \not\approx \neg\Box\phi_i \vee \neg\heartsuit?\phi_i$

A speaker using a (modal) disjunction implicates that for each disjunct $\phi_i$ either she doesn't know whether it is true or she doesn't care whether it is true.

Ignorance and free choice implicatures are obtained if we restrict competition to contexts in which the speaker cares about both disjuncts. In these cases, uses of (modal) disjunctions implicate that both disjuncts are epistemically possible.

(32)   a. $\phi_1 \vee \phi_2 \approx_{?\phi_1,?\phi_2} \Diamond\phi_1 \wedge \Diamond\phi_2$
    b. $\Box(\phi_1 \vee \phi_2) \approx_{?\Box\phi_1,?\Box\phi_2} \Diamond\phi_1 \wedge \Diamond\phi_2$
    c. $\Diamond(\phi_1 \vee \phi_2) \approx_{?\Diamond\phi_1,?\Diamond\phi_2} \Diamond\phi_1 \wedge \Diamond\phi_2$

Results (31b)-(32b) and (31c)-(32c) can be extended to non- epistemic modals $\Box'/\Diamond'$ under certain conditions that have been discussed by Zimmermann 2001, namely if we restrict competition to contexts in which the following principles hold: $\neg\Box\Box'\phi \to \neg\Box'\phi$ and $\neg\Box\Diamond'\phi \to \neg\Diamond'\phi$. Since existential statements can be seen as generalized disjunctions all these results extend to the case of indefinite expressions. In what follows we have a closer look at these results. We start with the ignorance and indifference implicatures of plain disjunctions.

*Plain disjunction.* Any context $C$ resulting optimal for $A \vee B$ according to the discussed ranked constraints, entails for each disjunct that either it is not believed to be true by the speaker or it is irrelevant (see (31a)).

We have three types of optimal contexts for $A \vee B$. In the first type, both disjuncts are relevant, $Q_C$ entails $?A$ and $?B$. The optimal state for the disjunction in this case is $[w_A, w_B]$. The stronger form $(A \vee B) \wedge \neg(A \wedge B)$ is ruled out by manner. The more informative states $[w_A]$, $[w_B]$ and $[w_{AB}]$ are blocked by quantity. The other states $[w_A, w_{AB}]$, $[w_B, w_{AB}]$ and $[w_A, w_B, w_{AB}]$ are ruled out by MMP. The optimal context entails that both disjuncts are epistemically possible.

(33) $A \vee B \mathrel{\approx\!\!\!\!\!\!\sim}_{?A?B} \Diamond A \wedge \Diamond B$ \hfill (ignorance)

But also that they are mutually exclusive.

(34) $A \vee B \mathrel{\approx\!\!\!\!\!\!\sim}_{?A?B} \neg(A \wedge B)$ \hfill (scalar implicature)

The ignorance implicature follows by quantity, the scalar implicature by MMP, as illustrated in the following tableau.

| | | QUAL, REL | MAN | QUAN | MMP |
|---|---|---|---|---|---|
| ⇒ | $A \vee B$ - $\langle Q_{?A?B}, [w_A, w_B]\rangle$ | | | ** | ** |
| | $(A \vee B) \wedge \neg(A \wedge B)$ - $\langle Q_{?A?B}, [w_A, w_B]\rangle$ | | !* | | ** |
| | $A \vee B$ - $\langle Q_{?A?B}, [w_A, w_{AB}]\rangle$ | | | ** | !*** |
| | $A \vee B$ - $\langle Q_{?A?B}, [w_A, w_B, w_{AB}]\rangle$ | | | ** | !*** |
| | $A \vee B$ - $\langle Q_{?A?B}, [w_A]\rangle$ | | !** | * | |
| ⇒ | $A$ - $\langle Q_{?A?B}, [w_A]\rangle$ | | * | * | |
| | $A \vee B$ - $\langle Q_{?A?B}, [w_{AB}]\rangle$ | | !** | *** | |
| ⇒ | $(A \wedge B)$ - $\langle Q_{?A?B}, [w_{AB}]\rangle$ | | | | *** |

The second type of optimal context for $A \vee B$ is one in which none of the disjuncts are relevant, but the disjunction is, $Q_C$ entails $?(A \vee B)$, but it does not entail $?A$ or $?B$. These contexts model the indifference reading, where it matters whether the disjunction is true, but the differences between the disjuncts are irrelevant.

(35) $A \vee B \mathrel{\approx\!\!\!\!\!\!\sim}_{?(A \vee B)} \neg\heartsuit?A \wedge \neg\heartsuit?B \wedge \heartsuit?(A \vee B)$ \hfill (indifference)

Note that in these contexts no conclusion can be drawn about the speaker's epistemic attitude towards the two disjuncts, beyond the fact that at least one of the two must be true. So no ignorance implicature arises in these cases. This is because QUANTITY does not play any role here. Since none of the stronger alternatives to the sentence are relevant in these contexts, stronger interpretation cannot be blocked. Scalar implicatures are blocked as well, because since the atoms $A$ and $B$ are irrelevant, all worlds are equally minimal in these contexts. This seems to be correct because like exhaustivity implicatures also scalar implicatures depend on the issue under discussion. Interestingly, as shown by (36), they do not arise on an indifference reading of disjunction.

(36) Q: Have you ever kissed a Russian or an American? A: Yes. $\not\Rightarrow$ not both

The following tableau illustrates these results. Note that none of the contexts in this tableau can compete with the contexts in the previous tableau with respect to MMP. This is because the two types of contexts have different issues thus they cannot be ordered by $\leq$. This means that the first candidate in the previous tableau is not ruled out by the following optimal contexts contrary to what is suggested by the number of *s in the MMP column.

| | QUAL | REL | MAN | QUAN | MMP |
|---|---|---|---|---|---|
| $\Rightarrow$  $A \vee B$ - $\langle \mathbf{Q}_{?(A \vee B)}, [w_A, w_B] \rangle$ | | | | ** | |
| $\Rightarrow$  $A \vee B$ - $\langle \mathbf{Q}_{?(A \vee B)}, [w_A, w_{AB}] \rangle$ | | | | ** | |
| $\Rightarrow$  $A \vee B$ - $\langle \mathbf{Q}_{?(A \vee B)}, [w_A, w_B, w_{AB}] \rangle$ | | | | ** | |
| $\Rightarrow$  $A \vee B$ - $\langle \mathbf{Q}_{?(A \vee B)}, [w_A] \rangle$ | | | | ** | |
| $A$ - $\langle \mathbf{Q}_{?(A \vee B)}, [w_A] \rangle$ | | !* | | * | |
| $\Rightarrow$  $A \vee B$ - $\langle \mathbf{Q}_{?(A \vee B)}, [w_{AB}] \rangle$ | | | | ** | |
| $(A \wedge B)$ - $\langle \mathbf{Q}_{?(A \vee B)}, [w_{AB}] \rangle$ | | !* | | | |

There is also a third option, in which only one of the disjuncts is relevant beside the disjunction itself, for example, if $Q_C$ entails $?(A \vee B)$ and $?A$, but it does not entail $?B$. In this case, the optimal state is $[w_B]$. Since $B$ is not relevant, this interpretation cannot be blocked by quantity and it is minimal by MMP.

| | QUAL | REL | MAN | QUAN | MMP |
|---|---|---|---|---|---|
| $\Rightarrow A \vee B$ - $\langle \mathbf{Q}_{?A?(A \vee B)}, [w_B] \rangle$ | | | | ** | |
| $B$ - $\langle \mathbf{Q}_{?A?(A \vee B)}, [w_B] \rangle$ | | !* | | * | |
| $A \vee B$ - $\langle \mathbf{Q}_{?A?(A \vee B)}, [w_A] \rangle$ | | | | !** | * |
| $\Rightarrow$   $A$ - $\langle \mathbf{Q}_{?A?(A \vee B)}, [w_A] \rangle$ | | | | * | * |
| $A \vee B$ - $\langle \mathbf{Q}_{?A?(A \vee B)}, [w_{AB}] \rangle$ | | | | ** | !* |
| $A \vee B$ - $\langle \mathbf{Q}_{?A?(A \vee B)}, [w_A, w_B] \rangle$ | | | | ** | !* |
| $A \vee B$ - $\langle \mathbf{Q}_{?A?(A \vee B)}, [w_A, w_{AB}] \rangle$ | | | | ** | !* |
| $A \vee B$ - $\langle \mathbf{Q}_{?A?(A \vee B)}, [w_A, w_B, w_{AB}] \rangle$ | | | | ** | !* |

Intuitions are not very sharp in this case. However, in support of this result consider a situation like the following. Suppose you are expecting Ann's call ($C \models \heartsuit?A$). Instead Bill calls ($C \models B$), about whom you don't care ($C \not\models \heartsuit?B$). We correctly predict then that in this situation you can say (37) signaling that you don't care of that particular person who called, namely Bill, that he called.

(37) Irgend jemand hat angerufen.                    'Irgend-one has called'

*Epistemic Modals* If both $A$ and $B$ are relevant, our analysis predicts the following implicatures for disjunction in the scope of an epistemic modal.

(38)  a. $\Box(A \vee B) \not\approx_{?\Box A, ?\Box B} \Diamond A \wedge \Diamond B$
      b. $\Diamond(A \vee B) \not\approx_{?\Diamond A, ?\Diamond B} \Diamond A \wedge \Diamond B$

Let us start with illustrating the case of necessity. If both $A$ and $B$ are relevant, then $[w_A, w_B, w_{AB}]$ is the unique optimal state for $\Box(A \vee B)$, which then implicates $\Diamond A$ and $\Diamond B$ (and $\neg\Box(A \wedge B)$).[5] Any other subset of this state is blocked either by an optimal non-modal form preferred by manner (e.g. $[w_A, w_B]$ by $(A \vee B)$), or by an optimal stronger modal form preferred by quantity (e.g. $[w_A, w_{AB}]$ by $\Box A$).

Let us now turn to the more interesting case of disjunction under possibility. If both $A$ and $B$ are relevant, then $[w_\emptyset, w_A, w_B]$ is the unique optimal state for $\Diamond(A \vee B)$, which then implicates $\Diamond A$ and $\Diamond B$ (but also the scalar implicatures $\neg\Diamond(A \wedge B)$, and $\neg\Box(A \vee B)$). The form-context pair $\Diamond(A \vee B)$-$\langle \mathbf{Q}_{?A?B}, [w_\emptyset, w_A, w_B] \rangle$ is optimal because no better alternative optimal form is available for such context ($\Diamond A \wedge \Diamond B$ that would be preferred by quantity is ruled out by manner) and no better optimal context is available for such form. All states not including $w_\emptyset$ would be blocked by optimal non-modal alternative forms (by manner), or in the case of $[w_A, w_B, w_{AB}]$ by the stronger $\Box(A \vee B)$ (by quantity). As for the states including $w_\emptyset$ consider the following tableau.

| | QUAL | REL | MAN | QUAN | MMP |
|---|---|---|---|---|---|
| a. $\Diamond(A \vee B)$ - $\langle \mathbf{Q}_{?A?B}, [w_\emptyset, w_A] \rangle$ | | | * | !* | * |
| $\Rightarrow$  $\Diamond A$ - $\langle \mathbf{Q}_{?A?B}, [w_\emptyset, w_A] \rangle$ | | | * | | * |
| b. $\Diamond(A \vee B)$ - $\langle \mathbf{Q}_{?A?B}, [w_\emptyset, w_B] \rangle$ | | | * | !* | * |
| $\Rightarrow$  $\Diamond B$ - $\langle \mathbf{Q}_{?A?B}, [w_\emptyset, w_B] \rangle$ | | | * | | * |
| $\Rightarrow$ c. $\Diamond(A \vee B)$ - $\langle \mathbf{Q}_{?A?B}, [w_\emptyset, w_A, w_B] \rangle$ | | | * | * | ** |
| $\Diamond A$ - $\langle \mathbf{Q}_{?A?B}, [w_\emptyset, w_A, w_B] \rangle$ | | | * | | !** |
| $\Diamond B$ - $\langle \mathbf{Q}_{?A?B}, [w_\emptyset, w_A, w_B] \rangle$ | | | * | | !** |
| d. $\Diamond(A \vee B)$ - $\langle \mathbf{Q}_{?A?B}, [w_\emptyset, w_A, w_B, w_{AB}] \rangle$ | | | * | * | !*** |

Here the contexts in (a) and (b) are blocked for $\Diamond(A \vee B)$ by the existence of alternative sentences which would be more appropriate choice for a speaker there, namely $\Diamond A$ and $\Diamond B$ respectively. Candidate (d) is ruled out by MMP. For $\Diamond(A \vee B)$ remains then as unique weakly optimal context the one in (c) which entails indeed the free choice implication $\Diamond A \wedge \Diamond B$.

The reasoning behind this implicature can be summarized as follows. Speaker said $\Diamond(A \vee B)$. Disregarding (d), three different interpretations are compatible with such a form.

(39)   a. The speaker believes: Possible A and not possible B.
   b. The speaker believes: Possible B and not possible A.
   c. The speaker believes: Possible A and possible B.

The third candidate wins, because the first two contents are blocked by the better alternative forms $\Diamond A$ and $\Diamond B$ respectively, which by the MMP automatically receive such exhaustive interpretations. Intuitively, we can reason as follows: if

---

[5] Note that also $\Diamond(A \wedge B)$ is among the predicted implicatures of the sentence. I don't know whether this is correct. It could be repaired by assuming that modal and non-modal sentence never compete with each other, but then we would predict that $\Box(A \vee B)$ implicates $\neg(A \wedge B)$, rather than $\neg\Box(A \wedge B)$. And that $\Box A$ implicates $\neg B$, rather than $\neg\Box B$.

speaker had known that B was not possible, she would have said $\Diamond A$. If she had known that A was not possible, she would have used $\Diamond B$. She didn't use these stronger forms. Therefore we can conclude that both $A$ and $B$ are possible.

Consider now the case in which the modal is not interpreted epistemically. A further possible interpretation arises for these cases:

e. The speaker doesn't know whether A is possible or B is possible.

This interpretation represents ignorance readings that can be paraphrased as 'You may do A or B, I don't remember which'. It is easy to see, however, that if we assume that the speaker is competent about what is possible or necessary, i.e. we restrict our competition to contexts satisfying the two following principles (I use $\Box'/\Diamond'$ for non-epistemic modals): $\neg\Box\Box'\phi \rightarrow \neg\Box'\phi$ and $\neg\Box\Diamond'\phi \rightarrow \neg\Diamond'\phi$, then the free choice interpretation (c) is optimal also for non-epistemic interpretation of the possibility operator.

To summarize, of the possible interpretations for $\Diamond(A \vee B)$, the 'exhaustive' interpretations (a) and (b) are blocked by the stronger forms $\Diamond A$ and $\Diamond B$. Candidate (e) represents the ignorance reading of the sentence and it is available only for non-epistemic interpretation of $\Diamond$. Candidate (c), representing the free choice interpretation, wins under the assumption that the speaker is competent about what is possible (this is always the case for epistemic $\Diamond$, and usually obtains when the sentence is used performatively).

# 5   Conclusion

I have presented a formal analysis of implicatures in the framework of Bi-directional OT, and have applied it to explain modal implicatures of disjunctions and indefinite expressions, but also scalar implicatures and exhaustification. A large number of further questions arise. The most urgent concerns implicatures of complex sentences. Another interesting question is whether free choice implicatures of non-epistemic modals could be derived as indifference implicatures rather than as I suggest in the previous section. A further open question concerns the exact relation between different kinds of indefinite pronouns (see Haspelmath, 1997). On the present account all indefinite expressions implicate speaker's ignorance or indifference. How do we account then for the difference between *irgend*-indefinites and plain indefinites. The implicatures of the latter have clearly a conversational nature. The implicatures of the former, instead, seem to have a double nature. On the one hand, they are derivable by the Gricean maxims like standard *conversational* implicatures. On the other, like *conventional* implicatures (e.g. those of *therefore* or *but*), they are hard to cancel, and somehow seem to be part of the lexical meaning of the pronoun. A proper investigation of this and other questions will have to be left to another occasion.

# References

Aloni, M.: Free choice and exhaustification: an account of subtrigging effects. Sinn und Bedeutung 11, Barcelona, Spain (2006)

Aloni, M., van Rooij, R.: Free choice items and alternatives. In: Bouma, G., Krämer, I., Zwarts, J. (eds.) Cognitive Foundations of Interpretation, 2004, Edita KNAW (to appear)

Alonso-Ovalle, L.: Distributing the disjuncts over the modal space. In: Bateman, L., Ussery, C. (eds.) Proceedings of the North East Linguistics Society 35, GLSA, University of Massachusetts, Amherst (2005)

Blutner, R.: Some aspects of optimality in natural language interpretation. Journal of Semantics 17, 189–216 (2000)

Chierchia, G.: Broaden your views. Implicatures of Domain Widening. Unpublished ms. University of Milan-Bicocca/Harvard University (2004)

Fox, D.: Free Choice and the theory of Scalar Implicatures (2006), available at http://mit.edu/linguistics/www/fox/free_choice.pdf

Gazdar, G.: Pragmatics. Academic Press, London (1979)

Groenendijk, J.: The logic of interrogation. In: Matthews, T., Strolovitch, D. (eds.) The Proceedings of the Ninth Conference on Semantics and Linguistic Theory, CLC Publications (1999)

Groenendijk, J., Stokhof, M.: Studies on the Semantics of Questions and the Pragmatics of Answers. Ph.D. thesis, University of Amsterdam (1984)

Grice, H.P.: Logic and Conversation, typescript from the William James Lectures, Harvard University (1967), Published in Grice, P., Studies in the Way of Words, pp. 22–40, Harvard University Press, Cambridge, Massachusetts (1989)

Haspelmath, M.: Indefinite Pronouns. Oxford University Press, Oxford (1997)

Hendriks, P., de Hoop, H.: Optimality theoretic semantics. Linguistics and Philosophy 24(1), 1–32 (2001)

Horn, L.: Towards a new taxonomy for pragmatic inference: Q-based and R-based implicatures. In: Schiffrin, D. (ed.) Meaning, Form, and Use in Context, pp. 11–42. Georgetown University Press, Washington (1984)

Kratzer, A.: Indefinites and the operators they depend on: From Japanese to Salish. In: Carlson, G., Pelletier, J. (eds.) Reference and Quantification: The Partee Effect, CSLI Publications, Stanford (2005)

Kratzer, A., Shimoyama, J.: Indeterminate pronouns: The view from Japanese. In: Proceedings of 3rd Tokyo Conference on Psycholinguistics (2002)

Prince, A., Smolensky, P.: Optimality Theory: Constraint Interaction in Generative Grammar. Blackwell, Oxford (1993/2004)

Sauerland, U.: Scalar implicatures of complex sentences. Linguistics and Philosophy 27, 367–391 (2004)

Schulz, K.: You may read it now or later. A case study on the paradox of free choice permission, Master thesis, University of Amsterdam (2004)

Schulz, K., van Rooij, R.: Exhaustive interpretation of complex sentences. Journal of Logic, Language, and Information 13, 491–519 (2004)

Schulz, K., van Rooij, R.: Pragmatic meaning and non-monotonic reasoning: the case of exhaustive interpretation. Linguistics and Philosophy 29, 205–250 (2006)

Spector, B.: Scalar implicatures: exhaustivity and Gricean reasoning. In: Aloni, M., Dekker, P., Butler, A. (eds.) Questions in Dynamic Semantics, 2003 (to appear)

Veltman, F.: Defaults in update semantics. Journal of Philosophical Logic 25, 221–261 (1996)

Zimmermann, T.E.: Free choice disjunction and epistemic possibility. Natural Language Semantics 8, 255–290 (2001)

# The Main Devices of Foregrounding in the Information Structure of Georgian Sentences[*]

Rusudan Asatiani

Oriental Institute, GAS
r_asatiani@hotmail.com

**Abstract.** Structuring of information proceeds through the foregrounding of certain parts of the information. In general, foregrounding can be realized on various linguistic levels and it is possible to distinguish: Conceptual, Functional, Discourse and Pragmatic devices, which can be represented by various formal means: Phonetic-Phonological, Morphological-Syntactic and Lexical-Pragmatic. All the devices can co-occur during the information packaging. Some of them are obligatory and are on the high level of the hierarchically organized processes of foregrounding (e.g. conceptual or functional foregrounding); some of them are optional and they are defined by the specific discourse and/or pragmatic values of a sentence (e.g. focus or topic); some forms of foregrounding are implicational (e.g. sometimes reordering implies emphasis of intonation) and so on. The relations between the different kinds of foregrounding are language specific, but it seems possible to speak about universal models of formalization of the information structures. In Georgian there is no morphological topic marker, but all other devices of foregrounding are possible. The paper examines the main models of such devices.

## 1 Introduction

Linguistic structuring of reality based on the notions 'same-different' proceeds through 'oppositions'. An opposition means that there are at least two items one of which is 'marked' and another is 'unmarked'. Structuring of the information, its packaging, also proceeds through oppositions where one part of the information stands out against a background of the other part of the information. From the communicational, pragmatic point of view, this information is highlighted, important and represents the foregrounding of a certain part of information. Any kind of 'foregrounding' (res. 'Highlighting', 'Logical Emphasis', 'Promotion', 'Standing out as the first, important' and etc) could be regarded as **one, common phenomenon** which represents the main strategy of structuring of linguistic structures. From this point of view Topic, Focus, Subject, Theme, Point of view and so on – are the same as far as they represent various forms of 'foregrounding'. It is supposed that such a wide, generalized interpretation of 'topicalization' make more clear, what happens when we have mixed forms of 'foregrounding'.

---

[*] This work was fulfilled within the Potsdam Project D2: "Information Structure of a sentence".

B.D. ten Cate and H.W. Zeevat (Eds.): TbiLLC 2005, LNAI 4363, pp. 21–30, 2007.
© Springer-Verlag Berlin Heidelberg 2007

Foregrounding, according to such a wide interpretation, can be realized on various linguistic levels:

## 1.1  Conceptual Foregrounding

During the linguistic structuring of the extra-linguistic situations some languages conventionally conceptualize as the central part of the information either Agent or Patient. In result, either Nominative (which shows agent's foregrounding) or Ergative (which shows patient's foregrounding) constructions arise. The first construction formally emphasizes *who is acting*, while the second emphasizes *what is done*.

From the grammatical point of view, conceptual foregrounding is represented by the unmarked, Nominative case: In the nominative languages it is the Agent, who always stands in nominative, while in the ergative languages it is the Patient (and not the Agent) who appears in nominative.

There are some languages which ignore semantic roles. The informational dimension plays a crucial role in the grammatical structures of such languages. This dimension helps the speaker and the hearer to package and retrieve the information: The highlighted part of the information (res. foregrounding of it) is formally marked by a special marker and it is possible to distinguish topicalized, foregrounding part of the information by morphological affixes.

## 1.2  Functional Foregrounding

Patient's foregrounding in the nominative languages, where agent is conceptually highlighted part, can further (on the second stage of foregrounding) be achieved by the changes of functional roles and as a result passive constructions rise. In the passive construction Patient is functionally promoted and it is defined as the Subject. The term *Subject* actually denotes foregrounding of a central part of information to *whom* or *what* the information concerns.

Active construction shows Agent's foregrounding (that means: Agent is the Subject), while Passive construction shows Patient's foregrounding (that means: Patient is the Subject).

## 1.3  Focus

During the communicative act, in the discourse, it is usual to stop the gap, which can occur in the information flow. In the dynamic linguistic structures, e.g. in dialogues such supplement of information is fulfilled by question-answer pairs: The demanded information in questions is given in the answers as the highlighted one: That is, foregrounding of the demanded information takes place. Such foregrounding can be reinterpreted as focusing and focal part of information is called *Focus*. In most cases, the Focus has a specific, marked intonation. It is represented in various languages by the different formal devices.

## 1.4  Topic

From the pragmatic point of view, sometimes it is necessary to make the information more exact, more precise and accurate or hypernymic in order to stress the contrast between the events, to clarify their implicational relations or bridging, to emphasize new or old information, to underline parallel events and so on. All these are reached by foregrounding of the contrasted parts of the information. This process is called topicalization and the foregrounding part of information is called *Topic*.

Conceptual and Functional foregrounding are obligatory. They are always represented in any linguistic structures. Focus is characteristic for the dialogue systems. As for the Topics, they are optional and defined only by the specific situations.

## 2  Grammatical Models of Foregrounding

From the formal point of view, foregrounding can be marked on various linguistic levels: *Phonetic-Phonological* (The almost universal device of foregrounding is the highlighting of a certain part of information by the marked intonation, which is different from the neutral one. Stress and other supra-segmental means are also possible.); *Morphological-Syntactic* (Some languages have special morphological markers (cases, particles, clitics) or specific syntactic constructions (reordering of unmarked word order, cleft constructions, different kinds of split, elliptic (short) answers and etc.); *Lexical-Pragmatic* (It is also possible to use special words, quantifiers or particles for the foregrounding (*indeed, certainly, also, just, only,* etc.) Besides the emphasis of the definite part of the information, such items add to the whole sentence specific semantics).

These devices denote the further foregrounding of any part of the information that is already structuralized and constructed on the conceptual or/and the functional linguistic levels.

All these devices can co-occur during the information packaging. Some of them are obligatory and are on the high level of the hierarchically organized processes of foregrounding (e.g. conceptual or functional foregrounding); some of them are optional and they are defined by the specific discourse and/or pragmatic values of a sentence (e.g. focus or topic); some of them are implicational (e.g. sometimes the reordering implies emphasis of intonation) and so on. Different devices and strategies are characteristic for the various languages. The relations between the different kinds of foregrounding are language specific, but it seems possible to speak about the universal signs of this linguistic processes.

## 3  Georgian Data

In the Georgian language there is no morphological topic marker but all other devices of foregrounding are possible.

### 3.1  Conceptual Foregrounding

The Georgian Language shows split ergativity: The Present Tense forms build the Nominative Constructions where conceptual foregrounding means to put the Agent in the central position:

**monadire-0**     k'l-av-s     irem-s ('The hunter kills the deer')
**hunter-Nom**   kill-Prs.-S.3   deer-Dat

The Aorist and Perfect Tense forms build the Ergative construction where conceptual foregrounding puts the Patient in the central position:

Aorist:     monadire-m mo-k'l-a                              **irem-i**
            hunter-Erg   Prev- kill-Aor.S.3.Sg               **deer-Nom**

Perfect:   monadire-s   mo-u-k'l-av-s                        **irem-i**
           hunter-Dat   Prev-Perf.Vers.-kill-Th.-S.3g        **deer-Nom**

### 3.2  Functional Foregrounding

The Passivization is a regular way for the Patient's foregrounding for the Present Tense forms:

Active:    **monadire-0**   k'l-av-s     irem-s ('The hunter kills the deer')
           **hunter-Nom**   kill-Prs.-S.3   deer-Dat

Passive:   **irem-i**       i-k'vl-eb-a      monadir-is mier
                                             ('The deer is killed by the hunter')
           **deer-Nom**     Prev.-Pass.-kill-Aor.-S.3        hunter-Gen by

The Passive construction is not always formally clearly distinguishable by the verb forms in the Aorist:

Active:    monadire-m mo-i-k'l-a          **irem-i**   tav-is-tvis
                                          ('The hunter killed the deer for himself')
           hunter-Erg   Prev.-S.Vers.-kill-Aor.S.3   **deer-Nom**   self-Gen-For

Passive:   **irem-i**       mo-i-k'l-a              monadir-is mier
                                                    ('The deer is killed by the hunter')
           **deer-Nom**     Prev.-Pass.-kill-Aor.S.3   hunter-Gen by

Finally, the Passive constructions are almost excluded in the Perfect Tense Forms.
Conceptually this fact is understandable: In ergative constructions (such constructions are characteristic for Aorist and Perfect) Patient is already defined as a conceptually foregrounding one and from the informational point of view its further functional foregrounding seems to be redundant.

### 3.3  Focus

The Focus in Georgian is represented by the special *rising* or *wave-like-raising* intonation, which differs from the non-focal, neutral intonation. Reordering and, especially, Fronting of the focal part of information is also characteristic. Because the Georgian language has free word order, all logically possible combinations of reordering can be realized as structures with different informational loading. It is difficult to describe and to explain all semantic or pragmatic nuances of these combinations. *Intonation+Fronting* seems to be the best and the clearest formal device of Focusing. Passivization is not an effective device for focusing because an answer usually has the same functional interpretation as the question has; That is, if a question is formulated by the active construction, an answer will be formulated as the active construction as well and vice versa: the passive question implies passive answer. Focus usually stands before   the verb; so, the best order is: *Focus - Verb*. This regularity must be a result of one the strongest syntactic restriction of word order in Georgian: Question words always are in preverbal position and consequently focus which replaces Wh-words in answers usually appears in the same position. The rising intonation of focus also should be a result of the regularity of intonation phrasing in Georgian: The verb has a tendency to be integrated into the p-phrase of a preceding or a following argument and as one unite it has the boundary tone of a prosodic phrase (p-phrase) which is canonically rising.

Here are some typical examples:

ra xdeba? (What is happening?)  monadire(hunter.Nom) k'lav-s(kills-Prs) irem-s(deer-Dat)
vin k'lavs irems? (Who kills the deer?)               **monadire** k'lavs irems
ras k'lavs monadire? (What does the hunter kill?)    **irems** k'lavs monadire
ras ak'etebs monadire? (What does the hunter do?)    **k'lavs** monadire irems
vin ras k'lavs? (Who kills what?)                    **monadire irems** k'lavs
                                                     **monadire** k'lavs **irems**
                                                     **irems monadire** k'lavs
                                                     **irems** k'lavs **monadire**

In answers (especially to repeated questions, which demand to give more accurate information) special particles and definite syntactic constructions arise:

**monadire** k'lavs irems? (Does **the hunter** kill the deer? Is it the hunter who kills the deer?)
          diax (yes.Pol), **monadire** k'lavs irems
          diaxac(yes.Pol-also=yes.mimicking), **monadire** k'lavs irems
          diax, **es** (this) **monadire-a**(is), vinc(who) k'lavs irems
          **namdvilad** (really) **monadire** k'lavs irems
          **sc'ored**(just,exactly) (**rom**(that),) **monadire** k'lavs irems
          **martlac** (indeed, right-also) (**rom** (that),) **monadire** k'lavs irems
          **martlacda** (indeed-and), **monadire** k'lavs irems

**irems** k'lavs monadire? (Does the hunter kill **the deer**?/Is it the deer which is killed by the hunter?)
          diax (yes.Pol), **irems** k'lavs monadire
          diaxac(yes.Pol-also=yes.mimicking), **irems** k'lavs monadire
          diax, **es** (this) **iremi-a**(is), visac(whom) monadire k'lavs
          **namdvilad** (really) **irems** k'lavs monadire
          **sc'ored**(just,exactly) (**rom**(that),) **irems** k'lavs monadire
          **martlac** (indeed, right-also) (**rom** (that),) **irems** k'lavs monadire
          **martlacda** (indeed-and), **irems** k'lavs monadire

monadire **k'lavs** irems? (Does the hunter **kill** the deer?/Does the hunter kill the deer or does he not?)

> diax (yes.Pol), **k'lavs** monadire irems
> diaxac(yes.Pol-also=yes.mimicking), **k'lavs** monadire irems
> **k'lavs** monadire irems, aba(well!) ara(no)? (Of course, the hunter do kill)
> **namdvilad** (really) **k'lavs** monadire **irems**
> **sc'ored**(just,exactly) (**rom**(that),) **k'lavs** monadire irems
> **martlac** (indeed, right-also) (**rom** (that),) **k'lavs** monadire irems
> **martlacda** (indeed-and), **k'lavs** monadire irems

And, so on.

Summarizing all the data, we can distinguish the following models for the Focusing:

1. Marked Intonation;
2. Reordering (Fronting) (+Intonation)
3. Syntactic Constructions (+Intonation)
4. Particles (+Syntax+Intonation)

### 3.4  Topic

The intonation is the main device for the Topicalization. The Topic intonation differs from the Focus and the Neutral intonations: it is ***rising-falling (L\*H\*L)***. All devices which are characteristic for the Focus are also possible for the Topic. There can be found also specific particles and constructions.

Here are some typical examples:

ra-s          it'q'vit        monadir-is        shesaxeb?  (What about the hunter?)
what-Dat  say.Fut-S.2.Pl  hunter-Gen      about
**monadire-m**    mo-k'l-a                    irem-i   ([The hunter]T killed the deer)
hunter-Erg      Prev-kill-Aor.S.3        deer-Nom

ici-t            rame          irm-is    shesaxeb? (Do you know something about the deer?)
know-Prs-S.2.Pl something.Nom deer-Gen  about
**irem-i**          mo-k'l-a                    monadire-m  (The hunter killed [the deer]T)
deer-Nom        Prev-kill-Aor.S.3        humter-Erg

**irem-i**    mo-i-k'l-a                      monadir-is    mier ([The deer]T is killed by the hunter)
deer-Nom  Prev-Pass-kill-Aor.S.3        hunter-Gen    by

ra-s          it'q'vi-t        am          monadir-is      shesaxeb?  (What about this hunter?)
what-Dat  say.Fut-S.2.Pl  this.Gen    hunter-Gen  about
**am**      **monadire-m**    mo-k'l-a            irem-i   ([This hunter]T killed a deer)
this.Erg hunter-Erg        Prev-kill-Aor.S.3 deer-Nom

**ai**      **am**          **monadire-m**    mo-k'l-a      irem-i  ([Precisely this hunter]T killed a deer.)
here.is this.Erg    hunter-Erg        Prev-kill-Aor.S.3    deer-Nom

**namdvilad** (really) **am monadirem** mo-k'l-a iremi ([Really this hunter]T killed a deer./ This is really so that this hunter (and not other) killed a deer./ It is really this hunter who killed a deer. )

**sc'ored** (just, exactly) (**rom**(that),) **am monadirem** mo-k'l-a iremi ([Exactly this hunter]T killed a deer./ This is exactly true, that this hunter killed a deer. It is just this hunter who killed a deer.)

**martlac** (indeed, right-also) (**rom** (that),) **am monadirem** mo-k'l-a iremi ([Indeed this hunter]T killed a deer./ It is indeed this hunter who killed a deer.)

**martlacda** (indeed-and), **am monadirem** mo-k'l-a iremi (Indeed, this is true that it is this hunter who killed a deer.)

| **es** | **is** | **monadire-a,** | vinc | iremi | mo-k'l-a |
|---|---|---|---|---|---|
| | | | (This is that hunter who killed a deer) | | |
| this.Nom | that.Nom | hunter.Nom=be.Prs.S.3 | who | deer | Prev-kill-Aor.S.3 |

| ici-t | rame | am | irm-is | shesaxeb? |
|---|---|---|---|---|
| | | | (Do you know something about this deer?) | |
| know-Prs-S.2.Pl | something.Nom | this.Gen | deer-Gen | about |

| **es** | **irem-i** | mo-k'l-a | monadire-m | (The hunter killed [this deer]T) |
|---|---|---|---|---|
| this.Nom | deer-Nom | Prev-kill-Aor.S.3 | hunter-Erg | |

| **ai** | **es** | **irem-i** | mo-k'l-a | monadire-m |
|---|---|---|---|---|
| | | | | (The hunter killed [precisely this deer]) |
| here.is | this.Nom | deer-Nom | Prev-kill-Aor.S.3 | hunter-Erg |

| **sc'ored rom** | **es** | **irem-i** | mo-k'l-a | monadire-m |
|---|---|---|---|---|
| | | | | (The hunter killed [just this deer]) |
| just | that | this.Nom | deer-Nom | Prev-kill-Aor.S.3 hunter-Erg |

| **martlac rom** | **es** | **irem-I** | mo-k'l-a | monadire-m |
|---|---|---|---|---|
| | | | | (The hunter killed [indeed this deer]) |
| indeed | that | this.Nom | deer-Nom | Prev-kill-Aor.S.3 hunter-Erg |

And so on.
Same constructions are usual also for the corresponding passive constructions:

| **ai es** | **irem-i** | mo-i-k'l-a | monadir-is | mier |
|---|---|---|---|---|
| | | | ([This deer]T is killed by the hunter) | |
| here.is | deer-Nom | Prev-Pass-kill-Aor.S.3 | hunter-Gen | by |

And so on.
In Georgian specific constructions more often classified as ways to introduce topics, like "As for", "As far as … is concerned", "Concerning", "As regards …", represent mostly syntactic devices of toplicalization:

| ra-c | she-e-x-eb-a | monadire-s, |
|---|---|---|
| what.Nom-Part | Prev-Pass-concern-Th.Suf-Pass.Pres.3.Sg | hunter-Dat |

| **sts'ored rom** | **is** | klav-s | irem-s |
|---|---|---|---|

exactly    that    he.Nom                    kill-Pres.3.Sg                  deer-Dat
(Concerning the hunter, [just it is he]T who kills a deer.)

Summarizing all the data, we can distinguish the following models for the Topicalization:

1. Marked Intonation (different from focus and neutral intonations);
2. Reordering (Fronting) (+Intonation)
3. Syntactic Constructions (+Intonation)
4. Particles (+Syntax+Intonation)

## 4  Mixed Forms of Foregrounding

Different kinds of foregrounding can co-occur and we can speak about the different degrees of 'Foregrounding': It is supposed that increasing of formal devices represents rising  of the degree of foregrounding and 'stages' can conventionally represent this complicated process.

As an example, let us consider the sentence:

> *kal-ma*      *gat'exa*      *magida* (The woman broke the table)
> woman-Erg    broke          Table.Nom

1st **stage** (Conceptual Foregrounding):
Ergative construction represents the Patient ( **magida** 'table.Nom') foregrounding;
2nd **stage** (Functional Foregrounding):
Active construction denotes the Agent (**kal-ma** 'woman-Erg') foregrounding

3rd **stage:** Intonation emphasis shows different kinds of different foregrounding. It depends on the wider context and on the type of intonation are these highlighting parts Focus or Topic ones? (Underlining in the below examples mark specific changes of an intonation):

> **_kalma_** *gat'exa magida*
> *kalma* **_gat'exa_** *magida*
> *kalma gat'exa* **_magida_**

4th **stage**: The reordering also works as the marker of foregrounding:

> *kalma gat'exa magida* (neutral word order)
> *kalma magida gat'exa* (neutral word order)
> **gat'exa** *kalma magida*
> **gat'exa magida** *kalma*
> **magida** *gat'exa kalma*
> **magida kalma** *gat'exa*

But the reordering with a certain pitch accent shows clearly a higher degree of foregrounding. The most usual position for Topic is the beginning of the sentence and for the Focus the position before the verb. Fronting together with intonation emphasis gives the highest degree of foregrounding:

**5<sup>th</sup> stage**:  *__kalma__ gat'exa magida*
*__gat'exa__ kalma magida*
*__magida__ gat'exa kalma*

It is also possible to use specific particles:

**6<sup>th</sup> stage**:  *__ai kalma__ gat'exa magida* (The woman (not the other one) broke the table)
*__ai magida__ gat'exa kalma* (The table (not the other thing) was broken by the woman)
*__ai gat'exa__ magida kalma* (The woman was broken (neither bought, nor made or etc.) the table')

(The particle *ai* ('here is') implies also fronting and specific intonation.)
Specific syntactic constructions (cleft, split...) along with the certain particles show the highlighted part of information as well.

**7<sup>th</sup> stage**:  *es **magidaa**, kalma rom gat'exa* ('It is the table that the woman broke')
***magida**, gat'exa kalma, xis* ('The table, the woman broke, wooden')
*sts'ored rom **magida** gat'exa kalma*
('(It is) precisely the table that the woman broke')

If we change the active construction into the passive one, the sentence *magida gat'q'da (kalis mier)* would show the different foregrounding on the **2<sup>nd</sup> stage** where *magida* has turned into the Subject. All the possibilities which are characteristic for the topicalization or focusing in active constructions can be used in the passive construction as well:

**3<sup>rd</sup> stage**:  *__magida__ gat'q'da (kalis mier)*
*magida __gat'q'da__ (kalis mier)*
*magida gat'q'da __kalis mier__*

**4<sup>th</sup> stage**:  *__gat'q'da__ magida (kalis mier)*
*__kalis mier__ gat'q'da magida*

**5<sup>th</sup> stage**:  *__ai magida__ gat'q'da (kalis mier)*
*__ai gat'q'da__ magida (kalis mier)*
*__ai kalis mier__ gat'q'da magida*

**6<sup>th</sup> stage**:       *__es magidaa__, (kalis mier) rom gat'q'da*
*__magida__ gat'q'da (kalis mier), xis*
*__sts'ored rom magida__ gat'q'da (kalis mier)*

So, the following hierarchy occurs:

**1st stage** – Aorist and Perfect show Patient's foregrounding, while the Present shows Agent's foregrounding;

**2nd stage** – Passive construction shows Patient's further foregrounding in Present;

**3rd stage** – Marked intonation shows different kinds of Topics or Focuses;

**4th stage** – Reordering+Intonation (Fronting+Intonation);

**5th stage** – Syntactic constructions (+Intonation);

**6th stage** – Particles (+Syntax+Intonation).

The first and second stages are obligatory, other stages are optional. We assume that the hierarchy of stages (1<2)<3<4<5<6 presents the rising of the degree of foregrounding.

# References

Asatiani, R.: subiekt'isa da obiekt'is akt'ualizaciis dziritadi mekanizmebi kartulshi (Main devices of the subject and object topicalization in the Arabic language). Typological Researches, IV, mecniereba, Tbilisi (2000)

Asatiani, R.: aktualizaciis dziritadi tipologiurad gansxvavebuli modelebi (Main typologically different models of topicalization). TSU publ., Tbilisi (2002)

Büring, D.: Topic. Electronic publication, Cologne University (1995)

Chikobava, A.: mart'ivi c'inadadebis problema kartulshi (Problem of the simple sentence in Georgian), mecniereba, Tbilisi (1968)

Shanidze, A.: kartuli gramat'ik'is sapudzvlebi (The foundations of the Georgian language), mecniereba, Tbilisi (1973)

Vallduvi, E.: Discourse Configurational Languages. Kiss, K.E. (ed.), Oxford Un.Press, New York-Oxford (1995)

# Focus and 'Only' in Hungarian

Kata Balogh

ILLC/Department of Philosophy
Universiteit van Amsterdam
k.balogh@uva.nl

**Abstract.** The main of this paper to investigate Hungarian focus interpretations. Hungarian has a special pre-verbal position for focussed
constituents, which receive an exhaustive interpretation. Since the focus
sensitive particle, 'only' goes together with this exhaustive focus, 'only'
seems to be redundant or superfluous. For this reasons, we will investigate focus and 'only' in answers and multiple focus constructions and
propose an analysis where exhaustivity-operator and only-operator are
distinct.

In the current syntactic, semantic and pragmatic literature focus, 'only' and
exhaustivity are a major subject of study. There are several proposals for the
semantics and pragmatics of *focus*, and the focus sensitive particle *'only'*, for
example, von Stechow (1991), Krifka (2004), Rooth (1985), Geurts and van der
Sandt (2004) – to mention just the most famous ones. The most famous analysis
of exhaustive interpretation of answers is from Groenendijk and Stokhof (1984,
1991), which is widely studied and used in recent work, for example, by van Rooij
and Schulz (to appear) on exhaustivity or Kratzer (2005) on questions. For many
languages – for example Basque, Catalan, Greek, Finnish, Hungarian – focus is
a significant syntactic matter as well. For Hungarian focus structure the most
prominent theories are from Bródy (1990), É. Kiss (1998), Horváth (2006) on
syntax, Szabolcsi (1981) on the syntax-semantics interface and Szendrői (2001)
on the syntax-phonology interface.

The issues of focus, 'only' and exhaustivity are often claimed to be interre-
lated, and from a linguistic perspective the study of Hungarian is a particularly
interesting case. Hungarian has a special pre-verbal position for focused constituents, which is assigned a pitch accent and gets an exhaustive interpretation.

The main aim of this paper is to investigate Hungarian focus constructions
and their interpretation and to point out that in order to give a proper analysis
of Hungarian focus constructions we have to bring together the above mentioned
issues: the syntactic structure of the sentence, the semantic interpretation, pragmatic effects and the intonation pattern. We hope this brings to bear on the
interpretation of focus, 'only' and exhaustivity in other languages as well.

The paper is organized as follows. In section 1 we will introduce the main
attributes of Hungarian focus structure. In section 2 we investigate the problem of identification/exhaustive focus and 'only' via question-answer relations
(section 2.1) and multiple focus constructions (section 2.2). Section 3 deals with

B.D. ten Cate and H.W. Zeevat (Eds.): TbiLLC 2005, LNAI 4363, pp. 31–44, 2007.
© Springer-Verlag Berlin Heidelberg 2007

complex focus and double focus interpretations and the role of intonation, syntax and the appearance of 'only' for distinguish them. Section 4 gives the conclusions and introduces some further work. At the end of the paper, the appendix contains some detailed technical proofs.

# 1  Focus in Hungarian

Hungarian belongs to the type of discourse-configurational languages (É. Kiss1 1995). A main property of these languages is that some discourse-semantic information is mapped into the syntactic structure of the sentences as well. Hungarian has special structural positions for *topics*, *quantifiers* and *focus*. The special structural position for the focused element(s) is the immediate pre-verbal position. In "neutral sentences" like (1a) the immediate pre-verbal position is occupied by the verbal modifier (VM) whereas in focused sentences like (1b) this position is occupied by the focused element, and the verbal modifier is behind the finite verb. The constituent in the focus-position is assigned a pitch accent and receives an *exhaustive* interpretation.[1]

(1)    a.  Anna felhívta    Emilt.           b.  Anna EMILT    hívta fel.
           Anna VM-called Emil.acc              Anna Emil.acc called VM
           'Anna called Emil.'                  'It is Emil whom Anna called.'

In her (1998) paper, É. Kiss distinguishes two types of focus: *identificational focus* and *information focus*. Her main claims are that these two types are different both in syntax and semantics, and that identificational focus is not uniform across languages. The main differences between the two types of focus in Hungarian according to É. Kiss are the following: a) *identificational focus*: expresses exhaustive identification, certain constituents are out, it takes scope, involves movement and can be iterated; b) *information focus*: merely marks the unpresupposed nature, is nonrestricted, does not take scope, does not involve movement and can project. For example, we can answer the question '*Where were you last summer?*' with (2a), which has identificational focus, or with (2b), which has information focus. From these two answers only (2a) gets an exhaustive interpretation.

(2)    a.  ANGLIÁBAN voltam.           b.  Voltam ANGLIÁBAN.
           England.loc was.1sg             was.1sg England.loc
           'It is England where I went.'     'I went to England.'
           [and nowhere else]              [among other places]

The pre-verbal focus in Hungarian falls under the category of identificational focus, whereas the status of the information focus in Hungarian is rather questionable (e.g. Szendrői1 2003). In the following we will concentrate on the pre-verbal (identificational focus) to point out several problems with the exhaustive meaning and 'only'. In Hungarian 'only' is always associated with identificational focus, it cannot go together with the *information* focus, see (3).

---

[1] Here and further on small capitals indicate pitch accent.

(3)   a.  Csak ANGLIÁBAN voltam.      b.  *Voltam csak ANGLIÁBAN.
         only England.loc was.1sg          was.1sg  only England.loc
         'I went only to England.'

Since in Hungarian both 'only' and identificational focus indicate exhaustivity, the question arises whether sentences with bare (identificational) focus (4a) and sentences with 'only' (4b) get the same interpretation or not and if they are not the same what the difference is.

In classical semantic analyses 'only' is identified with an exhaustivity operator, which suggests that identificational focus and 'only' get the same semantic interpretation with one *exh/only* operator. Later on we will see that this view cannot be applied to some focus constructions in Hungarian.

(4)   a.  ANNA hívta  fel   Emilt.        b.  Csak ANNA hívta  fel   Emilt.
         Anna  called VM Emil.acc            only Anna  called VM Emil.acc
         'It is Anna who called Emil.'        'Only Anna called Emil.'

An important question here is if 'only' in Hungarian has an exhaustive semantic content or not. If we suppose that 'only' gets exhaustive semantics, then examples like (3a) invole two exhaustivity operators. We will see in section 2.1 that for the semantics this solution is not a problem, since exhaustification of an exhaustified term does not have semantic effect. However, example (3b) suggests the opposite, since 'only' cannot go together with information focus, only with identificational focus, which is already exhaustive. This fact can be an argument in favour of the view that 'only' in Hungarian is not responsible for exhaustive meaning, or it can be an argument against the existence of information focus.

In this paper I choose for the second option, to give exhaustive semantics for 'only'. I will suggest an analysis for Hungarian focus and 'only' with two distinct operators, $\mathcal{EXH}$ and $\mathcal{ONLY}$. The two operators both get exhaustive semantic content, but $\mathcal{ONLY}$ has a pragmatic effect on top of it.[2] We will see later that for some multiple focus constructions this distinction is crucial to get the intended interpretation.

## 2   Exhaustivity and 'Only' in Hungarian

The constituents in the pre-verbal focus position are interpreted as exhaustive identification (É. Kiss 1998, Horváth 2006). Accordingly, the semantic interpretation of identificational focus involves an exhaustivity operator. In the focus-analysis of Horvath (2006) exhaustivity operators already appear in the syntactic structure of the sentence. She assumes a quantificational *exclusive identification* operator in the Focus-head which triggers Focus-movement.

---

[2] This is an alternative of the analysis in my previous work (Balogh 2005, 2006) where 'only' has no semantic content, only a pragmatic effect on the expectations.

In their dissertation from (1984), Groenendijk and Stokhof give an elegant analysis of the exhaustification of answers. I would like to extend their analysis to apply it to focus, especially to Hungarian identificational focus.[3]

For the semantics of linguistic answers they define an answer formation rule introducing an exhaustivity operator, which gives the minimal elements from a set of sets.

(5)   a.  *the rule of answer formation:* if $\alpha'$ is the interpretation of an n-place term, and $\beta'$ is the relational interpretation of an n-constituent interrogative, the interpretation of the linguistic answer based on $\alpha$ in the context of the interrogative $\beta$ is $(EXH(\alpha'))(\beta')$, where $EXH$ is defined as follows:

   b.  $EXH = \lambda\mathbb{P}\lambda P[\mathbb{P}(P)\wedge \neg\exists P'[\mathbb{P}(P') \wedge P \neq P' \wedge \forall x[P'(x) \rightarrow P(x)]]]$

$EXH$ is defined as a semantic operation which takes a term $T$ (GQ) and filters the set $D$ of sets $D'$ in the denotation of $T$ where the set containing $T$ is included and there is no other set in $D$ which is the subset of $D'$. In this model, $EXH$ equals the interpretation of 'only': *"(...) the semantic content of EXH can be verbalized as the term modifier 'only' (...)"* (Groenendijk and Stokhof 1984 p. 295). If we give the answer *'Anna$_F$ called Emil.'* to the question *'Who called Emil?'*, then it is interpreted as *'Only Anna called Emil.'*:

(6)   $(EXH(\lambda P.P(Anna)))(\lambda x.called(x, Emil)) =$
      $\lambda P\forall x[P(x) \leftrightarrow [x = Anna]](\lambda x.called(x, Emil)) =$
      $\forall x[called(x, Emil) \leftrightarrow [x = Anna]]$

Along Groenendijk and Stokhof (1984) both the interpretation of (7a) and (7b) – with the underlying question: *Who called Emil?* – involves one *EXH* operator (8):

(7)   a.  ANNA hívta  fel   Emilt.    (=4a)
          Anna  called VM  Emil.acc
          'It is Anna who called Emil.'

      b.  Csak ANNA hívta  fel   Emilt.    (=4b)
          only  Anna  called VM  Emil.acc
          'Only Anna called Emil.'

(8)   $(EXH(Anna))(called\text{-}Emil)$

In the following sections, I will propose an analysis for Hungarian where the two operators are distinct. In this way we can explain certain differences in answers with identificational focus versus 'only' (section 2.1) and we can interpret multiple focus constructions where the two focused constituents go together with

---

[3] Since my aim in this paper is not the comparison of several focus/exhaustivity theories, I will not discuss here the Alternative Semantics (Rooth 1985) or the Structured Meaning Account (Krifka 1991). For the particular aims of this paper they face similar problems as the Partition Theory (Groenendijk and Stokhof 1984).

two 'only's (section 2.2). My proposal is to assume two distinct operators: $\varepsilon \varkappa \mathcal{H}$ and $\mathcal{ONLY}$. The two operators get the same exhaustive semantic content defined by Groenendijk and Stokhof (5b). In case the two operators modify the same term, 'only' has no semantic but a pragmatic effect on the previous expectations.

## 2.1  Question–Answer Pairs

The first example where we have to distinguish between bare (identificational) focus and 'only'-sentences resides in question-answer pairs. As we saw in the previous section, in the classical analyses (9a) and (9b) get the same interpretation involving one operator: *exh* or *only*. For the question in (9) the answers with or without 'only' are semantically equivalent, saying that Anna and nobody else called Emil. The focus in (9a) expresses exhaustive identification, thus the interpretation is $\forall x[called(x, e) \leftrightarrow x = a]$. In example (9) this seems to be not problematic, since both sentences are equally felicitous answers. This suggest that a sentence with bare (identificational) focus and an 'only'-sentence are the same, so the appearance of 'only' in (9b) does not make any difference.

> (9)  Ki  hívta  fel  Emilt?
>      who called VM Emil.acc
>      'Who called Emil?'
>
>   a.  ANNA hívta  fel  Emilt.
>       Anna  called VM Emil.acc
>       'It is Anna who called Emil.'
>
>   b.  Csak ANNA hívta  fel  Emilt.
>       only Anna  called VM Emil.acc
>       'Only Anna called Emil.'

Consider, however, example (10) where the same question is posed in plural, so we have an explicit expectation of more persons who called Emil.

> (10)  Kik   hívták  fel  Emilt?
>       who.pl called.pl VM Emil.acc
>       'Who called Emil?'
>
>   a.  #ANNA hívta fel Emilt. (=9a)
>
>   b.  Csak ANNA hívta fel Emilt. (=9b)

Question (10) cannot be answered with a simple identificational focus, but (10b) – with 'only' – is felicitous. Considering the above example I propose that it is not the 'only' that is responsible for the exhaustive meaning. The function of 'only' here is cancelling the expectation.[4]

Semantically we have two operators – $\varepsilon \varkappa \mathcal{H}$ and $\mathcal{ONLY}$ – that have the same exhaustive content as defined by Groenendijk and Stokhof (1984, 1991). Thus,

---

[4] In different contexts there can be different expectations/presuppositions. Here I will only discuss this simple case, so we will analyze (9) without any expectations. Still there is the question what cancels then 'only' in (9a). I claim that in this case only gives information about the *answerers* previous expectations, but according to the questioners information state this additional information is irrelevant.

semantically both sentences get the interpretation that nobody else but Anna called Emil, but the 'only' in (10b) has a pragmatic effect on top of it, saying that it is against the expectations. According to this proposal in this cases it is not the focus particle 'only' that is the main responsible for the exhaustive meaning, exhaustivity comes from the semantics of the identificational focus.

The exhaustivity operator defined by Groenendijk and Stokhof (1984, 1991) filters the minimal element of a set of sets. Accordingly, if we apply it twice on the same term we get the same semantic interpretation: $\varepsilon \chi \mathcal{H}(\varepsilon \chi \mathcal{H}(\alpha)) = \varepsilon \chi \mathcal{H}(\alpha)$ (see the appendix). In this way semantically both (10a) and (10b) get the same interpretation as: $\forall x.called(x, e) \leftrightarrow x = a$. The difference between the two sentences is of a pragmatic nature, which is a consequence of the appearance of 'only'. In the partition semantics(Groenendijk and Stokhof 1984, 1991), the meaning of a question like (9) and (10) is a partition. In this theory the meaning of an interrogative determines what its possible complete semantic answers are. The semantic interpretation of an interrogative is an equivalence relation over the set of possible worlds, thus an interrogative sentence denotes a partition of logical space. Every block of the partition induced by $?\phi$ contains the possible worlds where the extension of $\phi$ is the same, thus the meaning of a question is a set of propositions, the set of complete semantic answers to the question. $[\![?x\phi]\!] = \{(w, v) \in W^2 \mid [\![\lambda x\phi]\!]^w = [\![\lambda x\phi]\!]^v\}$ In case of a domain of three persons $\{Anna, Rena, Tomi\}$ the meaning of question (9) is an eight-block partition (*part A*). Question (10) is posed in plural, so it has an explicit expectation from the questioner's side: (s)he thinks that there was more than one person (from the relevant domain) who came. This expectation should be interpreted as a *restriction* on the partition (*part B*).

part A

| nobody | anna and rena |
|--------|---------------|
| anna   | anna and tomi |
| rena   | rena and tomi |
| tomi   | everybody     |

part B

| nobody | anna and rena |
|--------|---------------|
| anna   | anna and tomi |
| rena   | rena and tomi |
| tomi   | everybody     |

The question in example (9) is equated with the partition *part A*. The focus expresses exhaustive identification, thus it contains an exhaustivity operator. Consequently, the proposition that a sentence with identificational focus denotes is one of the propositions in the partition induced by the underlying question. Thus identificational focus selects one block from the partition, or equivalently, it eliminates all blocks but one from the partition. In case of (9a) the focus selects the block containing the proposition *only Anna called Emil*.

In example (10), for the identificational focus in the answer only the restricted area (dashed lines) is accessible to select a block. Therefore we cannot reply to (10) with (10a), because the block where the proposition is *only Anna called*

*Emil* is not among the available ones, but we can reply with (11), so it is not the case that the bare identificational focus is out as an aswer for plural questions.

(11)   ANNA és   TOMI hívta      fel   Emilt.
       Anna  and Tomi  called.3sg VM Emil.acc
       'It is Anna and Tomi who called Emil.'

In fact, for question (10) it is not excluded to give an answer that expresses that Anna and nobody else called Emil, but in case of (10) we need 'only' to go explicitly against the previous expectation of the questioner as in (10b). Thus 'only' cancels the restriction, whereby the blocks which were excluded before can "pop-up" again, so they become accessible for the identificational focus to select one of them. It follows that the exhaustive identification – namely selecting a block from the partition – is the function of the identificational focus, and 'only' has an additional pragmatic effect on the domain restriction.

Given these observations we may wonder 'What is happening in (9b)?' In question (9) the questioner does not have any expectation about how many people came, but we can answer with an 'only'-sentence. I claim that in this case the use of 'only' in the answer gives information about the answerer's previous expectations, namely the answerer expected more people to come. But according to the questioner's information state this additional information is irrelevant. Nevertheless, it shows, too, that (9a) and (9b) are slightly different and the use of 'only' in (9b) is not redundant.

## 2.2   Multiple Foci

An other example from Hungarian in favour of the distinction of $\mathcal{EXH}$ and $\mathcal{ONLY}$ can be found in multiple focus constructions. In case of sentences containing two (or more) prosodic foci there are two possible interpretations: the two foci can form a complex focus where semantically a pair of constituents is in focus (12), or the first focus-phrase takes scope over the second one (13).

(12)   complex focus (pair-reading)

       a.  John only introduced BILL to SUE. (from Krifka 1991)

       b.  ANNA hívta  fel   EMILT.
           Anna  called VM Emil.acc
           'It is the Anna, Emil pair of whom the first called the second.'

(13)   double focus (scope-reading)

       a.  Even$_1$ JOHN$_1$ drank only$_2$ WATER$_2$. (from Krifka 1991)

       b.  Csak ANNA hívta  fel   csak EMILT.
           only Anna  called VM only Emil.acc
           'Only Anna called only Emil. [the others nobody or more persons]'

In the following I will use the more informative terminology for these two types: *pair-reading* for the complex focus and *scope-reading* for the double focus/real multiple foci. The above examples show that these two different readings are present in Hungarian. However, interestingly, example (14) can have both readings: the scope-reading (14a) and the pair-reading (14b).

(14)    Csak ANNA hívta fel   csak EMILT.   (=13b)
        only Anna called VM only Emil.acc
        a. 'Only Anna called only Emil.' [the others nobody or more persons]
        b. 'It is the Anna, Emil pair of whom the first called the second.'

For multiple terms, Groenendijk and Stokhof (1984, 1991) gives the generalized definition of exhaustivity ($EXH^n$). This operator gives the right result for examples where exhaustivity applies to pairs, thus for example for (12b):

(15)    $(EXH^2(\lambda R[R(a,e)]))(\lambda x\lambda y.called(x,y)) =$
        $\lambda R\forall x\forall y[R(x,y) \leftrightarrow [x = a \wedge y = e]](\lambda x\lambda y.called(x,y)) =$
        $\forall x\forall y[called(x,y) \leftrightarrow [x = a \wedge y = e]]$

This is the intended interpretation saying that the only pair of persons of whom the call-relation holds is: Anna and Emil. The problem arises if we try to get the meaning in (14b). In Groenendijk and Stokhof's (1984, 1991) framework 'only' and the exhaustivity operator are not distinct, thus the two 'only's are the operators that exhaustify the phrases respectively: $EXH(a)$ called $EXH(e)$. Following this, the interpretation of (14) goes as follows:

(16)    $(EXH(\lambda P.P(a)))((EXH\lambda P.P(e))(\lambda x\lambda y.called(x,y)))=$
        $(\lambda P\forall y[P(y) \leftrightarrow y = a])((\lambda P\forall x[P(x) \leftrightarrow x = e])(\lambda x\lambda y.called(x,y)))=$
        $\forall y[\forall x[called(x,y) \leftrightarrow x = a] \leftrightarrow y = e]$

It says that only Anna is such that she called only Emil, so we get the 'scope-reading' (14a). Exhaustifying the terms separately we cannot get the complex focus interpretation (14b). As a solution we can suppose there is an exhaustivity operator that takes a pair of constituents and there are two 'only's modifying the two terms as above.[5] In this way the semantic interpretation goes as follows:

(17)    $\varepsilon x\mathcal{H}\langle o\mathcal{N}\mathcal{L}y(anna),\ o\mathcal{N}\mathcal{L}y(emil)\rangle(\lambda x\lambda y.called(x,y))$

Like singular terms, multiple terms as well may need not only exhaustification of the $o\mathcal{N}\mathcal{L}y$ operators, but also exhaustification of the identificational focus – $\varepsilon x\mathcal{H}$ – on top of it. The exhaustification of the pair of exhaustified terms does not lead to scopal meaning, but gives the pair-reading:

(18)    $\varepsilon x\mathcal{H}\langle o\mathcal{N}\mathcal{L}y(\alpha),\ o\mathcal{N}\mathcal{L}y(\beta)\rangle = \varepsilon x\mathcal{H}\langle \alpha,\beta\rangle$

With distinct $\varepsilon x\mathcal{H}$ and $o\mathcal{N}\mathcal{L}y$ operators we can account for both readings for (14), but we have to take into consideration the discourse-structure as well. An important fact is that in case of a scope-reading the second focus contains always given information, and the new information goes to the (identificational) focus position which is associated with an $\varepsilon x\mathcal{H}$ operator.[6]

---

[5] One might say that this example is an instance of concord phenomena where only one of the 'only'-operators is semantically visible. I think this is not the case here since $\langle only(\alpha), only(\beta)\rangle$, $\langle only(\alpha), \beta\rangle$, $\langle \alpha, only(\beta)\rangle$ and $\langle \alpha, \beta\rangle$ can have the very same interpretation.

[6] There is more evidence for this in section 3 on intonation.

(19)  Q:  Ki   hívott fel   kit?
           who called VM whom
           'Who called whom?'

      A:  Csak ANNA hívta   fel    csak EMILT.
          only Anna  called VM   only Emil.scc
          'It is the Anna, Emil pair of whom the first called the second.'
          #'Only Anna called only Emil. [the others nobody or more persons]'

Following this proposal the interpretation goes as follows. For the pair-reading of (14b) both *Anna* and *Emil* are new information, so a pair of constituents, ⟨*Anna, Emil*⟩ is in focus and associated with an $\varepsilon x \mathcal{H}$ operator, while both constituents are modified by 'only'. This gives us semantically the pair-reading.

(20)  $\varepsilon x \mathcal{H} \langle \mathcal{ONLY}(anna), \mathcal{ONLY}(emil) \rangle (\lambda x \lambda y.called(x, y)) =$
      $\forall x, y[called(x, y) \leftrightarrow [x = anna \wedge y = emil]]$

In the case of the scope-reading of (14a) only *Anna* is new information, so it will serve as (identificational) focus associated with $\varepsilon x \mathcal{H}$.

(21)  $(\varepsilon x \mathcal{H}(\mathcal{ONLY}(anna)))((\mathcal{ONLY}(emil))(\lambda x \lambda y.called(x, y))) =$
      $(\varepsilon x \mathcal{H}(anna))((\varepsilon x \mathcal{H}(emil))(\lambda x \lambda y.called(x, y))) =$
      $\forall y[\forall x[called(x, y) \leftrightarrow x = a] \leftrightarrow y = e]$

Information structure plays a crucial role for the disambiguation between the pair-reading and the scope-reading. The different information structure is assigned by different intonation patterns. In the following section we will investigate further what what linguistic factors play a role to disambiguate between the two meanings.

## 3  Multiple Focus Readings

In this section we will discuss important linguistic factors which determine the two different multiple focus readings, the pair-reading and the scope-reading. Our claim here is that in order to interpret multiple foci we have to take into consideration all three factors: intonation, syntactic structure and the appearance of 'only'.

First of all we discuss intonation, which seems to have a very important role here. For sentence (14) two different intonation patterns lead to two meanings. In (22a) both focussed constituents get pitch accent, before the second focused element there is a little stop (end of an intonation phrase) and just before this break there is a rising intonation. This intonation pattern gives us the complex focus (pair) reading. In (22b) all words between the focussed constituents are deaccented and there is no break[7]. This pattern gives the double focus (scope) reading. For the above examples intonation indicates the information structure,

---

[7] I will not discuss the question here whether the second focused phrase here is deaccented as well or gets pitch accent. There are different opinions on this topic, according to my intuitions the second focus is not deaccented.

for (22a) both focused constituents are new information which leads to the semantic interpretation that a pair of constituent is in (identificational) focus: $(\varepsilon x \mathcal{H}^2(\langle o \mathcal{N} \mathcal{L} \mathcal{Y}(foc_1), o \mathcal{N} \mathcal{L} \mathcal{Y}(foc_2)\rangle))(R) \Rightarrow$ pair-reading; for (22b) only the first focus is new information, the second one is second occurence/old information which leads to the semantic interpretation: $(\varepsilon x \mathcal{H}(foc_1))((\varepsilon x \mathcal{H}(foc_2))(R)) \Rightarrow$ scope-reading.

(22)   Csak ANNA hívta fel csak EMILT. (=14)

    a.  Csak Anna hívta fel      csak Emilt.
          H*-L L      L-H%      H*-L  $\Longrightarrow$ pair / *scope
        'It is the Anna, Emil pair of whom the first called the second.'

    b.  Csak Anna hívta fel csak Emilt. $\Longrightarrow$ *pair / scope
          H*-L L      L L      H*-L
        'Only Anna called only Emil. [the others more or nobody]'

Consequently, intonation has the role to yield the intended meaning, however, there is no one-to-one correspondence between intonation patterns and meanings, since for (23) and (24) the pair-intonation leads to the pair-reading, but the scope-intonation leads either to the pair-reading again or ungrammaticality. Interestingly only for structure (22) we can get the scope-reading, for structures (23) and (24) the scope-reading is out.

(23)   Csak ANNA hívta fel EMILT.

    a.  Csak Anna hívta fel      Emilt.
          H*-L L      L-H% H*-L  $\Longrightarrow$ pair-reading / *scope-reading

    b.  Csak Anna hívta fel Emilt.
          H*-L L      L H*-L  $\Longrightarrow$ *pair-reading / *scope-reading

(24)   ANNA hívta fel EMILT.

    a.  Anna hívta fel      Emilt.
        H*-L L      L-H% H*-L  $\Longrightarrow$ pair-reading / *scope-reading

    b.  Anna hívta fel Emilt.
        H*-L L      L H*-L  $\Longrightarrow$ *pair-reading / *scope-reading

This suggests that the scope-reading is only possible with 'only'-phrases. We cannot even use (25a) to ask *Who is that, who called Emil and nobody else?*, but we can by using (25b). Thus it seems that to express scope-meaning without 'only' we need a special syntactic structure.

(25)   a.  *Ki hívta fel  EMILT?
        who called VM Emil.acc
        'Who called Emil (and nb. else)?'

      b.  Ki  hívta EMILT   fel?
        who called Emil.acc VM
        'Who called Emil (and nb. else)?'

É. Kiss (1998) proposes an elegant syntactic analysis of multiple focus constructions. She claims that F(ocus)P(hrase) (Bródy 1990) iteration is possible. According to this analysis, the second focused constituent also moves to an FP position, while the verb moves to the first F-head going through the second one. This syntactic analysis assumes two Focus Phrases, hence two focus/exhaustivity operators, accordingly in the semantic interpretation we have two focussed elements where the first takes scope over the second one.

(26)   Csak ANNA hívta csak EMILT   meg.
       only Anna  called only Emil.acc VM
       'Only Anna called only Emil. [the others more or nobody]'

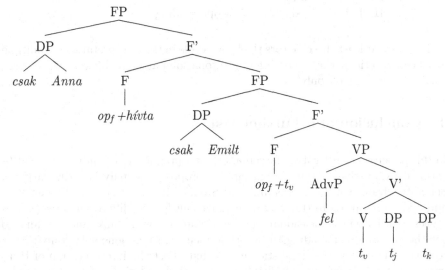

This structure generates only the word order: Foc$_1$ Verb Foc$_2$ VM, but cannot give an account of the word order where the second focus is at the and of the sentence: Foc$_1$ Verb VM Foc$_2$, which can get the scope-reading as well.

For the latter Alberti and Medve (2000) gives a different syntactic analysis which they assign the pair-reading. They call this structure "mirror focus" construction (27) versus the "double focus" construction from É. Kiss.

(27)   (Csak) ANNA hívta fel  (csak) EMILT.
       (only) Anna  called VM (only) Emil.acc
       'It is the Anna, Emil pair of whom the first called the second.'
       ... [$_{FP}$ [$_{VP}$ ... $t_k$ $t_u$ XP $t_l$ ...]$_i$ [$_{F'}$ F+(V+V$_k$)$_s$ [$_{VP}$ $t_s$ $t_i$ $t_u$ XP$_l$ ...] $t_i$]]

The advantage of this analysis is that it assigns a different syntactic structure for the complex focus, where there is only one focus phrase and consequently only one focus/exhaustivity operator which is applied to an ordered pair of arguments. The disadvantage is that the above distinction suggest a correspondence between the two readings and the two structures respectively. However, the picture is not as simple as that, since it can be the case that structure (26) gets the pair reading or structure (27) gets the scope reading. Consider, for example, the following example with the same word order as in (26), but with the strong intonation pattern we can get the complex focus reading.

(28)   ANNA hívta   EMILT   fel.
       Anna  rescued Emil.acc VM

   a.  Anna hívta Emilt fel.
       H*-L L-H% H*-L L%$\Longrightarrow$ pair-reading

   b.  Anna hívta Emilt fel.
       H*-L L      H*-L L% $\Longrightarrow$ scope-reading

There are at least three factors that play a role in the interpretation of multiple focus constructions: the use of different intonation patterns, different word order and the occurence of 'only'.

# 4   Conclusion and Further Issues

In this paper we investigated the semantics and pragmatics of 'only' and identificational/exhaustive focus in Hungarian. We proposed an analysis in the Partition Semantics framework (Groenendijk and Stokhof 1984, 1991) with distinct $\varepsilon\mathcal{X}\mathcal{H}$ and $\mathcal{ONLY}$ operators. In this way we can account for the difference between sentences with bare identificational focus and sentences with 'only' and we can also get the two different readings of multiple focus constructions with 'only'. Next to this we looked at the linguistic factors that affect the interpretation of Hungarian sentences containing multiple prosodic foci and give rise to the *complex focus* reading with a pair of constituents in focus or to the *double focus* reading with two foci where the first takes scope over the second one. Our claim is that in order to interpret multiple focus (in Hungarian) we have to take into consideration the different intonation patterns (hence the information structure), the occurrence of only, and the syntactic structure as well.

There are several matters about the exhaustive semantics of Hungarian focus that should be further investigated. The most important issues for further research are the following: (1) a proper syntactic analysis of multiple focus constructions mentioned in section 3, with special interest on sentences like (28) where the word order suggest an iterated FP-structure proposed by É. Kiss (1998), but the intonation can force the pair-reading (28); (2) we should have a closer look at negation, identificational focus and 'only' in Hungarian; (3) an analysis of scalar reading of 'only' sentences, and scalar readings and scope-relations. According to Hungarian data scalar only and non-scalar only behave differently in scope-relations: if we have two only-phrases where the first takes scope over the second one, then the first one cannot be scalar, but has to be exhaustive and distributive.

# References

Alberti, G., Medve, A.: Focus constructions and the "scope-inversion puzzle" in Hungarian. In: Kenesei, I., Alberti, G. (eds.) Approaches to Hungarian 7, JATEPress, Szeged (2000)

Balogh, K.: 'Only' and Exhaustivity in Hungarian. Wh-questions and Focusation of Answers. In: Extended abstract and talk at the ESSLLI workshop 'Formal Semantic and Cross-Linguistic Data', Edinburgh (2005)

Bródy, M.: Some remarks on the focus field in Hungarian. UCL Working Papers in Linguistics, vol. 2 (1990)

Kiss, K.É.: Identificational focus versus information focus. Language 74(2) (1998)

Kiss, K.É. (ed.): Discourse Configurational Languages. Oxford University Press, New York, Oxford (1995)

Geurts, B., van der Sandt, R.: Interpreting focus. Theoretical Linguistics 30 (2004)

Groenendijk, J., Stokhof, M.: Studies on the Semantics of Questions and the Pragmatics of Answers. PhD thesis, University of Amsterdam, Amsterdam (1984)

Groenendijk, J., Stokhof, M.: Partitioning Logical Space. Annotated handout at the 2nd ESSLLI, Leuven (1991)

Horváth, J.: Separating "focus movement" from focus. Clever and Right: a Festschrift for Joe Edmonds (2006)

Kratzer, A.: Exclusive questions. Talk at the 10th Sinn und Bedeutung, Berlin (2005)

Krifka, M.: A compositional semantics for multiple focus constructions. In: Jacobs, J. (ed.) Informationsstruktur und Grammatik, Sonderheft der Linguistische Berichte, Westdeutscher Verlag, Opladen (1991)

Krifka, M.: The semantics of questions and the focusation of answers. In: Chungmin, L., Gordon, M., Büring, D. (eds.) Topic and Focus: A Cross-Linguistic Perspective, Kluwer Academic Publishers, Dordrecht (2004)

Rooth, M.: Association with Focus. PhD thesis, University of Massachusetts, Amherst (1985)

Szabolcsi, A.: The semantics of topic-focus articulation. In: Groenendijk, J., Janssen, T., Stokhof, M. (eds.) Formal Methods in the Study of Language, Mathematisch Centrum, Amsterdam (1981)

Szendrői, K.: Focus and the syntax-phonology interface. PhD thesis, University College, London (2001)

Szendrői, K.: A stress-based approach to the syntax of Hungarian focus. The Linguistic Review 20(1) (2003)

van Rooij, R., Schulz, K.: Only: Meaning and implicature. In: Aloni, M., Butler, A., Dekker, P. (eds.) Questions in Dynamic Semantics. CRiSPI Series, Elsevier, Amsterdam (to appear)

von Stechow, A.: Focusing and backgrounding operators. In: Abraham, W. (ed.) Discourse Particles, Benjamins, Amsterdam/Philadelphia (1991)

# Appendix

$$(\varepsilon\mathcal{XH}(\varepsilon\mathcal{XH}(T))) = (\varepsilon\mathcal{XH}(T))$$

$$\varepsilon\mathcal{XH} = \lambda\mathbb{P}\lambda P[\mathbb{P}(P) \wedge \neg\exists P'[\mathbb{P}(P') \wedge P' \neq P \wedge \forall x[P'(x) \to P(x)]]]$$

1. $\forall P(\varepsilon\mathcal{XH}(U)(P) \to U(P))$ by definition of $\varepsilon\mathcal{XH}$ $U$ instantiates $\mathbb{P}$

2. $\forall P(\varepsilon\varkappa\mathcal{H}(\varepsilon\varkappa\mathcal{H}(T))(P) \to \varepsilon\varkappa\mathcal{H}(T)(P))$ directly from 1., $\varepsilon\varkappa\mathcal{H}(T)$ instantiates $U$

3. $\forall P(\varepsilon\varkappa\mathcal{H}(T)(P) \to \varepsilon\varkappa\mathcal{H}(\varepsilon\varkappa\mathcal{H}(T))(P))$

   proof by contradiction: suppose this is not the case

   then $\exists P.\varepsilon\varkappa\mathcal{H}(T)(P) \land \neg\varepsilon\varkappa\mathcal{H}(\varepsilon\varkappa\mathcal{H}(T))(P)$;

   then (by definition of $\varepsilon\varkappa\mathcal{H}$) $\exists P'((P' \neq P \land \forall x(P'(x) \to P(x))) \land \varepsilon\varkappa\mathcal{H}(T)(P))$

   but then $\neg\varepsilon\varkappa\mathcal{H}(T)(P)$

4. $\varepsilon\varkappa\mathcal{H}(\varepsilon\varkappa\mathcal{H}(T)) = \varepsilon\varkappa\mathcal{H}(T)$ [from 2. and 3.]

$$(\varepsilon\varkappa\mathcal{H}^2(\langle\varepsilon\varkappa\mathcal{H}(\lambda P.P(\alpha)),\ \varepsilon\varkappa\mathcal{H}(\lambda Q.Q(\beta))\rangle)) =$$
$$(\varepsilon\varkappa\mathcal{H}^2(\langle\lambda P.P(\alpha), \lambda Q.Q(\beta)\rangle))$$

$\varepsilon\varkappa\mathcal{H}^2 = \lambda\mathbb{R}\lambda R[\mathbb{R}(R) \land \neg\exists R'[\mathbb{R}(R') \land R' \neq R \land \forall x,y[R'(x,y) \to R(x,y)]]]$

- $(\varepsilon\varkappa\mathcal{H}^2(\langle\lambda P.P(\alpha), \lambda Q.Q(\beta)\rangle))$

$\langle\lambda P.P(\alpha), \lambda Q.Q(\beta)\rangle = \lambda R[(\lambda P.P(\alpha))(\lambda x((\lambda P.P(\beta))(\lambda y[R(x,y)])))]$
which this reduces to $\lambda R.R(\alpha,\beta)$

$(\varepsilon\varkappa\mathcal{H}^2(\lambda R.R(\alpha,\beta))$

$(\lambda\mathbb{R}\lambda R[\mathbb{R}(R) \land \neg\exists R'[\mathbb{R}(R') \land R' \neq R \land \forall x,y[R'(x,y) \to R(x,y)]]])(\lambda R.R(\alpha,\beta))$

$\lambda R[R(\alpha,\beta) \land \neg\exists R'[R'(\alpha,\beta) \land R' \neq R \land \forall x,y[R'(x,y) \to R(x,y)]]]$
which reduces to: $\lambda R.\forall x,y[R(x,y) \leftrightarrow [x = a \land y = b]]$

- $(\varepsilon\varkappa\mathcal{H}^2(\langle\varepsilon\varkappa\mathcal{H}(\lambda P.P(\alpha)),\ \varepsilon\varkappa\mathcal{H}(\lambda Q.Q(\beta))\rangle))$

$\langle\varepsilon\varkappa\mathcal{H}(\lambda P.P(\alpha)),\ \varepsilon\varkappa\mathcal{H}(\lambda Q.Q(\beta))\rangle =$
$\lambda R[(\lambda P.\forall x[P(x) \leftrightarrow x = \alpha])(\lambda x((\lambda P.\forall y[P(y) \leftrightarrow y = \beta])(\lambda y[R(x,y)])))] =$
$\lambda R[\forall x[\forall y[R(x,y) \leftrightarrow y = \beta] \leftrightarrow x = \alpha]]$

$(\varepsilon\varkappa\mathcal{H}^2(\lambda R[\forall x[\forall y[R(x,y) \leftrightarrow y = \beta] \leftrightarrow x = \alpha]]))$

$(\lambda\mathbb{R}\lambda R[\mathbb{R}(R) \land \neg\exists R'[\mathbb{R}(R') \land R' \neq R \land$
$\qquad \forall x,y[R'(x,y) \to R(x,y)]]])(\lambda R[\forall x[\forall y[R(x,y) \leftrightarrow y = \beta] \leftrightarrow x = \alpha]])$

$\lambda R[\forall x[\forall y[R(x,y) \leftrightarrow y = \beta] \leftrightarrow x = \alpha] \land$
$\qquad \neg\exists R'[\forall x[\forall y[R'(x,y) \leftrightarrow y = \beta] \leftrightarrow x = \alpha] \land R' \neq R \land$
$\qquad\qquad \forall x,y[R'(x,y) \to R(x,y)]]]$

which is equivalent to $\lambda R\forall x,y[R(x,y) \leftrightarrow [x = \alpha \land y = \beta]]$

# Duals of Simple and Subdirectly Irreducible Distributive Modal Algebras

Be Birchall

ILLC, University of Amsterdam
ebirchal@science.uva.nl

**Abstract.** Simplicity and subdirect irreducibility of complex algebra duals of Kripke frames can be readily characterized in terms of roots of the corresponding Kripke frames.

Here these characterizations are generalized to the case of distributive modal algebras $(A, \vee, \wedge, 0, 1, \Diamond, \Box, \rhd, \lhd)$, and their duals. Such an algebra consists of a distributive bounded lattice $(A, \vee, \wedge, 0, 1)$ together with a join preserving operator $\Diamond$, a meet preserving operator $\Box$, a join reversing operator $\rhd$, and a meet reversing operator $\lhd$.

After introducing the problem in §1, we arrive at the characterizations of simple and subdirectly irreducible distributive modal algebras in §2. The final section sketches a more transparent characterization.

## 1 The Problem

This first section introduces the key notions figuring in the title, and we see what characterizations we are aiming to generalize.

### 1.1 Simple and Subdirectly Irreducible Algebras

The *direct product* of a collection of algebras is the usual product for algebras, generalizing that based on the cartesian product of the underlying sets of a finite collection of algebras. We might wonder if every algebra can be expressed as the direct product of algebras that cannot themselves be further reduced to a direct product of other algebras. For finite algebras this is indeed the case. That is, where a *directly indecomposable* algebra is one that is not isomorphic to a direct product of two nontrivial algebras, every finite algebra is isomorphic to a direct product of directly indecomposable algebras.

This does not, though, obtain for infinite algebras in general. However, something similar does hold for a weaker notion of product. An algebra $A$ is a *subdirect product* of a collection of algebras if it is a subalgebra of the direct product of that collection such that the natural projection map of $A$ to each algebra in the collection is surjective. If one such projection map is an isomorphism for every collection of algebras of which $A$ is a subdirect product, then $A$ is *subdirectly irreducible*. That is, informally, an algebra is subdirectly irreducible iff it cannot be reduced to other algebras via subdirect product. A theorem of Birkhoff

B.D. ten Cate and H.W. Zeevat (Eds.): TbiLLC 2005, LNAI 4363, pp. 45–57, 2007.

states that every algebra is isomorphic to a subdirect product of subdirectly irreducible algebras. In this sense, subdirectly irreducible algebras are the basic building blocks of algebras.

An alternative characterization of subdirect irreducibility, in terms of the congruence lattice of an algebra, follows from the definition of subdirect irreducibility. Where $\mathbb{A}, \mathbb{A}'$ are algebras and $\mathbb{A}$ has underlying set $A$, a *congruence* of $\mathbb{A}$ is the kernel $\theta_h := \{(a,b) \in A \times A : h(a) = h(b)\}$ of a homomorphism $h : \mathbb{A} \to \mathbb{A}'$. The set of congruences $Con(\mathbb{A})$ of $\mathbb{A}$ forms a lattice under $\subseteq$. This *congruence lattice* of $\mathbb{A}$ has top element $A \times A$, and bottom element $\{(a,a) : a \in A\}$. This bottom element is known as the *trivial* congruence. According to the alternative characterization (which is sometimes taken as the definition, rather than established as an immediate consequence of our initial definition), an algebra is subdirectly irreducible iff it is trivial or has a smallest nontrivial congruence. Simple algebras are the special case of subdirectly irreducible algebras having only a least and a greatest congruence. Thus we have the following working definitions:

- An algebra is *subdirectly irreducible* if it is trivial or has a smallest nontrivial congruence.
- An algebra is *simple* if it is trivial or its smallest nontrivial congruence is its maximal congruence.

A more detailed presentation of the above can be found in § II.8 of [2].

## 1.2   Kripke Frame Duals

Simplicity and subdirect irreducibility of complex algebra duals of Kripke frames can be readily characterized (see [6]) in terms of roots of the corresponding Kripke frames:

1. *A Kripke frame $(W, R)$ has a root iff its dual $(\mathcal{P}(W), \cup, \cap, \emptyset, \backslash, W, \langle R \rangle)$ is subdirectly irreducible;*
2. *All elements of a Kripke frame $(W, R)$ are roots iff its dual $(\mathcal{P}(W), \cup, \cap, \emptyset, \backslash, W, \langle R \rangle)$ is simple.*

A *Kripke frame* $(W, R)$ consists of a binary relation $R$ on a nonempty set $W$. *Roots* are elements of $W$ from which every element of $W$ can be reached in a finite number of $R$-steps; that is, where $R' \subseteq W \times W$ is the smallest transitive superset of $R$, $r \in W$ is a root iff $rR'w$ for every $w$ in $W$. The complex algebra dual of a Kripke frame $(W, R)$ is its representation as the Boolean algebra $(\mathcal{P}(W), \cup, \cap, \backslash, \emptyset, W, \langle R \rangle)$ based on the power set of $W$. The operator $\langle R \rangle$ here is given by $\langle R \rangle a = \{w : wRv \text{ for some } v \in a\}$, for $a \subseteq W$.

As is well known, the class of Kripke frames is not adequate for the representation of Boolean algebras with operators ($BAO$'s); the collection of Kripke frame duals is only a proper subset of the collection of all $BAO$'s. Instead, Kripke frames are generalized to descriptive general frames, structures involving a topology, to yield the duals of $BAO$'s. Venema in [7] generalized the above characterization of subdirect irreducibility from the special case of Kripke frame duals to arbitrary $BAO$'s.

The aim of this paper is to see how the above two characterizations generalize to the distributive setting. This involves generalizing the notion of rootedness to take aspects of the dual structure into account.

## 1.3  Priestley Duality

Before introducing the generalization of Kripke frame duals, distriibutive modal algebras, we pause to review some facts about Priestley spaces. All results here without proof are proved in chapter 11 of [3].

An *ordered topological space* is a triple $\mathbb{X} = (X, \leqslant, \tau)$ where $(X, \leqslant)$ is a partially ordered set and $(X, \tau)$ is a topological space. Terminology for partially ordered sets and topological spaces is applied also to ordered topological spaces. For example, where $\mathbb{X} = (X, \leqslant, \tau)$ is an ordered topological space, $\mathbb{X}$ is closed iff the associated topological space $(X, \tau)$ is closed. And a closed down-set of $\mathbb{X}$ is a subset of $X$ that is both a closed set of $(X, \tau)$ and a down-set of $(X, \leqslant)$.

The set of clopen down-sets of an ordered topological space $\mathbb{X}$ is denoted $\mathsf{cl}\mathcal{D}(\mathbb{X})$. For $a \subseteq X$, $\downarrow a := \{x \in a : x \leqslant y \text{ for some } y \in a\}$ and $\uparrow a := \{x \in a : x \geqslant y \text{ for some } y \in a\}$. For $x \in X$, $\downarrow\{x\}$ and $\uparrow\{x\}$ are abbreviated (respectively) $\downarrow x$ and $\uparrow x$.

An ordered topological space $\mathbb{X} = (X, \leqslant, \tau)$ is a *Priestley space* if it is compact and such that for any $x, y \in X$ with $x \not\geqslant y$ there is a clopen down-set $a$ such that $x \in a$ and $y \notin a$.

The following states properties of Priestley spaces that we will make use of later:

**Proposition 1.** *Let $\mathbb{X} = (X, \leqslant, \tau)$ be a Priestley space. Then*

1. *Where $c \subseteq X$ is a closed down-set of $\mathbb{X}$ with $x \notin c$, there is some $a \in \mathsf{cl}\mathcal{D}(\mathbb{X})$ for whch $c \subseteq a$ and $x \notin a$,*
2. *Where $c, d \subseteq X$ are disjoint closed sets, if $c$ is a down-set while $d$ is an up-set then there is some $b \in \mathsf{cl}\mathcal{D}(\mathbb{X})$ for which $c \subseteq b$ and $d \cap b = \emptyset$,*
3. *$\downarrow x$ is closed for $x \in X$, and*
4. *$\downarrow c, \uparrow c$ are closed for $c \subseteq X$.*

A Priestley space $\mathbb{X} = (X, \leqslant, \tau)$ gives rise to two "weaker" topologies $T_1, T_2 \subseteq T$ on $X$. Let $T_1 = \{\bigcup U : U \subseteq \mathsf{cl}\mathcal{D}(\mathbb{X})\}$ and let $T_2 = \{\bigcup\{(X \setminus a) : a \in U\} : U \subseteq \mathsf{cl}\mathcal{D}(\mathbb{X})\}$.

**Proposition 2.** *$T_1$ and $T_2$ are topologies on $X$*

*Proof.* Since $\emptyset, X \in \mathsf{cl}\mathcal{D}(\mathbb{X})$, also $\emptyset = \bigcup\{\emptyset\}$, $X = \bigcup\{X\} \in T_1$. And certainly $T_1$ is closed under arbitrary union. To see that $T_1$ is closed under finite intersection, consider $U_1, \ldots, U_n \subseteq \mathsf{cl}\mathcal{D}(\mathbb{X})$. Observe that since $a_1 \cap \cdots \cap a_n \in \mathsf{cl}\mathcal{D}(\mathbb{X})$ for $a_1, \ldots, a_n \in \mathsf{cl}\mathcal{D}(\mathbb{X})$, we have

$$\bigcup U_1 \cap \cdots \cap \bigcup U_n = \bigcup\{a_1 \cap \cdots \cap a_n : a_1 \in U_1, \ldots, a_n \in U_n\} \in T_1.$$

Thus $T_1$ is a topology on $X$; the reasoning to establish that $T_2$ is a topology on $X$ is similar.

$T_1$ is the *upper topology (for $\mathbb{X}$)*, and has basis $\mathsf{cl}\mathcal{D}(\mathbb{X})$. $T_2$ is the *lower topology (for $\mathbb{X}$)*, and has basis $\{X \setminus a : a \in \mathsf{cl}\mathcal{D}(\mathbb{X})\}$.

The dual of a Priestley space is a bounded distributive lattice:

**Proposition 3.** Where $\mathbb{X} = (X, \leqslant, \tau)$ is a Priestley space, $\mathbb{X}^* = (\mathsf{cl}\mathcal{D}(\mathbb{X}), \cup, \cap, \emptyset, X)$ is a bounded distributive lattice.

Next the notion of the Priestley dual of a bounded distributive lattice is formulated, with some useful notation introduced along the way:

**Definition 1.** *Let $\mathbb{A} = (A, \vee, \wedge, 0, 1)$ be a bounded distributive lattice. For $a \in A$,*

$$\hat{a} := \{I \in \mathcal{I}_{\mathcal{P}}(\mathbb{A}) : a \notin I\}.$$

*The Priestley dual of $\mathbb{A}$ is $\mathbb{A}_* := (\mathcal{I}_{\mathcal{P}}(\mathbb{A}), \subseteq, \tau)$, where $\tau$ is the topology on $\mathcal{I}_{\mathcal{P}}(\mathbb{A})$ with basis $\{\hat{a} \cap (\mathcal{I}_{\mathcal{P}}(\mathbb{A}) \setminus \hat{b}) : a, b \in A\}$.*

Here $\mathcal{I}_{\mathcal{P}}(\mathbb{A})$ denotes the set of prime ideals of $\mathbb{A}$.

**Proposition 4.** The Priestley dual $\mathbb{A}_*$ of a bounded distributive lattice $\mathbb{A}$ is a Priestley space.

Now we are ready to look at a generalization of Priestley duality, between distributive modal algebras and their extended Priestley space duals.

### 1.4 Distributive Modal Algebras and Their Duals

A *distributive modal algebra (DMA)*. $\mathbb{A} = (A, \vee, \wedge, 0, 1, \Diamond, \Box, \rhd, \lhd)$ is an algebra with an underlying bounded distributive lattice $(A, \vee, \wedge, 0, 1)$ and modal operators $\Diamond, \Box, \rhd, \lhd$ satisfying:

$$\Diamond(a \vee b) = \Diamond a \vee \Diamond b , \qquad \Diamond 0 = 0,$$
$$\Box(a \wedge b) = \Box a \wedge \Box b , \qquad \Box 1 = 1,$$
$$\rhd(a \vee b) = \rhd a \wedge \rhd b , \qquad \rhd 0 = 1,$$
$$\lhd(a \wedge b) = \lhd a \vee \lhd b , \qquad \lhd 1 = 0.$$

Notice that while *DMA*'s contains a function symbols for disjunction and conjunction ($\vee$ and $\wedge$, respectively), they don't contain a function symbol for negation. However, $\Box$ behaves as $\neg\Diamond\neg$ would in a modal algebra, and $\rhd$, $\lhd$ behave as $\neg\Diamond$ and $\Diamond\neg$ respectively. Since negation is not present, $\Box$ and $\Diamond$ are not interdefinable as would be the case with a modal algebra. This explains the need for modal operators $\Box$, $\lhd$ and $\rhd$ in addition to $\Diamond$.

A duality for *DMA*'s is developed extending Priestley duality, in which distributive algebras without modal operators are represented as Priestley spaces. This extension is similar to the duality developed in [5], which also extends Priestley duality but to a setting with only two modal operators.

An *extended Priestley space* is a tuple $\mathbb{X} = (X, \leqslant, \tau, R_\Diamond, R_\Box, R_\rhd, R_\lhd)$ such that $(X, \leqslant, \tau)$ is a Priestley space, and the *operator relations* $R_\Diamond, R_\Box, R_\rhd, R_\lhd \subseteq X \times X$ satisfy

- If $a \in clD(\mathbb{X})$ then so are $\langle R_\diamond \rangle a$, $[R_\square] a$, $[R_\triangleright] a$ and $\langle R_\triangleleft \rangle a$,
- For all $x \in X$, $R_\diamond[x]$ and $R_\triangleright[x]$ are closed in the upper topology $(X, \leqslant, \tau)$, and $R_\square[x]$ and $R_\triangleleft[x]$ are closed in the lower topology for $(X, \leqslant, \tau)$,
- $\leqslant \circ R_\diamond \circ \leqslant \, \subseteq R_\diamond$, $\geqslant \circ R_\square \circ \geqslant \, \subseteq R_\square$, $\geqslant \circ R_\triangleright \circ \leqslant \, \subseteq R_\triangleright$, and $\leqslant \circ R_\triangleleft \circ \geqslant \, \subseteq R_\triangleleft$.

For $R \subseteq X \times X$ with $x \in X$, $R[x]$ denotes the set of $x$'s $R$-successors. That is, $R[x] = \{y \in X : xRy\}$. $clD(\mathbb{X})$ is the set of clopen down-sets of $(X, \leqslant, \tau)$. The following defines $\langle R_\diamond \rangle$, $[R_\square]$, $[R_\triangleright \rangle$ and $\langle R_\triangleleft]$ :

**Definition 2.** *Where $R \subseteq X \times X$, the operations $\langle R \rangle$, $[R]$, $[R \rangle$ and $\langle R]$ on $\mathcal{P}(X)$ are given by*

$$\langle R \rangle a = \{u : \exists v(uRv \text{ and } v \in a)\},$$
$$[R] a = \{u : \forall v(uRv \rightarrow v \in a)\},$$
$$[R \rangle a = \{u : \forall v(uRv \rightarrow v \notin a)\}, \text{ and}$$
$$\langle R] a = \{u : \exists v(uRv \text{ and } v \notin a)\}.$$

The dual $\mathbb{A}_*$ of a *DMA* $\mathbb{A} = (A, \vee, \wedge, 0, 1, \diamond, \square, \triangleright, \triangleleft)$ is defined by

$$\mathbb{A}_* = (\mathcal{I}_\mathcal{P}(\mathbb{A}), \subseteq, \tau, R_\diamond, R_\square, R_\triangleright, R_\triangleleft),$$

where $(\mathcal{I}_\mathcal{P}(\mathbb{A}), \subseteq, \tau)$ is the Priestley dual of the algebra $(A, \vee, \wedge, 0, 1)$ and $R_\diamond$, $R_\square$, $R_\triangleright$, $R_\triangleleft \subseteq \mathcal{I}_\mathcal{P}(\mathbb{A}) \times \mathcal{I}_\mathcal{P}(\mathbb{A})$ are defined by

$I R_\diamond J$ iff $\diamond a \in I$ implies $a \in J$,
$I R_\square J$ iff $\square a \notin I$ implies $a \notin J$,
$I R_\triangleright J$ iff $\triangleright a \notin I$ implies $a \in J$, and
$I R_\triangleleft J$ iff $\triangleleft a \in I$ implies $a \notin J$, for $a \in A$.

The dual $\mathbb{X}^*$ of an extended Priestley space $\mathbb{X} = (X, \leqslant, \tau, R_\diamond, R_\square, R_\triangleright, R_\triangleleft)$ is defined by

$$\mathbb{X}^* = (clD(\mathbb{X}), \cup, \cap, \emptyset, X, \langle R_\diamond \rangle, [R_\square], [R_\triangleright \rangle, \langle R_\triangleleft]).$$

The result that the classes *DMA*'s and of extended Priestley spaces are dual to one another is summarized by the following:

**Proposition 5.** *Where $\mathbb{A}$ is a DMA and $\mathbb{X}$ is an extended Priestley space,*

- $\mathbb{A}_*$ *is an extended Priestley space and $\mathbb{X}^*$ is a DMA;*
- $\mathbb{A} \cong (\mathbb{A}_*)^*$ *and $\mathbb{X} \cong (\mathbb{X}^*)_*$.*

Notice that Kripke frames correspond to the special case of extended Priestley spaces with a discrete topology (in which all subsets of the underlying set are closed), a trivial ordering (the identity relation) and with all operator relations except for the $R_\diamond$ relation empty.

## 2   Characterizations

To obtain the characterizations, we begin by looking at the duals of homomorphisms between *DMA*'s. This allows us to translate the generalized notion of root for extended Priestley spaces, that we arrive at in §2.2, back to *DMA*'s. By then we are almost ready to provide the characterizations, which is done in §2.4.

## 2.1  Homomorphisms as Duals

Our working definitions of subdirect irreducibility and simplicity, recall, are stated in terms of congruences. So the next definition describes the connection between the subdirect irreducibility and simplicity of an algebra, and the homomorphisms from the algebra:

**Definition 3.** *Let* $\mathbb{A} = (A, \vee, \wedge, 0, 1, \Diamond, \Box, \triangleright, \triangleleft)$ *and* $\mathbb{A}' = (A', \vee', \wedge', 0', 1', \Diamond',$ $\Box', \triangleright', \triangleleft')$ *be DMA's. A homomorphism* from $\mathbb{A}$ to $\mathbb{A}'$ *is a function* $\eta : A \to A'$ *satisfying*

$$\eta(0) = 0' \text{ and } \eta(1) = 1',$$
$$\eta(a \vee b) = \eta(a) \vee \eta(b) \text{ and } \eta(a \wedge b) = \eta(a) \wedge \eta(b) \text{ for } a, b \in A$$

*and*

$$\eta(\triangle\, a) = \triangle' \, (\eta a) \text{ for } a \in A,$$

*for each operator* $\triangle \in \{\Diamond, \Box, \triangleright, \triangleleft\}$ *with corresponding operator* $\triangle'$ *of* $\mathbb{A}'$. *The kernel* $\{(a, b) : \eta(a) = \eta(b)\}$ *of a homomorphism* $\eta$ *is called a* congruence.

Homomorphisms between two $DMA$'s correspond to certain dual maps between the $DMA$'s extended Priestley space duals:

**Definition 4.** *A* continuous order-preserving bounded morphism *(abbreviated* morphism *where no confusion is likely to result)* $\chi$ *between extended Priestley spaces* $\mathbb{X}$ *and* $\mathbb{X}'$ *is a function* $\chi : X \to X'$ *between the underlying sets of these algebras such that*

- $\chi$ *is continuous,*
- $\chi$ *is order-preserving; i.e.,* $x \leqslant y$ *implies* $\chi(x) \leqslant' \chi(y)$ *for* $x, y \in X$,
- *(forth)* $xR_\triangle y$ *implies* $\chi(x)R_\triangle\chi(y)$ *for* $\triangle \in \{\Diamond, \Box, \triangleright, \triangleleft\}$,
- *(back)* $\chi(x)R'_\Diamond y$ *($\chi(x)R'_\Box y, \chi(x)R'_\triangleright y, \chi(x)R_\triangleleft y$) implies* $\exists z \in X$ *with* $xR_\Diamond z$ *$(xR_\Box y, xR_\triangleright y, xR_\triangleleft y)$ and* $\chi(z) \leqslant' y$ *$(y \leqslant' \chi(z), \chi(z) \leqslant' y, y \leqslant' \chi(z))$, respectively).*

Readers familiar with bounded morphisms between Kripke frames will notice that these last two conditions correspond to the "forth" and "back" conditions in the definition of those maps. The first two conditons above account for the topological, and (respectively) order aspects of the duals of $DMA$'s.

For a function $\chi : X \to X'$ between extended Priestley spaces $\mathbb{X}$ and $\mathbb{X}'$, define the dual
$\chi^* : clD(\mathbb{X}') \to \mathcal{P}(X)$ by

$$\chi^* : a \mapsto \{x \in X : \chi(x) \in a\}.$$

And the dual $\eta_* : \mathcal{I}_\mathcal{P}(\mathbb{A}') \to \mathcal{P}(A)$ of a function $\eta : A \to A'$ is defined by

$$\eta_* : I \mapsto \{a \in A : \eta(a) \in I\}.$$

The duality results about maps are summarized by the following proposition.

**Proposition 6.** *Where* $\chi : X \to X'$ *is a morphism between extended Priestley spaces* $\mathbb{X}$ *and* $\mathbb{X}'$, *and* $\eta : \mathbb{A} \to \mathbb{A}'$ *is a homomorphism between DMA's* $\mathbb{A}$ *and* $\mathbb{A}'$,

- $\chi^*$ *is a homomorphism from* $\mathbb{X}'^*$ *to* $\mathbb{X}^*$, *and* $\eta_*$ *is a morphism from* $\mathbb{A}'_*$ *and* $\mathbb{A}_*$;
- *Where* $f : \mathbb{X} \to (\mathbb{X}^*)_*$, $f' : \mathbb{X}' \to (\mathbb{X}'^*)_*$ *are given by* $f : x \mapsto \{a \in cl\mathcal{D}(\mathbb{X}) : x \notin a\}$ *and* $f' : x \mapsto \{a \in cl\mathcal{D}(\mathbb{X}') : x \notin a\}$,

$$f'_{\mathbb{X}'}(\chi(x)) = (\chi^*)_*(f_{\mathbb{X}}(x)), \text{ for all } x \in X,$$

*and where* $g : \mathbb{A} \to (\mathbb{A}_*)^*$, $g' : \mathbb{A}' \to (\mathbb{A}'_*$ *are given by* $g : a \mapsto \{I \in \mathcal{I}_P(\mathbb{A}) : a \notin I\}$ *and* $g' : a \mapsto \{I \in \mathcal{I}_P(\mathbb{A}') : a \notin I\}$,

$$g'_{\mathbb{A}'}(\eta(a)) = (\eta_*)^*(g_{\mathbb{A}}(a)), \text{ for all } a \in A.$$

## 2.2 Generalizing the Notion of Root

The characterizations (stated in § 1.2) that we are aiming to generalize are in terms of the roots of Kripke frames. So me must find an appropriate notion of root for our new structures, extended Priestley spaces. To do this, it would help to understand how Kripke frame roots are related to aspects of Kripke frames that we already know how to generalize. And, as we saw in the previous section, we do have a generalization of the notion of bounded morphism.

We can describe roots in terms of $R$-*hereditary* sets of a Kripke frame $(W, R)$. A subset of $W$ is $R$-*hereditary* if it is closed under $R$; that is, $X \subseteq W$ is $R$-hereditary iff for all $x, v \in W$, $w \in X, wRv$ implies $v \in X$. Now observe that

- An $R$-hereditary set contains a root only if it is equal to the whole $W$. That is, the roots are the elements of $W$ that are not contained in any proper hereditary subset of $W$.
- The $R$-hereditary sets are the images of bounded morphisms.

So our strategy is to define a notion of heredity for extended Priestley spaces so that the hereditary sets are the images of continuous order-preserving bounded morphisms. Proposition 7 proves that the following definition succeeds in doing this.[1]

**Definition 5.** *For an extended Priestley space* $\mathbb{X} = (X, \leqslant, \tau, R_\diamond, R_\Box, R_\triangleright, R_\triangleleft)$, *a subset* $c \subseteq X$ *is a topo-hereditary subset of* $\mathbb{X}$ *if* $c$ *is topologically closed, and for* $x, y \in X$

*if* $x \in \chi[X']$ *and* $xR_\diamond y$ ($xR_\Box y, xR_\triangleright y, xR_\triangleleft y$) *then there is a* $z \in \chi[X']$ *such that*
$xR_\diamond z$ ($xR_\Box z, xR_\triangleright z, xR_\triangleleft z$) *and* $z \leqslant y$ ($z \geqslant y, z \leqslant y, z \geqslant y$, *respectively*).

---

[1] Actually, only one direction of this claim is proved below, since it turns out that we don't need to appeal to the other direction.

Now we are ready to define the generalized notion of root for extended Priestley spaces:

**Definition 6.** A topo-root *of an extended Priestley space* $\mathbb{X} = (X, \leqslant, \tau, R_\Diamond, R_\Box, R_\triangleright, R_\triangleleft)$ *is an element of $X$ not contained in any proper topo-hereditary subset of* $\mathbb{X}$.

Notice that topo-roots are indeed the roots of the special case of extended Priestley spaces (those with trivial ordering, discrete topology, and all operator relations except $R_\Diamond$ empty) coinciding with Kripke frames. This is because topo-hereditary subsets of those special cases of extended Priestley spaces coincide with hereditary subsets of the corresponding Kripke frames.

## 2.3  Dualizing

The collection $\mathcal{H}(\mathbb{X})$ of topo-hereditary subsets of the extended Priestley space $\mathbb{X}$ forms a lattice under $\subseteq$ with smallest element $\emptyset$ and largest element the non proper topo-hereditary subset $X$. Similarly, $(\mathcal{H}(\mathbb{X}), \supseteq)$ forms a lattice, now with largest element $\emptyset$. We will see that this latter lattice is isomorphic to the congruence lattice $(Con(\mathbb{X}^*), \subseteq)$ of $\mathbb{X}^*$. This gives us a connection betweeen congruences of *DMA*'s and topo-hereditary subsets – and so topo-roots – of their duals, which is just what we're looking for.

To have an idea of why this connection obtains, recall that topo-hereditary subsets are the images of continuous order-preserving bounded morphisms, which in the dual structure correspond to pre-images of homomorphisms, which are in turn closely related to congruences. This line of thought is made precise in the proofs of the next two propositions below.

For the remainder of this paper, let $\mathbb{X} = (X, \leqslant, \tau, R_\Diamond, R_\Box, R_\triangleright, R_\triangleleft)$ be an extended Priestley space.

**Proposition 7.** *Let* $\mathbb{X}' = (X', \leqslant', \tau', R'_\Diamond, R'_\Box, R'_\triangleright, R'_\triangleleft)$. *If* $\chi : X' \to X$ *is a morphism then the image $\chi[X']$ of $X'$ is a topo-hereditary subset of* $\mathbb{X}$.

*Proof.* Since $\chi$ is continuous and $(X, \tau)$ is compact and Hausdorff, standard topological considerations guarantee that $\chi[X']$ is closed.

So it remains to ensure that for $x, y \in X$,

> if $x \in \chi[X']$ and $xR_\Diamond y$ ($xR_\Box y, xR_\triangleright y, xR_\triangleleft y$) then there is a $z \in \chi[X']$ such that
> $xR_\Diamond z$ ($xR_\Box z, xR_\triangleright z, xR_\triangleleft z$) and $z \leqslant y$ ($z \geqslant y, z \leqslant y, z \geqslant y$, respectively).

Since the cases for the other operator relations are similar, we will show that this obtains only for $R_\Diamond$. So consider $x \in \chi[X']$ for which $xR_\Diamond y$. Let $x' \in X'$ be such that $\chi(x')R_\Diamond y$. Then by the "back" condition in the definition of morphism, there is some $y' \in X'$ such that $x'R'_\Diamond y'$ and $\chi(y') \leqslant y$. Making use of the "forth" condition, from $x'R'_\Diamond y'$ we obtain $\chi(x')R_\Diamond \chi(y')$. Thus $z := \chi(y')$ is as required.

**Proposition 8.** $(\mathcal{H}(\mathbb{X}), \supseteq)$ *is isomorphic to the congruence lattice* $(Con(\mathbb{X}^*), \subseteq)$ *of* $\mathbb{X}^*$.

*Proof.* We will see that $\varepsilon : c \mapsto \theta_c$ is the required isomorphism, where $\theta_c \subseteq clD(\mathbb{X}) \times clD(\mathbb{X})$ is defined by

$$(a, b) \in \theta_c \text{ iff } a \cap c = b \cap c.$$

Notice that for $c, d \in \mathcal{H}(\mathbb{X})$ we have $c \subseteq d$ iff $\theta_d \subseteq \theta_c$. To see this, consider $c, d \in \mathcal{H}(\mathbb{X})$, and suppose first that $c \subseteq d$. Then for $(a, b) \in \theta_d$ we have $a \cap d = b \cap d$, and so since $c \subseteq d$ also $a \cap c = b \cap c$; thus $(a, b) \in \theta_c$. Proposition 1 is useful in proving the converse. Suppose $c \not\subseteq d$, letting $x \in c \setminus d$. To ensure that $\theta_d \not\subseteq \theta_c$, it suffices to find $a, b \in clD(\mathbb{X})$ such that $a \cap d = b \cap d$ and $x \in b \setminus a$. Since $d \in \mathcal{H}(\mathbb{X})$, $d$ is closed. So using proposition 1 (3) and (4), we see that $\downarrow(d \cap \downarrow x)$ is a closed down-set. And since $x \notin d$, also $x \notin \downarrow(d \cap \downarrow x)$. So by proposition 1 (1) there is some $a \in clD(\mathbb{X})$ such that $x \notin a$ and $\downarrow(d \cap \downarrow x) \subseteq a$. Now observe that by proposition 1 (3), $a \cup \downarrow x$ is a closed down-set. And since $a$ is open while $d$ is closed, $d \setminus a$ is closed and so by proposition 1 (4) $\uparrow(d \setminus a)$ is a closed up-set. To use proposition 1 (2), we must ensure that $a \cup \downarrow x$ and $\uparrow(d \setminus a)$ are disjoint. For consider $y \in \uparrow(d \setminus a)$ so that $y \geqslant z$ for some $z \in d \setminus a$. Then since $a$ is a down-set and $z \notin a$, also $y \notin a$. And from $z \in d \setminus a$, we have $z \in d$ but $z \notin d \cap \downarrow x$. But then $z \not\leqslant x$, which together with $z \leqslant y$ implies $y \not\leqslant x$. That is, $y \notin \downarrow x$, and so we have shown that $y \notin a \cup \downarrow x$. With the hypothesis of proposition 1 (2) now in place, we can conclude that there is some $b \in clD(\mathbb{X})$ such that $(a \cup \downarrow x) \subseteq b$ and $\uparrow(d \setminus a) \cap b = \emptyset$. To see that $a$ and $b$ are as required, notice that $a \subseteq b$ while $(d \setminus a) \cap b = \emptyset$.

It remains to show that $\varepsilon$ is surjective. So consider $\theta \in Con(\mathbb{X}^*)$. Since $\theta$ is a congruence, $\theta$ is the kernel of some homomorphism $\eta : \mathbb{X}^* \to \mathbb{X}'^*$ from $\mathbb{X}^*$ into another distributive modal algebra $\mathbb{X}'^*$. The duality results ensure that $\eta$ is the dual of a morphism $\chi : \mathbb{X}' \to \mathbb{X}$. Now let $c := \chi[X']$ be the $\chi$-image of the underlying set $X'$ of $\mathbb{X}$. Then by proposition 7 above, $c \in \mathcal{H}(\mathbb{X})$. Finally, observe that $\theta = \theta_c$. For we have

$$
\begin{aligned}
(a, b) \in \theta &\text{ iff } (a, b) \in \ker \chi^*, \\
&\text{ iff } \chi^*(a) = \chi^*(b), \\
&\text{ iff } \{x \in X' : \chi(x) \in a\} = \{x \in X' : \chi(x) \in b\}, \\
&\text{ iff } a \cap \chi(X') = b \cap \chi(X'), \\
&\text{ iff } (a, b) \in \theta_{\chi(X')} = \theta_c.
\end{aligned}
$$

## 2.4 The Greatest Topo-Hereditary Subset

With the correspondence between hereditary sets of a *DMA* and congruences of their duals in place, we are almost ready to provide our characterizations. Since we are interested in the smallest non-trivial congruence of a *DMA*, we are correspondingly interested in the largest proper topo-hereditary subset of its dual. The following proposition characterizes the greatest proper topo-hereditary subset of an extended Priestley space.

**Proposition 9.** *Let* $\mathbb{X} = (X, \leqslant, \tau, R_\diamond, R_\square, R_\triangleright, R_\triangleleft)$ *be an extended Priestley space, with* $a \subseteq X$. *Then* $a$ *is the greatest proper topo-hereditary subset of* $\mathbb{X}$ *iff*

1. *$a$ is a proper closed subset of $X$, and*
2. *$X \setminus a$ is the set of topo-roots of $\mathbb{X}$.*

*Proof.* First suppose that $a \subseteq X$ is the greatest proper topo-hereditary subset of $\mathbb{X}$. Then condition 1 in the statement is satisfied, since $a$ is proper and (since topo-hereditary) closed. To see that condition 2 is satisfied, consider an element $x$ of $X$. If $x$ is a topo-root, then since $a$ is a proper topo-hereditary subset, $x \notin a$. And if, conversely, $x$ is not a topo-root then $\mathbb{X}$ has a proper topo-hereditary subset $b$ such that $x \in b$. Then $b \subseteq a$, since $a$ is the greatest proper topo-hereditary subset of $\mathbb{X}$, and thus $x \in a$.

Now for the converse, suppose that $a \subseteq X$ satisfies conditions 1 and 2. By condition 1, $a$ is proper. And since condition 1 also guarantees that $a$ is closed, to check that $a$ is topo-hereditary it suffices to ensure that for $x, y \in X$,

if $x \in a$ and $xR_\diamond y$ ($xR_\square y, xR_\triangleright y, xR_\triangleleft y$) then there is a $z \in a$ such that $xR_\diamond z$ ($xR_\square z, xR_\triangleright z, xR_\triangleleft z$) and $z \leqslant y$ ($z \geqslant y, z \leqslant y, z \geqslant y$, respectively).

Since the cases for the other operator relations are similar, we will show that this obtains only for $R_\diamond$. So consider $x \in a$ for which $xR_\diamond y$. Since $x \in a$, $x$ is not a topo-root and so $x \in b$ for some proper topo-hereditary subset $b$. The definition of topo-heredity then guarantees the existence of some $z \in b$ for which $z \leqslant y$ and $xR_\diamond z$. Now since $z$ is in the proper topo-hereditary subset $b$, $z$ is not a topo-root; so $z$ is in $a$, and so is as required. Thus $a$ is a proper topo-hereditary subset of $\mathbb{X}$. To see that $a$ is the greatest such set, consider any proper topo-hereditary set $c$. Every element of $c$ is not a topo-root, and os by ocnditon 2 must be in $a$. Thus $c subseteq a$.

The characterizations of simplicity and subdirect irreducibility now follow almost immediately from this last result together with.

**Theorem 1.** *A nontrivial DMA* $\mathbb{A}$ *is subdirectly irreducible iff the set of topo-roots of its dual* $\mathbb{A}_*$ *is open and non-empty.*

*Proof.* $\mathbb{A}$ is subdirectly irreducible iff $\mathbb{A}$ has a smallest nontrivial congruence, iff (by proposition 8) $\mathbb{A}_*$ has a greatest proper topo-hereditary subset, iff (by proposition 9) iff the set of topo-roots of $\mathbb{A}_*$ is open and non-empty.

**Theorem 2.** *A nontrivial DMA* $\mathbb{A}$ *is simple iff all the elements of its dual* $\mathbb{A}_*$ *are topo-roots.*

*Proof.* $\mathbb{A}$ is simple iff $\mathbb{A}$'s smallest nontrivial congruence is its maximal congruence, iff (by proposition 8) $\mathbb{A}_*$'s greatest proper topo-hereditary subset is $\emptyset$, iff (by proposition 9) all elements of $\mathbb{A}_*$ are topo-roots.

# 3    Refinements

This last section makes steps towards more transparent characterizations of subdirectly irreducible and simple *DMA*'s, and results are obtained for *DMA*'s that satisfy a certain simplifying condition. Finally, we look at a class of *DMA*'s – Ockham algebras – that do satisfy that simplifying condition. The results here are only sketched; a detailed development can be found in chapter 4 of [1].

## 3.1    Heredity Again

Recall that the definition 5 of topo-heredity involves a topological condition together with four conditions relating the ordering to each of the four operator relations. Isolating these latter conditions, we obtain the notion of order-heredity:

**Definition 7.** *Where* $\mathbb{X} = (X, \leqslant, \tau, R_\Diamond, R_\Box, R_\rhd, R_\lhd)$ *is an extended Priestley space, a subset* $c \subseteq X$ *is* order-hereditary *if*

$x \in c$ *and* $xR_\Diamond y$ $(xR_\Box y, xR_\rhd y, xR_\lhd y)$ *implies there is a* $z \in c$ *such that* $xR_\Diamond z$ $(xR_\Box z, xR_\rhd z, xR_\lhd z)$ *and* $z \leqslant y$ $(z \geqslant y, z \leqslant y, z \geqslant y,$ *respectively).*

It turns out that a set is order-hereditary iff it is hereditary with respect to a certain restriction $M \subseteq R_\Diamond \cup R_\Box \cup R_\rhd \cup R_\lhd$, to be defined in terms of the maximal and minimal elements of the set of successors of an element of $\mathbb{X}$.

For a partially ordered set $(X, \leqslant)$ with $a \subseteq X$, $\mathsf{min}\,a$ is the set of all minimal element of $a$. That is, $\mathsf{min}\,a = \{x \in a : \forall y \in a(y \leqslant x \rightarrow y = x)\}$. Similarly, $\mathsf{max}\,a = \{x \in a : \forall y \in a(x \leqslant y \rightarrow y = x)\}$. If $R$ is a binary relation on $X$ and $x \in X$ then $R[x] := \{y \in X : xRy\}$ is the set of $R$-successors of $x$.

**Definition 8.** *Where* $\mathbb{X} = (X, \leqslant, \tau, R_\Diamond, R_\Box, R_\rhd, R_\lhd)$ *is an extended Priestey space, let* $M \subseteq X \times X$ *be defined by*

$$xMy \text{ iff } y \in \{\min R_\Diamond[x] \cup \max R_\Box[x] \cup \min R_\rhd[x] \cup \max R_\lhd[x]\}.$$

*A subset* $a \subseteq X$ *is* M-hereditary *if* $y \in a$ *for all* $x, y \in X$ *with* $x \in a$ *and* $xMy$.

Notice that $M \subseteq R_\Diamond \cup R_\Box \cup R_\rhd \cup R_\lhd$. This next proposition, not proved here, depends on the fact that the set $R_\triangle[x]$ of points $R_\triangle$-accessible from $x$ is topologically closed.

**Proposition 10.** *Where $X$ is the underlying set of an extended Priestley space and $a \subseteq X$, $a$ is order-hereditary iff $a$ is $M$-hereditary.*

## 3.2    Alternative Characterizations

Alternative characterizations of simplicity and subdirect irreducibility can be made by basing a notion of root on our new notion of M-heredity in place of topo-heredity. Some notation is useful for this. For a binary relation $R$ on a set $X$ with $x \in X$, $R^\omega[x]$ denotes the set of elements of $X$ that can be reached from $x$ in any finite number of $R$-steps. That is, $R^\omega[x] = \bigcup_{n \in \mathbb{N}} R^n[x]$, where

$$R^0[x] = \{x\},$$
$$R^{n+1}[x] = \{y \in X : xRy \text{ and } x \in R^n[x]\}, \text{ for } n \neq 0.$$

If $a \subseteq X$ then $\bar{a}$ denotes the topological closure of $a$.

Not surprisingly, our alternative rootedness notion depends on the topology of the extended Priestley space as well as the relation $M$:

**Definition 9.** *Where $x$ is an element of $X$, the underlying set of an exteded Priestley space, $x$ is an $M$-toporoot of $\mathbb{X}$ if $\overline{M^\omega[x]} = X$.*

**Theorem 3.** *Suppose that for all $x$ in $\mathbb{X}$, $\overline{M^\omega[x]}$ is $M$-hereditary. Then:*

1. $\mathbb{X}^*$ *is subdirectly irreducible iff the set of $M$-tooporoots of $\mathbb{X}$ is open and nonempty.*
2. $\mathbb{X}^*$ *is simple iff all elements of $\mathbb{X}$ are $M$-toporoots.*

### 3.3   An Example: Ockham Algebras

Finally, we see how to view Ockham Algebras as $DMA$'s and notice that they satisfy the hypothesis of theorem 3.

An *Ockham algebra* $\mathbb{A} = (A, \vee, \wedge, 0, 1, \sim)$ is an algebra with $(A, \vee, \wedge, 0, 1)$ a bounded distributive lattice with a weak negation $\sim$ reversing top and bottom elements and satisfying de Morgan's laws. That is, $\sim$ is a unary operator on $A$ such that

(1) $\sim(a \vee b) = \sim a \wedge \sim b,\ \sim 0 = 1,$
(2) $\sim(a \wedge b) = \sim a \vee \sim b,\ \sim 1 = 0.$

Notice that the conditions (1) are those that must be satisfied by the $\triangleright$ operator in a $DMA$, and the conditions (2) are those required of $\triangleleft$. Thus Ockham algebras can be seen as $DMA$'s $(A, \vee, \wedge, 0, 1, \Diamond, \Box, \triangleright, \triangleleft)$ satisfying $\Diamond a = 0, \Box a = 1$ and $\triangleright a = \triangleleft a$ for all $a \in A$.

The dual of such an algebra is $\mathbb{A}_* = (\mathcal{I}_\mathcal{P}(\mathbb{A}), \subseteq, \tau, R_\Diamond, R_\Box, R_\triangleright, R_\triangleleft)$, where $R_\Diamond$ and $R_\Box$ are empty relations and $R_\triangleright$ and $R_\triangleleft$ are binary relations on $\mathcal{I}_\mathcal{P}(\mathbb{A})$ satisfying

$$I R_\triangleright J \text{ iff } a \notin J \to \sim a \in I \text{ for all } a \in A,$$
$$I R_\triangleleft J \text{ iff } a \in J \to \sim a \notin I \text{ for all } a \in A.$$

Here $\sim a := \triangleright a = \triangleleft a$ for $a \in A$.

Consider $R_\sim \subseteq \mathcal{I}_\mathcal{P}(\mathbb{A}) \times \mathcal{I}_\mathcal{P}(\mathbb{A})$ defined by $R_\sim := R_\triangleright \cap R_\triangleleft$. $\mathbb{A}$'s being subdirectly irreducible will be characterized it terms of this relation $R_\sim$ on the dual $\mathbb{A}_*$. It turns out (see [1] for a proof) that the relation $M$ figuring in the previous section coincides in this special case with $R_\sim$, and that $\overline{M^\omega[I]}$ is $M$-hereditary for $I \in \mathcal{I}_\mathcal{P}(\mathbb{A})$. $R_\sim$-toporoots coincide with $M$-toporoots, so that:

**Definition 10.** $I \in \mathcal{I}_\mathcal{P}(\mathbb{A})$ *is an $R_\sim$-toporoot of $\mathbb{A}_*$ if $\mathcal{I}_\mathcal{P}(\mathbb{A}) = \overline{R_\sim^\omega[I]}$.*

**Proposition 11.** *An Ockham algebra $\mathbb{A} = (A, \vee, \wedge, 0, 1, \sim)$ is subdirectly irreducible iff the set of $R_\sim$-toporoots of its dual $\mathbb{X} = (\mathcal{I}_\mathcal{P}(\mathbb{A}), \subseteq, \tau, R_\sim)$ is open and nonempty.*

# References

[1] Birchall, B.: Duality for Distributive Modal Algebras. Master's Thesis, ILLC, University of Amsterdam, available at www.illc.uva.nl/Publications

[2] Burris, S., Sankappanaar, H.: A Course in Universal Algebra. Graduate Texts in Mathematics. Springer, Heidelberg (1981)

[3] Davey, B., Priestley, H.: Introduction to Lattices and Order. Cambridge University Press, New York (2002)

[4] Gehrke, M., Nagahashi, H., Venema, Y.: A Sahlqvist Theorem for Distributive Modal Logic. Annals of Pure and Applied Logic 131, 65–102 (2005)

[5] Goldblatt, R.: Varieties of Complex Algebras. Annals of Pure and Applied Logic 44(3), 173–242 (1989)

[6] Sambin, G.: Subdirectly Irreducible Modal Algebras and Initial Frames. Studia Logica 62(2), 269–282 (1999)

[7] Venema, Y.: A Dual Characterization of Subdirectly Irreducible BAOs. Studia Logica 77, 105–115 (2004)

# Productivity, Polysemy, and Predicate Indexicality

Peter Bosch

Institute of Cognitive Science
University of Osnabrück, D-49069 Osnabrück, Germany
pbosch@uos.de

**Abstract.** This paper argues that at least some cases of productive language use, specifically cases of apparent variation in word sense, require a treatment at the conceptual level rather than a lexical semantic solution. It is argued that the lexical semantics should be left underspecified in these cases, and the observed variation in truth-conditions should be attributed to differences in conceptual representation that result from differences in the utterance context. This involves rather drastic changes in our conception of the semantics-pragmatics interface, which are discussed in this paper.

## 1 Introduction: The Semantics-Pragmatics Interface

Language comprehension is concerned in the first instance with linguistic utterances. But, as much recent work emphasizes (e.g. Trueswell & Tanenhaus 2005), language comprehension also makes essential use also of non-linguistic information as it may be available concurrently with the comprehension process. How exactly the processing of linguistic and non-linguistic information interact is still largely an open issue. In this paper I am exploring an architecture of the language processing system that is decidedly *modular* in that it clearly distinguishes different subsystems, but that is also *incremental* in the sense that it permits current processes to take advantage of information as soon as it becomes available to any one of the subsystems. Similar views were proposed in the language processing literature already in Marslen-Wilson & Tyler (1980) and Altmann & Steedman (1988), and are receiving additional support from recent eye-tracking studies (Hartmann 2005, Karabanov e.a. to app.) .

The assumption of modularity and incrementality seems to lead to a better fit between theory and observation. But it makes it harder to maintain classic ideas about the semantics-pragmatics interface: It becomes more difficult, in particular, to understand the relation between compositional processes that construct the sentence-semantic content of an utterance, and subsequent pragmatic processes that would finally yield a truth-evaluable content adequate to the utterance context.

There may well be additional reasons, and not necessarily all them empirical, to rediscuss the role of sentence-semantic contents or propositions (Bach 1999, Bosch 1982, Recanati 2002). I will skip these arguments here and start directly by exploring an architecture that assumes that sentence comprehension uses information from the

B.D. ten Cate and H.W. Zeevat (Eds.): TbiLLC 2005, LNAI 4363, pp. 58–71, 2007.
© Springer-Verlag Berlin Heidelberg 2007

utterance context immediately and results in truth-evaluable utterance contents – without the intermediate construction of sentence contents. The idea, in brief, is that we dispense with semantic contents that are not context-relative.

Perhaps surprisingly it seems that already Gottlob Frege, in his later writings, held a similar view of sentence contents:

> *Wenn mit dem Tempus* Praesens *eine Zeitangabe gemacht werden soll, muß man wissen, wann der Satz ausgesprochen worden ist, um den Gedanken richtig aufzufassen. Dann ist also die Zeit des Sprechens Teil des Gedankenausdrucks.*[1] (Frege 1918/1966:38f.; my emphasis, PB)

The currently probably most widely discussed, if not also the most widely accepted, theory that takes utterance context into account in the construction of semantic values is David Kaplan's theory of Demonstratives (1989). Kaplan distinguishes *characters* of linguistic expressions from their *contents*. If the linguistic expression is a declarative sentence, its *character* is a function that, much like one would expect of the 'meaning' of the sentence, yields for each context in which the sentence may be uttered the proposition it expresses relative to that context. This proposition then is the truth-evaluable *content* of the sentence for that context.

This way Kaplan can cater for many forms of explicit context dependence. In particular the reference of personal pronouns of the first and second person can be handled this way, but also many other indexical expressions, like *here, now, tomorrow*. While a majority of lexical expressions look as if they had constant semantic values, the exceptional class of indexical expressions is handled separately; they take specific contextual parameters as their values: *here* takes the place of the utterance as its value and *I* the speaker of the utterances, etc. It is not entirely clear though that Kaplan's account could be applied equally directly to the indexical interpretation of tense, as in Frege's example. And it seems likely that the account is not applicable to certain forms of implicit reference to the utterance context. John Perry (1998) and others have claimed that there are such implicit, or as Perry calls them "unarticulated" constituents that function indexically. He argues, for instance, that each utterance of the sentence

(1)    It's raining,

contains an implicit place reference and hence cannot be assigned a semantic value without first making the place reference explicit: We cannot evaluate a statement made by (1) for its truth unless we know *where* it is supposed to be raining at the time of utterance.

## 2   More Context Dependence

Cases like in Perry's example form a serious problem for the architecture of the Semantics-Pragmatics interface. They seem to show that the utterance context cannot be

---

[1] "If the present tense is used as an indication of time one needs to know when the sentence was uttered in order to grasp the thought correctly. The time of speaking thus is part of the expression of the thought".

satisfactorily modelled with the help of a set of parameters that could, as it were, be extracted from a list of expressions that occur explicitly in the linguistic utterance and that refer to features of the utterance context.

I want to argue that the situation may actually be even more difficult than Perry's argument suggests. Not only are there *implicit* indexical constituents that make the semantic value of a sentence depend on the utterance situation, much in the way that Kaplan proposed for explicit indexicals, but also a large proportion of the *explicit* constituents that are not in Kaplan's class of indexicals depend on properties of the utterance context in the contribution that they make to the truth-evaluable content of the sentence. These constituents do not seem to have lexically fixed constant semantic values.

Take the verb *rain* in sentence (1). Is there a constant semantic value for it in all utterances of the sentence *It's raining*? Is there a semantic value for *rain* that is independent of utterance situation and speakers' intentions? Are the truth-conditions for (1) really the same when the sentence is uttered as a reply to questions such as those in (2)?

(2)    a. Is it still snowing?
       b. Are you saying it's still drizzling?
       c. Is it still pouring like this morning?
       d. Can we go for a walk now?
       e. Why did you bring the washing in?
       f. Why did you call a taxi?

The kind of modification that such contexts bring about in the interpretation of a lexical item is *productive*: Modification that is made and understood automatically and with no effort. It remains unnoticed by the language user, and it can yield, in principle, infinitely many variants of arbitrarily fine granularity. The *rain* example already hints this direction. Also, and perhaps even more clearly, there is the familiar kind of variation that we find in the interpretation of common verbs like *run*. Different truth conditions result for the utterance, depending on the argument to which the verb is applied: No constant semantic value for *run* will cover the cases of a running sportsman, a running water tap, a watch, a lecture, a program (or programme), or a stocking that are "running".

## 3 Productive Modification of Lexical Meaning

Productive modification of lexical meaning is not, as may be thought, appropriately modelled as lexical disambiguation, i.e., as the mapping of the occurrence of an expression onto one of a certain number of semantically different lexical entries. Lexical disambiguation is well suited particularly for cases of homonymy, for instance, an occurrence of *bass* must be mapped onto either of the lexical items $bass_1$ or $bass_2$, depending on the intended meaning.

Lexical disambiguation implies a cognitive choice and is a task that inhibits comprehension processes. It should be distinguished from processes that lead to a differentiation of word senses. The former task is accomplished fairly reliably also without much contextual information while the latter is not (cf. Veronis 1998, 2001). It has also been shown that homonymous words, which require disambiguation, slow down lexical access, while polysemous words, which activate a multiplicity of word senses, speed up lexical access (Rodd e.a. 2002).

However, both the productive modification of semantic values and the straightforward choice between lexically different items have in common that they require additional non-lexical information.

Suppose we had two lexical entries for the English verb *work*, as it is used in the sentences *The telephone wasn't working this morning* and *The caretaker wasn't working this morning*.

(3)    Lexical Representation

        Lexical entry 1:   $[[work_1]] = \lambda xWORK_1(x)$

        Lexical entry 2:   $[[work_2]] = \lambda xWORK_2(x)$

Each of the two senses is here given as a different concept, and in our knowledge representation or conceptual representation we would explicate the difference between the two concepts $\lambda xWORK_1(x)$ and $\lambda xWORK_2(x)$ by different inferences that they may license:

(4)    Conceptual Representation

$$\forall x\ (WORK_1(x) \rightarrow DEVICE(x)\ ...)$$
$$\forall x\ (WORK_2(x) \rightarrow HUMAN(x)\ ...)$$

If we do not assume that *work* is lexically ambiguous in this way, we still have two different concepts for the two sentences at hand, and we still have the very same difference in the conceptual representation. Only the lexical entry would give us just a single denotation: A concept $\lambda xWORK(x)$ that has, as it were, less content and is a super-concept of $\lambda xWORK_1(x)$ and $\lambda xWORK_2(x)$.

Note that the conceptual or denotational differentiation of the occurrence of a lexical item in the case at hand, just as in the case of disambiguation, requires access to semantic values, i.e., to the intended reference situation, and not just to lexical entries. An utterance of (5) does not contain relevant information to differentiate the denotation of *work* between $\lambda xWORK_1(x)$ and $\lambda xWORK_2(x)$ as long we know nothing about the intended reference of the name *Charley*.

(5)    Charley isn't working this morning.

If Charley is a computer, another interpretation would be appropriate than in a case where Charley is our caretaker. But the relevant information  comes from the utterance situation, or the intended reference situation, not from the lexicon.

Although it is quite clear in this case that differentiation or disambiguation is brought about by the argument and not by the argument expression, many argument expressions are apt to mislead about this point, as the examples in (6) may demonstrate.

(6)    a.    *cut*:    hair, bread, lawn, cake, ...
      b.    *open*:   book, letter, door, bottle, buffet, ...

The fact that the information required for the differentiation comes from the intended reference and not from the argument expressions, and hence cannot be thought of as being recoverable from lexical knowledge, is brought home when we consider pronouns as argument expressions: Plainly you can't get a differentiated denotation for utterances of *cut it*, or *open it* until you know what the pronoun refers to.

In the kind of case we have been considering one could argue, as in the case of Kaplan's indexicals, that the relevant information for disambiguation is found in one specific feature of the utterance context: in our case the argument. But not all cases of productive modification are like this. Here is a type of case where the denotation of argument expressions won't help:

(7)    a. Where is Fred? He's working.

(8)    a. How can Fred afford these expensive holidays? He's working.

If *He's working* figures as an answer to *Where is Fred?* the utterance is interpreted as giving information about Fred's location, and if it figures as an answer to *How can Fred afford these expensive holidays?* it must carry information about Fred's financial situation.

(7)    b. $\text{WORK}_i(\text{fred}) \rightarrow \varphi(\text{LOCATION\_OF}(\text{fred}))$

(8)    b. $\text{WORK}_j(\text{fred}) \rightarrow \psi(\text{WEALTH\_OF}(\text{fred}))$

The denotation of *work* can do this only if it is enriched by contextual knowledge, and in different ways for (7a) and (8a)[2]. The difference between the semantic values of the two occurrences of *work*, i.e., the concepts $\lambda x \text{WORK}_i(x)$ and $\lambda x \text{WORK}_j(x)$, is truth-conditionally relevant and licences different inferences: Nothing follows, for instance, about Fred's location when *He is working* is an answer to *How can Fred afford these expensive holidays?*

The difference between $\lambda x \text{WORK}_i(x)$ and $\lambda x \text{WORK}_j(x)$ in (7) and (8) is stable within the utterance context, as is demonstrated by VP anaphora:

(9)    Fred is working and so is Pete.

An utterance of (9) cannot be interpreted as saying, e.g., that Fred is in his office and Pete can afford expensive holidays.

What then is the exact difference between the occurrences of *work* in (7) and (8)? It can't be a difference in lexical meanings (Kaplan's *characters*) - because the variation correlates with a change in the utterance context. So I conclude that it is a difference in the semantic values (*contents*) of the two occurrences of *work*. Following the footsteps of Frege, who argued that the semantic values of predicate expressions are concepts, i.e. truth functions, I call these semantic values *Contextual Concepts* (CCs) (Bosch 1991, 1997).

CCs are the contextual referents or semantic values of predicate expressions. They are truth functions that are completely defined for arguments in the intended context. And what's more, CCs are linguistically real: they define the required notion of identity in VP anaphora, VP ellipsis, coordination, question-answer coherence, and they define the units in counting (cf. Bosch 2006).

---

[2] It may be thought that the difference in interpretation between the two replys *He's working* should be a matter of Gricean implicature. I have no objection to this. Note, however, that this formulation is no more informative than what I'm saying.

As for VP anaphora, VP ellipsis, and coordination we observe, as hinted above, that the property ascribed to Fred and Pete in (10)-(12) is identified with the interpretation of the first occurrence of *working* in these sentences.

(10)   Fred is working and so is Pete.

(11)   Fred is working, and Pete too.

(12)   Fred is working and Pete is working.

When these sentences occur as answers to a question like *Where is Fred?* then this context enforces a CC $\lambda xWORK_i(x)$ that is a sub-concept of a more general location concept, somewhat like "to be at one's workplace" – only as such can the CC figure in an answer to *where* questions. If, in a different context, the sentences (10)-(12) are used to answer a question like *Is Fred still unemployed?* the CC induced by that context, $\lambda xWORK_j(x)$ is a sub-concept of a concept of employment status that could perhaps be paraphrased as "to be employed".

Finally, also the identity of countable objects rests on CC identity. When we are talking of Fred, Pete, and a few others and I say:

(13)   I wonder how many of them are working.

then we are not allowed to re-interpret *be working* for each of the individuals we are counting. The question is how many of them have the one property in common that is identified by the contextual interpretation of *be working*. If the answer is *Two of them*, then this cannot mean that one is working in the sense of being at his place of work right now and the other in the sense of being able to afford expensive holidays or just in the sense of being employed. Whatever CC is chosen as the semantic value for *work*, it must be the same for all of them.

Note that CCs are not meanings or senses in any sense. This is clearly seen from (14).

(14)   Fred is working for her, and so is Pete.

The relevant observation here is that the reference of *her* must be the same for both conjuncts: Both Fred and Pete must be working for the same woman[3]. The reference of *her* is part of the specification of the CC that is asserted of both Pete and Fred. – If this observation is correct then it would follow that the identity of CCs depends on identity of reference. This would exclude the option of regarding CCs in any sense as meanings – at least under most current accounts of "meaning".

## 4   How Are Contextual Concepts Computed?

The computability of the content of indexicals along the lines of the Kaplan approach rests on the assumption that we are concerned with a process of variable saturation: One variable at a time that is evaluated by the context (speaker, listener, place, time, etc.).

---

[3] Readers who have any doubt about this observation, as one of the reviewers had, are reminded that sloppy identity readings of VP anaphora are irrelevant here. The argument only requires that there is at least one reading of (14) in which the referential identity of the pronoun is decisive. One situation in which such a reading is unavoidable is one in which the pronoun is accompanied by a pointing gesture.

This assumption won't work for the context dependence of predicate expressions we have been discussing, i.e., for *predicate indexicality*, as one might call it. The reason is that there are arbitrarily many parameters with respect to which CCs can differ from each other, and there can be no finite parameterisation of contexts (hence no context-independent identity of contexts, cf. Bosch 1982). – So how can we compute CCs, given whatever little information about contexts we have?

First of all there is an important difference to note: The computation of CCs differs for different information structure status of the constituent we are concerned with (Bosch 1999). *Anaphoric constituents* are interpreted by reference to objects that are already given in the established discourse representation. There is no modification and no lexical semantics involved. *Focal constituents*, on the other hand, are interpreted via their lexical entries, plus disambiguation and modification. The "disambiguation" and modification here are however not linguistic, but conceptuall processes: We are concerned more with reasoning than with linguistic semantics. I will return to this point below.

But let me first explain the relevance of the distinction between *anaphoric* and *focal constituents*. Let's take as an example a question like (15) that is being asked about our friend Fred. *Working* would here have a *focal* occurrence: Its interpretation cannot be derived from any preceding discourse context, but depends largely on the lexical semantics of the expression plus, possibly, other factors that are not our concern at the moment. If now (15) is answered by (15a), then the interpretation of *working* in (15a) must be exactly the same as in (15) – whatever the interpretation in (15) may have been – on pains of (15a) not being an answer to the question. This is what it means to say that the occurrence of *working* in (15a) is *anaphoric*. – Now suppose the answer is not (15a) but (15b), which would have exactly the same effect in the dialogue and be truth-conditionally fully equivalent; perhaps it would sound even more natural as a reply to (15). But the word *working* does not occur in (15b). So, clearly, if both (a) and (b) mean the same in this context, then the lexical semantics of *working* in (a) can't be making a semantic contribution to the interpretation of (a).

(15)  Is Fred working?
   a.      No, he isn't working. He's sick.
   b.      No, he isn't. He's sick.

Coming back to our question about the computation of focal and anaphoric constituents, we can now say that anaphoric constituents select their denotation from a small and finite domain: The current discourse representation. The information used in their interpretation is discourse-structural information, as in the interpretation of anaphoric pronouns, such as salience status.

Focal constituents on the other hand are mapped onto their semantic values in two steps:

(i) The expression selects a lexical entry, which contains a pointer to a lexical concept, and

(ii) conceptual processes and information from non-linguistic sources complete the construction of semantic values. – This requires that the lexical concept that is identified in (i) is part of a conceptual representation and is linked to other concepts via its internal structure, via subsumption, and possibly also via various axioms. It may still be underspecified with regard to what is the eventual semantic value.

The properly speaking semantic part of this interpretation ends after step (i) and the more complex and clearly more interesting part is in step (ii), which is the business of conceptual processing or reasoning – and with no specifically linguistic ingredients.

So far I have given a rough sketch of how semantic values are computed in the case of anaphorically occurring predicate expressions and I have assigned the computation of semantic values for focal constituents to conceptual processes. This means that what I referred to earlier as *productivity of interpretation* ends up in the conceptual system. – Well, not entirely: The semantic values of sub-sentential constituents that are computed via conceptual processes may (and ordinarily should) still combine with each other compositionally in the construction of a semantic value for the entire utterance – and here we are of course back in the semantics. The crucial point is rather that, in order to compute the semantic values also for sub-sentential constituents, we need to step outside of the semantics and get into conceptual processing before we can return to compositional semantic processing. If you like, you may call this "compositional pragmatics".

## 5   Some Applications

In the following I want to look at the consequences of our proposals from the preceding sections for the treatment of some relevant phenomena,  here in particular the transitive-intransitive alternation and the interpretation of argument expressions, as exemplified in (16) and (17) respectively.

(16)   a.      Fred is reading a novel.
         b       Fred is reading.

(17)   a.      Fred began reading the novel.
         b.      Fred began the novel.
         c.      Fred began.

How many lexical entries and how many lexical meanings for the verbs *read* and *begin* do we need?

### 5.1   Transitive-Intransitive Alternation

Let me first discuss the difference between (16a) and (16b). At least intuitively, one would like to have just one lexical entry for the verb *read*. Perhaps like the one represented in (18). Here the direct object is syntactically optional, but is co-indexed with the semantic object. Although we don't mention explicitly the object that is being read every time that we talk about reading, the relevant concept of reading still requires something that is being read as much as it requires a reader.

..

(18)

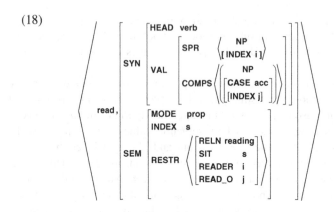

The denotation of the verb *read* is a lexical concept, which may be partially specified in the conceptual representation as in (19).

(19)   $[[read]] = \lambda y \lambda x \exists s(\text{READING}(s) \wedge \text{READER}(x,s) \wedge \text{READ\_O}(y,s))$

What happens in the comprehension process if the linguistic utterance mentions no object that is being read (no READ_O), as in (16b)? Nothing very serious. Note that (19) forms part of the conceptual representation. This is the level of representation where information from all sources available, not just from the linguistic utterance, gets integrated into to the comprehension process. If the utterance does not say what it is that is being read, the listener will still assume that such an object exists in the READING situation, because it is conceptually required. This is clear from a "bridging inference", as in (20).

(20)   Fred is reading. But he's bored by the book.

The definiteness of *the book* demonstrates that the referent is regarded as identifiable and familiar. The assumption would be reasonable then that some object read by Fred was either already assumed in the comprehension of the first sentence in (20) or is at least easily accommodated. This follows directly from our concept of reading situations.

(21)   $\forall s(\text{READING}(s) \, \delta \, (\exists x \text{READER}(x,s) \wedge \exists y \text{READ\_O}(y,s)))$

The verb *walk*, for comparison, does not denote a concept that would introduce a reading object or would allow easily for the accommodation of one, cf. (22).

(22)   [#]Fred is walking. But he's bored by the book.

Similarly, if the READER is not explicitly mentioned, as in (23), we still may assume that there is a reader, albeit a generic reader:

(23)   This book reads beautifully. The reader never gets bored.

Since, as would seem plausible in the absence of other evidence, the intransitive, the transitive, and the ergative construction of *read* all denote the same concept, we assume no lexical semantic difference. The difference is exclusively syntactic[4].

## 5.2  Argument (re-)interpretation

The second set of cases I want to look at are those in (17), repeated here.

(17)  a.      Fred began reading the novel.
     b.      Fred began the novel.
     c.      Fred began.

The question here is how we can lexically specify the verb *begin* so that (17a) – (17c) are all licensed and interpretable in the intended sense. A suitable lexical entry is provided by the feature structure in (24) and an appropriate partial conceptual representation follows in (25).

(24)

$$\left\langle \text{begin},\ \left[ \begin{array}{l} \text{SYN} \left[ \begin{array}{l} \text{HEAD  verb} \\ \text{VAL} \left[ \begin{array}{l} \text{SPR} \quad \langle [\text{INDEX } i] \rangle \\ (\text{COMPS} \langle [\text{INDEX } j] \rangle) \end{array} \right] \end{array} \right] \\ \text{SEM} \left[ \begin{array}{l} \text{MODE} \quad \text{prop} \\ \text{INDEX} \quad s \\ \text{RESTR} \left\langle \left[ \begin{array}{l} \text{RELN beginning} \\ \text{SIT} \qquad s \\ \text{AGENT} \quad i \\ \text{EVENT} \quad j \end{array} \right] \right\rangle \end{array} \right] \end{array} \right] \right\rangle$$

(25)   $\Downarrow begin \lozenge = \lambda y \lambda x \exists s (\text{BEGINNING}(s) \wedge \text{AGENT}(x,s) \wedge \text{EVENT}(y,s)$
        $\wedge -\exists z (\text{PART\_OF}(z,y) \wedge \text{EARLIER\_THAN}(z,s)))$

Both (24) and (25) say that the concept [[*begin*]] requires an event argument. Accordingly the comprehension process would attempt to recover information about the event argument from utterances of sentences like those in (17) or, alternatively, from the utterance situation.

This is straightforward for (17a): Reading is an event (as should be represented in the conceptual representation by a subsumption relation for the concept [[*read*]]), and so is reading a novel, which should be represented as a subconcept of [[*read*]]. (17c) is treated along the same lines as already (16b): There is no reason to specify every relevant conceptual ingredient linguistically if it can also be retrieved from other sources. Hence *Fred began* is perfectly normal in contexts where the required event can be recovered from contextual knowledge, as must be the case for an utterance of (26):

(26)  Everybody was waiting. But not Fred. Fred began.

---

[4] The lexical entry in (18) licenses only the transitive and intransitive, but not the ergative construction. I take it that there is a semantically empty lexical rule that derives the ergative structure which takes care of the argument linking.

When we consider (17b), however, we are encountering a new problem: What do we do with the surface object argument of *begin*, the NP *a novel*? Can we interpret *a novel* as referring to an event?

Following the general line suggested in this paper, we assume underspecified lexical representations, as in (27) for *novel*, and leave the conceptual content to the conceptual representation, as in (28).

(27)

$$
\left\langle \text{novel}, \begin{bmatrix} \text{SYN} & \begin{bmatrix} \text{HEAD} & \begin{bmatrix} \text{noun} \\ \text{AGR 3sing} \end{bmatrix} \\ \text{VAL} & \begin{bmatrix} \text{SPR} & <\text{HEAD det}> \\ \text{COMPS} <> \end{bmatrix} \end{bmatrix} \\ \text{SEM} & \begin{bmatrix} \text{MODE} & \text{ref} \\ \text{INDEX} & i \\ \text{RESTR} & \left\langle \begin{bmatrix} \text{RELN novel} \\ \text{INST} & i \end{bmatrix} \right\rangle \end{bmatrix} \end{bmatrix} \right\rangle
$$

(28)  $[[novel]] = \lambda x \text{NOVEL}(x)$

Admittedly, (28) is not any more informative than the semantic restrictions in (27). But we must take care, because the noun *novel* is highly polysemous. We can refer to a physical object as "a novel" (when the weight of the book is at issue), we can refer to a set of ideas as "a novel" (when we are saying that an author is working on one, while there is not a single printed copy of it yet, nor even a finished typescript), we can refer to a publication as "a novel" (when we are talking about an author's most recent novel), etc. If we want to maintain just one lexical entry for *novel* it must remain underspecified in many respects (though eventually we will probably need to add some such attribute as perhaps RELATED_ TO_A_BOOK-LENGTH_PROSE_ NARRATIVE.)[5]

How are these different senses of *novel* represented? The simple proposal I have to make (Bosch 1997) is that the various senses each represent a different *view* of our underspecified concept [[*novel*]]. We may view a novel as a physical object, as a text, an object of the publishing industry, etc. Each of these views is represented in the knowledge representation by different subsumption relations. The concept [[*novel*]] may be subsumed by concepts like PHYSICAL_OBJECT, TEXT, PUBLICATION, etc. In each such view the resulting CCs for *novel* (in all cases sub-concepts of the lexical concept [[*novel*]]) inherit different attributes from the different superconcepts under which they are being subsumed. Allowing, as we do, multiple inheritance relations, nothing prevents the formation of CCs that are subconcepts of NOVEL and are also subordinate to TEXT and PHYSICAL_OBJECT. This latter concept would be required, e.g., in the comprehension of (29).

(29)  Peter was reading the novel that he had found at the bus stop.

---

[5] This adopts an idea of Manfred Bierwisch (1982), who used "has as its goal processes of education" for the polysemous *school*.

Which *views* of a concept are actually possible is a further question that we cannot start investigating here (but cf. Bierwisch 1982:93 for discussion).

Returning to our current problem about *novel* as the grammatical object of *read*, we can now say that in one class of CCs a novel is viewed as an event, i.e., it is subsumed by a higher concept EVENT. These event concepts of *novel* are still different from each other: Reading events, writing events, production events, etc. These *novel*-CCs are partially specified by their subsumption relations as in (30) via which they inherit some of their attributes.

(30)  $\lambda xNOVEL_i(x) \subset \lambda xTEXT(x)$

$\lambda xNOVEL_j(x) \subset \lambda xPUBLICATION(x)$

$\lambda xNOVEL_k(x) \subset \lambda xPHYS\_OBJ(x)$

And indeed all attributes of these higher concepts are inherited (by default) by the concepts they subsume. Accordingly, whatever attributes we can gnerally attach to physical objects, we can attach to novels under the appropriate physical object view of novels, and analogously for other superconcepts of [[*novel*]] on the respective views.

For our current problem the question is if novels may indeed be viewed as events. In general, anything may presumably be viewed as anything we please, provided the resulting concept does not become inconsistent or remains without sub-concepts or without instances for other reasons. With sufficiently general concept specifications, however, this happens less frequently than one may expect. As for our case at hand, i.e., for the subsumption of the lexical concept NOVEL under EVENT, it follows first of all, that under this view we can attribute any properties that we can generally attribute to events also to novels, and secondly that, under this view, a novel may figure as an event argument, as it does in (17b).

The approach to productive polysemy I am here proposing receives additional support when we look at examples like (31), that was discussed by several authors (Godard & Jayez 1993, Copestake 2001).

(31)  Fred began the tunnel.

It was claimed that this could mean (if anything) that Fred began building the tunnel, but not, for instance, that he began walking through the tunnel. Even though, admittedly, this would certainly not be the most plausible interpretation when (31) is considered out of context, it seems like an entirely natural interpretation if the appropriate context is provided. All you need to know is that there is this somewhat weird group of people who call themselves "The Royal Tunnel Walkers Society" who spend their weekends travelling to the mountains and walking through tunnels, regarding this as some kind of an exciting sport. Having introduced these people into our context, the desired interpretation of (32) should come about fairly naturally.

(32)  The first group began the tunnel at 5:15.

What we need in our conceptual representation is a view of a tunnel as an event. The role of the context here is simply in suggesting event types that may be related to tunnels, like building tunnels or, in our case, walking through tunnels, and of which our group could be the agent.

The proposal about polysemy I have been making differs somewhat from the 'generative lexicon' approach (Pustejovsky 1995). The central difference is, I believe, that

I make a clear distinction between the lexical representation on the one hand, and conceptual or factual information on the other. In Pustejovsky's lexical entries we find a considerable amount of conceptual and contingent information, which is not linguistic information and which really belongs into the conceptual system and the representation of factual knowledge. My proposal in this paper follows rather the line of a 'disquotational' view of lexical semantics (Fodor & Lepore 1998), in an attempt to keep linguistic and conceptual information apart and allocate them to different modules of the cognitive system.

## 6 The Semantics-Pragmatics Boundary - from the Perspective of Semantic Minimalism

According to the approach taken in this paper, language comprehension is fed by information from many sources, only some of which are properly speaking linguistic. A considerable part of the semantic productivity that we observe in language is attributed to the workings of the conceptual system. This becomes apparent when we consider how linguistic utterances are mapped onto truth-evaluable contents that cannot be derived from the current linguistic input alone, but contain conceptual material from other sources: preceding discourse, background knowledge, the intended reference situation, and the current utterance situation. I want to suggest that it is worth continuing this line investigation, if only for the reason that the classic semantics-pragmatics interface – first constructing a semantic representation and then using pragmatic knowledge – holds little promise for an account of productive language use.

## Acknowledgements

Various earlier versions of this paper were presented at a workshop on "The (In-) Determinacy of Meaning: Issues in Formal Pragmatics" organised by Regine Eckardt and Markus Egg at the 27. Jahrestagung of the Deutsche Gesellschaft für Sprachwissenschaft in February 2005 in Cologne, at the Semantikzirkel at the Zentrum für Allgemeine Sprachwissenschaft, Berlin in a talk on 3rd June, 2005, at the Sixth International Symposium on Language, Logic and Information, 12-16 September 2005, in Batumi, Georgia, and in a talk at the DIP Colloquium at the Institute for Logic, Language and Computation in Amsterdam on 18th Nov, 2005. I am very grateful for the opportunity to present these ideas on these occasions and all the comments and criticism that I received at these meetings, in particular to Michiel van Lambalgen who had prepared a critical reply to my talk at the DIP Colloquium and to two anonymous reviewers who read the paper for his volume.

## References

Altmann, G.T.M., Steedman, M.J.: Interaction with context during human sentence processing. Cognition 30, 191–238 (1988)

Bach, K.: The semantics–pragmatics distinction: What it is and why it matters. In: Turner, K. (ed.) The Semantics–Pragmatics Interface from Different Points of View, pp. 65–84. Elsevier, Oxford (1999)

Bierwisch, M.: Semantische und konzeptuelle Repräsentation lexikalischer Einheiten. In: Růžička, R., Motsch, W. (eds.) Untersuchungen zur Semantik, pp. 61–99. Akademie-Verlag, Berlin (1982)

Bosch, P.: The Role of Propositions in Natural Language Semantics. In: Leinfellner, W., Kraemer, E., Schank, J. (eds.) Proceedings of the 6th International Wittgenstein Sym- posium, Hoelder, Pichler Tempsky, pp. 282–285. Wien (1982)

Bosch, P.: The Bermuda Triangle: Natural Language Semantics Between Linguistics, Knowledge Representation, and Knowledge Processing. In: Herzog, O., Rollinger, C.-R. (eds.) Text Understanding in LILOG. LNCS, vol. 546, pp. 243–258. Springer, Heidelberg (1991)

Bosch, P.: Dynamik kontextueller Konzepte. In: Umbach, C., Grabski, M., Hoernig, R. (eds.) Perspektive in Sprache und Raum, pp. 195–209. Deutscher Universitätsverlag, Wiesbaden (1997)

Bosch, P.: Presupposition, Focus, and Lexical Semantics. Semantica lessicale. Studi Italiani di Linguistica Teoretica e Applicata XXVIII(2), 249–264 (1999)

Bosch, P.: VP Anaphora at the Semantics-Pragmatics Interface. Talk at the 2006 Milan Meeting, Palazzo Feltrinelli, Gargnano, June 15-17, 2006 (2006), http:// www. cogsci. uos. de/~pbosch/

Copestake, A.: The semi-generative lexicon: limits on lexical productivity. In: Proceedings of the 1st International Workshop on Generative Approaches to the Lexicon, Geneva (2001)

Fodor, J.A., Lepore, E.: The emptiness of the lexicon. Linguistic Inquiry 29, 269–288 (1998)

Frege, G.: Der Gedanke. In: Patzig, G. (ed.) Gottlob Frege: Logische Untersuchungen, pp. 30-53. Vandenhoeck & Ruprecht, Göttingen (1918, 1966)

Godard, D., Jayez, J.: Towards a proper treatment of coercion phenomena. In: EACL-93. Proceedings of the Sixth Conference of the European Chapter of the Association for Computational Linguistics, Utrecht, The Netherlands, pp. 168–177 (1993)

Hartmann, N.: Processing Grammatical Gender in German. Bachelor Thesis, unpubl. Univ. of Osnabrück, Cognitive Science (2005), http://www.cogsci.uni-osnabrueck.de/~CL/download/Hartmann_GramGender.pdf

Kaplan, D.: Demonstratives. In: Almog, J., Wettstein, H., Perry, J. (eds.) Themes from Kaplan, pp. 481–563. Oxford University Press, New York (1989)

Karabanov, A., Bosch, P., König, P.: Eye Tracking as a Tool to Investigate the Comprehension of Referential Expressions. In: Featherston, S., Sternefeld, W. (eds.) Proceedings from the Workshop on Linguistic Evidence, Tübingen, 2006 (to appear)

Marslen-Wilson, W.D., Tyler, L.K.: The temporal structure of spoken language understanding. Cognition 8, 1–71 (1980)

Perry, John: Indexicals, Contexts, and Unarticulated Constituents. In: Proceedings of the 1995 CSLI-Armsterdam Logic, Language and Computation Conference, CSLI Publications, Stanford (1998)

Pustejovsky, J.: The Generative Lexicon. MIT Press, Cambridge, MA (1995)

Rodd, J., Gaskell, G., Marslen-Wilson, W.: Making sense of semantic ambiguity: Semantic competition in lexical access. J. of Memory and Learning 46, 245–266 (2002)

Recanati, F.: Unarticulated Constituents. Linguistics and Philosophy 25, 299–345 (2002)

Trueswell, J.C., Tanenhaus, M.K. (eds.): Approaches to Studying World-Situated Language Use. MIT Press, Cambridge (2005)

Veronis, J.: A study of polysemy judgements and inter-annotator agreement. In: Programme and Advanced Papers of Senseval Workshop, Herstmonceux Castle, UK (1998)

Veronis, J.: Sense tagging: does it make sense? In: Corpus Linguistics 2001 Conference (2001)

# Argument Dependencies in Tukang Besi
## A Formal Account

Alastair Butler[1] and Mark Donohue[2]

[1] Department of English Language and Literature, National University of Singapore
Blk AS5, 7 Arts Link, Singapore, 117570
[2] School of Languages, Cultures and Linguistics, Faculty of Arts, Linguistics
Department, Monash University, Victoria 3800, Australia

**Abstract.** This paper uses standard syntactic scoping properties (as found with lambda calculus and predicate logic) to account for linking dependencies in Tukang Besi, an Austronesian language of Indonesia. Basic argument dependencies are established with a combination of verbal agreement, case marking and constituent order. If taken alone, no one of these is sufficient to determine the grammatical relations in the clause. Rather these different factors operate in combination to yield unambiguous clauses. What is shown is that scope taking options determine which combinations are possible and which are impossible.

## 1  Syntactic Scope and Accidental Hiding

First we introduce some basic formulas that look much like lambda terms. We will call such formulas core syntax forms or **CS forms**. The data we cover will be seen to match the scoping requirements of this syntax.

**Definition 1 (core syntax).**

Let a set $V$ of variables be given. $CS$, the core syntax, is the smallest set such that:

$$\text{P}(x_1, ..., x_n) \in CS \quad \text{for any } n\text{-ary predicate P}, x_1, ..., x_n \in V$$
$$\lambda x\phi \in CS \quad \text{for any } \phi \in CS, x \in V$$
$$\phi\psi \in CS \quad \text{for any } \phi, \psi \in CS$$

This gives predicate formulas, an operator $\lambda x$, which opens a fresh $x$-scope, and a means of concatenating formulas. Since there is only one means of joining formulas, an operator for concatenation is left implicit. We can picture the types of binding relations we get with (1).

(1)

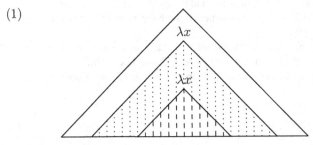

We see from (1) how $\lambda x \phi$ opens an $x$-scope that continues to remain open throughout $\phi$ (the dotted shading); unless another $\lambda x$ is met, whereupon the $x$-scope will be that of the new binding (the dashed shading).

As an example, consider (2), with its distinct variable names $x$ and $y$.

(2)   $\lambda x(\mathtt{P}\,\lambda y(\mathtt{Q}\,\lambda x \mathtt{R}(x)))$

Assume the subformula $\mathtt{R}(x)$ is a formula of arbitrary complexity that contains $x$ free. Then each free occurrence of $x$ in $\mathtt{R}(x)$ is captured by the inner $\lambda x$, so that the binding of the outermost $\lambda x$ is hidden from the viewpoint of $\mathtt{R}(x)$. There is no way to refer to the outermost $\lambda x$ from within $\mathtt{R}(x)$. In contrast, $\lambda y$ remains accessible from within $\mathtt{R}(x)$. Following Stehr (2002), we will refer to this property of scoping formulas as **accidental hiding**.

Accidental hiding is generally no cause for concern, since the treatment of binding constructs in most logical formalisms allows for working with formulas "up to the renaming of bound variables."[1] This allows for the general convention that bindings can be renamed at any moment (see e.g., Barendregt 1984), and thus accidental hiding can always be avoided. This convention works well in the abstract, but what if we had to pre-choose a single representation for each formula; and in particular, what if we needed to decide how occurrences of binders were to be represented without the option of future change. Such concerns are very real for computer scientists who wish to implement logical formalisms, and we will suppose they are just as real for natural language, which, after all, has implemented languages.

In what follows, instances of accidental hiding with CS forms will be found to match up either with unobtainable scope readings for sentences of Tukang Besi or with sentences that are ungrammatical in Tukang Besi.

Before proceeding, we first need to introduce some argument structure terminology.

### 1.1   Some Argument Structure Terminology

In argument structure terms we can identify three 'positions' in terms of the ordered arguments of a verb:

1. the highest role;
2. the lowest role (/the second highest role);
3. a position that is both the highest and lowest role; that is, it is the sole argument in the subcategorisation frame.

Following (approximately) Comrie (1978) and Andrews (1985) we will use the abbreviations A, P and S to refer to the positions (loosely) described in 1, 2 and 3, respectively. More specifically:

– An A is the most agent-like argument of a polyvalent verb, the highest role, which is not simultaneously the lowest role.

---

[1] This property is usually referred to as $\alpha$-equality.

- The label P refers to the non-A argument in a prototypical bivalent verb, and to the argument in a trivalent (or quadrivalent) predicate which shows the same morphosyntactic behaviour. It is the lowest (/second highest) role in the verb's subcategorisation frame, but it is not simultaneously the highest.
- An S is the single argument of a monovalent verb; it is the highest role in the verb's subcategorisation frame, and can simultaneously be described as the lowest role in the frame.

These are syntactic roles in the sense of relationships existing at argument structure that can frequently be shown to affect morphosyntactic categories in languages. These are not descriptors of grammatical status, though the identity of grammatical functions such as 'subject' and 'object' may be defined, after examining the properties of appropriate constructions in the language, in terms of the appropriate groupings of these roles. While grammatical functions may be defined with appropriate groupings in say English, this turns out not to be possible for Tukang Besi.

## 2   Some Tukang Besi Data

Tukang Besi is a language with a mix of head-marking and dependent-marking morphology, with agreement on verbs and case marking on all nominals (see Donohue 1999). In this section, we look at examples of clauses in Tukang Besi with monovalent and bivalent verbs. These examples will show both grammatical and ungrammatical versions of 'neutral' and pragmatically marked sentences. The subject, and agreement with the subject, will be shown in bold.

In (3) we see examples of a simple monovalent clause consisting of a verb and a single argument. While other elements are possible (such as time expressions and other adjuncts), these are examples of minimal fully-specified clauses. The verb is marked for agreement with a third person argument with the prefix *no-*, which is also specified for realis mood.

(3)  a.  **No**-tinti **na**   **mo'ane**.
        3R-run   NOM man
        'The man has run (away).'
    b.  *\***No**-tinti **te mo'ane**.
    c.  **Te**    **mo'ane** **no**-tinti.
        CORE man      3R-run
        'The man, he has run (away).'
    d.  *\***Na mo'ane no**-tinti.

The nominal *mo'ane* 'man' appears with the case marker *na* in (3a). This is the only possible case marker for this argument in this position; marking with the only other plausible case marker, *te*, is not grammatical, as can be seen in (3b). The *te* case marker is found on the same argument, if this argument appears preverbally, as in (3c). As (3d) shows, a preverbal argument cannot appear with the case marker *na*, even when *na* is the case marker that it would appear with postverbally.

The lexical semantic content of (3a) and (3c) is the same, but, as indicated approximately by the translations provided, the pragmatic implications of the two sentences are different. While (3a) is a 'neutral' statement, without any particular emphasis or contrast implied, (3c) is used with particular identificational focus on 'the man'.

Taking the clause in (3a) with a postverbal subject to be more 'basic' than the clause in (3c), we can also see that Tukang Besi is a verb-initial language. We address the question of the positioning of adjuncts in section 4.

In (4) and (5) we have examples of polyvalent clauses, formed with the verb *tu'o* 'chop down'. In (4a) we can see that the generalisations we formed about case marking and verbal agreement in monovalent clauses on the basis of an examination of (3) are just as valid here, the only addition being that now a postverbal *te*-argument is licensed, the object of the verb taking the *te* case marker. (4b) shows that the order of the subject and the object following the verb is fixed: the object must occur closer to the verb than the subject. In (4c–d) we see that bivalent clauses also allow for an argument to appear in the preverbal position; only the 'man' argument is eligible to appear preverbally, as shown in (4c), and when preverbal it must appear with the *te* case marker, just as in (3c). It is not grammatical for the 'tree' argument to appear preverbally, (4d).

(4)  a.  **No**-tu'o te      kau **na** **mo'ane**.
         3R-chop CORE tree NOM man
         'The man chopped down the tree.'

    b.  \***No**tu'o **na mo'ane** te kau.

    c.  **Te    mo'ane no**-tu'o te      kau.
         CORE man      3R-chop CORE tree
         'The man, he chopped down the tree.'

    d.  \*Te kau **no**tu'o **na mo'ane**.

The clauses in (5) are in many ways the 'reverse' of the clauses in (4). Having the same verb as the clauses in (4), the clauses in (5) are still bivalent, but they show a change in verbal agreement: the prefixal agreement is unchanged, but there is an additional enclitic agreement marker that indexes the 'tree' argument of the clause. Furthermore, we see that the case markers *te* and *na*, while still appearing in (5), have exactly the opposite functions, in terms of syntactic roles, to their functions in (4). In (4a) *na* appeared marking the A, 'man', while *te* was used to mark the P, 'tree'. In (5) it is the P which is marked with *na*, while the A is marked with *te*. (5b) demonstrates another difference between the bivalent clause type in (5) that shows agreement for P and the clause type in (4) that does not: while (4b) shows that the relative order of the postverbal A and P is fixed in a clause without P-agreement, (5b) shows that no such word order restrictions are found in clauses with P-agreement. (5c) and (5d) show that while preverbal positioning is still possible, the argument which may appear preverbally is the P, and not the A, as in (4).

(5)  a.  **No**-tu'o=**ke** te      mo'ane **na**   **kau**.
         3R-chop=3P CORE man       NOM tree
         'The man chopped down the tree.'

b.   Notu'o**ke na kau** te mo'ane.

c.   **Te     kau** no-tu'o=**ke**  te     mo'ane.
CORE tree 3R-chop=3P CORE man
'The tree, the man chopped it down.'

d.   *Te mo'ane notu'o**ke na kau**.

It is worth emphasising some additional points. We have seen from (4c) and (5c) that the (CORE) case marker *te* may appear multiple times in the clause, marking all terms. It follows that *te* cannot be considered to be confined to a particular semantic or syntactic role in the clause, and so case labels such as 'ergative', 'accusative' etc. will not apply to it. We have seen that the argument which in more 'neutral' contexts (e.g., (3a), (4a), (5a,b)) appears postverbally with the *na* case marker can, in discourse-prominent contexts, appear preverbally, marked with *te*, a different case marker (e.g., (3c), (4c), (5c)). In expressions without a P enclitic (such as (4a) or (4c)), the *na* marked phrase (or the preverbal *te*-marked phrase) is associated with the highest argument position; while in expressions with a P enclitic (e.g., (5a–c)) the *na* marked phrase (/preverbal *te* phrase) is associated with the second highest argument position of the verb's subcategorisation frame. Put more intuitively, in (4a,c) the *na* marked phrase (/preverbal *te* phrase) is the 'man', while in (5a–c), it is the 'tree,' yet this change in the association of arguments and case appears with the verb 'chop' remaining constant (that is, there are no valency-affecting operations that distinguish (4) from (5)). Finally, we note that, as (4d) and (5d) show, a fronted *te* NP is not compatible with a postverbal *na* NP.

## 3   Establishing Basic Argument Dependencies

From the data in (3)–(5), we see that basic argument dependencies are established with a combination of verbal agreement, case marking and constituent order. None of them is enough on its own to determine the syntactic relations; the identities of the A and P are clear from verbal agreement, but their syntactic 'status' is not. The case marking alternatives available to bivalent clauses show quite clearly that we cannot uniquely associate any one case with any one syntactic role or relation. The order of elements in the clause shows enough variation that there can be no simple declaration that there is one basic order for the language. Rather, these different factors operate in combination to yield (usually) unambiguous clauses.

Excluding the pragmatic fronting seen in (3c), (4c) and (5c), the possibilities for a clause are shown in (6), where *no* is the prefix for S/A, *ke* is the clitic for P, *na* is the nominative case, and *te* is the non-nominative CORE case. The make-up of a clause with an intransitive verb is illustrated in (6a). (6b–d) illustrate options for the encoding of a clause with a polyvalent verb. The choice of (6b) versus (6c,d) depends on the need, pragmatic or syntactic, for the P to be the nominative argument in the clause. There is no pragmatic difference between (6c) and (6d); they are essentially free variants of each other.

(6) a.  no V na S
    b.  no V te P na A
    c.  no V ke na P te A
    d.  no V ke te A na P

With preverbal fronting (a position of pragmatic focus or contrast) the number of word order possibilities increases, as shown in (7).

(7) a.  te S no V
    b.  te A no V te P
    c.  te P no V ke te A

The argument in the preverbal position is always marked with *te*, and must be the argument that would have been marked with the nominative case if it were to have appeared postverbally, hence the contrast between the acceptable (5c) and the ungrammatical (5d).[2]

## 3.1  Assumptions for the Analysis

We now turn to a sketch of how the Tukang Besi data of (3)–(5) can be found to match the syntax of definition 1. We will quickly see that the scoping properties of definition 1, complete with the prospect of accidental hiding, are the key to replicating which argument links are possible and which argument links are not possible.

To get things started, we need to make assumptions about what links to a scope and what opens a scope where:

- An S/A-prefix opens a *no*-scope over the verb and all postverbal material. This binds (possibly among other things) the highest argument position of the verb.
- A P-enclitic opens a *ke*-scope, which takes narrowest scope with respect to the verb. This binds (possibly among other things) the second highest argument position of the verb.
- The case marker *te* opens a *te*-scope from its syntactic location. This binds nominals, and is somehow linked to the verb.
- The case marker *na* plays a 'dummy' role: it does not open a scope.
- All nominals of core arguments link to a *te*-scope, having predicate form: P(*te*).
- A *te*-scope is always opened as the outermost scope.

We will call the outermost *te*-scope that is always opened, the **discourse scope** (DS). In sentences with a preverbal *te* NP, like (3c), (4c) and (5c), the preverbal *te* NP opens the DS. For sentences without a preverbal *te* NP, the current discourse will have opened the DS.

## 3.2  The Emerging Picture

What picture of Tukang Besi emerges from these assumptions? NPs do one of two things: either they open a new *te*-scope (when *te* case marked), or else they link to an already open *te*-scope (when *na* case marked). Verbs themselves carry

---

[2] It is also possible for a time expression to appear in this preverbal position, but no Tukang Besi predicate subcategorises for a time expression as a basic argument.

open scope operators: they always carry an S/A prefix to open a *no*-scope that takes wide scope with respect to the verb and postverbal material, and they can in addition carry a P enclitic to open a narrow *ke*-scope. That verbs themselves carry open scope instructions comes as a necessity, since NP linking is itself so impoverished, showing no differentiation among the different core arguments, which all link to a *te*-scope.

We have already noted the assumption that each *te*-scope must *somehow* link to the verb. As an assumption this should not be controversial. It is just a way to spell out that an opened scope should play a role in the interpretation of the clause.

We can be very noncommittal regarding how links are established and simply assume that they are made if and when they can be. In practise, this will either be by binding of a vacant argument slot of the verb, or by linkage to an open *no*- or *ke*-scope that binds an argument slot of the verb. These assumptions bring about a lot of interesting, and importantly testable, consequences. It is exactly these consequences that we see reflected in the Tukang Besi data.

Let us see the machinery in operation. First off, we see how things play out for (3b), an example that codes its single argument with a preverbal *te* NP. This can be matched to the CS form (8). The *te* NP opens a *te*-scope with widest scope, making it the DS. The DS binds the nominal MAN(*te*) and links to the verb with the aid of the *no*-scope opened by the verb's S/A prefix, via the *no* = *te* link.

(8)   $\lambda\underline{te}($ MAN(*te*)   $\lambda no(no = te$   RUN(*no*) ))
      **Te   mo'ane   no-**            tinti

Here, and in what follows, we underline the operator that opens the DS. This underlining has no formal or theoretical significance, and is added purely to ease reference to the DS.

Now we consider (9) (= (3a)). This is identical to (8), except for the positioning (and case marking) of the 'man' argument in the clause. Also, in (9), it is the discourse that opens the DS. (9) is not a felicitous way to commence a stretch of discourse, as (8) is. Rather, (9) is a felicitous way to continue a stretch of discourse with a previously identified DS. This DS links to the verb via the *no*-scope opened by the verb's S/A prefix, giving the DS a role to play in the interpretation. Since *na* acts as a dummy, that is, it doesn't itself open a scope, the NP it case marks links to the active *te*-scope, which happens to be the DS, and so the only possible interpretation is that *mo'ane* 'man' is linked as the S of the verb.

(9)   $\lambda\underline{te}$ $\lambda no(no = te$   RUN(*no*)   MAN(*te*)     )
      **No-**            tinti   **na mo'ane**

Now we consider the basic bivalent clause without agreement for P, as in (10) (= (4a)). We see with (10) how the added complication of an extra argument leads to an only slightly more complicated analysis, since the scoping requirements eliminate many of the putative linking possibilities we might try to apply. As with (9), (10) is felicitous only if the discourse has already opened the DS, which links to the verb via the *no*-scope opened by the verb's S/A prefix; also the *na* marked NP links to the active *te*-scope, which is the DS. What is new, compared to (9), is that a second *te*-scope is opened by the postverbal *te* marked NP. This binds the nominal *kau* 'tree', and the free slot of the verb's subcategorisation frame, which happens to be the P.

(10)  $\underline{\lambda te}$ $\lambda no(no = te$  $\lambda te($ CHOP$(no, te)$  TREE$(te)$ ) MAN$(te)$      )
      **No-**            tu'o        te kau        **na mo'ane**

Keeping the fact that the S/A prefix of the verb opens a single *no*-scope, could the linking have been different? The answer is no. Underlying the scope requirements is the fact that the verb and DS must link. This is achieved in (10) because of the coidentity $no = te$. Since *na* does not open a scope, there is no scope opened by *na mo'ane* 'the man' to prevent $no = te$ bringing about a link with the DS. Instead, *mo'ane* is left to also link with the DS.

The best we can do to get an alternative linking, that links the DS to the P of the verb, is to have $te = te$. But this just gives the infelicitous (11), with its embedded *te* hiding the DS, with the effect that the DS is left without a link to the verb, linking only to the nominal MAN$(te)$.

(11)  $\#\underline{\lambda te}\lambda no(\lambda te(te = te$ CHOP$(no, te)$ TREE$(te))$ MAN$(te))$

We might instead try to link the P of the verb, *kau* 'tree', with the DS by changing the word order, as in (12) (= (4b)). But, as the star of (12) tells us, such attempts are doomed. (12a–c) give possible CS forms that we might reasonably give the sentence, and each is bad.

(12)  *\***Notu'o **na mo'ane** te kau.
      a.  $\#\underline{\lambda te}\lambda no(no = te$ $\lambda te($CHOP$(no, te)$ MAN$(te)$ TREE$(te)))$
      b.  $\#\underline{\lambda te}\lambda no(no = te$ CHOP$(no, te)$ MAN$(te)$ $\lambda te(te = no$ TREE$(te)))$
      c.  $\#\underline{\lambda te}\lambda no(no = te$ CHOP$(no, te)$ MAN$(te)$ $\lambda te(te = te$ TREE$(te)))$

First we note that, in contrast to (10), the *te*-scope opened by *te*-tree of (12) cannot scope over the verb. When it does, as in (12a), it also scopes over *na*-man. As a result, *na*-man links to *te*-tree rather than the DS, which is left without a link to the clause. But perhaps *te*-tree could itself open an independent scope and then try to link to another open scope. The problem here is that there is no useful scope for *te*-tree to link to: in (12b) we try and link to *no*, but all we get is a linking of MAN$(te)$ and TREE$(te)$; in (12c) we try to link to the DS, but of course we cannot because *te*-tree itself, in opening up a *te*-scope, hides access to the DS.

Let us now consider a different basic bivalent clause type, one that appears with the enclitic *ke* on the verb, such as (13) (= (5b)). How does the linking in this example work? The discourse has already opened the DS. A *no*-scope is opened by the verb's S/A-prefix, which takes wide scope over the verb and all postverbal material. The *te* marked NP opens a *te*-scope that is kept local to the nominal and linked to the verb via the open *no*-scope. The *na* marked NP, unable to open any scope itself, links to the open *te*-scope, which is the DS. The DS is itself linked to the verb via the *ke*-scope opened narrowly to the verb by the P suffix. A notable feature of the success of this linking of the DS to the verb is the lack of any interference from the scope opened by the *te* NP, which was kept narrow.

(13)   $\underline{\lambda te}$ $\lambda no($ $\lambda ke(ke = te$   CHOP$(no, ke)$ )      TREE$(te)$   $\lambda te(te = no$
     No-                                    tu'o                    **-ke   na kau**   te

MAN$(te)$) )
mo'ane

Could the linking for (13) have gone differently? The answer is no. Here are some alternatives:

(14)   a.  $\#\underline{\lambda te}\lambda no(no = te\ \lambda te(\lambda ke(ke = te\,\text{CHOP}(no, ke))\,\text{TREE}(te)\,\text{MAN}(te)))$
     b.  $\#\underline{\lambda te}\lambda no(no = te\ \lambda ke(\text{CHOP}(no, ke))\,\text{TREE}(te)\,\lambda te(te = no\,\text{MAN}(te)))$
     c.  $\#\underline{\lambda te}\lambda no(no = te\ \lambda ke(\text{CHOP}(no, ke))\,\text{TREE}(te)\,\lambda te(te = ke\,\text{MAN}(te)))$

In (14a), $te$-man scopes over the verb. This is out since it prevents $ke$ from linking to the DS. As a consequence in (14a), while the DS links to MAN$(te)$, it fails to link to the verb. In (14b), $no$ links to the DS. This has the unfortunate result of linking the two arguments MAN$(te)$ and TREE$(te)$: MAN$(te)$ links to $no$ and TREE$(te)$ links to the DS. In (14c) we try and avoid the problem that befalls (14b) by linking $te$-man to $ke$. The problem here is that $te$-man is outside the scope of $ke$, which can only take narrow scope with respect to the verb. From this last example we see that $ke$ must link to the DS, since this is its only hope of, in effect, extending its scope to link to an NP.

So much for (13), but we might wonder about alternative word orders when the verb comes with $ke$. Alternative orders are possible, and an example of a sentence with a different order, maintaining postverbal alignment for all arguments, is given in (15) (= (5a)):

(15)   $\underline{\lambda te}$ $\lambda no($ $\lambda ke(ke = te$   CHOP$(no, ke)$ )      $\lambda te(te = no$   MAN$(te)$)
     No-                                    tu'o             **-ke** te                mo'ane

TREE$(te)$)
**na kau**

The CS form given is perfectly acceptable, much as was the case with (13). Could things have been different? No they could not, since alternatives would fall into the same types of traps as we saw in (14b,c). However, there is one possible contender:

(16)   $\underline{\lambda te}\lambda no(no = te\ \lambda te(\lambda ke(ke = te\,\text{CHOP}(no, ke))\,\text{MAN}(te))\,\text{TREE}(te))$

Here $te$-man scopes over the verb to link to the $ke$-scope and there is no intervening TREE$(te)$ to worry about, like there was with (14a). As a consequence, TREE$(te)$ lies outside the scope of $te$-man and so is bound by the DS, which is linked to the $no$-scope. As a result, (16) gives an interpretation in which tree chopped down man. This is not just an unlikely interpretation for (5a), but an impossible interpretation. (5a) is unambiguously about man chopping down tree.

Our one recourse is to fall back on the constituency of Tukang Besi to rule out (16) as an available CS form. To scope directly over the verb, as it does in (16), $te$ $mo'ane$ 'the man' would need to be part of the verb-phrase (cf. $te\ kau$ 'the tree' in (10)). From constituency tests, we know that this is not the case (see section 4). Hence, $te\ mo'ane$ 'the man' cannot scope directly over the verb. Rather, it is forced to take a local scope (which recall was required in (13)), which returns us back to (15) as the only available CS form. While we cannot rule (16) out with scoping principles alone, we see that the language independently rules out the option — on the basis of its required constituency. The same effect arises to make (5c) unambiguous.

## 3.3  Summary

We can summarise the findings of this section with (17). This illustrates the scoping properties of the clause types of (6) and (7), that we have found our assumptions to enforce.

(17)

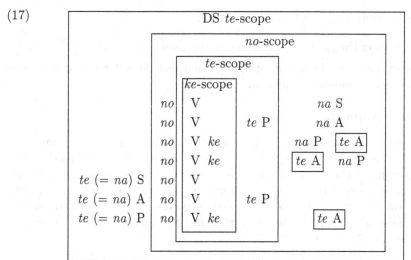

## 4  Constituency

The assumptions we have made about scope give a clear idea of what constituency is expected to be like in Tukang Besi. This is something we can test for empirically.

In what follows, the symbol △ indicates positions in the sentence where the tested element may appear; * indicates an ungrammatical placement. Only positions outside NPs are considered.

### 4.1  Locative Adjuncts

Locative adjuncts, by which we mean any expressions denoting an inner or outer locative, a goal, or a source, referring to space, must occur to the right of the VP. In (18)–(21) we can see this principle, and the right edge of the VP that it delimits, by testing with the locative phrase *di koranga* 'in the garden'. While (18) and (19) show a pattern in which the *na*-marked argument is always to the right of any locative expressions, and a *te*-marked argument is to the left, in (20) and (21) we can see that both the arguments are to the right of this boundary.

(18) [VP   Notinti]     na ana.
          *          △         △
     'The child ran in the garden.'

(19) [VP   Notu'o   te kau]     na mo'ane.
          *        *          △          △
     'The man chopped down the tree in the garden.'

(20) [VP   Notu'oke]    te mo'ane    na kau.
          *          △           △          △
     'The man chopped down the tree in the garden.'

(21) [VP   Notu'oke]    na kau    te mo'ane.
          *          △         △         △
     'The man chopped down the tree in the garden.'

In summary, locative adjuncts must appear following the VP, but may intervene between other arguments of the clause.

## 4.2   Time Adjuncts

Time adjuncts are found to the right of the IP that immediately dominates the VP. Many time adjuncts occur with the same general oblique case marker that is found with locations, but nonetheless show the same placement as non-case marked time expressions. Here the placement options have been tested with *sio'oloo* '(in the) afternoon'. We can see that *sio'oloo* is strictly constrained to appear clause-finally in (22) and (23), while in (24) and (25) the two arguments may follow *sio'oloo*.

(22) [IP [VP   Notinti]    na ana].
              *          *         △
     'The child ran in the afternoon.'

(23) [IP [VP   Notu'o   te kau]     na mo'ane].
              *        *          *          △
     'The man chopped down the tree in the afternoon.'

(24) [IP [VP   Notu'oke]]    te mo'ane    na kau.
              *           △           △          △
     'The man chopped down the tree in the afternoon.'

(25) [IP [VP   Notu'oke]]    te mo'ane    na kau.
              *           △           △          △
     'The man chopped down the tree in the afternoon.'

The evidence of (22)–(25) is that time adjuncts appear following the IP that immediately governs the VP.

## 4.3   Adverbs

In (26)–(28), possibilities for the placement of the adverbial *merimba* 'quick' are shown.

(26)  [VP    Notinti    ] na ana.
          △          △              *
       'The child ran quickly.'

(27)  [VP    Notu'o    te kau    ] na mo'ane.
          △          △        △              *
       'The man chopped down the tree quickly.'

(28)  [VP    Notu'oke    ] te mo'ane    na kau.
          △            △          *          *
       'The man chopped down the tree quickly.'

The positional possibilities for adverbs clearly delimit the extent of the VP, since adverbs can be found anywhere inside the VP (there are some additional restrictions which do not concern us here — see Donohue 1999: 177–179).

## 4.4   Summary

With the data we have collected, we can model the clause in Tukang Besi as shown in (29).

(29)

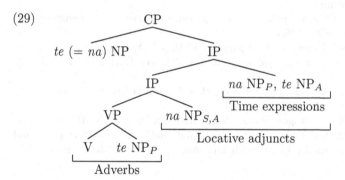

The structure of (29) matches exactly the scope results pictured in (17). While we cannot claim that scope results determine *all* aspects of constituency (see e.g., the discussion of (16) above), it seems likely that scope considerations have had a strong influence in determining Tukang Besi's constituency. Notably, it is scope considerations that allow this constituency to pull off the encodement of argument dependencies unambiguously.

# 5   Summary

In summary we wish to simply point out that it is surprising that such basic scoping properties as we have assumed in this paper can already be used to account for so much grammatical data in a language. Not only were the CS forms shown to closely replicate the Tukang Besi data, they also provided a rational for why the data is the way that it is.

An obvious concern will be how the outlook of this paper scales-up, since the simple syntactic scoping requirements of section 1 cannot possibly account for *all* data in a natural language. Indeed, the present account falls short as soon as we look at data involving clause embeddings in Tukang Besi. This can be remedied with an extension of the CS language that includes a more involved *semantic* scope to realise localities (as in Butler 2006), but this we leave for another occasion.

## Acknowledgements

We would like to thank the two anonymous reviewers for their very helpful suggestions and thought-provoking critical remarks.

## References

[1985] Andrews, Avery: The major functions of noun phrase. In: Shopen, T. (ed.) Language typology and syntactic description. Clause structure, vol. I, pp. 62–154. Cambridge University Press, Cambridge (1985)

[1984] Barendregt, H.P.: The lambda calculus: Its syntax and semantics. North-Holland, Amsterdam (1984)

[2006] Butler, Alastair: Binding effects with scope control. Research on Language and Computation 4, 54–76 (2006)

[1978] Comrie, Bernard: Ergativity. In: Lehmann, W.P. (ed.) Syntactic typology: Studies in the phenomenology of language, pp. 329–394. The Harvester Press, Sussex (1978)

[1999] Donohue, Mark: A Grammar of Tukang Besi. Grammar Library Series, vol. 20. Mouton de Gruyter, Berlin (1999)

[2002] Stehr, Mark-Oliver: Programming, specification, and interactive theorem proving: Towards a unified language based on equational logic, rewriting logic, and type theory. Ph.D. thesis, Fachbereich Informatik, Universität Hamburg (2002)

# The Marking of Verb-Actant Relations in Georgian

G. Chikoidze

Georgian Academy of Sciences
gogi@gw.acnet.ge

The purpose of our research is to find a transparent and consistent basis for representing the relations between the Georgian verb and its actants. We use the metaphor of an "action chain" as a means to elucidate the complex interdependencies representing the most general aspects of the verbal meaning, as well as the core component of the utterance as a whole, namely the standpoint from which the speaker considers the event described in the utterance.

The metaphor of an "action chain" was first discussed in Langacker (1990). Its main feature is a linear ordering of event participants corresponding to the interpretation of their functions as exerting influence on the immediate "neighbor" lower in the chain (nearer to its "tail"), presuming that both the constituents are present in the event representation. At the same time, the participants' options, which may be explicitly expressed on the "highest" layer of a sentence, that is - in the frames of its verb-actant construction, are essentially restricted by grammatical rules defining the marking of actants by the verbal form, on the one hand, and case forms on the other hand.

Georgian verbs can be marked for up to four participants of an event (though not simultaneously). The participants may be ordered according to the action chain as:

$$C \rightarrow Ag \rightarrow P \rightarrow Ad, \tag{1}$$

where the letters correspond to actants with the semantic roles of causer - C, agent - Ag, patient - P and addressee - Ad. Only these entities can be marked with different verbal inflections, though not more than two of them can be addressed simultaneously. All possible combinations of the chain positions are given in Fig.1.

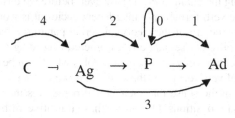

**Fig. 1.** Action chain positions that may be marked by verbal inflections on a single verb form

The list of all possible combinations is given below; each of them followed by the corresponding example using the verb *tboba* – 'to warm':3

B.D. ten Cate and H.W. Zeevat (Eds.): TbiLLC 2005, LNAI 4363, pp. 85–95, 2007.

0)  P: *otaxi* (P) *tbeba* - 'the room (P) is being warmed,

1)  P→Ad: *otaxi* (P) *mas* (Ad) *utbeba* -'the room (P) is being warmed for somebody (Ag),

2)  Ag→P: *is* (Ag) *atbobs otaxs* (P) -'she/he (Ag) is warming the room(P)',

3)  Ag→Ad: *is* (Ag) *mas* (Ad) *utbobs otaxs* (P)-'she/he (Ag) is warming the room (P) for somebody (Ag),

4)  C→Ag: *is* (C ) *atbobinebs mas*(Ag) *otaxs* (P) – 'she/he (C)  causes somebody (Ag) to warm the room (P)'.

The relation between the verbal inflection and the actants becomes obvious when the actant's person/number change values:

**subject (sb):**
*me v-tbebi* - 'I am being warmed',
*shen tbebi* - 'You are being warmed',
*chven v-tbebi-t* -'we are being warmed', etc.                                    (3)

Besides the subject-oriented set of affixes there are two other, object-oriented complex markers (direct and indirect) which may be demonstrated by the following examples:

**direct object (do):**
*is m-a-tbob-s* - 'she/he is warming me',
*is g-a-tbob-s* - 'she/he is warming you',
. . . . . . . . . . .
*is gv-a-tbob-s* -'she/he is warming us',
etc.                                                                              (4)

**indirect object (io):**
*is m-i-tbob-s mas* -'she/he is warming something for me',
*is g-i-tbob-s mas* - 'she/he is warming something for us',
etc.                                                                              (5)

In all the examples listed in (4) and (5), the Ag is represented by the third person, singular -*s* suffix; as for objects, they are expressed by the *m*-(first p., sing.), *g*-(second p., sing.) and *gv*- (first. p., plr.) prefixes, followed by –*a*- in case of direct object markers (P) and -*i*- for markers of indirect objects (Ad).

The main feature of these markers in the context of the present approach is their peculiar distribution along the chain in Fig.1. However, before we turn our attention to this particular aspect of the verb form/actant interdependencies, it is worthwhile to present a sketch of the general structure of the Georgian verbal paradigm, based on the relations of its components to different semantic roles ordered according to the chain in Fig.1. Note that the chain includes only such semantic roles which can be explicitly addressed by at least one group of verb forms. At the same time, we restrict ourselves here to verbs which are "maximal" in the sense that their global paradigms include verb forms relevant to each of the chain positions. Of course, these transitive verbs (*šeneba* -'to build', *tboba* -'to warm', etc.) do not fully represent  the repertoire of Georgian verbs, but they provide the most convenient and transparent means to demonstrate a whole range of possible verb-actant relations. The sketch given in Fig. 2 arranges the members of one such typical verb paradigm (*šeneba* - 'to build') according to the chain positions explicitly addressed by the verb form, including their semantics. We assume that the chain positions in Fig.1 represent the total range of grammatical means to build the foreground of event representation corresponding to the semantics of the given verb. At the same time, each particular verb form chooses one or two of the possible chain positions to place them at the core of the foreground, while other elements are considered to be secondary or even suppressed into the background.

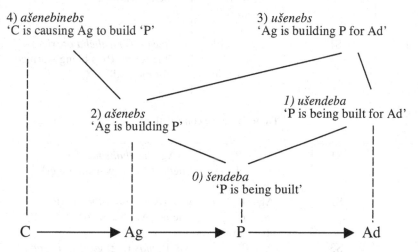

4) *ašenebinebs*
'C is causing Ag to build 'P'

3) *ušenebs*
'Ag is building P for Ad'

2) *ašenebs*
'Ag is building P'

1) *ušendeba*
'P is being built for Ad'

0) *šendeba*
'P is being built'

C ——————▶ Ag —————▶ P—————————▶ Ad

**Fig. 2.** Scheme of super-paradigm of Georgian verb šeneba – 'to build'. Enumeration of verb forms 0 – 4 corresponds to the list in (2).

As indicated in Fig. 2, the role of the semantic core component is allotted to the passive form (0), the only one marking a single P- participant. The second-level forms (1, 2) both incorporate the semantic component represented by the 0-core form, both imply that P' is being built' and for that call forth into the core of the foreground an additional participant: Ad in (1) and Ag in (2). The last (third) level entities slightly vary in their behavior: The causative construction in (4) "absorbs" the meaning of (2) with the additional role of a causer (C) who exerts its immediate influence on Ag. The semantics of the third form includes the meanings of the first and second form, adding to the core foreground the role of Ad (with respect to (2)), and Ag (with respect to (1)). In spite of these differences in foreground core composition, it is obvious that all super-paradigm members include the meaning of the passive 0-form with its single P-participant and  this fact makes us consider the scheme in Fig. 2 to represent the super-paradigm of the verb. In turn, each component of the super-paradigm itself represents a paradigm, including up to 11 mini-paradigms ("skriva"): the mini-paradigms of one and the same paradigm differ from each other   in mood, aspect, tense and some other categories; their elements, that is the verb forms included in a single mini-paradigm, differ from each other only in person and number  (Shanidze (1955)).

Essentially, case realizations of actants are not stable but depend, first, on the core lexical meaning of the verb, i.e., on the super-paradigm;   second, on the specific member of the super-paradigm (its paradigmatic entry); and third, on the choice of the specific mini-paradigm. The first of these conditions (lexical meaning) determines the selection of roles on the chain in Fig.1, as well as possible case variations.

**Table 1.** Passive constructions

| 0 | S1,2,3: | P<br>n<br>sb | *me* (P) *v-tbebi* - 'I (P) am<br>being warmed |
|---|---------|--------------|-------------------------------------------------|
| 1 | S1,2 | P→Ad<br>n    d<br>sb   io | '*me* (Ad) *mi-tbeba otaxi*(P)'-<br>'the room (P) is being warmed<br>for me (Ad)' |

**Table 2.** Active constructions

| 2 | S1 | Ag →P<br>n      d<br>sb     d | *is* (Ag) *ma-tbobs me* (P) -<br>'she/he (Ag) is warming me(P)' |
|---|----|------------------------------|-----------------------------------------------------------------|
|   | S2 | Ag→P<br>e      n<br>sb    do | *man* (Ag) *ga-ma-tbo me* (P)<br>'she/he (Ag) has warmed me (P)' |
|   | S3 | Ag→P<br>d      n<br>io     sb | *me* (P) *mas* (Ag) *ga-u-tb-i-v-ar*<br>(it turns out that just)<br>she/he (Ag) has warmed me (P) |
| 3 | S1 | Ag→P→Ad<br>n    d    d<br>sb   -    io | *me*(Ag) *mas* (Ad)<br>*v-u- tbob otaxs* (P) - 'I (Ag) am<br>warming the room (P) for her/him<br>(Ad)'. |
|   | S2 | Ag→P→Ad<br>e    n    d<br>sb   -    io | '*me* (A) *ga-gi-tbe shen* (Ad)<br>*otaxi* (P) - 'I (Ag) have warmed<br>the room (P) for you (Ad)' |
|   | S3 | -    -    - | |

**Table 3.** Causative constructions

| 4 | S1 | C→Ag→P<br>n    d    d<br>sb   do   - | *is* (C) *me* (Ag) *ma-tbobinebs*<br>*otaxs* (P) - 'she/he (C)<br>couses me(Ag) to warm<br>the room |
|---|----|--------------------------------------|------------------------------------------------------------------|
|   | S2 | C→Ag→P<br>e    d    n<br>sb   do   - | *man* (C) *me* (Ag)<br>*ga-ma-tbobina otaxi* (P)-<br>'she/he (C) has caused me (Ag)<br>to warm the room(P) |

As we have seen above (viz. Fig.2), the chain positions explicitly expressed by the verb form define the choice of the corresponding paradigm (0 - 4 in Fig.2). However, even after choosing a specific paradigm, the case realization of verb valences may vary from one group ("series") of mini - paradigms to another within a single paradigm. The character of these variations for a verb with the maximal range of valences is given above in the tables (1)-(3).

The numbers in the left-most column of each table refer to the paradigms in Fig.2 marked with the same number to define the general scheme of a construction. The next column shows the "series" symbols (S1, S2, S3) which single out specific instances of a given construction (depending on Si) with the same verb-actant relations. These relations are shown in the next (third) column, where they are represented by three-level structures: the first string defines the relevant chain  positions (C, Ag, P, Ad); the second and the third ones define the appropriate actant markers (e-ergative, n-nominative, d-dative) and verbal morphemes (sb-subject affixes, do-direct object, io-indirect object). The right-most, fourth column gives  examples that illustrate the construction types identified by the first three columns.

All the three tables in (1)-(3) have a similar structure but the first of them corresponds to the types 0 and 1 of passive constructions, the second to the types (2) and (3) of active constructions and the third one to the causative construction in (4).

In what follows we  attempt to schematize the  relations between case values (CV), verb markers (VM) and their corresponding positions (CP) in  a given construction, using the symbol h  for the head of the construction, i.e. the member nearest to the "absolute' head of the chain (in Fig.1); t for the last component (nearest to the "absolute" tail), and m for any  component situated in the middle, between h and t. However,  the schemes given below in Fig. 3 do not include the third series (S3) of active constructions (viz. table 2) because its structure significantly deviates  from the behavior of the rest, as represented in tables (1)-(3). Later ,we shall hypothesize about possible reasons of this fact.

Now we can represent the relations between construction positions CP=(h,m,t), verb markers VM=(sb,do,io) and actant cases CV=(e,n,d) as indicate in the schemes (1,2,3)  in Fig.3.

Both the schemes (1) and (2) in Fig. 3 indicate the tendency of CV and VM to be ordered according to the chain in Fig.1 as:

$$e, \quad n, \quad d; \tag{6}$$
$$sb, \quad do, \quad io \tag{7}$$

In compliance with the tables (1)-(3) and  (6) we can suppose that the semantics of the case values is subjected to the following tendencies:

1. The core component of the dative (d) meaning is based on the concept of "possession" in the widest sense; the dynamic aspect of this concept is more characteristic for it than, e.g., for the genitive; that is, it presupposes an action directed towards the d-marked object, as a result of which the object becomes a "possessor".

2. The abstract meanings of the nominative (n) and the ergative (e) include a common component: they are both oriented towards the actor, the source of the action, exerting influence on some other object or at least carrying out an "independent" process without any external causation. At the same time, though, we assume that a characteristic feature of the nominative is that it expresses the source of an action that has, as yet, not been accomplished, while the ergative expresses the source of an interrupted process, which may not have resulted as presupposed.

These definitions are obviously congruent with the general tendency of d to occupy the positions shifted to the right, i.e, towards the "tail"/"sink" of the chain, where they are subjected to the influence of their left-hand "neighbor" (P) or represent the ultimate purpose of its activity (Ad). On the contrary, n and e obviously tend to occupy left-hand positions and exert some kind of influence on their right-hand neighbors.

The tendency to shift in opposite directions is most evident at the ends of the chain: C may be marked by e or n and Ad by d only. The choice between e and n is conditioned by the above mentioned semantic difference correlated with the aspect values in the following way: n corresponds to the head position in the course of the event (S1) and is replaced by e when the process was either accomplished or interrupted, i.e., when its influence on P already belongs to the past (S2). This opposition stands behind the n/e alternation in Ag position of active constructions. More peculiar is the emergence of the d-case in the Ag-position in S1, S2 of causative constructions.

1) CP→CV

2) CP→VM

3) VM→CV

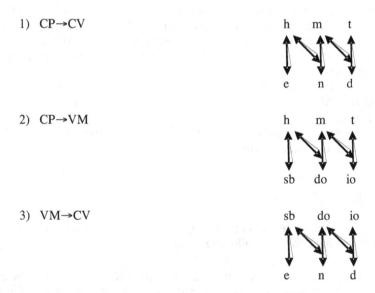

**Fig. 3.** Schemes of relations between positions within construction (CP) and corresponding case values (CV) and kind of verb address (VM) to those positions (1,2). The third scheme mirrors relations between CV and VM directly.

It may be supposed that the influence of the absolute head position C dominates its next right-hand neighbor Ag which is otherwise itself a source of influence/action directed at its own right-hand successor: as a result of this clash of interests, subdued by C the agentive position Ag receives the d-case, otherwise more fit for role of "sink".

The n/d alternations in the P position may be explained by similar reasoning: n marks the P position when it is not influenced in a direct (issuing from Ag) or indirect (from C) manner, but concedes its function to d otherwise. Note also that C exerts its influence on P over the Ag.

Now let us turn to the complex problem of inversive case distribution in the S3 series where d appears in the independent Ag position and nominative (n) in the next right-hand point (P). It seems that the only domain where we may find an explanation for this fact is the peculiar semantics of the S3 series; in particular, the event profiled by its forms is presented as hearsay information and as a result not fully trustworthy, perhaps even contradicting the presuppositions of the speaker, who was not a direct witness of the process itself: S*3: *mas* (Ag,d) *aušenebia saxli* (P,n) - 'she/he (it seems, it turned out, I heard that) has built the house'.

We hypothesize that this pragmatic aspect of the construction prevails over the semantics of the action chain: the only factual witness of the event (P) acquires the status of the sole possible information source, on the basis of which something can be concluded about the process and its actor (Ag). In this context, n becomes the most appropriate marker for P given its above discussed characteristic features and the same could be said about the Ag-d relation in S3.

In spite of the scarcity of the examples considered here, the action chain approach seems promising in structuring the quite complicated Georgian verbal paradigm and in elucidating the semantic basis of its relations to the event participants. Even if other constructions are found that deviate from the scheme, we still assume it to be prototypical for the relations under consideration.

In the final part of this paper, we will consider some examples which on the face of it significantly deviate from the proposed prototypical scheme but, when examined closely, can actually be explained in accordance with it.

We begin with the prototypical verb of possession,- *akvs* - 'he has'. It is quite natural that in the context of the action chain, the possessor is marked by dative as it has the  strongest tendency to shift towards the end ("sink", "target", Ad) of the chain. Accordingly, the verb itself carries a marker for objects : m-*akv-s* ('I have"), g-*akv-s* ('you have'), 0-akv-s ('she/he has'). As for the verb *qavs*, which is a substitute for *akvs* when the possessed object (P) is animate, the first and second person forms incorporate the auxiliary verb *aris* - 'to be' with subjective markers for the possessed object:

$$m\text{-}qev\text{-}[h\text{-}ar] \text{ - 'I have you',}$$
$$g\text{-}qev[(v)\text{-}ar] \text{ - "you have me",} \tag{8}$$

where the m-, g- prefixes mark the "possessor" (Ad), and h-, v- are the subjective markers of *aris* ('to be'):

$$v\text{-}ar \text{ ('I am'), } h\text{-}ar \text{ ('you are').} \tag{9}$$

The only difference is the possible omitting of the v-prefix due to the preceding v of the verb root (*qav*). Thus, the verb-actant relations of this pair of verbs (*akv, qav*) are quite alike to  point 1 of Fig.2 (*ušendeba*).

According to Langacker (1991), the action chain sometimes correlates with 'energy flow'. It seems convenient to interpret the "energy" of this expression as a metaphor or generalization subsuming the concepts of emotion and information flow as well. Then the behaviour of the so-called inversive verbs like *miqvars, momcons, mdzuls* ('I love, like, hate') becomes transparent in the action chain: the Ad of emotion (its target) is marked by  verbal markers for objects  and by dative case on the noun. In addition, these verbs show the same peculiarity as the verb *qav*, in that their corresponding forms behave according to scheme given in (8):

$$mi\text{-}qvarhar \text{ - 'I love you',}$$
$$giqvarvar \text{ -0 'you love me'} \tag{10}$$

Another peculiarity characterizes the verb-actant relations of the verbs expressing anxiety:

$$ešinia \text{ - 'he fears',}$$
$$scxvenia \text{ - he is ashamed',}$$
$$erideba \text{ - 'he feels shy' etc.} \tag{11}$$

The point here is that the source of these negative emotions is marked by genitive (not by nominative, as it was in (10)). In Chikoidze (2003) we proposed that the genitive with its prototypical relation of possession has a tendency to express domination, which is obviously  the case for the verbs in (11), where something dangerous or at least utterly undesirable exerts influence on Ad. Interestingly, a similar situation can be observed for Russian, despite its typological distance from Georgian. In particular, Russian verbs with semantics equivalent to (11) (пугаться, страшиться, стесняться) are construed with genitive as the source case as well.

Another example of a   strong - though this time positive - dependence on the source of the emotion are verbs like

$$mdjera, \text{ } mçams \text{ -'I believe/trust'} \tag{12}$$

which require genitive case for their source marking as well.

It seems that yet another deviation from the action chain scheme occurs in case of the reflexive forms noted below (*sataviso kceva* - in Georgian):

$$v\text{-}i\text{-}šeneb \text{ - 'I'm building for myself',}$$
$$i\text{-}šeneb \text{ - 'you're building for yourself',}$$
$$i\text{-}šeneb\text{-}s \text{ - 'she/he's building for her/him-self'}$$
$$v\text{-}i\text{-}šeneb\text{-}t \text{ - 'we're building for ourselves', etc.} \tag{13}$$

Unlike with the usual reflexivity (cf. Russian 'купаться ' or German 'sich baden'), the Georgian expressions imply the confluence of the subject/agent with the indirect (not direct) object/addressee. For the examples in (13), the left-most position represented by Ag is blended with the right-most one, i.e., Ad. We could assume that the action chain in such cases turns into a closed circle with a single point representing both the Ag and the Ad. A more preferable explanation though, is that the different positions in the action chain may in some cases be filled with actants having the same denotation. This supposition appears to be acceptable  both  for the representation of usual reflexivity, as well as the Georgian data. One more fact to note about (13) is that in the Ag/Ad "blends", the Ag dominates the Ad both verbally and nominally, i.e., both the markers correspond just to Ag:

> *is* (n) *išeneb-s* (subst, marker) *saxls* (d),
> 'she/he is building a house for her/himself'
> '*man (e) aišen-a* (subst, marker) *saxli* (n),
> 'she/he has built a house for her/himself'. (14)

Finally, we shall briefly consider one more lexical domain of the Georgian predicate – actant relation, namely expressions of information flow. Let us consider the most prototypical instance given by the verb *sçavlobs* – 'she/he is learning':

0)  *matemaţiķa* (P) *isçavleba (sķolashi)* – 'Math is beeing studied (in a school)'
1)  *matemaţiķa* (P) *esçavlebat moçapeebs* (Ad) – ' Math is being studied by pupils'
2)  *gogo* (Ag) *sçavlobs matemaţiķas* (P) – 'The girl is studying/learning math'
  3*) *peţre* (C*) *asçavlis gogos* (Ag) *matemaţiķas* (P)– 'Peter is teaching math to the girl'
  4*) *pavle* (C) *peţres* (C*) *asçavlebinebs gogostvis* (Ad) *matemaţiķas* (P) – 'Paul   causes Peter to teach math to the girl' (15)

The first three strings in (15) obviously repeat the scheme of *šeneba* ('to build') verb represented in Fig. 2 under the same numbers. However, 3* and 4* definitely deviate from examples 3, 4 of *šeneba* ('to build'), viz. (Fig. 2). The difference is that 3* and 4* demonstrate that the verb has at least two levels of causation, C and C*. Here, as usual, C exerts its influence from a position external to the situation profiled by the core component of the verb's lexical content. C*, on the other hand, is far more intrinsic to the core component, while obviously exerting some influence on the literal Agent, that is on the girl, who is studying math. In particular, C* is an Agent of the enhanced event, including the process of teaching itself, and so may be considered both causative and agentive. This nuance in causativity is often marked by the prefix a- (*a-sçavlis*), which characterizes many other instances of causativity (*a-▢inebs* – '(she/he) causes (somebody) to fall asleep', *a-rçmunebs* - '(she/he) causes (somebody) to believe (in something)', etc.), though this correlation is not strict and constant: in *a-šenebs* ((she/he) is building (something)) the Ag (she/he) exerts  influence on the P (something) directly, without any human mediator. It could be the case that the prefix a- simply expresses a high degree of the influence (cf. also *a-ngrevs* – '(she/he) is demolishing (something)'), which is typical for the causative role.

One more peculiarity of the examples in (15) is that the Ag  ("the girl") is at the same time the Ad of the process profiled by the verb, in the sense that she not only makes effort to acquire some knowledge but at the same time serves as the target for the results of her endeavor. This case of the Ag/Ad blending remains unmarked in the imperfective examples in (15) but the perfective forms of the same verb are again prefixed by i-morph characteristic for this kind of a blend. In particular. *i-scavla-* '(she/he) has learned (something)', that is the girl has accomplished the process of learning (Ag) and acquired the corresponding knowledge (Ad). Another example of the same construction would be the core verb of the same semantic domain: *i-cis-* '(she/he) knows (something)'.

The above considered examples are in no way exhaustive, however, we hope that they nevertheless demonstrate some possibilities and perspectives of the proposed approach to the interpretation of Georgian verb-actant relations by means of the action chain.

As a conclusion, let us summarize the claims made in the present paper. Our goal was to describe the Georgian verb-actant relations using the metaphor of an action chain.

These relations as such are expressed by verbal (person, number) and actant (case) markers. Verbal markers are of three different kinds, expressing subject (sb), direct object (do) and indirect object (io); the markers may address actants characterized by three case values: ergative (e), nominative (n), dative (d). Fig.3 mirrors the interconnections and their relation to the positions in the action chain (C, Ag, P, Ad). We assumed that these relations are signs, with the latter (positions and semantic roles) corresponding to their meaning and the former (markers) representing their expression.

The above described form of verb-actant relations is characteristic for most Georgian verbs that are regular in this respect: their paradigms are organized according to the scheme of Fig.2.

However, the concept of these relations demonstrates a radial structure: besides the prototypical domain represented by the schemes in Fig.1, 2 and 3, there are some verbs which deviate from the centre of the concept. Some of them differ from it only seemingly (verbs of emotion flow), others more substantially (information flow) and there are cases that really pose a problem to the approach (the third series' forms – S3). For the last (S3) type, an additional metaphor seems to be needed, taking into account the informational/pragmatic peculiarities of the paradigm (hearsay information, etc.).

Finally, it should be underlined that the Georgian verb can demonstrate a set of prototypical constructions (Fig.2, tables 1, 2, 3) within a single paradigm, that is with grammatical inflections of a unique lexical item, and that the relations of these constructions to the action chain positions are expressed by a pair of related morphologic units (verb markers and cause of actant). Both these qualities are somewhat peculiar to Georgian: they distinguish it, e.g., from such languages as Russian, where the single feature coordinated with the action chain is actant's case (see L. Janda's article (to appear) on this matter).

# References

Langacker, R.: Concept, Image and Symbol. Cognitive Basis of Grammar. Mouton De Gruyter, Berlin, New York (1991)

Shanidze, A.: Grammar of Georgian Language (in Georgian). Tbilisi University Publishing, Hause (1955)

Melikishvili, D.: Conjugation System of Georgian Language (2001) Publ. Hause: Logos Presi, Tbilisi (in Georgian)

Chikoidze, G.: The Semantics of Georgian genetive case. In: Asatiani, R., Balogh, K., Chikoidze, G., Dekker, P., de Jongh, D. (eds.) Proceedings of the fifth Tbilisi International Symposium on Language, Logic and Computation, pp. 59–66 (2003)

Janda, L.: Transitivity in Russian from a Cognitive Perspective. In: A festschrift for Elena Paducheva (to appear)

# Uniform Interpolation, Bisimulation Quantifiers, and Fixed Points

Giovanna D'Agostino*

University of Udine, Department of Mathematics and Computer Science
Viale delle Scienze 206, 33100 Udine, Italy
dagostin@dimi.uniud.it

**Abstract.** In this paper we consider some basic questions regarding the extensions of modal logics with bisimulation quantifiers. In particular, we consider the relation between bisimualtion quantifiers and uniform interpolation for modal logic and the $\mu$-calculus. We first consider these questions over the whole class of frames, and then we restrict to specific classes, where we see that the results obtained before can be easily falsified. Finally, we introduce classes of frames where we found the same good behaviour than in the whole class of frames. The results presented in this paper have been obtained in collaboration with other authors during the last years; in alphabetical order: Tim French, Marco Hollenberg, and Giacomo Lenzi.

**Keywords:** Bisimulation, Fixed Points, Bisimulation Quantifiers, Mu-Calculus.

## 1 Introduction

Bisimulation quantifiers were first introduced in [11] in the context of intuitionistic logic, and then used in [8] and [12] as a tool to prove uniform interpolation for modal logic; this technique was then reconsidered in [1] to show uniform interpolation for the modal $\mu$-calculus. The uniform interpolant of a formula $\phi$ with respect to a sublanguage $L'$ of the language of $\phi$ is a formula $\theta$ in the language $L'$ such that $\phi$ and $\theta$ imply the same formulas $\psi$ with $L(\phi) \cap L(\psi) \subseteq L'$: it is a uniform interpolant because the formula $\theta$ behaves as an interpolant between $\phi$ and any other $\psi$ which is a logical consequence of $\psi$ and for which $L(\phi) \cap L(\psi) \subseteq L'$. A logic containing all uniform interpolants of its formulas is said to enjoy uniform interpolation. Since uniform interpolation implies Craig interpolation, which in turn implies properties as the Beth one, a logic having uniform interpolation has a good interplay between syntax and semantics. Moreover, uniform interpolation allows *modularization*: if we are interested only in $L'$-consequences of $\phi$ then we may consider the (hopefully simpler) uniform interpolant $\psi$ instead of $\phi$, and *derive* all its $L'$-consequences (which are the same as the $L'$-consequences of $\phi$) in an appropriate calculus: this would be like a module for this subtask. Notice that modularization is not granted if only Craig interpolation is present.

---

* Partially supported by grant INTAS Nr. 04-77-7080 and by the McTafi Project.

B.D. ten Cate and H.W. Zeevat (Eds.): TbiLLC 2005, LNAI 4363, pp. 96–116, 2007.

Suppose $\theta$ is the uniform interpolant of $\phi$ with respect to $L(\phi) \setminus \{P\}$ (say in modal logic): then for all formulas $\psi$ not containing $P$ we have

$$\models \phi \to \psi \quad \Leftrightarrow \quad \models \theta \to \psi;$$

this suggests that the formula $\theta$ behaves as an existential propositional closure of $\phi$: the implication

$$\models \phi \to \psi \quad \Rightarrow \quad \models \theta \to \psi$$

can be seen as the elimination rule for $\exists P \phi = \theta$, while the arrow from right to left is equivalent to $\models \phi \to \theta$, which in turn can be seen as an instance of existential introduction for $\exists P \phi = \theta$.

However, we will not consider the standard semantics for the quantifier $\exists P$ here: neither modal logic nor the $\mu$-calculus allow the elimination of this kind of quantifiers. We consider a non standard semantics instead, and to motivate its introduction we consider the use of (extended) modal logics as a specification language for describing properties of reactive systems. Such systems are modeled using Kripke-structures, and the problem of characterizing the equivalence relation which holds between two Kripke structures when they model the same system can be answered in many different ways, one of the most popular being the relation of bisimulation equivalence. In this case, properties of systems will be expressed by properties which are invariant under bisimulation and modal logic and the $\mu$-calculus express indeed such properties. Let's now make a further step: existential propositional properties assert the existence of a subset having some characteristic. Since we are interested in the system more than in any model of it, it is reasonable to look for this subset not only in the model we are in, but also in any other representation of the same system, that is, in any model which is bisimilar, except for $P$, to the original one. In other words: $\exists P \phi(P)$ is true in a model if we can find a subset $P$ satisfying $\phi(P)$ in any other model which is bisimilar (up to $P$) to the given one (notice the use of the notation $\widetilde{\exists} P$ to emphasize the non standard semantics of the existential quantifier).

Let us return to uniform interpolation. One can prove that any logic which is invariant under bisimulation and closed under the existential bisimulation quantifier (that is: given $\phi$ in the logic, there exists a formula $\psi$ in the logic with the same semantics as $\widetilde{\exists} P \phi$) enjoys uniform interpolation: the uniform interpolant of a formula $\phi$ with respect to the language $L'$ being simply (the formula equivalent to) $\widetilde{\exists} P_1 \ldots \widetilde{\exists} P_n \phi$, where $L(\phi) \setminus L' = \{P_1 \ldots P_n\}$. We shall see that modal logic and the $\mu$-calculus are closed under bisimulation quantifiers over the class of all frames, and consider what happens if we restrict to specific levels of the fixed point alternation hierarchy of the $\mu$-calculus. We then try to see if the closure under bisimulation quantifier generalizes to other classes of frames.

We also investigate the opposite direction of the relation between uniform interpolation and bisimulation quantifiers: a logic with uniform interpolation will be necessarily closed under bisimulation quantifiers? As we shall see, the answer depends on the class of frames we are considering.

The paper is organized as follows. In Section 2 we introduce the $\mu$-calculus and give two possible formalizations of the semantics of bisimulation quantifiers. In Section 3 we investigate under which conditions the bisimulation quantifier commutes with other operators of the logic. In Section 6 we state the results concerning the fixpoint alternation hierarchy and the bisimulation quantifier, and in Section 7 we consider what happens if we restrict the semantics of the bisimulation quantifier to a class $C$ of frames. Finally in Section 9 axiom systems for modal logic extended with bisimulation quantifiers are considered. We will not prove all these results here, but only sketch some proof, and refer to papers where a full proof can be found.

## 2   Preliminary Notions

### 2.1   The Modal $\mu$-Calculus

First of all, we recall the definition of the extension of modal logic known as the modal $\mu$-calculus.

**Definition 1.** *The language of the $\mu$-calculus over a set of propositions Prop and a set of atomic programs $\Lambda$ is defined as the least set $\mu$ which contains Prop, and satisfies:*
*if $\phi, \psi \in \mu$ then $\neg\phi, \phi \vee \psi, \Diamond_a\phi$ belong to $\mu$;*
*if $P \in Prop$ occurs just positively in $\phi$ (that is: under an even number of negations) then $\mu P\phi$ belongs to $\mu$.*

The derived operators $\phi \wedge \psi, \phi \rightarrow \psi$, $\phi \leftrightarrow \psi, \Box_a\phi$, and $\nu P\phi$ are defined as usual. The proposition $P$ is said to be bound in $\mu P\phi$, $\nu P\phi$. Free occurrences of propositions in a formula and sentences are defined as usual. If $\phi$ is a formula, then $L(\phi)$ is defined as the set of propositions which occur free in $\phi$. We call $\phi$ a *modal formula* if it is constructed without using the fixpoint operators.

A $\mu$-calculus formula is interpreted in pointed Kripke models, i.e. first order structures for the language $\{r\} \cup \{R_a : a \in \Lambda\} \cup Prop$, where $r$ is a constant symbol, $R_a$ is a binary relational symbol for each $a \in A$, and $P$ is a unary relational symbol for each $P \in Prop$. Hence, a pointed Kripke model ( a *model* from now on) consists of a non-empty domain $D^M$, an element $r^M \in D^M$ (the *initial* point of the model), a binary relation $R_a^M$ on $D^M$, for each $a \in \Lambda$, and subset $P^M$ of $D^M$, for each $P \in Prop$.

Given a model $M$, a $\mu$-formula is interpreted in $M$ as a subset $[\![\phi]\!]_M$ of $D^M$, defined as follows:

$$
\begin{aligned}
[\![P]\!]_M &:= P^M \\
[\![\neg\phi]\!]_M &:= D^M \setminus [\![\phi]\!]_M \\
[\![\phi \vee \psi]\!]_M &:= [\![\phi]\!]_M \cup [\![\psi]\!]_M \\
[\![\Diamond_a\phi]\!]_M &:= \{s \in D^M \mid [\![\phi]\!]_M \cap \{t : sR^M t\} \neq \emptyset\} \\
[\![\mu P\phi]\!]_M &:= \bigcap\{S \subseteq D^M \mid [\![\phi]\!]_{M[P:=S]} \subseteq S\}
\end{aligned}
$$

where $M[P := S]$ is equal to $M$ except that the proposition $P$ is evaluated as $S$. Note that $[\![\mu P\phi]\!]_M$ is the least fixpoint of the monotone operator $S \mapsto [\![\phi]\!]_{M[P:=S]}$.

In the following, we denote $s \in \llbracket \phi \rrbracket_M$ by $(M, s) \models \phi$. $M \models \phi$ is used to denote $(M, r^M) \models \phi$. $\Gamma \models \phi$ denotes logical consequence: if $M \models \Gamma$ then $M \models \phi$ for every model $M$.

If $C$ is a class of pointed Kripke frames (i.e. of first order structures for the language $\{r\} \cup \{R_a : a \in \Lambda\}$), we say that a Kripke model $M$ is a *C-model* (or $M \in C$) if the frame underlying $M$ is in $C$; $\Gamma \models_C \phi$ means that, for all $M \in C$, if $M \models \Gamma$ then $M \models \phi$. A formula $\phi$ is said to be *C-valid* (notation: $\models_C \phi$) if $M \models \phi$, for all $M \in C$. The set of $\mu$-formulas (modal formulas) which are valid in $C$ is denoted by $\mu(C)$ (ML(C), respectively).

An alternative syntax for the $\mu$-calculus is obtained by substituting a set of *cover operators* for the $\Diamond_a$ operators. For each $n \geq 1$ there is a cover operator of arity equal to $n$: if $\Theta = \{\phi_1, \ldots, \phi_n\}$ is a finite set of formulas, then

$$\text{COVER}_a(\Theta),$$

is a formula. We also allow the constant operator $\text{COVER}_a(\emptyset)$.

The cover operators are interpreted in a Kripke model $M$ as follows: $\text{COVER}_a(\emptyset)$ is true in $M$ if and only if the root of $M$ does not have any $R_a$-successor, while $\text{COVER}_a(\{\phi_1, \ldots, \phi_n\})$ is true in $M$ if and only if the $R_a$-successors of the root are *covered* by $\phi_1, \ldots, \phi_n$. More formally, $(M, s) \models \text{COVER}_a(\{\phi_1, \ldots, \phi_n\})$ if and only if:

1. for every $i = 1, \ldots, n$ there exists $t$ with $(s, t) \in R_a^M$ and $(M, t) \models \phi_i$;
2. for every $t$ with $(s, t) \in R_a^M$ there exists $i \in \{1, .., n\}$ with $(M, t) \models \phi_i$.

Since $\text{COVER}_a(\{\phi_1, \ldots, \phi_n\})$ is equivalent to

$$\Diamond_a(\phi_1) \wedge \ldots \wedge \Diamond_a(\phi_n) \wedge \Box_a(\phi_1 \vee \ldots \vee \phi_n),$$

cover operators are definable in the $\Diamond$ syntax. Conversely,

$$\Diamond_a \phi \Leftrightarrow \text{COVER}_a(\{\phi, \top\}).$$

Hence, the $\mu$-calculus obtained from the covers-syntax is equivalent to the familiar $\mu$-calculus constructed using the $\Diamond$-syntax.

We now introduce an important class of $\mu$-formulas.

**Definition 2.** *The* class of *disjunctive $\mu$-formulas is the least class containing* $\top, \bot$, *all non-contradictory conjunctions of literals, and which is closed under:*

1. *disjunctions;*
2. *special conjunctions: if $a_1, \ldots a_n$ are distinct atomic actions, $\Theta_1, \ldots \Theta_n$ are finite sets of formulas in the class and $\sigma$ is a non-contradictory conjunction of literals, then*

$$\sigma \wedge \bigwedge_i \text{COVER}_{a_i}(\Theta_i)$$

*is in the class;*

3. *fixpoint operators: if $\phi$ is disjunctive, $\phi$ does not contain $P \wedge \gamma$ as a subformula for any formula $\gamma$, and $P$ is positive in $\phi$, then $\mu P \phi, \nu P \phi$ are in the class.*

The disjunctive formulas are representative of the whole $\mu$-calculus:

**Theorem 1.** *[10] Any $\mu$-calculus formula is equivalent to a disjunctive one.*

The same is true for the class of modal formulas with respect to disjunctive modal formulas (which are defined as in Definition 2 but without closing for fixpoint operators). In the modal case the proof of Theorem 1 is a simple consequence of the following validity:

$$\mathrm{COVER}_a(\Theta_1) \wedge \mathrm{COVER}_a(\Theta_2) \leftrightarrow \bigvee_B \mathrm{COVER}_a(\{\phi \wedge \psi : (\phi, \psi) \in B\})$$

where the disjunction ranges over all relations $B \subseteq \Theta_1 \times \Theta_2$ satisfying:
for all $\phi \in \Theta_1$ exists $\psi \in \Theta_2$ with $(\phi, \psi) \in B$;
for all $\psi \in \Theta_2$ exists $\phi \in \Theta_1$ with $(\phi, \psi) \in B$.

   The equivalence above allows to eliminate *non-disjunctive* conjunction from any modal formula.

## 2.2   Bisimulation Quantifiers Modal Logic

We consider the extension of modal logic by means of propositional quantifiers:

**Definition 3.** *The language of Bisimulation Quantifiers Modal Logic over a set of propositions Prop and a set of atomic programs $\Lambda$ is defined as the least set BQL which contains Prop and satisfies:*
*if $\phi, \psi \in BQL$, then $\neg \phi, \phi \vee \psi, \Diamond_a \phi$ belong to $BQL$;*
*if $P \in Prop$ and $\phi$ belongs to $BQL$ then $\exists P \phi \in BQL$.*

*BQL*-formulas are interpreted in pointed Kripke models. To introduce their semantics we first need the notion of *bisimulation*.

**Definition 4.** *Let $M$, $N$ be models with $D^M, D^N$ as respective domains. Let $Prop' \subseteq Prop$. A relation $Z \subseteq D^M \times D^N$ is a Prop'-bisimulation between $M$ and $N$ if:*

1. *$r^M Z r^N$;*
2. *if $wZv$ then $w \in P^M$ iff $v \in P^N$, for every $P \in Prop'$;*
3. *if $wZv$, $a \in \Lambda$, and $wR_a^M w'$, then there exists a $v'$ such that $vR_a^N v'$ and $w'Zv'$;*
4. *if $wZv$, $a \in \Lambda$, and $vR_a^N v'$, then there exists a $w'$ such that $wR_a^M w'$ and $w'Zv'$.*

Two models $M, N$ are *Prop'-bisimilar* (notation: $M \sim_{Prop'} N$) if there exists a *Prop'*-bisimulation between them; we write $M \sim N$ if $Prop' = Prop$, and $M \sim_{\neq P} N$ if $Prop' = Prop \setminus \{P\}$.

## 2.3  Bisimulation Quantifiers: Local and Global Version

As we outlined in the introduction, a formula $\tilde{\exists}P\phi$ holds in a $C$-model $M$ if it is possible to find a $C$-model $N$ which is bisimilar to $M$ up to $P$ and satisfies $\phi$. This gives the global version of the semantics of $\tilde{\exists}P\phi$ in a class of frames $C$:

$$M \models^g_C \tilde{\exists}P\phi \Leftrightarrow \exists N \in C, N \sim_{\neq P} M, \text{ and } N \models^g_C \phi,$$

where the $g$ stays for *global* since we require that the model $N$ is bisimilar to $M$ w.r.t. to the whole set of propositional variables, except for $P$; the semantics for the other operators of the logic is standard and we do not repeat it here.

As an example, consider the class $C$ of all frames and the formula

$$\phi := \tilde{\exists}P(\Diamond_a(P) \wedge \Diamond_a(\neg P)).$$

Then, for all models $M$ we have

$$M \models^g_C \phi \Leftrightarrow M \models \Diamond_a(\top).$$

On the other hand, if $C$ is the class of frames where the root as only one immediate successor, and $M \in C$ then $M \not\models^g_C \phi$.

This semantics validates some natural and basic principles on bisimulation quantifiers as

$$\models^g_C \phi \rightarrow \tilde{\exists}P\phi, \qquad \models^g_C \tilde{\exists}P(\phi \vee \psi) \leftrightarrow (\tilde{\exists}P\phi \vee \tilde{\exists}P\psi),$$

but not all the ones we would expect. In particular, under this semantics the principle of existential elimination is not valid in general, that is, there are classes of frames $C$ and modal formulas $\phi, \psi$ such that:

1. $P$ does not appear in $\psi$;
2. $\models^g_C \phi \rightarrow \psi$;
3. $\not\models^g_C \tilde{\exists}P\phi \rightarrow \psi$.

This peculiarity was first noticed by Tim French in [6]. The problem with the global definition is that under this semantics $BQL$-fomulas are not in general invariant under bisimulation: there could be two models $M, N$ which are bisimilar w.r.t. the language of a formula, but disagree on the formula. In this case it is possible that $\models^g_C \phi \rightarrow \psi$ but there exists an $M$ with $M \models^g_C \tilde{\exists}P\phi$ and $M \not\models^g_C \psi$. We borrow the following example from [6].

*Example 1.* Over an arbitrary class of frames $C$ the logic $BQL$ is not necessarily bisimulation invariant. Let $\Lambda = \{a\}$ and $C$ be the class consisting of a single frame $F$, having the set $S = \{a, b, c\}$ as domain, $R_a = S \times S$, and where $a$ is the root. Then there exists a $BQL$-formula $\phi$ and models $M, M'$ based of $F$ such that $M' \models \phi$, $M \not\models \phi$ but $M \sim_{L(\phi)} M'$.

Let $Q, R, S \in Prop$ be different propositions, and let $M$ be the model based on $F$ where $Q^M = \{a\}$, $R^M = \{c\}$ and $P^M = \emptyset$ for $P \in Prop \setminus \{Q, R\}$; let $M'$ be the model based on $F$ where $R^M = \{b, c\}$, $S^M = \{b\}$, and $P^{M'} = \emptyset$ for $P \in Prop \setminus \{R, S\}$. Notice that the models $M, M'$ are bisimilar w.r.t. the language

$\{R\}$. Let $\phi = \widetilde{\exists}S(\Diamond(R\wedge S)\wedge\Diamond(R\wedge\neg S))$; then $L(\phi) = \{R\}$; $M' \models \phi, M \not\models \phi$. the reason why $M \not\models \phi$ is simply that any model $K$ which is bisimilar to $M$ w.r.t. $\{Q,R\}$ and satisfies $\Diamond(R\wedge S)\wedge\Diamond(R\wedge\neg S)$ must have at least four distinct worlds: there must be one satisfying $R\wedge S$ and a different one satisfying $R\wedge\neg S$; moreover, since $K \sim_{\{Q,R\}} M$ we must also have a world satisfying $Q\wedge\neg R$, which is then necessarily different from the previous ones, and another one satisfying $\neg Q\wedge\neg R$, which will be different from all previous worlds. This means that $K$ must have at least four words, which is impossible for a $C$-model. Tim French showed that the same example can be exploited to show that Bisimulation Quantifier Logic does not satisfy the principle of existential elimination.                                   $\square$

In [6] it is proved that the well known property of amalgamability of a class of frames is a condition that ensures the invariance under bisimulation of Bisimulation Quantifiers Logic. One could ask if it would not be possible to change the semantics of the bisimulation quantifiers in order to obtain, in any class of frames, a logic which is bisimulation invariant. The idea is to move from a global to a local definition:

$$M \models^l_C \widetilde{\exists}P\phi \Leftrightarrow \exists N \in C, N \sim_{L(\phi)\setminus\{P\}} M, \text{ and } N \models^l_C \phi.$$

The difference with the global definition is that we do not pretend that the model $N$ is bisimilar to $M$ with respect to all variables except $P$, but only bisimilar to $M$ with respect to the free variables of $\widetilde{\exists}P\phi$. The advantage of the local definiton w.r.t. the global variant is that now it is easily proved by induction that a $BQL$-formula is invariant under bisimulation: if $M \models^L_C \phi$ and $M \sim_{L(\phi)} M'$ then $M' \models \phi$. Unfortunately, the rule of existential elimination is still not valid in general using the local definition. This can be seen as follows: let $C, M, M'$ be as in Example 1. Let $\phi$ be the formula $\Diamond(R\wedge S)\wedge\Diamond(R\wedge\neg S)$, and $\psi$ be the formula $\neg(\Diamond(Q\wedge\neg R)\wedge\Diamond(\neg Q\wedge\neg R))$. Then $\models^l_C \phi \to \psi$; on the other hand, $M \models^l_C \widetilde{\exists}S\phi$ (because $M' \models^l_C \phi$, and $M \sim_{L(\phi)\setminus\{S\}} M'$), but $M \not\models^l_C \psi$.

In the next Lemma we see that if we impose the amalgamability property over a class of frames then the global and local definition of the semantics of bisimulation quantifiers coincide, and, as a consequence, the rule of existenial elimination holds.

First we remember the definition of an amalgamable class of frames:

**Definition 5.** *A class $C$ of frames is amalgamable if, whenever we have two $C$-models $M, N$ with $M \sim_{\theta_1\cap\theta_2} N$, then there exists a $C$-model $K$ with*

$$K \sim_{\theta_1} M, \quad K \sim_{\theta_2} N.$$

**Lemma 1.** *([6,2] ) Let $C$ be an amalgamable class of frames. Then the global and local semantics of Bisimulation Quantifiers Modal Logic coincide, and the logic satisfies the principle of existential elimination.*

*Proof.* We first show French results: amalgamability of $C$ implies that $BQL$-formulas are bisimulation invariant w.r.t. the global semantics. That is, we prove by induction on $\phi$ that for all $C$-models $M, N$, if $M \sim_{L(\phi)} N$ and $M \models^g_C \phi$, then

$N \models_C^g \phi$. Amalgamation is needed in the case when $\phi = \widetilde{\exists}P\psi$. If $M \models \widetilde{\exists}P\psi$, there exists a $C$-model $M'$ with $M' \sim_{\neq P} M$ and $M' \models_C^g \psi$; it follows that $N \sim_{(L(\psi)\backslash\{P\})} M'$, and, by amalgamability, there is a $C$-model $K$ with $K \sim_{L(\psi)} M'$, $K \sim_{(Prop\backslash\{P\})} N$. By induction $K \models_C^g \psi$, and hence $N \models_C^g \widetilde{\exists}P\psi$.

Having that the global semantics is bisimulation invariant, we can prove, by induction on $\phi$, that for all $C$-models $M$ it holds:

$$M \models_C^g \phi \Leftrightarrow M \models_C^l \phi.$$

The only interesting case is $M \models_C^l \widetilde{\exists}P\psi \Rightarrow M \models_C^g \widetilde{\exists}P\psi$: suppose there exists a model $N$ with $N \sim_{L(\psi)\backslash\{P\}} M$ and $N \models_C^l \psi$, then $M \models_C^g \widetilde{\exists}P\psi$; otherwise $M \models_C^g \neg\widetilde{\exists}P\psi$ and by bisimulation invariance of the global semantics this would imply $N \models_C^g \neg\widetilde{\exists}P\psi$, which is not since (by induction) $N \models_C^g \psi$.    □

Hence, if $C$ is an amalgamable class of frames, there is no difference between the two versions of bisimulation quantifiers semantics; hence, in amalgamable classes we will drop the $g, l$ notation, writing simply $M \models_C \phi$; if $C$ is the class of all frames we drop the $C$ as well, writing $M \models \phi, \models \phi$ etc.

A similar analysis can be done for another natural principle that we expect to hold, that is, the principle of existential introduction: if the modal formula $\psi$ is free for the substitution of $P$ in the modal formula $\phi$, then $\models_C \phi[P|\psi] \rightarrow \widetilde{\exists}P\phi$. As in the case of existential elimination, it is possible to prove that the principle of existential introduction holds for an amalgamative class of frames (see [6]). *From now on, unless otherwise stated, we implicitly assume that the class $C$ enjoys amalgamation.*

We finally notice that the discussion above is not restricted to modal logic. We could as well consider the extension of the $\mu$-calculus with bisimulation quantifiers, and the same results would hold: in particular the principles of existential elimination and introduction are valid for the mu-calculus extended with bisimulation quantifiers over an amalgamable class of frames.

## 3    Commutativity Principles

As we already noted, bisimulation quantifiers always commute with disjunctions. Not surprisingly, the commutativity with modal operators depends on the class $C$. In this section we consider in particular the commutativity with the Cover Operator, that is, the principle

$$\models_C \widetilde{\exists}P(\sigma \wedge \text{COVER}_a(\phi_1, \ldots, \phi_n)) \leftrightarrow \widetilde{\exists}P\sigma \wedge \text{COVER}_a(\widetilde{\exists}P\phi_1, \ldots, \widetilde{\exists}P\phi_n),$$

where $\sigma$ is a conjunction of literals (notice that from this principle we obtain the commutativity of $\widetilde{\exists}$ with the $\square$ and $\diamond$ operators). The arrow from left to write of this equivalence holds in every class of frames $C$. We now introduce a sufficient property for the other arrow.

## 3.1   The Glueing Property

**Definition 6.** *If $\mathcal{F}$ is a family of pointed frames, then the frame $Glue_a(\mathcal{F})$ is defined as the frame obtained from the disjoint union of all frames of the family by adding a new initial point $s$, and an accessibility relation $R_a$ between $s$ and all the initial points of the frames in the family. This definition is extended to a family of models $\mathcal{M}$ and a set of propositions $\Theta$: we consider the family $\mathcal{F}$ of the corresponding frames, we copy the valuation of the propositions from the $M_i$ to the corresponding copies in $Glue_a(\mathcal{F})$, and we let the new root $s$ agree with $\Theta$ (in the sense that $s$ verifies all propositions in $\Theta$ and falsifies all propositions outside $\Theta$). The new model is denoted by $Glue_a(\mathcal{M}, \Theta)$.*

**Definition 7.** *A class $C$ of pointed frames enjoys the* glueing *property if the following holds: suppose we have $F \in C$ with initial point equal to $r$ and a class $\mathcal{K}$ of $C$-frames such that*

1. *if $K \in \mathcal{K}$ there exists $w$ with $rR_aw$ and $K \sim (F, w)$;*
2. *for all $w$ with $rR_aw$ there exists $K \in \mathcal{K}$ with $K \sim (F, w)$;*

*then, $Glue_a(\mathcal{K}) \in C$.*

**Lemma 2.** *If $C$ is a class of frames satisfying the glueing property, then*

$$\models_C \widetilde{\exists} P\sigma \wedge \text{COVER}_a(\widetilde{\exists} P\phi_1, \dots, \widetilde{\exists} P\phi_n) \rightarrow \widetilde{\exists} P(\sigma \wedge \text{COVER}_a(\phi_1, \dots, \phi_n)).$$

*Proof.* Let $M$ be a $C$-model such that

$$M \models_C \widetilde{\exists} P\sigma \wedge \text{COVER}_a(\widetilde{\exists} P\phi_1, \dots, \widetilde{\exists} P\phi_n).$$

This implies that there is a family $\mathcal{K}$ of $C$-models with the following properties:

1. *if $K \in \mathcal{K}$ there exists $w$ with $r^M R_a w$ and $K \sim_{\neq P} (M, w)$;*
2. *for all $w$ with $r^M R_a w$ there exists $K \in \mathcal{K}$ with $K \sim_{\neq P} (M, w)$;*
3. *for all $i$ there exists $K \in \mathcal{K}$ with $K \models \phi_i$;*
4. *for all $K \in \mathcal{K}$ there exists $i$ with $K \models \phi_i$.*

Let $\Theta = \{Q \in Prop \setminus \{P\} : M \models Q\} \cup \{P^*\}$, where $P^*$ is $P$ if $P$ is a conjunct in $\sigma$, and $P^* = \neg P$, otherwise. Then the model $Glue_a(\mathcal{K}, \Theta)$ is a $C$-model, by hypothesis. Moreover one can easily verifies that

$$Glue_a(\mathcal{K}, \Theta) \models \sigma \wedge \text{COVER}_a(\phi_1, \dots, \phi_n),$$

and that the model $Glue_a(\mathcal{K}, \Theta)$ is bisimilar to $M$ up to $P$. It follows

$$M \models_C \widetilde{\exists} P(\sigma \wedge \text{COVER}_a(\phi_1, \dots, \phi_n)). \qquad \square$$

Since the class of all pointed frames trivially satisfies the glueing property we see that the commutativity of $\widetilde{\exists}$ with the Cover Operators is valid over this class. Unfortunately, the glueing property and the commutativity of $\widetilde{\exists}$ with the Cover Operators are very easily destroyed, e.g. they do not hold in the class of transitive frames. Consider the formula

$$\text{COVER}_a(\widetilde{\exists} P(P \wedge \square_a(\neg P))) \rightarrow \widetilde{\exists} P\text{COVER}_a(P \wedge \square_a(\neg P)).$$

Then, the antecedent is true in the finite transitive $a$-chain of lenght three, but the consequent is false.

## 3.2 Disjunctive Modal Formulas and $\widetilde{\exists}$

From the commutativity of $\widetilde{\exists}$ with disjunctions and Cover Operators (see Lemma 2) we easily prove by induction:

**Lemma 3.** *If $\delta$ is a modal disjunctive formula, then, over a class $C$ satisfying the glueing property we have:*

$$\models_C \widetilde{\exists}P\delta \leftrightarrow \delta[P|\top, \neg P|\top],$$

*where $\delta[P|\top, \neg P|\top]$ denotes the formula in which $P$ and $\neg P$ are simultaneously substituted by $\top$.*

Notice that by definition a disjunctive formula will never contain $P$, $\neg P$ in the same conjunction.

## 3.3 Commutativity of $\widetilde{\exists}$ with Fixed Points

One can easily show that the bisimulation quantifier does not commute in general with fixed points; indeed, the following formula is not valid:

$$\widetilde{\exists}P\nu X(P \wedge \Box(\neg P) \wedge \Box(X)) \rightarrow \nu X(\widetilde{\exists}P(P \wedge \Box(\neg P) \wedge \Box(X))).$$

However, if we restrict to disjunctive formulas, we have:

**Lemma 4.** *(see [3]) If $\delta$ is disjunctive, then $\widetilde{\exists}P\delta$ is equivalent (over the class of all frames) to $\delta[P|\top, \neg P|\top]$. In particular, if $\mu Q\phi, \nu Q\phi$ are disjunctive formulas, then the following equivalences are valid over the class of all frames:*

$$\widetilde{\exists}P\nu Q\phi \leftrightarrow \nu Q\widetilde{\exists}P\phi; \qquad \widetilde{\exists}P\mu Q\phi \leftrightarrow \mu Q\widetilde{\exists}P\phi.$$

This theorem can be proved using either automata or tableaux for disjunctive formulas. The problem with a direct inductive proof relies on the greatest fixed point operator, which, being equivalent to an infinitary conjunction of its approximations does not allow an easy access to the inductive step.

## 4 Closure Under Bisimulation Quantifiers

From Lemma 1 we know that every modal formula is equivalent to a disjunctive modal formula and every $\mu$-formula is equivalent to a disjunctive $\mu$-formula. Moreover, by Lemma 4 we know that disjunctive (modal or $\mu$) formulas are closed under bisimulation quantifiers over the class of all frames, that is, for any disjunctive (modal or $\mu$) formula $\delta$ there exists a (modal or $\mu$ ) formula $\theta$ having the same semantics as $\widetilde{\exists}P\delta$. Since existential elimination and introduction holds over this class, we have

$$\models \phi \leftrightarrow \psi \quad \Rightarrow \quad \models \widetilde{\exists}P\phi \leftrightarrow \widetilde{\exists}P\psi,$$

and hence:

**Theorem 2.** *Modal Logic and the $\mu$-calculus are closed under bisimulation quantifiers over the class of all frames.*

In Section 8 we shall generalize this Theorem to special classes of frames, but first we investigate the relation between bisimulation quantifiers and uniform interpolation.

## 5   Bisimulation Quantifiers and Uniform Interpolation

If a class $C$ of frames is amalgamable, then we know from Lemma 1 that both $BQML(C)$ (modal logic extended with bisimulation quantifiers) and $BQ\mu(C)$ (the $\mu$-calculus extended with bisimulation quantifiers) satisfies the rule of existential elimination. Let us denote by $\mathcal{L}$ one of the two logics: then for all pairs $\phi, \psi$ of $\mathcal{L}$-formulas and for all $P$ which is not free in $\psi$ we have:

$$\models_C \phi \to \psi \quad \Leftrightarrow \quad \models_C \tilde{\exists} P \phi \to \psi.$$

This means that the formula $\tilde{\exists} P \phi$ of $\mathcal{L}$ is an interpolant for $\phi$ in $\mathcal{L}$ with respect to all formulas non containing $P$; in other words, the interpolant does not depend on $\psi$: the same interpolant can be used for all formulae which are implied by $\phi$ and do not contain $P$. We call such an interpolant a *uniform interpolant* for $\phi$ w.r.t. $P$.

From the discussion above we have:

**Theorem 3.** *Let $C$ be a class of frames such that the $\mu$-calculus is closed under bisimulation quantifiers over $C$. Then $\mu(C)$ enjoys uniform interpolation over $C$. Similarly, if Modal logic is closed under bisimulation quantifiers over $C$, then $ML(C)$ enjoys uniform interpolation over $C$. In particular, Modal logic and the $\mu$-calculus enjoy uniform interpolation over the class of all frames.*

## 6   The Existential Bisimulation Quantifier and the Fixed Point Hierarchy

We consider now the behaviour of the existential bisimulation quantifier with respect to the fixpoint alternation levels of the $\mu$-calculus. In this section we consider the $\mu$-formulas as constructed from a set of propositional constants *Prop*, their negations $\{\neg P : P \in Prop\}$, and a set of atomic programs $\Lambda$ using the following operators: if $\phi_1, \phi_2 \in \mu$ then

$$\phi_1 \vee \phi_2, \ \phi_1 \wedge \phi_2, \ \Diamond_a(\phi_1), \ \Box_a(\phi_1), \ \mu P \phi_1, \ \text{and} \ \nu P \phi_1 \text{ belong to } \mu$$

(in the last two cases: provided $P$ is positive in $\phi_1$) .

This definition is equivalent to the one adopted in the previous sections, but avoids the use of explicit negation.

**Definition 8.** *The fixpoint alternation-depth hierarchy of the $\mu$-calculus is the sequence $N_0 = M_0, N_1, M_1, \ldots$ of sets of $\mu$-formulas defined inductively as follows:*

1. $N_0 = M_0$ *is defined as the set of all modal fixpoint free formulas;*
2. $N_{k+1}$ *is the closure of* $N_k \cup M_k$ *under the operations described in* (a), (b) *below.*

    (a) *(Positive Substitution) If* $\phi(P_1, \ldots P_n), \phi_1, \ldots, \phi_n$ *are in* $N_{k+1}$, *then* $\phi(\phi_1 \ldots \phi_n)$ *is in* $N_{k+1}$, *provided* $P_1, \ldots, P_n$ *are positive in* $\phi$ *and no occurrence of a variable which was free in one of the* $\phi_i$ *becomes bound in* $\phi(\phi_1 \ldots \phi_n)$.

    (b) *If* $\phi$ *is in* $N_{k+1}$, *then* $\nu P \phi \in N_{k+1}$.

3. *Likewise,* $M_{k+1}$ *is the closure of* $N_k \cup M_k$ *under positive substitution and the* $\mu$-*operator.*

Since the 0-level of the $\mu$-calculus coincides with modal logic, Theorem 2 says that this level and the set of all levels are closed under the existential bisimulation quantifier. It is then natural to ask whether any single level of the $\mu$-calculus is closed, or, equivalently, if the uniform interpolant of a formula in a certain level of the hierarchy belongs to the same level. Since the best model checking algorithm known so far for $\mu$-calculus formulas depends on the fixpoint alternation level of the formula (the lower the level, the easier it is to check whether the formula is true in a finite model), and most of the temporal logics used in applications can be embedded into the low levels of the hierarchy, it would be good to know whether the low levels are closed.

As an easy corollary of Lemma 4 we have that the uniform interpolant of a disjunctive formula $\phi$ belongs to the same level as $\phi$. It is however possible to prove (see [3]) that this is not true in general: levels $0, 1$ and $2$ of the fixpoint alternation-depth hierarchy of the $\mu$-calculus are closed under the existential bisimulation quantifier, while the third level is not, since the closure of this level is the whole $\mu$-calculus. and the fixed point alternation hierarchy is strict.

## 7   Restricting the Semantics to Smaller Classes of Frames: Negative Results

We now consider what happens to the preceding discussion when, instead of considering the semantics of bisimulation quantifiers over the class of all frames, we restrict to some specific smaller amalgamable class $C$. In particular, we consider the following questions:

1. If a modal formula $\phi$ has a uniform interpolant $\theta$ w.r.t. $P$ in $ML(C)$, then it is always the case that $\theta$ behaves semantically as $\tilde{\exists}P\phi$ over $C$?
2. If $ML(C)$ enjoys the uniform interpolation property then it is true that $ML(C) = BQML(C)$?

Notice that the first property implies the second one, and that we may as well ask the same questions for $\mu(C)$ instead of $ML(C)$. Since uniform interpolation is a property of the logic while the closure under bisimulation quantifiers depends on the class of frames, the second property above can be easily falsified:

*Example 2.* We consider the class $C$ consisting of all well founded transitive frames and the class $C'$ of all finite, transitive, well-founded frames plus the following well founded frame:

- the domain of the frame is the infinite set $\omega + 1 = \{0, 1, 2, \ldots, \omega\}$;
- the accessibility relation is $\alpha R \beta \Leftrightarrow \beta \in \alpha$;
- $\omega$ is the initial point of the frame.

We have $ML(C) = ML(C') = GL$, the Gödel-Löb logic. It is well known that modal logic is closed under bisimulation quantifiers over $C$ (see e.g. [12]), hence by Theorem 3 we know that $ML(C')$ enjoys uniform interpolation. On the other hand, we shall prove that modal logic over $C'$ it is not closed under bisimulation quantifiers. Consider the formula

$$\phi \equiv \Diamond^2(T) \to \tilde{\exists} P (\Diamond(P \wedge \Diamond(T) \wedge \Box(\neg P)) \wedge \Diamond(\neg P \wedge \Diamond(T) \wedge \Box(P))).$$

This formula is true in all frames of $C' \setminus \{\omega + 1\}$ because we can always duplicate nodes remaining inside this class. On the other hand, it is false in $\omega + 1$ because the only frame in the class $C'$ which is bisimilar to $\omega + 1$ is $\omega + 1$, and we cannot interpret $P$ in this frame in such a way that the formula

$$\Diamond(P \wedge \Diamond(T) \wedge \Box(\neg P)) \wedge \Diamond(\neg P \wedge \Diamond(T) \wedge \Box(P))$$

becomes true. But no modal formula can be true in all frames in $C \setminus \{\omega + 1\}$ and false in $\omega + 1$, hence the above bisimulation quantifier formula is not equivalent to a modal formula. □

On the other hand, the logic $\mu ML(C)$ gives an affirmative answer to the first question, provided we restrict to classes of finite frames (the same holds for $ML(C)$, provided we restrict to classes of finite transitive frames).

**Theorem 4.** *Let $C$ be a class which only contains finite frames. Then if $\beta$ is the uniform interpolant of the $\mu$-formula $\alpha$ w.r.t. $P$, then $\beta$ sematically behaves as $\tilde{\exists} P \alpha$ over $C$. In particular, $\mu ML(C)$ enjoys uniform interpolation iff $\mu ML(C)$ is closed under bisimulation quantifiers.*

*Proof.* The proof is an adaptation of the proof of the modal version which can be found in [2]. We sketch the proof below. Given a finite model $M$ with initial point $w_0$, let $\{w_0, \ldots, w_m\}$ be the points which are reachable from $w_0$ in a finite number of steps. Given a finite set of propositions $\Theta$, there is a $\mu$ formula $\phi_M(\Theta, P_0, \ldots, P_m)$ using variables from $\Theta$ and new variables $P_0, \ldots, P_m$ such that for all model $K$ it holds:

$$K \models \phi_M(\Theta, P_0, \ldots, P_m)$$
$$\Updownarrow$$

$\rho = \{(v, w_i) \in K^* \times M : (K, v) \models P_i\}$ is a functional bisimulation between $K^*$ and $M$ over $\Theta$, (where $K^*$ is the model $K$ restricted to reachable points).

The formula $\phi_M(\Theta, P_0, \ldots, P_m)$ is the $\mu$-formula expressing the following properties:

- $P_0$ contains the initial point;
- $P_0, \ldots, P_m$ is a partition of the set of reachable points;
- the formula $P_i \rightarrow \bigwedge_{a \in \Lambda} \text{COVER}_a \{P_j \ : \ w_i R_a^M w_j\}$ is true in all reachable points;
- the formula $P_i \rightarrow \bigwedge \{Q : Q \in \Theta, M, w_i \models Q\}$ is true in all reachable points,

(notice that we need greatest fixed points to express the last three conditions ).

Suppose $\alpha$ is a $\mu$ formula and consider its uniform interpolant $\beta$ w.r.t. $P$. We want to prove that $\beta$ has the same semantics as $\tilde{\exists} P \alpha$. We first claim that for any $C$ model $M$ it holds:

$$M \models \beta \Leftrightarrow \text{ there exists a model } K \in C \text{ with } K^* \rightarrow_{L(\alpha) \setminus \{P\}} M \text{ and } K \models \alpha,$$

where $K^* \rightarrow_{L(\alpha) \setminus \{P\}} M^*$ stands for: there exists a functional bisimulation between $K^*$ and $M$ over the language $L(\alpha) \setminus \{P\}$.

Before proving the claim, we notice that it implies that the uniform interpolant $\beta$ behaves like $\tilde{\exists} P \alpha$, that is:

$$M \models \beta \Leftrightarrow \text{ there exists a model } K \in C \text{ with } K \sim_{\neq P} M \text{ and } K \models \alpha$$

The implication from right to left is straightforward. As for the other implication, if $M \models \beta$, then the claim above implies the existence of a model $K \in C$ with $K^* \rightarrow_{L(\alpha) \setminus \{P\}} M$ and $K \models \alpha$; let $f$ be the $p$-morphism from $K^*$ to $M$. We can now change the value of the variables in $Prop \setminus L(\alpha)$ by letting, for $Q \in Prop \setminus L(\alpha)$ and $v \in K^*$.

$$Q \text{ is true in } v \ \Leftrightarrow M, f(v) \models Q.$$

In this way we obtain a new model where $\alpha$ still holds, but which is $Prop \setminus \{P\}$-bisimilar to $M$.

We are left to prove the claim. The direction from right to left is obvious. For the other direction let us fix a $C$ model $M$. From the property of the uniform interpolant we know that for any $\gamma$ not containing the variable $P$ it holds:

$$\models_C \alpha \rightarrow \gamma \ \Leftrightarrow \models_C \beta \rightarrow \gamma.$$

We apply this to the formula $\gamma = \neg \phi_M(L(\alpha) \setminus \{P\}, P_0, \ldots, P_m)$, where $\phi_M(L(\alpha) \setminus \{P\}, P_0, \ldots, P_m)$ is the $\mu$-formula defined above (where the $P_i's$ are all new w.r.t. $L(\alpha)$). We first notice that $\models_C \beta \rightarrow \gamma$ is equivalent to $M \models \neg \beta$ (from left to right: we consider the model $M'$ which is like $M$ except for the values of the $P_i$ which are given to the singletons of the $w_i$; then $M' \models \neg \gamma$ and hence $M' \models \neg \beta$. But $M$ and $M'$ are bisimilar w.r.t. the variables in $\beta$, hence $M \models \neg \beta$ as well.) Together with

$$\models_C \alpha \rightarrow \gamma \ \Leftrightarrow \models_C \beta \rightarrow \gamma,$$

this implies that

$$M \models \beta$$

$$\Downarrow$$

there exists a model $K \in C$ with $K^* \rightarrow_{L(\alpha) \setminus \{P\}} M$ and $K \models \alpha$    □

Hence: although uniform interpolation does not imply in general closure under bisimulation quantifiers, this is true over classes of finite frames. Can't we say more? Since a modal logic can be described as the logic of different classes of frames, it is reasonable to consider as a natural environment for bisimulation quantifiers the largest class, that is, the class of frames which validates the logic, and not only a subclass of it (although it gives the same logic). Hence we may reformulate the two properties above in terms of the the largest class of frames validating the logic: let $C$ be the largest class for $ML(C)$.

1a) If a modal formula $\phi$ has a uniform interpolant w.r.t. $P$ then it is always true that this formula behaves semantically as $\widetilde{\exists} P\phi$ over $C$?

2a) If $ML(C)$ enjoys the uniform interpolation property then it is true that $ML(C) = BQLML(C)$?

In the following example, we show that the answer to the first question is not always affirmative, even under the proposed restriction.

*Example 3.* We consider the logic $GL.3 = ML(C)$ where $C$ is the class of frames over $\Lambda = \{a\}$ where $R_a$ is a strict, linear ordering without strictly ascending $R_a$-chains. Let $\phi(S, T)$ be the following formula

$$(T \Rightarrow S) \wedge (S \Rightarrow \Box(\neg T)) \wedge (T \vee \Diamond(T)),$$

where $A \Rightarrow B$ is $(A \to B) \wedge \Box(A \to B)$.

Then $\psi = S \vee \Diamond(S)$ is the uniform interpolant w.r.t. $\{S\}$, because:

- $\models_C \phi(S, T) \to \psi(S)$.
- If $\theta$ is a formula not containing $T$ and $\models_C \phi(S, T) \to \theta$, then $\models_C \psi \to \theta$: by the finite model property of $GL.3$, it is enough to show the validity of $\psi \to \theta$ over finite strict linear orders, and this is easily verified.

Hence, the uniform interpolant of $\phi(S, T)$ in $GL.3$ is $S \vee \Diamond(S)$. On the other hand, $S \vee \Diamond(S)$ does not behave as $\widetilde{\exists} T\phi(S, T)$ over $C$. To see this, notice that $S \vee \Diamond(S)$ is true in the model based on the frame $\omega + 1$ of Example 2, where all points in $\omega$ satisfies $S$, but $\omega$ does not. On the other hand one can easily show that the formula $\widetilde{\exists} T\phi(S, T)$ is not true in this model. Hence, property 1a) is false.    □

The question whether property 2a) holds is, to my knowledge, open.

In Section 8 we will return to these questions by introducing a family of classes of frames where bisimulation quantifiers and uniform interpolants always correspond to each other.

## 7.1    Uniform Interpolation Closure of a Modal Logic

Not all modal logics enjoy uniform interpolation: there are natural examples of classes $C$ of frames, such as the class of all transitive frames or the class of all transitive and reflexive frames, where $ML(C)$ does not have the uniform interpolation property, although it has the non uniform one (see [8,9,12]). If the class $C$ enjoys amalgamation, then we know that $BQML(C)$ is a logic containing modal logic that enjoys uniform interpolation: hence, in $BQML(C)$ we find all uniform interpolants which where missing in $ML(C)$. Hence, from $ML(C)$ to $BQML(C)$ we gain a nice property, but are we preserving some other useful properties such as decidability, finite model property, etc. ?

Unfortunately, this is not true. In [6] Tim French gives examples of decidable modal logics which become undecidable when extended with bisimulation quantifiers ($S5 \times S5$ is such an example); moreover, in $BQGL3$ the formula

$$FIN := \widetilde{\forall}X(\Diamond(X) \wedge \neg X \rightarrow \widetilde{\exists}Y(\Diamond(Y) \wedge (X \Rightarrow \Box(\neg Y)) \wedge (Y \Rightarrow X)))$$

is true in all finite $GL3$ frames (that is well founded, linear, transitive frames) but false in all infinite $GL3$ frames. Hence, $BQGL3$ does not have the finite model property, although $GL3$ does have it.

Do we have a better candidate to play the role of an extension of $ML(C)$ with uniform interpolation? We already proved that over the class of all frames the $\mu$-calculus enjoys the uniform interpolation property, hence it is natural to ask whether this is still true if we restict to a class $C$, and, when this is indeed the case, to compare the two logics $BQML(C), \mu(C)$ w.r.t. expressive power.

We notice that in general $\mu(C)$ is not a good choice, because it can even lack interpolation. This is the case for the class $C$ of well founded, linear, transitive frames, because in this case $ML(C) = \mu(C) = GL3$ and $GL3$ does not have interpolation (the equality $ML(C) = \mu(C)$ holds for all subclass $C$ of the well founded transitive frames, see Section 8.1). This example also shows that closure under monotone fixed points is not a sufficient condition to ensure (uniform) interpolation over an arbitrary class of frames.

In the next Section we will isolate classes of frames where the $\mu$ calculus always enjoys uniform interpolation, is decidable, has the finite model property, and where uniform interpolants behave as bisimulation quantifiers.

## 8    Reducible Classes and Transduction Invariant Logics

We consider classes of frames which are *reducible* to the class of all frames:

**Definition 9.** *A class $C$ of frames is called a $\mu$-reducible class if there exists a surjective function $\Pi$ from arbitrary models to $C$-models, and a function $\pi$ from $\mu$-formulas to $\mu$-formulas such that*

1. *$\Pi(\Pi(M)) = \Pi(M)$, for all models $M$;*
2. *$\Pi(M) \models \phi \Leftrightarrow M \models \pi(\phi)$;*
3. *if $M \sim_\Theta N$ then $\Pi(M) \sim_\Theta \Pi(N)$.*

*The class $C$ is called* modal reducible *if the function $\pi$ takes modal formulas to modal formulas.*

We show that $\mu$-reducible classes are well behaved with respect to bisimulation quantifiers:

**Lemma 5.** *(see [5] ) If the class $C$ is $\mu$-reducible (modal reducible) then $\mu(C)$ ($ML(C)$, respectively) is closed under bisimulation quantifiers.*

*Proof.* From Theorem 2 we know that there exists a $\mu$-formula $\psi$ behaving semantically as $\widetilde{\exists}P\pi(\phi)$ over the class of all frames, that is:

$$M \models \psi \quad \Leftrightarrow \quad \text{there exists } N, \text{ with } N \sim_{\neq P} M, N \models \pi(\phi).$$

From the property of the functions $\Pi, \pi$ above we prove that $\psi$, restricted to $C$, behaves as $\widetilde{\exists}P\phi$ over the class $C$. Suppose first that $\Pi(M) \models \psi$. Then if $N$ is such that $N \sim_{\neq P} \Pi(M), N \models \pi(\phi)$, we have $\Pi(N) \sim_{\neq P} \Pi(M)$, and $\Pi(N) \models \phi$. On the other hand, if a $C$-model $K$ satisfies $\phi$ and $K \sim_{\neq P} \Pi(M)$ holds then, $K \models \pi(\phi)$ (because the second property implies that $\phi$ and $\pi(\phi)$ are equivalent over $C$ ) and $\Pi(M) \models \psi$. Hence

$$\Pi(M) \models \psi \quad \Leftrightarrow \quad \text{there exists a } C\text{-model } K \text{ with } K \sim_{\neq P} \Pi(M), K \models \phi,$$

and hence the $\mu$-formula $\psi$ behaves as $\widetilde{\exists}P\phi$ on $C$.

If $C$ is modal reducible, then $\pi(\phi)$ is a modal formula, and, by applying the modal version of Theorem 2 we see that the formula $\psi$ above is a modal formula. $\quad\Box$

In order to give examples of $\mu$-reducible classes of frames, we consider an extension of the $\mu$-calculus by means of programs. This extension is easily seen to be expressively equivalent to the $\mu$-calculus, but the explicit definition of program constructs will allow us to define the class of Transduction Invariant Logics.

**Definition 10.** *Let $\Lambda$ be a set of atomic programs. The $\mu$-programs $p$ over $\Lambda$ are:*

$$p := a|p; p|p \cup p|p^*|\alpha?;$$

*where $a \in \Lambda$ and*

$$\alpha := P \mid \neg\alpha \mid \alpha \vee \alpha \mid \Diamond_p\phi \mid \mu P\alpha,$$

*(in the last case, provided $P$ appears under an even number of negation in $\alpha$).*

A $\mu$-program is closed if it contains no free propositions. The set of closed $\mu$-programs over $\Lambda$ is denoted by $Progr(\Lambda)$. If $a \in \Lambda$, then $a^*$, $a; a^*$, $a \cup (\top)?$, $(\mu P\Box_a P)?; a; a^*$ are examples of closed $\mu$-programs over $\Lambda$.

The semantics of $\mu$-programs and $\mu$-formulas is defined in the usual way. E.g., given a Kripke models $M$, and a $\mu$-program $p$, $p^M$ is a binary relation on $M$ defined inductively in such a way that

$$a^M = R_a^M, \quad (\alpha?)^M = \{(w, w) \in M^2 : M \models \alpha\},$$

$(p^*)^M$ is the reflexive and transitive closure of $p^M$.

**Definition 11.** *A transduction is defined as a function $\pi$ from $\Lambda$ to $Progr(\Lambda)$.*

A transduction is extended in a unique way from atomic programs to programs and to extended $\mu$-formulas by imposing that $\pi$ commutes with the operators over programs and formulas: if $p$ is a program and $\alpha$ is a $\mu$-formula then $\pi(p)$ is a program and $\pi(\alpha)$ is an extended $\mu$-formula, and both are obtained by *shifting* inside $\pi$; e.g. if $\pi(a) = (\mu Q \Box_a Q)?; a; a^*$ and $\pi(b) = a^*$, then

$$\pi(a \cup b) = ((\mu Q \Box_a Q)?; a; a^*) \cup a^*, \text{ and } \pi(\mu P \Box_a P) = \mu P \Box_{(\mu Q \Box_a Q)?;a;a^*} P.$$

We now use the function $\pi$ to define a function $\Pi$ from frames to frames: $\Pi(F)$ is the frame which has the same domain as $F$ while the interpretation of an atomic relation $R_a$ is given by:

$$(R_a)^{\Pi(M)} = R^M_{\pi(a)};$$

if $M$ is a model based on a frame $F$ we define $\Pi(M)$ as the model over $\Pi(F)$ which has the same interpretation of propositional variables as $M$.

We denote by $C_\Pi$ the result of applying the transduction $\Pi$ to the class of all frames.

$$C_\Pi = \{\Pi(F) : F \text{ is a frame}\}.$$

One can show that the function $\Pi$ satisfies the third condiction of Definition 9 (see [7,6]), and the pair $\Pi, \pi$ satisfies the second one.

A trandsuction $\pi$ is called *idempotent* if the corresponding function $\Pi$ verifies the first condition of Definition 9:

**Definition 12.** *A transduction* $\pi : \Lambda \rightarrow Progr(\Lambda)$ *is* idempotent *if, for all models $M$ it holds:*

$$\Pi(\Pi(M)) = \Pi(M).$$

From Lemma 9 it follows:

**Lemma 6.** *(see [5]) If $\pi$ is an idempotent transduction then $C_\Pi$ is $\mu$-reducible. In particular, $\mu(C_\Pi) = BQL\mu(C_\Pi)$ and $\mu(C_\Pi)$ enjoys uniform interpolation.*

*Example 4.* Consider the following transductions: $\pi_1 = \top? \cup a$, $\pi_2 = a^*$, $\pi_3 = a; a^*$, $\pi_4 = (\mu P \Box_a P)?; a; a^*)$. Each transduction $\pi_i$ is idempotent. The corresponding classes of frames are:

1. $C_{\Pi_1}$ is the class of all reflexive frames;
2. $C_{\Pi_2}$ is the class of all transitive and reflexive frames (i.e.) the class of all $S4$ frames;
3. $C_{\Pi_3}$ is the class of all transitive frames (i.e.) the class of all $K4$ frames;
4. $C_{\Pi_4}$ is the class of all well founded and transitive frames (i.e.) the class of all $GL$ frames.

Hence, from Lemma 6 we obtain that the logics $\mu T := \mu(C_{\Pi_1})$, $\mu K4 := \mu(C_{\Pi_2})$, $break \mu S4 := \mu(C_{\Pi_3})$, $\mu GL := \mu(C_{\Pi_4})$ are all closed under bisimulation quantifiers. In the first and the last case we can actually say that modal logic is closed under bisimulation quantifiers over the class, and use this to have a proof of uniform interpolation for the modal logics $T$ and $GL$. This closure follows from 5 in the first case, because $\pi_1$ sends modal formulas to modal formulas. In the case of $GL$ we have $\mu GL = GL$, because $GL$ is closed under fixed points of monotone operators: this is a consequence of the De Jongh-Sambin Theorem on $GL$. A proof of the uniform interpolation of $GL$ using a syntactical reduction to the $\mu$-calculus can be found in [13].

## 8.1  Transitive Transductions

We finally consider the case of transitive classes of frames. Then (if the class is amalgamable) bisimulation quantifiers are stronger than fixed points because

$$\models_C \nu X \phi \leftrightarrow \widetilde{\exists} X (X \wedge X \Rightarrow \phi),$$

where $X \Rightarrow \phi$ stays for $(X \to \phi) \wedge \Box(X \to \phi)$.

**Definition 13.** *A transduction $\pi$ is transitive if $C_\Pi$ only contains transitive frames.*

If $\pi$ is transitive and idempotent, than it is possible to prove that in $ML(C_\Pi)$ uniform interpolants always behave as bisimulation quantifiers, and, moreover, that $\mu(C_\Pi)$ is minimal between the extension of $ML(C_\Pi)$ having uniform interpolation. More precisely, given a class $C$ of frames, we consider a set $L$ of $\mu$-formulas which contains all modal logic formulas and is closed under substitutions: if $\phi(P_1, \ldots, P_n), \psi_1, \ldots, \psi_n \in L$ then $\phi(\psi_1, \ldots, \psi_n)$ is (equivalent over $C_\Pi$ to) a formula in $L$. Given such an $L$, we let

$$L(C) = \{\phi \in L : \ \phi \text{ is } C\text{-valid}\}.$$

$L(C)$ is called a $\mu$-extension of $ML(C)$.

**Theorem 5.** *(see [5] ) If $\pi$ is transitive and idempotent then uniform interpolants of modal formulas always behave as bisimulation quantifiers over $C_\Pi$. Moreover, $\mu(C_\Pi)$ is minimal w.r.t. expressive power between the $\mu$-extension of $ML(C_\Pi)$ having uniform interpolation.*

# 9  Axiomatizations

Although modal logic and the $\mu$-calculus are closed under bisimulation quantifiers over the class of all frames, it still makes sense to look for axiomatizations of bisimulation quantifiers over these logics: if we want to *use* the uniform interpolant of a modal or $\mu$ formula $\phi$ in order to find all consequences of $\phi$ in a given sublanguage, then we should have a deductive system for the extended logic. From the results in Section 4 we easily obtain such a calculus for modal logic and the $\mu$-calculus over the class of all frames; for modal logic we need all modal axioms, the rule of existential elimination, the axiom of existential introduction, and the commutativity of $\widetilde{\exists}$ with Covers:

$$\widetilde{\exists} P(\sigma \wedge \text{COVER}_a(\phi_1, \ldots, \phi_n)) \leftrightarrow \sigma[P|\top, \neg P|\top] \wedge \text{COVER}_a(\widetilde{\exists}\phi_1, \ldots, \widetilde{\exists}\phi_n);$$

for the $\mu$-calculus we have to add the commutativity of $\widetilde{\exists}$ with disjunctive formulas to the above axioms: if $\mu Q \phi, \nu Q \phi$ are disjunctive, then

$$\widetilde{\exists} P \mu Q \phi \leftrightarrow \mu Q \widetilde{\exists} P \phi, \quad \widetilde{\exists} P \nu Q \phi \leftrightarrow \nu Q \widetilde{\exists} P \phi.$$

These systems are complete because the commutativity axioms allow to prove into the system that any formula is equivalent to a quantifier free formula (see [3] for a detailed proof).

For different languages the problem of the axiomatization of bisimulation quantifiers becomes more difficult. An interesting case is the one of Propositional Dynamic Logic $PDL$. In [7] it is proved that by extending $PDL$ with bisimulation quantifiers we obtain a logic which is equivalent to the $\mu$-calculus. Hence, an axiomatization for the bisimulation quantifiers over $PDL$ would give an alternative view of a useful logic. In [4] such an axiomatization is proposed, although some rules of the system are not very natural.

## 10   Conclusions

In these notes we proposed an overview of the properties of bisimulation quantifiers over modal logics, and their relations with the uniform interpolants of the logics. Some point remains open, e.g.: the implications between the property of uniform interpolation of the logic and the closure of the largest class of frames validating the logic under bisimulation quantifiers; axiomatizations for bisimulation quantifiers over modal logics, in particular, for logics defined from an idempotent tranduction, such as $BQK4, BQS4$: notice that the logics $\mu K4, \mu S4$ (which have the same expressive power than $BQK4, BQS4$) can be axiomatized by adding the specific modal axioms of the logic to the $\mu$-axioms for the class of all frames. However, we cannot do the same with bisimulation quantifiers, because the axioms we found for the class of all frames are not valid over the class of transitive frames. A related question is the axiomatization of $PDL$ plus bisimulation quantifiers. Here it would be interesting to find a natural axiomatization for $BQPDL$, and use this axiomatization to find a new proof of the completeness of Kozen axiomatization for the $\mu$-calculus (which is equivalent to $BQPDL$).

Another question regards modal logics which do not have uniform interpolation such as $K4, S4$. Can we find an useful characterization of the formulas having uniform interpolants? Is this set decidable?

## References

1. D'Agostino, G., Hollenberg, M.: Logical questions concerning the $\mu$-calculus. Journal of Symbolic Logic 65, 310–332 (2000)
2. D'Agostino, G., Lenzi, G.: A Note on Bisimulation Quantifiers and Fixed Points over Transitive Frames, University of Pisa, Department of Mathematics. Mathematical Logic Section (preprint n. 1626, March 2006 )
3. D'Agostino, G., Lenzi, G.: On Modal $\mu$-Calculus with Explicit Interpolants. Journal of Applied Logic (accepted for publication)
4. D'Agostino, G., Lenzi, G.: An axiomatization of bisimulation quantifiers via the mu-calculus. Theoretical Computer Science 338, 64–95 (2005)
5. D'Agostino, G., Lenzi, G., French, T.: $\mu$-Programs, Uniform Interpolation and Bisimulation Quantifiers for Modal Logics (submitted)

6. French, T.: Bisimulation Quantifiers for Modal Logics. PhD thesis, University of Western Australia (in preparation)
7. Hollenberg, M.: Logic and Bisimulation. PhD Thesis, University of Utrecht, vol. XXIV, Zeno Institute of Philosophy (1998)
8. Ghilardi, S., Zawadowski, M.: Sheaves, Games and Model Completions (a categorical approach to non classical propositional logics). Trends in Logic Series. Kluwer, Dordrecht (2002)
9. Ghilardi, S., Zawadowski, M.: Undefinability of Propositional Quantifiers in the Modal System $S4$. Studia Logica 55, 259–271 (1995)
10. Janin, D., Walukiewicz, I.: On the expressive completeness of the propositional $\mu$-calculus w.r.t. monadic second-order logic. In: Sassone, V., Montanari, U. (eds.) CONCUR 1996. LNCS, vol. 1119, pp. 263–277. Springer, Heidelberg (1996)
11. Pitts, A.: On an interpretation of second-order quantification in first-order intuitionistic propositional logic. Journal of Symbolic Logic 57, 33–52 (1992)
12. Visser, A.: Uniform interpolation and layered bisimulation. In: Gödel '96 (Brno, 1996). Lecture Notes Logic, vol. 6, pp. 139–164. Springer, Heidelberg (1996)
13. Visser, A.: Löb's Logic Meets the mu-Calculus. In: Middeldorp, A., van Oostrom, V., van Raamsdonk, F., de Vrijer, R. (eds.) Processes, Terms and Cycles: Steps on the Road to Infinity. LNCS, vol. 3838, pp. 14–25. Springer, Heidelberg (2005)

# The Problem of Learning the Semantics of Quantifiers

Nina Gierasimczuk

Institute of Philosophy, Warsaw University Institute for Logic, Language and Computation, University of Amsterdam

**Abstract.** This paper is concerned with a possible mechanism for learning the meanings of quantifiers in natural language. The meaning of a natural language construction is identified with a procedure for recognizing its extension. Therefore, acquisition of natural language quantifiers is supposed to consist in collecting procedures for computing their denotations. A method for encoding classes of finite models corresponding to given quantifiers is shown. The class of finite models is represented by appropriate languages. Some facts describing dependencies between classes of quantifiers and classes of devices are presented. In the second part of the paper examples of syntax-learning models are shown. According to these models new results in quantifier learning are presented. Finally, the question of the adequacy of syntax-learning tools for describing the process of semantic learning is stated.

## 1 Introduction

According to an old philosophical idea, the meaning of a natural language construction can be identified with a representation of its denotation [Frege 1892]. This thought has been developed in the direction of identifying the meaning of an expression with a procedure for finding its extension [Tichy 1969, Moschovakis 1990, van Lambalgen, Hamm 2004, Szymanik 2004]. In the case of words: the meaning of "Poland" is the procedure of checking if the object in question satisfies the conditions for being Poland. In the case of sentences: the meaning is a procedure for finding a sentence's logical value. The meaning of "Alice has a cat." is a procedure for checking if Alice really has a cat. Therefore, we can say that someone understands a sentence (knows its meaning), if he knows a procedure for checking whether it is true or not.

In this paper we assume that for modelling ordinary linguistic behaviour finite models are sufficient. We state this assumption for both theoretical and practical reasons. First of all we claim that most natural language sentences have natural interpretations in finite universes. The practical reason is that if we restrict ourselves to finite models, then the objects computational semantics is concerned with, namely procedures for finding denotations, become effective (algorithmizable).

B.D. ten Cate and H.W. Zeevat (Eds.): TbiLLC 2005, LNAI 4363, pp. 117–126, 2007.

## 2   Quantifiers

Many authors have already considered the semantics of quantifiers from a computational point of view (see e.g. [van Benthem 1986, M. Mostowski 1998]); there have also been a few such attempts in linguistics (see e.g. [Suppes 1982, Cooper 1994, Bunt 2003]).

The presence and importance of quantifiers in natural language and consequently in linguistic research is beyond discussion. We use quantifiers very often in various contexts: "all", "some", "every other", "half of"... examples can be multiplied. Computational semantics gives us an idea of the meaning of quantifier constructions. We know the meaning of the sentence:

1. Every other European is depressed

if we know how to check its logical value. The first solution for this sentence would be: we just count to two on our Europeans. One – normal, two – depressed, one – normal, two – depressed.... If this procedure is satisfied on the whole set of Europeans, then we can say that our sentence is true. If we made a wrong prediction somewhere and some "one" appeared to be depressed or some "two" was normal, we can conclude that the sentence is false in our universe of Europeans. Of course the meaning of "every other" explained above is not very obvious and common. In most usages of this quantifier we would say that "every other" is a more pictorial version of "exactly half" and means the same thing. This is the case especially when we have no natural ordering on our universe. Therefore let us now consider the second meaning of "every other". In order to check whether every other European is depressed, we can execute one of following procedures:

1. Count Europeans; count depressed Europeans; if *Number of Europeans* = 2 × *Number of depressed Europeans*, then the sentence is true, otherwise it is false.
2. Make Europeans stand in pairs: every normal European with a depressed European; if our pair-ordering does not leave any European alone, then the sentence is true, otherwise it is false.

Our example shows not only the trivial fact that some words or phrases are ambiguous, but also that we can use many non-equivalent procedures to operate "inside" one established meaning. Here arises the problem of identifying algorithms, which partially justifies our failures in explaining the phenomenon of synonymy (see [Moschovakis 2001, Szymanik 2004]).

In order to use these ideas and to apply them to finite models, we should think about quantifiers as classes of finite models satisfying some special conditions.[1] We make here the not very controversial restriction to monadic quantifiers. This subclass we consider sufficient for linguistic considerations. Let us define a quantifier as follows:

---

[1] For a detailed review of results on monadic quantifiers in computational semantics, see [M. Mostowski 1998].

**Definition 1.** *Let $K$ be a class, closed under isomorphism, of finite models of the form $(U, R_1, \ldots, R_n)$, where $U \neq \emptyset$ and $R_i \subseteq U$, for $i = 1, \ldots, n$. $K$ is an interpretation of monadic quantifier $Q_K$. For every model $M$ and valuation $\bar{a}$ on $M$:*

$$M \models Q_K x(\varphi_1(x), \ldots, \varphi_n(x))[\bar{a}] \iff (|M|, \varphi_1^{M,x,\bar{a}}, \ldots, \varphi_n^{M,x,\bar{a}}) \in K,$$

*where $|M|$ is universe of model $M$, and $\varphi^{M,x,\bar{a}}$ is a set indicated by $\varphi$ in $M$ with respect to variable $x$ by the valuation $\bar{a}$. Quantifier $Q_K$ of type*

$$\underbrace{(1, 1, \ldots, 1)}_{n}$$

*binds one first-order variable in $n$ formulae.*

Let us give an example of a quantifier defined in the way described above:

**Existential quantifier** $(\exists)$ For all $M$:

$$M \models \exists x \varphi(x)[\bar{a}] \iff \text{card}(\varphi^{M,x,\bar{a}}) \geq 1 \iff (|M|, \varphi^{M,x,\bar{a}}) \in K_E$$

The class of models $K_E$ which determines the interpretation of the existential quantifier we define as follows:

$$K_E = \{(|M|, R) : R \subseteq |M| \wedge R \neq \emptyset\}$$

We have identified quantifiers with classes of appropriate finite models. This step allows us to encode models as words with certain features. Classes of models will be encoded as sets of words (languages). This encoding can be done by means of the concept of constituents (see [M. Mostowski 1998]).

**Definition 2.** *The class $K_Q$ of finite models of the form $(M, R_1, \ldots, R_n)$ can be represented by the set of nonempty words $L_Q$ over the alphabet $A = \{a_1, \ldots, a_{2^n}\}$ such that: $\alpha \in L_Q$ if and only if there is $(U, R_1, \ldots, R_n) \in K_Q$ and a linear ordering $U = \{b_1, \ldots, b_k\}$ such that $\text{lh}(\alpha) = k$ and the $i$-th character of $\alpha$ is $a_j$ exactly when $b_i \in S_1 \cap \cdots \cap S_n$, where:*

$$S_l = \begin{cases} R_l & \text{if the integer part of } \frac{j}{2^l} \text{ is odd,} \\ U - R_l & \text{otherwise.} \end{cases}$$

Such defined intersections $S_1 \cap \cdots \cap S_n$ are called constituents of the proper model. Characters $a_1, \ldots, a_{2^n}$ are names for these constituents. Our definition says that the $i$-th character of $\alpha$ is $a_j$ exactly when element $b_i$ belongs to the $j$-th constituent. In other words, $\alpha$ uniquely encodes the model by giving information on the constituent to which every element belongs. We illustrate the idea for $n = 2$. We consider $M = (U, R_1, R_2)$, where $U = \{b_1, b_2, b_3, b_4, b_5\}$. Our model is represented by the word $\alpha_M = a_1 a_2 a_4 a_3 a_3$ over the alphabet $A = \{a_1, a_2, a_3, a_4\}$ which says that element $b_1 \in S_1 = U - (R_1 \cup R_2)$, $b_2 \in S_2 = R_1 - R_2$, $b_3 \in S_4 = R_1 \cap R_2$, and $b_4, b_5 \in S_3 = R_2 - R_1$.

Let us think of classes of monadic quantifiers as languages obtained by means of this encoding. We can now define what it means that some class of monadic quantifiers is recognized by some class of devices.

**Definition 3.** *Let $\mathcal{D}$ be a class of recognizing devices, and $\Omega$ be a class of monadic quantifiers. We say that $\mathcal{D}$ accepts $\Omega$ if and only if for every monadic quantifier $Q$:*

$$(Q \in \Omega \iff \text{there is some device } A \in \mathcal{D} \text{ such that } A \text{ accepts } L_Q).$$

Using this definition, we can now recall the following results describing dependences between classes of quantifiers and classes of devices:

**Theorem 1.** [van Benthem 1984] *Quantifier $Q$ is first-order definable $\iff$ $L_Q$ is accepted by some acyclic finite automaton.*

**Theorem 2.** [M. Mostowski 1998] *Monadic quantifier $Q$ is definable in the divisibility logic $FO(D_\omega) \iff L_Q$ is accepted by some finite automaton.*

**Theorem 3.** [van Benthem 1986] *Quantifier $Q$ of type (1) is semilinear (elementary definable in the structure $(\omega, +)) \iff L_Q$ is accepted by a push-down automaton.*

Additionally we can state that there are many natural language quantifiers which lie outside the context-free languages [Clark 1996].

## 3   Learning

### 3.1   Identification in the Limit

After stating some assumptions and preliminary definitions in computational linguistics and quantifiers, we would like to present the basic ideas of formal learning theory.[2] This part of the paper is needed to establish final results.

The *identification in the limit* model [Gold 1967] shows what the process of learning can look like in general and what results we can obtain using it. This model describes the learnability of a given class of languages. One language from the class is chosen. The learner gains some information about it. The information can be presented in several possible ways (the *data presentation method*). The learner's task is to guess the name of the language in question. Names of languages are simply grammars. The aim of the learner is to find a correct grammar for the presented sequence of linguistic data.

In each step of the procedure the learner is given a unit of data about the unknown language. Therefore, the learner always has only a finite set of information. In each step the learner chooses a name of a language.

The procedure is infinite. The language is identified in the limit if, after some time (finite but not specified in advance), the guesses remain the same and are correct. Identifiability concerns classes of languages. The whole class of languages is identifiable in the limit, if there is a guessing algorithm (learner) such that it identifies in the limit every language from this class. It is worth mentioning that the learner

---

[2] For a detailed analysis of various learning algorithms see [Gierasimczuk 2005].

does not know when his guesses are correct. The learner proceeds infinitely, because it is not able to check if the next step won't force it to change its decision.

Identification in the limit depends on three factors: data presentation method, naming relation and chosen class of languages.

The learner has the information presented in one of two ways:

**Definition 4.** *A **TEXT** for language $L$ is an $\omega$-sequence, $I$, of words $\alpha_1, \alpha_2, \ldots \in L$, such that every word $\alpha \in L$ occurs at least once in $I$.*

**Definition 5.** *An **INFORMANT** for language $L$ is an $\omega$-sequence, $I$, of elements of $(A^* \times \{0,1\})$, such that for each $\alpha \in A^*$:*

$$(\alpha, 1) \text{ is in } I \text{ if } \alpha \in L$$
$$(\alpha, 0) \text{ is in } I \text{ if } \alpha \notin L.$$

The learner can use one of two naming relations:

**Definition 6.** *A **GENERATOR** for language $L$ is a Turing Machine, $e$, such that:*

$$L = \{\alpha \in A^* : \{e\}\{\alpha\} \downarrow\}.$$

**Definition 7.** *A **TESTER** for language $L$ is a Turing Machine that computes the function $\chi_L$ such that for each $\alpha \in A^*$:*

$$\chi_L(\alpha) = \begin{cases} 0 & \text{if } \alpha \notin L \\ 1 & \text{if } \alpha \in L. \end{cases}$$

Let us now present Gold's table of results for learnability and non-learnability of languages from the Chomsky hierarchy.[3]

**Table 1.** Identifiability results. (Anomalous text is primitive recursive text with a generator naming relation. A superfinite class of languages is a class containing all finite languages and at least one infinite language.)

| | |
|---|---|
| Anomalous text | Recursively enumerable |
| | Recursive |
| Informant | Primitive recursive |
| | Context-sensitive |
| | Context-free |
| | Regular |
| | Superfinite |
| Text | Finite cardinality languages |

## 3.2   Syntax Learning Algorithms

We give here examples of learning algorithms effective for a certain class of languages. Firstly let us describe the $L^*$-algorithm proposed by Dana Angluin [Angluin 1987]. In her paper she analyses the possibility of finite and effective identification of regular languages from an informant. The algorithm identifies the language by finding a deterministic finite automaton adequate for the

---

[3] For details and proofs see [Gold 1967].

unknown language. This procedure is controlled by the so-called *Minimally Adequate Teacher*. He answers two types of questions:

1. Membership queries: Is sequence $\alpha$ in the unknown language?
2. Extensional equivalence queries: Is the deterministic finite automaton currently being guessed by the $L^*$-algorithm extensionally equivalent[4] to the deterministic finite automaton which corresponds to the unknown language being learned? If it is not, then the teacher gives a counterexample.

The algorithm $L^*$ is able to identify every regular language. $L^*$ works in time polynomial in the number of states of the minimal DFA for the language being learned and in the maximum length of the counterexample given by the teacher.

The idea of learning with queries has been further explored, particularly in the direction of wider classes of languages. An example of such an attempt is the algorithm of Yasubumi Sakakibara [Sakakibara 1990]. It is a quite straightforward translation of the $L^*$-algorithm described in the previous paragraph for context-free grammars. The $LA$-algorithm learns a given context-free grammar on the basis of so-called structural data: skeletons of derivation trees of the given grammar. The following facts allow identification in the limit:

1. The set of derivation trees of any given context-free grammar is regular.
2. A regular set of trees is recognized by some tree automaton.
3. The procedure of changing derivation trees into their structural descriptions preserves the regularity of the set.
4. The problem of learning a context-free grammar from structural descriptions is therefore reducible to the problem of learning a certain tree automaton.

It should be stressed that the aim of $LA$ learning is not a context-free language but some particular context-free grammar. It is known that for each context-free language there are infinitely many adequate grammars, therefore such a restriction is indispensable here.

## 4   Quantifier Learning

The problem of quantifier learning was raised and explored in [van Benthem 1986, Clark 1996, Florêncio 2002, Tiede 1999]. These were similar to our attempts to use syntax-learning models to describe learning of the semantic aspect of language.

Persisting in the declared paradigm of computational semantics leads us to the assumption that acquisition of natural language quantifiers consists essentially in collecting procedures for computing their denotations. Additionally assumptions about the adequacy of finite models and restriction to monadic quantifiers gives

---

[4] We say that two finite automata are extensionally equivalent if they accept the same set of strings.

us an opportunity to analyse many natural language quantifiers from the point of view of syntax-learning models. We can encode a quantifier and check its learnability according to results known from the field of inference theory. For instance, one such known fact is:

**Theorem 4.** [Tiede 1999] *There are subclasses of FO quantifiers which are identifiable in the limit using text, e.g. the set of first-order left upward monotone quantifiers.*

We now present similar results which can be inferred from previous considerations and theorems:

**Proposition 1.** *The classes of $FO$, $FO(D_\omega)$ and semilinear quantifiers are not identifiable in the limit using text but are identifiable using informant.*

**Proof.** This result follows directly form Theorems 1, 2, 3, and the fact that regular and context-free languages are not identifiable using text but are identifiable using informant. □

**Proposition 2.** *The monadic $FO(D_\omega)$-definable quantifiers are learnable using the $L^*$-algorithm.*

**Proof.** By Theorem 2 every monadic $FO(D_\omega)$-definable quantifier can be represented by the set $L_Q$, which is accepted by some deterministic finite automaton. We know that deterministic finite automata are learnable by Angluin's $L^*$-algorithm. Therefore, the monadic $FO(D_\omega)$-definable quantifiers are learnable using the $L^*$-algorithm. □

**Proposition 3.** *Semilinear quantifiers of type (1) are learnable using the LA-algorithm.*

**Proof.** From Theorem 3 we know that a quantifier of type (1) is semilinear iff it can be represented by a set $L_Q$ which is accepted by some pushdown automaton. Pushdown automata are a class of devices equivalent to context-free grammars, which are effectively learnable using Sakakibara's $LA$-algorithm. Therefore, the semilinear quantifiers of type (1) are learnable using the $LA$-algorithm. □

## 5 Conclusions

The approach presented in this paper can be treated as a strictly theoretical proposal. Nevertheless, let us now discuss some problems connected with modelling the natural process of semantic learning. First of all we can pose the question about the adequacy of tools of syntactic learning theory for describing the process of semantic learning. Let us present some intuitions about the construction of semantic competence.

$$\text{Semantic competence} \begin{cases} \begin{array}{l} \text{ability to check the logical value} \\ \text{input: } M \text{ and } \varphi; \ M \models \varphi? \\ \\ \text{ability to recognize} \\ \text{inferential relations} \\ \text{input: } \bar{\varphi}, \bar{\psi}; \text{ e.g. } \bar{\varphi} \vdash \bar{\psi}? \\ \\ \text{ability to generate} \\ \text{adequate descriptions} \\ \text{input: } M; \text{ find } \bar{\varphi} \text{ s.t. } M \models \bar{\varphi} \end{array} \end{cases}$$

The learnability models presented so far do not distinguish between the ability to check the logical value of a sentence and the ability to describe a given situation. There is of course a mutual translation between automata (testing devices) and grammars (generating devices). But are we allowed to treat these abilities as equivalent? Is it the case that if we can recognize the logical value of some sentence $\varphi$ in a given model $M$, then we can also generate the sentence $\varphi$ as the description of $M$? Some research concerning the relation between comprehension and production (equivalents of testing and generating) has already been done. It shows that the respective acquisitions of testing and generating competence are not parallel. First we can understand semantic constructions and only then are we able to use them in descriptions (see e.g. [Bates et al. 1995, Benedict 1979, Clark 1993, Fraser et al. 1979, Goldin-Meadow et al. 1976, Layton, Stick 1979]). Generating is more complicated than testing and the assumption of mutual reducibility of these two competences seems unrealistic.

To state another problem with our approach we should focus on the distinction between referential and inferential meaning.

The referential meaning of a sentence $\varphi$ is given by determining a method of establishing the truth-value of $\varphi$ in all possible situations. This kind of meaning is what we mainly refer to in this paper.

However, having a sentence $\varphi$ we can establish its truth-value by means of inferences (recognized by our logical competence) between $\varphi$ and other sentences. For example, knowing that a sentence $\psi$ is true and $\psi \Rightarrow \varphi$ we know that $\varphi$ is true; knowing that $\varphi$ is false and $\psi \Rightarrow \varphi$ we know that $\psi$ is false. In this way we determine the inferential meaning of $\varphi$.

Semantic learning models which are based on the syntax-learning approach seem to have no application in the case of learning inferential meaning. The nontrivial enterprise would be to describe possible learning mechanisms responsible for the acquisition of various semantic devices. Therefore we conclude that the learnability model presented so far is not compatible with the proposed description of semantic competence. If one wants to propose a psychologically and linguistically plausible model of semantic learning, one must fight the aforementioned subtle difficulties.

# References

| | |
|---|---|
| [Angluin 1987] | Angluin, D.: Learning Regular Sets from Queries and Counterexamples. Information and Computation 75, 87–106 (1987) |
| [Bates et al. 1995] | Bates, E., Dale, P.S., Thal, D.: Individual Differences and their Implications. In: Fletcher, P., MacWhinney, B. (eds.) The Handbook of Child Language, Oxford (1995) |
| [Benedict 1979] | Benedict, H.: Early Lexical Development: Comprehension and Production. Journal of Child Language 6, 183–200 (1979) |
| [van Benthem 1984] | van Benthem, J.: Semantic Automata, Stanford. Raport of the Center for the Study of Language and Information (1984) |
| [van Benthem 1986] | van Benthem, J.: Essays in Logical Semantics. Reidel Publishing Company, Amsterdam (1986) |
| [Bunt 2003] | Bunt, H.: Underspecification in Semantic Representations: Which Technique for What Purpose? In: Proceedings of the Fifth International Workshop on Computational Semantics, pp. 37–54 (2003) |
| [Clark 1993] | Clark, E.V.: The Lexicon in Acquisition, Cambridge (1993) |
| [Clark 1996] | Clark, R.: Learning First–Order Quantifiers Denotations. An Essay in Semantic Learnability, IRCS Technical Report, University of Pennsylvania, pp. 19–96 (1996) |
| [Cooper 1994] | Cooper, R.: A Framework for Computational Semantics, Edinburgh (1994) |
| [Florêncio 2002] | Florêncio, C.C.: Learning Generalized Quantifiers. In: Proceedings of Seventh ESSLLI Student Session (2002) |
| [Fraser et al. 1979] | Fraser, C., Bellugi, U., Brown, R.: Control of Grammar in Imitation, Production, and Comprehension. Journal of Verbal Learning and Verbal Behaviour 2, 121–135 (1979) |
| [Frege 1892] | Frege, G.: Über Sinn und Bedeutung. Zeitschrift für Philosophie und philosophische Kritik 100, 25–50 (1892) |
| [Gierasimczuk 2005] | Gierasimczuk, N.: Algorithmic Approach to the Problem of Language Learning (in polish). MA Thesis, Warsaw University, also in Studia Semiotyczne, 2005 (to appear) |
| [Gold 1967] | Gold, E.M: Language Identification in the Limit. Information and Control 10, 447–474 (1967) |
| [Goldin-Meadow et al. 1976] | Goldin-Meadow, S., Seligman, M.E.P., Gelman, R.: Language in the Two Year Old. Cognition 4, 189–202 (1976) |
| [van Lambalgen, Hamm 2004] | Van Lambalgen, M., Hamm, F.: Moschovakis' Notion of Meaning as applied to Linguistics. In: Baaz, M., |

Friedman, S., Krajicek, J. (eds.) Logic Colloquium '01. ASL Lecture Notes in Logic (2004)

[Layton, Stick 1979]    Layton, T.L., Stick, S.L.: Comprehension and Production of Comparatives and Superlatives. Journal of Child Language 6, 511–527 (1979)

[Moschovakis 1990]    Moschovakis, Y.: Sense and Denotation as Algorithm and Value. In: Oikkonen, J., Väänänen, J. (eds.). Lecture Notes in Logic, vol. 2, pp. 210–249 (1994)

[Moschovakis 2001]    Moschovakis, Y.: What is an Algorithm? In: Mathematic Unlimited — 2001 and beyond, pp. 919–936. Springer, Heidelberg (2001)

[M. Mostowski 1998]    Mostowski, M.: Computational Semantics for Monadic Quantifiers. Journal of Applied Non-Classical Logics 8(1-2), 107–121 (1998)

[Sakakibara 1990]    Sakakibara, Y.: Learning Context-free Grammars from Structural Data in Polynomial Time. Theoretical Computer Science 75, 223–242 (1990)

[Suppes 1982]    Suppes, P.: Variable-Free Semantics with Remarks on Procedural Extensions. In: Bunt, H., Sluis, I., Morante, R. (eds.) Language, Mind, and Brain, pp. 21–31 (1982)

[Szymanik 2004]    Szymanik, J.: Computational Semantics for Monadic Quantifiers in Natural Language (in polish). MA Thesis, Warsaw University, also in Studia Semiotyczne, 2004 (to appear)

[Tichy 1969]    Tichy, P.: Intension in terms of Turing Machines. Studia Logica XXIV, 7–23 (1969)

[Tiede 1999]    Tiede, H.J.: Identifiability in the Limit of Context–Free Generalized Quantifiers. Journal of Language and Computation 1, 93–102 (1999)

# Towards a Cross-Linguistic Production Data Archive: Structure and Exploration*

Michael Götze[1], Stavros Skopeteas[1], Torsten Roloff[1], and Ruben Stoel[2]

[1] SFB 632 "Information Structure", Institut für Linguistik, Universität Potsdam,
Postfach 60 15 53, 14415 Potsdam, Germany
goetze@ling.uni-potsdam.de,
{troloff,skopetea}@rz.uni-potsdam.de,
http://www.sfb632.uni-potsdam.de
[2] Leiden University Centre for Linguistics, van Wijkplaats 4, P.O. Box 9515,
2300 RA Leiden, The Netherlands
R.B.Stoel@let.leidenuniv.nl

**Abstract.** The present paper presents the structure of a cross-linguistic database of production data. The database contains annotated texts collected from a sample of fifteen different languages by means of identical data gathering methods, which are designed to enable studies on typology and universals of information structure. The special property of this database is that it combines the features of a natural language corpus and the features of a typological database. The challenge for the exploration interface is to provide user-friendly support for exploiting this particular type of resource, thus facilitating empirical generalizations about the collected data in the individual languages and comparison among them.

## 1 Introduction

The developments of the two past decades have given rise to the creation of a large number of electronic archives of language data. Nowadays there are several typological databases designed to empirically support linguistic comparison across different grammatical systems (e.g., *WALS* in [15] which includes features of all layers of grammar in a large sample of the world's languages, *Autotyp* in [2] which is especially designed to allow for typological and areal generalizations, as well as several databases on particular grammatical domains such as deponency in [6], systems of lexical tones in [16], agreement phenomena in [4], intensifiers and reflexives in [18] and reduplication phenomena in [19]). These resources are designed for the archiving of grammatical features for typological comparisons. Primary data are only available in some of them in the form of illustrative examples. In recent

---

* We would like to thank Sam Hellmuth and two anonymous reviewers for their valuable comments. This paper is part of the projects D1 "Linguistic Databases for Information Structure: Annotation and Retrieval" and D2 "Typology of Information Structure" at the University of Potsdam (sponsored by the German Research Foundation).

B.D. ten Cate and H.W. Zeevat (Eds.): TbiLLC 2005, LNAI 4363, pp. 127–138, 2007.

years, there have been some attempts to create typological archives containing primary data (texts and sound files). A well-known example is the *LACITO Archive*[1], which contains texts or single sentences collected from Oceanic languages, Caucasian languages, and languages of Nepal. This is a new and promising type of resource for typological studies, that combines the properties of a typological database and the properties of a natural language corpus containing a large collection of primary language data.

In this paper we present a contribution to the development of typological archives of this type. Two properties of the resource we are presenting in this paper are innovative with respect to previous attempts: first, the data from the different languages is collected by identical data collection methods, i.e., the data set is a type of a parallel corpus, and not just a resource for the archiving of data from more than one language; second, the data is richly annotated with a large number of linguistic layers (phonology, morphology, syntax, semantics, and information structure), hence allowing the user to explore the occurrence of grammatical categories in the entire set of archived data.

The aim of this paper is to present the structure of this resource along with the means of exploring it. In Section 2, the data contained in the database is described in more detail. In Section 3, we discuss the requirements of an exploration interface and present our current solutions, and Section 4 summarizes the main points of this article.

## 2 A Cross-Linguistic Production Data Archive

The cross-linguistic empirical data is collected using the *Questionnaire on Information Structure* (henceforth, QUIS, see [13]).[2] The aim of this tool is to provide methods for the collection of data for the study of information structure (henceforth, IS) in the object language. QUIS comprises a set of translation tasks and production experiments for the collection of primary data (see Sect. 2.2). The "translation tasks" contain a number of simple sentences in particular contexts and question/answer pairs illustrating a range of IS categories that are translated into the object language from a contact language. The "production experiments" contain a range of experimental settings that induce spontaneous expressions (e.g., picture descriptions, map tasks, etc.; see details in Sect. 2.2). Finally, QUIS provides a section with questions about the grammatical structure of the language (see Sect. 2.3).

On the basis of these data collection methods, a corpus of primary data is currently being built up from fifteen languages belonging to different language families and spoken in different parts of the world, with about 2,000 sentences per language:

---

[1] See http://lacito.vjf.fr/archivage/index.html.

[2] The cross-linguistic production data archive is being developed within the Sonderforschungsbereich 632 "Information Structure" at the University of Potsdam and the Humboldt University Berlin funded by the German Scientific Society (DFG). The development of this archive is collaborative work of the projects D1 "Linguistic Database for Information Structure: Annotation and Retrieval" (S. Dipper, M. Götze, J. Ritz, M. Stede), and the project D2 "Typology of Information Structure" (G. Fanselow, C. Féry, I. Fiedler, M. Krifka, A. Schwarz, R. Stoel, and S. Skopeteas). For more information, see http://www.sfb632.uni-potsdam.de.

Chinese, French, Dutch, Georgian, German, Greek, English, Hungarian, Japanese, Konkani (India: Indo-Iranian), Maung (Australia: Non-Pama-Nyungan), Niue (Niue: Austronesian), Prinmi (China: Tibeto-Burman), Teribe (Panama: Chibchan), and Yucatec Maya (Mexico: Mayan). For every collected sentence, the database contains the following:

    (a) sound file;
    (b) transcription;
    (c) annotation;
    (d) metadata.

Besides the data from the individual languages, the database contains full documentation of the experiments and translation tasks and further supporting documents concerning the performance of the experiments and the archiving methods.

## 2.1 Primary Data and Annotation

The primary data is collected in the place where each language is spoken. Translation tasks and production experiments are performed by native speakers under the guidance of researchers specialized in the grammatical description of the object language. The data is recorded in the field then digitized and prepared for insertion in the database using *Praat* (see [3]).

The sound files are transcribed and annotated using *EXMARaLDA* (see [20]). The annotation is based on detailed annotation guidelines (see [10]), with an annotation scheme providing a comprehensive description on the following layers: phonological (orthographic and phonemic transcription, lexical tones, intonational tones, breaks, and prosodic structure, as well as further optional features), morphological (morphemic transcription, glossing, and word class), syntactic (grammatical functions, semantic roles, and constituent structure), semantic (free translation, definiteness, countability, animacy, and quantificational properties) and information structural annotations (givenness, topic, and focus). The development of the detailed annotation guidelines is the collaborative product of interdisciplinary working groups in which researchers of different projects of the Collaborative Research Center participated.

The annotation files are illustrated in Fig. 1 by means of a Georgian sentence (screenshot from the *EXMARaLDA* editor). In Fig. 1, only a part of the annotation tiers is displayed for illustrative purposes. The tier *words* contains a phonological transcription of the spoken utterance and the tier *int-tones* indicates in auto-segmental-metrical notation the tonal events that accompany it. The utterance is morphologically transcribed in *morph*, which indicates morpheme boundaries. The tier *gloss* presents a morpheme-to-morpheme translation following the glossing conventions established in typological studies (see *Eurotyp* in [17] or *LGR* in [1]) and the tier *class* contains information about the word class (the abbreviations follow the general conventions established in EAGLES[3]). Subsequent tiers describe the syntactic properties of the utterance: $cs_n$ represent the constituent structure, *function* and *role* provide information about syntactic function and semantic role, respectively. After

---

[3] http://www.ilc.cnr.it/EAGLES96/browse.html

the free translation of the example, the last three tiers illustrate the annotation of information structure: since the example has been elicited in an out-of-the blue context, all referential nominal phrases (NPs) bear new information.

| | 0 | 1 | 2 | 3 | 4 |
|---|---|---|---|---|---|
| **words** | bitS'ma | lamp'a | gat'exa | . | |
| **int-tones** | LHp | LHp | L | Li | |
| **morph** | bitS'-ma | lamp'a-0 | ga-t'ex-a | | |
| **gloss** | boy-ERG | lamp-NOM | PFV-break-AOR.SUBJ.3.SG | | |
| **class** | NCOM | NCOM | VTRA | | |
| **cs1** | | NP | V | | |
| **cs2** | | VP | | | |
| **cs3** | S | | | | |
| **function** | SUBJ | DO | | | |
| **role** | AG | THEME | | | |
| **translation** | A boy broke a lamp. | | | | |
| **given** | new | new | | | |
| **topic** | | | | | |
| **focus** | | | | | |

**Fig. 1.** Annotated expression (Georgian, annotated by R. Asatiani)

## 2.2 Data Gathering Methods

This Section presents the data gathering methods that are used in QUIS: translation tasks and production experiments.

Elicitation through translation is a commonly used method for data collection, especially in cross-linguistic comparison (see [7]). Following this research tradition, QUIS contains 252 simple discourse units that are given in English and are translated and recorded by native speakers in the object languages (when necessary through the medium of a further contact language). These discourse units contain a target sentence often preceded by a context sentence (either a question or a declarative). The context is used to manipulate the discourse condition in which the target sentence is produced, hence evoking information structural effects on it. For instance, the sentence *The boy ate the beans* is translated and recorded as an answer to the questions: (a) *What did the boy eat?* and (b) *Who ate the beans?* Depending on the object language, the context questions may trigger different syntactic, morphological and/or prosodic structures in the answer. Further translation tasks are used to induce several types of topic and focus or manipulations of the discourse status of the referents.

The translation tasks are labeled for the discourse conditions in which the target sentence is assumed to be realized. So, the context question presented in translation task "4" in Fig. 2 evokes the discourse condition "the agent is given and the theme is solicited through the question". The definite expression of the theme in the target sentence requires that the theme is accessible information for the discourse participants. Translation task "5" is designed to evoke the reverse discourse conditions for the same target sentence.

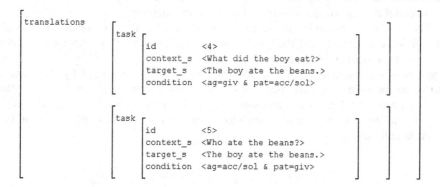

**Fig. 2.** Structure of the translation tasks

QUIS also contains 30 production experiments which all make use of visual stimuli (either pictures or films), so that the data from the different languages is induced by a cross-linguistically invariant perceptual input. Each experiment aims to compare among different discourse conditions which are established through the stimuli and the experimental instruction. Each condition is factorially implemented with a set of different stimuli (for example, different pictures that correspond to different events), in order to ensure that the resulting observations are not influenced by event- or item-particular effects. Depending on the experimental design, the production experiments are performed by four to eight native speakers, who each see the same items but in different conditions.

As an illustrative example we will discuss a production experiment that is intended to induce manipulations of the discourse status of the arguments through the description of picture sequences. The picture sequences implement several discourse conditions of which two are described here. Condition A is intended to induce the production of a sentence in which the agent is given information and the theme is new. In order to achieve this discourse condition, the first picture of the sequence (context situation) presents an entity $x$, e.g. "a man", and the second picture (target situation) presents an event, in which entity $x$ is involved as an agent and a new entity $y$ is involved as a theme, e.g., "the man is kicking a ball". The data from Condition A is compared with the data from Condition B, which is intended to induce the production of a sentence in which the agent is new information and the theme is given. In order to induce this information structure, the first picture of a sequence (context situation) presents the entity that is involved as a theme in the event of the second picture (target situation), e.g. picture 1 presents "a ball" and picture 2 presents "a man kicking the ball". The native speakers are shown the pictures one after the other and are instructed to describe the situations which are presented to them as a coherent story. The data gathered through this experiment might allow for generalizations concerning the use of pronouns, the use of different word orders, and the occurrence of active/passive voice in the object languages.

The following examples illustrate the kind of data that are obtained through production experiments and their annotations. Condition A of the experiment under discussion induced in Modern Greek the target sentence shown in Fig. 3. The given agent is not encoded through a lexical NP, but is cross-referenced by the subject suffix on the verb. The new theme is encoded through an indefinite NP. Only the overtly encoded referents are annotated in the layer of information structure: The object constituent is annotated as *new* (see the givenness tier, labelled "*given*" in the leftmost column).

| | 0 | 1 | 2 | 3 | 4 | 5 |
|---|---|---|---|---|---|---|
| **words** | tóra | klotsái | mía | bála | | . |
| **int-tones** | H- | L*H | | H*L   L-L% | | |
| **morph** | tóra | klotsá-i | mía | bála | | |
| **gloss** | now | kick-3.SG | INDEF.ACC.SG.F | ball-ACC.SG.F | | |
| **class** | ADV | VTR | DET | NCOM | | |
| **cs1** | | V | NP | | | |
| **cs2** | | VP | | | | |
| **cs3** | S | | | | | |
| **function** | | | DO | | | |
| **role** | | | THEME | | | |
| **translation** | Now, he kicks a ball. | | | | | |
| **given** | | | new | | | |
| **topic** | | | | | | |
| **focus** | | | nf | | | |

**Fig. 3.** Target sentence in Condition A (Modern Greek)

Condition B is illustrated in Fig. 4. The given theme is left dislocated in this example; it is annotated as *given* in the givenness tier (label "*given*") and as an aboutness topic (*ab*) in the tier *topic*. The new agent is encoded through the postverbal subject NP.

Data gathered through production experiments contains the spontaneous reactions of native speakers. In consequence, the structure that the native speaker produces during the performance of the experiment often deviates from the predicted structure. The example in Fig. 4 illustrates a deviation of this kind. Although the agent 'the man' is a new referent (i.e., not mentioned in the previous discourse), it is encoded as a definite NP in the illustrated example. This is captured through the annotation: the gloss shows that the native speaker has used a definite article, but the givenness tier (label "*given*") shows that this constituent is new information.

| | 0 | 1 | 2 | 3 | 4 | 5 | 6 | 7 | 8 |
|---|---|---|---|---|---|---|---|---|---|
| **words** | ti | bála | ti | glotsái | tóra | o | ádras | | . |
| **int-tones** | | L*H  H- | | L*H | | | H*L  L-L% | | |
| **morph** | ti | bála | ti | glotsá-i | tóra | o | ádra-s | | |
| **gloss** | DEF:ACC.SG.F | ball:ACC.SG.F | 3.SG.F:ACC | kick-3.SG | now | DEF:NOM.SG.M | man-NOM.SG.M | | |
| **class** | DET | NCOM | PRON | VTR | ADV | DET | NCOM | | |
| **cs1** | NP | | | V | | NP | | | |
| **cs2** | VP | | | | | | | | |
| **cs3** | S | | | | | | | | |
| **function** | DO | | | | | SUBJ | | | |
| **role** | THEME | | | | | AG | | | |
| **translation** | The ball, a man kicks it. | | | | | | | | |
| **given** | given | | | | | new | | | |
| **topic** | ab | | | | | | | | |
| **focus** | | | | | | nf | | | |

**Fig. 4.** Target sentence in Condition B (Modern Greek)

Besides simple picture descriptions, the production experiments of QUIS include several types of tasks, such as map tasks, spontaneous answers to questions, instruction games between two informants (e.g., an informant gives instructions to the other for the development of a spatial configuration), role games (e.g., two informants see a short film and perform a negotiation), etc.

## 2.3 General Questions on the Grammar

This component of the cross-linguistic production data archive relies on the tradition of typological questionnaires (see [5]) and has the structure of a typological feature database such as those mentioned in Section 1. It contains several questions on the typological properties of the grammar (phonology, morphology, syntax, and information structure) of the object language, that are necessary for the interpretation of the collected data. Each section contains a number of grammatical features that are presented to the user as questions, e.g. "Is there a passive/active distinction?", or "what is the canonical position of subject, object, verb?". The fragment in Fig. 5 presents the hierarchical structure of this component in the database. Each feature is accompanied by a finite set of values, that represent the typologically possible options: For the first example ("Is there a passive/active distinction?"), the possible options are "yes" and "no"; for the second example the possible options are the word orders encountered in world's languages: "SOV", "SVO", "VSO", "VOS", "OSV", and "OVS". The answers for these questions are not inferred from the archived data, but are collected from available grammatical descriptions and from the grammatical knowledge of language experts.

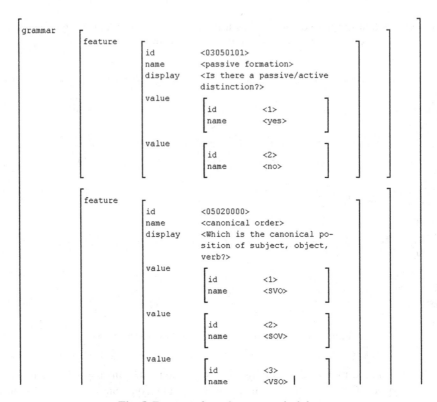

**Fig. 5.** Fragment from the grammatical data

The grammatical information contained in this component is indispensable for the interpretation of the production data. For instance, the data gathered in the condition "agent=new information" in the experiment presented above contains a large number of passive sentences in languages like English and German, but only active sentences in the data from Prinmi and Georgian.[4] Crucially for the interpretation of the result, the grammar of Prinmi does not have a passive formation rule (see [8]), while passive formation is available for the Georgian verb (see [14]). I.e., in these two languages the same experimental result is observed, but for completely different reasons: in Prinmi, passive is not an available option, whereas in Georgian passive is available but is not chosen in the discourse condition at issue. This information about the grammar is given through the values of Georgian ("yes") and Prinmi ("no") in the feature "passive formation" of Fig. 5.

## 3 Exploring the Archive

In sum, our production data archive differs from other typological data archives in providing: (a) primary data with rich multilevel annotations, (b) information about the

---

[4] The production data archive contains 16 sentences in each language gathered through this experimental condition (produced by eight different speakers per language).

discourse condition that induces the archived data, and (c) grammatical information about the object language. In this section, we present the solutions we have chosen in order to develop the production data archive and we illustrate the possibilities currently available for exploration of the archive. We do not illustrate in detail how searches are performed within the annotated data, since these do not substantially differ from exploration in text corpora (the reader is referred to [12] for natural language data and annotation instead), but we focus on the possibilities that emerge from the integration of the various components presented above into a single exploration environment.

As representation formats for individual archive components, we employ both existing formats and formats developed within the framework of the *Collaborative Research Center 632 "Information Structure"*. For representation of the natural language data and their annotations, the generic standoff XML exchange format PAULA is used, which facilitates easy addition of further annotation layers and supports import from a number of annotation tool formats (ref. [9]). For accessing of this data, we use ANNIS, a web application that allows for visualization and querying of the heterogeneous multilevel annotation via the internet ([11]).

We are currently developing an XML-format for QUIS, in particular for the grammatical questionnaire and the documentation of the data gathering methods. For visualization and querying of the Questionnaire, we are developing an exploration system, which will integrate as an interface to ANNIS, such that the production data archive can be viewed in a single environment.

An elementary way of searching within the production data archive is to query the annotations. For this purpose, the user of the archive may formulate query expressions that address any aspect of the information that is archived within the production data archive. A standard query would retrieve all sentences of a given language that match certain properties in the annotation, e.g.: "For the language with the name *Teribe* (TFR), retrieve sentences in which the agent (tag *ag* of type *role*) is the part of the sentence that constitutes the answer to a previous question (tag *ans* of type *focus*)".

$$\text{role=ag \& focus=ans \& doc=TFR*} \qquad (1)^5$$

The result of the query in (3) is shown in the screen-shot from ANNIS in Fig. 6:

As discussed in Section 2, a powerful property of the production data archive is that it not only provides an annotated text corpus, but also a description of the discourse environments (experimental conditions) in which this expression was induced. Experiments and experimental conditions are specified through the file names. In Section 2.2, for example, we have shown that an agent that is assumed to be new according to the experimental manipulation may be encoded through definite NPs in the resulting data. In order to retrieve examples like the one in Fig. 4, the user may address a particular experimental condition, e.g.: "For the language with the name *Greek* (GRK), retrieve sentences gathered in experiment 42, condition B, in which the agent (tag *ag* of type *role*) is encoded through an NP that contains a definite article (tag *def* of type *gloss*)."

$$\text{role=ag \& gloss=def \& doc=GRK*42-B \& \#1\_=\_\#2} \qquad (2)$$

---

[5] The expressions "doc=TFR" and "doc=GRK" (below) restrict the search to documents of Teribe (language code: TFR) or Greek (language code: GRK).

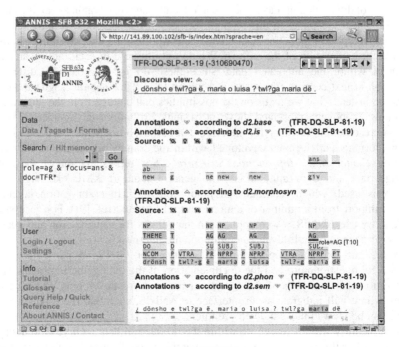

**Fig. 6.** ANNIS

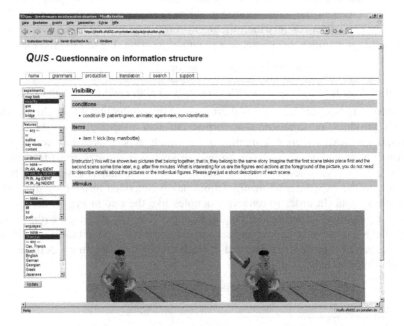

**Fig. 7.** QUISViewer

For browsing of the documentation of the experiments in QUIS, we are currently developing a tool "QUISViewer". The documentation includes an outline of each experiment and its experimental conditions, the procedure and instructions that were used during performance of the experiment, as well as the stimuli which were shown to the informant. A pilot version of this browser is shown in Fig. 7. At the left frame of this interface, the user may also browse the collected data restricting his query to particular experimental conditions, experimental items, or a subset of languages.

The aim of the component of QUIS which provides general questions on the grammar (see Sect. 2.3) is to support typological queries within our archive. Currently, the information about grammatical features of each languages is available in a separate database. In a future development this information will be integrated into ANNIS to allow for queries of the type: "For a language $L_i$ such that it has either value 'VOS' or 'VSO' in the feature 'canonical order', retrieve sentences in which a noun phrase precedes a verb".

## 4  Summary

We have presented our work on a cross-linguistic production data archive, which includes detailed information about data collection methods and about grammatical features of the languages involved, in addition to richly annotated natural language data from 15 typologically diverse languages. The special property of our archive is that it contains a parallel corpus of sentences and texts induced in the different languages through identical methods. We argue that this is a new type of resource that integrates features from both typological databases and natural language corpora. Finally, we have sketched the possibilities available for exploration of this archive on the basis of our current implementation, emphasizing operations that take place at the interfaces between the database components, in order to give an insight into the special properties of our complex archive architecture.

We believe that the type of resource presented in this paper represents a substantial enrichment of existing resources for language comparison, since it permits formulation of generalizations about the occurrence of language specific patterns in identical conditions. The *Collaborative Research Center 632 "Information Structure"* plans in future to expand the database with data from additional languages. Parallel to the integration of further data, we will also further develop the archiving infrastructure towards an integrated environment containing all of the components reported in this paper.

## References

1. Bickel, B., Comrie, B., Haspelmath, M.: Leipzig Glossing Rules. Ms. University of Leipzig (2004)
2. Bickel, B., Nichols, J.: Autotypologizing Databases and their Use in Field Work. In: Proc. Int. LREC Workshop on Resources and Tools in Field Linguistics (2002)
3. Boersma, P., Weenink, D.: Praat. doing phonetics by computer (Version 4.3.14) (2005), Computer program: http://www.praat.org/

4. Brown, D., Corbett, C., Tiberius, C., Barron, J.: The Surrey Database of Agreement (2005), Online database: http://www.smg.surrey.ac.uk/Agreement/explore.aspx
5. Comrie, B., Smith, N.: Lingua Descriptive Studies: Questionnaire. Lingua 42, 1–72 (1977)
6. Corbett, C., Baerman, M., Brown, D., Hippisley, A.: Extended Deponency: The Right Morphology in the Wrong Place (2005), Online database: http://www.surrey.ac.uk/ LIS/ MB/WALS/WALS.htm
7. Dahl, Ö. (ed.): Tense and Aspect in the Languages of Europe. Mouton de Gruyter, Berlin, New York (2000)
8. Ding, S.: Fundamentals of Prinmi. A Tibeto-Burman Language of Northwestern Yunnan, China. PhD. dissertation, Australian National University (1998)
9. Dipper, S.: XML-Based Stand-off Representation and Exploitation of Multi-Level Linguistic Annotation. In: BXML 2005. Proceedings of Berliner XML Tage 2005, Berlin, pp. 39–50 (2005)
10. Annotation Guidelines. In: Dipper, S., Götze, M., Skopeteas, S. (eds.) Interdisciplinary Studies on Information Structure (ISIS). Working Papers of the SFB 632, vol. 8, Universitätsverlag Potsdam, Potsdam (2006)
11. Dipper, S., Götze, M., Stede, M., Wegst, T.: ANNIS. A Linguistic Database For Exploring Information Structure. In: Interdisciplinary Studies on Information Structure (ISIS). Working Papers of the SFB 632, pp. 245–279. Universitätsverlag Potsdam, Potsdam (2004)
12. Dybkjaer, L., Berman, S., Bernsen, N.O., Carletta, J., Heid, U., LListerri, J.: Requirements Specification for a Tool in Support of Annotation of Natural Interaction and Multimodal Datad. ISLE Natural Interactivity and Multimodality Working Group. D11.2 (2001)
13. Skopeteas, S., Fiedler, M., Hellmuth, I., Schwarz, S., Stoel, A., Fanselow, R., Féry, G., Krifka, C.: Questionnaire on Information Structure. In: Interdisciplinary Studies on Information Structure (ISIS). Working Papers of the SFB 632, vol. 6, Universitätsverlag Potsdam, Potsdam (2006)
14. Harris, A.C.: Georgian Syntax. Cambridge University Press, Cambridge (1981)
15. Haspelmath, M., Dryer, M.S., Gil, D., Comrie, B. (eds.): The World Atlas of Language Structures. Oxford University Press, Oxford (2005)
16. Hyman, L., Mortensen, D., Allison, D.: X-tone: Cross-linguistic Tonal Database (2005), Online database: http://xtone.linguistics.berkeley.edu/display/index.php
17. König, E., Bakker, D., Dahl, Ö., Haspelmath, M., Koptjevskaja-Tamm, M., Lehmann, C., Siewierska, A.: EUROTYP Guidelines. European Science Foundation Programme in Language Typology (1993)
18. König, E., Gast, V., Hole, D., Siemund, P., Töpper, S.: Typological Database of Intensifiers and Reflexives. Freie Universität Berlin (2006), Online Database: http:// noam. philologie.fu-berlin.de/ gast/tdir/
19. Hurch, B., Mattes, V.: The Graz Database on Reduplication. Faits de Langues (to appear)
20. Schmidt, T.: Transcribing and Annotating Spoken Language with EXMARaLDA. In: Proceedings of the LREC-Workshop on XML Based Richly Annotated Corpora, Lisbon 2004. ELRA, Paris (2004)
21. Wittenburg, P., Mosel, U., Dwyer, A.: Methods of Language Documentation in the DOBES Project. In: Proceedings of LREC 2002, pp. 34–42 (2002)

# Case Attraction in Ancient Greek

Scott Grimm

Department of Linguistics, Stanford University
sgrimm@stanford.edu

**Abstract.** Case attraction has stood as a puzzling, and elusive, oddity of older Indo-European languages. This paper focuses on attraction in Ancient Greek, establishing both the regularity of the operation and its underlying motivation. A novel method is proposed for grounding case in terms of a feature-based representation of agentivity properties, loosely based on Dowty's proto-role theory, but reformulated in terms of privative opposition and hierarchically organized via a lattice. This structure is then used to model the case system of Ancient Greek and derive a hierarchical ordering on the case system in terms of agentivity. Modelling the interaction between this hierarchy and the other factors involved in case attraction in the Optimality Theory framework yields a full solution, predicting both its distribution and frequencies therein.

The attempt to describe case as a stable, syntactic phenomenon is belied by instances of what is known as *case conflict*. This paper investigates a particular type of case conflict, case attraction, which involves relative pronouns and their antecedents. Case attraction has long been seen as an exception to the general rule of case assignment, but I will argue in what follows that, once the conditions under which case attraction are clarified, and a given case's relation to semantic content is secured, case attraction must no longer be seen as an aberration, but rather as consistent with the general principles of case assignment.

The organization of the paper is as follows. I begin by summarizing the data from Ancient Greek, paying particular attention to the distribution of the phenomenon and the frequencies therein. Case attraction will be seen as crucially linked to the thematic, or agentivity, properties associated with a given case, and a general framework for connecting case and agentivity via a lattice structure will be exposed in section 2. The case system of Ancient Greek is then mapped upon the lattice, determining a hierarchical relation on the case system. Section 3 unifies the foregoing analysis of case attraction with the semantic agentivity properties to account for case attraction and its distribution within the Optimality Theory (OT) framework.

## 1 Delimiting Case Attraction

Languages which dispose of case systems use case in order to display the syntactic function of lexical items within the clause. Yet, case assignment can also be

B.D. ten Cate and H.W. Zeevat (Eds.): TbiLLC 2005, LNAI 4363, pp. 139–153, 2007.

subject to agreement constraints, e.g., an adjective modifying a noun must share the noun's case, if both are marked for case. When the agreement constraints are discordant with the functional role of case assignment, case conflict occurs. This conflict is commonly resolved by selecting to manifest either syntactic function or agreement. In most circumstances, Ancient Greek selects the former, and while a relative pronoun agrees with its antecedent in gender, number, and person, its case is determined by the construction of the clause in which it stands. However, under certain circumstances, Greek prioritizes agreement, as in (1)[1], where the case of the pronoun shifts to agree with the nominal. Although the focus here is on Greek, such fluctuation also occurs in other languages, e.g., Anglo-Saxon, Old High German, and Latin.

(1)  Xenophon, Anabasis, 1.7.3

andres     axioi        tēs        eleutheriās   hēs
Men.NOM worthy.NOM the.GEN freedom.GEN which.GEN
[hēn]           kektēsthe
[which.ACC]  possess.2nd.PL

Men worthy of-the freedom which you possess.

I will refer to the type of attraction in (1) as 'proper attraction'. Additionally, it occurs that it is not the relative pronoun which is provoked into another case, but the antecedent which shifts case to accord with the case of the relative pronoun, as in (2)[2]. Since the roles are reversed, this variety of attraction is known as 'inverse attraction'.

(2)  Sophocles, Oedipus Rex, 449

ton andra    touton    [ho anēr      touto]    hon        palai
the man.ACC this.ACC [the man.NOM this.NOM] who.ACC long-ago
zēteis          ... houtos estin enthade
search-2nd... this one.NOM is      here

The man who you long ago searched ... is here.

Inverse attraction "regularly occurs when the antecedent stands at the head of the sentence and precedes the relative clause, which itself precedes the main clause" [4], i.e., the antecedent is in a focus position and distanced from its governing verb.

---

[1] The examples of case attraction phenomena were gathered from grammars [3], [8] and [13], and cross-checked against a corpus of the relative pronoun in Xenophon's Anabasis gathered from [10].

[2] It will be noted that this example contains a resumptive pronoun, which would lead one to posit that inverse attraction can be analyzed as left-dislocation, as was done by [11] for Old and Middle High German. However, resumptive pronouns, while possible, do not appear to be the rule in Greek (cf. (4) below), and so left-dislocation will not suffice to explain the data at hand.

The languages which have been the source of discussion for case attraction provide little in the way of variation. If a language exhibits proper attraction, it exhibits inverse attraction as well, as is the case in Latin, Greek, and Old High German.[3] This indicates that an account of attraction would optimally posit the same underlying reason for proper and inverse attraction. I now examine the conditions which appear to trigger case attraction based on data from Ancient Greek.

## 1.1 The Distribution of Cases

The details of the distribution in terms of case provide the main challenges for an account. Proper attraction canonically occurs when the relative pronoun is in the accusative and the antecedent is in the dative or genitive, as in (1).[4] Less frequently, relative pronouns standing in the nominative or the dative are attracted. Inverse attraction also affects the accusative most frequently, which is then coerced into a genitive or dative. However, it is possible with the nominative as well, which can be realized as an accusative. The possible combinations and attested attractions are summarized in table 1 below.

**Table 1.** Distribution of Case Attraction

| antecedent | relative pronoun | output pair | antecedent | relative pronoun | output pair |
|---|---|---|---|---|---|
| nominative | nominative | — | nominative | dative | no change attested |
| accusative | nominative | no change attested | accusative | dative | no change attested |
| dative | nominative | (dat, dat) | dative | dative | — |
| genitive | nominative | (gen, gen) | genitive | dative | (gen, gen) |
| nominative | accusative | (acc, acc) | nominative | genitive | (gen, gen) |
| accusative | accusative | — | accusative | genitive | (gen, gen) |
| dative | accusative | (dat, dat) | dative | genitive | (gen, gen) |
| genitive | accusative | (gen, gen) | genitive | genitive | — |

It is important to note that there are types of attraction not found—one does *not* see a relative pronoun in the nominative attracting an antecedent in the genitive into the nominative.[5] This can be explained systematically if a case hierarchy which orders the cases is adopted, as was done in [7]:

nominative < accusative < dative < genitive

This hierarchy can be adduced from the table of the distribution of case attraction. A comparison among the input/output pairs in table 1 makes it

---

[3] A notable exception is Anglo-Saxon, where one does not find inverse attraction. But this arises for entirely different reasons—the relative particle 'þe' is indeclinable, so it does not have a case with which to attract the nominal.

[4] It must be noted that case attraction, which in certain circumstances is expected, is ultimately optional in Ancient Greek. [3, 51.10.2] notes that a lack of attraction tends to add emphasis, and is primarily found in the works of the Greek orators.

[5] Note that case attraction does not coincide with the 'inherent case' and 'structural case' partition [7], since an accusative can attract a nominative (cf. (4) below), yet both are 'structural' cases.

evident that attraction only occurs in Ancient Greek when the relative pronoun or antecedent can take a case that is located higher on the case hierarchy. In addition, it is identical to so-called markedness hierarchies of case found in the literature (cf. [14]).

While the case hierarchy has indeed captured a generalization about how case attraction operates, this in itself has not led to a satisfactory account of what underlies case attraction. More generally, earlier attempts to explain case attraction have left room for improvement in two directions. Some accounts, despite their virtues, have not incorporated the case hierarchy, thereby missing an aspect of the phenomenon's regularity and the ability to predict which case attracts which, e.g., [2], who proposes a Principles and Parameters account. [6] models the conflict between a relative pronoun displaying syntactic function versus agreement in terms of Optimal Theoretic parsing, yet without reference to the case hierarchy, their analysis will over-generalize to instances in which attraction has not been attested in Greek. On the other hand, the hierarchy has been used by itself to explain case attraction [7]. Yet, there are two fundamental issues at stake when using this case hierarchy as an explanatory device for case attraction. First, claiming that a certain case is more marked than another leaves open the question of what actually underlies this markedness. In other words, what are the principles upon which the hierarchy is founded? Second, if it were only a matter of blindly applying the hierarchy to clauses conjoined by a relative pronoun, the disparity between the frequency of attraction from the accusative and from the nominative and dative is left unexplained. The first sort of attraction is the most frequent, indeed regular, while the latter two are rare.

## 1.2    Agentivity and Prominence

Further insight into the factors at play can be gleaned by examining the argument structures of the examples, in particular, regarding what type of thematic content is associated with the attracted items. The pronouns that underwent proper attraction referred to arguments which would have been quite low in agentivity—often referring to the object of verbs such as 'legō' ('to say') or 'echō' ('to have'), i.e., patients, broadly speaking. This observation holds for attracted items of all cases. No pronoun which referred to an accusative argument that would have been high in agentivity was found to undergo proper attraction. A nominative is attracted only when the argument is the subject of a passive or middle verb, where the grammatical subject of the verb is not an agent. Finally, attraction from the dative only seems to occur when the argument represented by the pronoun refers to the theme or beneficiary, as in (3), where attraction affects the direct object of the verb 'entetucheka' ('meet with').

(3)    Plato, Republic 531e

oligoi    hōn      [toutōn    hois]      ego      entetucheka
few.NOM  who.GEN  [those.GEN  which.DAT]  I.Nom  meet.PERF

A few of those whom I have met with.

It can be adduced that proper attraction is contingent on the relative pronoun representing an argument low in agentivity. So it is with inverse attraction which was only observed with subjects that are low in agentivity: subjects of passive constructions or of the "to be" copula, or unaccusatives, as in (4).

(4)   Isokrates 6. 48

politeiān       [politeiā]              hoian           einai
Constitution.ACC [Constitution.NOM] of.such.a.sort.ACC to.be.INF
chrē         para monois hēmin   estin
necessary.3rd for    alone    us.DAT is

We alone have a constitution such as it ought to be.

Intuitively, this is what one would expect. It has often been remarked (cf. [1] and references there) that the subject of a sentence is the least marked and most prominent argument. Conversely, the object, typically associated with arguments low in agentivity, is more marked yet less prominent. So it stands to reason that case attraction, which results in a case-marking which ranks higher on the case hierarchy, would most likely affect the class of arguments that is most apt to be marked, those low in agentivity.

All the instances of attraction share another characterization: all the attracted items are in positions which indicate high discourse prominence—either (topicalized) subjects or heads of relative clauses. Therefore, a generalization arises: attracted items are low in agentivity and high in discourse prominence. This gives cause to suspect that case attraction has a functional explanation—these two competing factors, low agentivity and high prominence, are disharmonious, and set the conditions for attraction to occur. After a detailed examination of the connection between case and agentivity, I will give this generalization a more precise formulation.

## 2   Case and Agentivity

A full account of case attraction must both incorporate the case hierarchy and at the same time constrain its application, and ideally demonstrate what the case hierarchy is grounded in. Having noted above agentivity constrains the possibility of attraction, it is plausible that a more precise account of the connection between case and agentivity can meet the above requirements. The following section pursues this connection and will ultimately demonstrate that the degree of agentivity associated with a case determines its position on the case hierarchy. This will simultaneously provide an explanation for the observed frequency patterns of case attraction.

The connection between case and agentivity follows from cases' relation to argument structure. An argument structure representation of a predicate states that the predicate requires certain types of participants as its subject, object, etc.—e.g., the verb *hit* in English requires that the subject be an agent, one that performs the action, and that the object be a patient, one who submits to the effects of the action. Marking argument structure is the primary reason for having a case system in the first place—to signal what is the subject, object, etc., of the predicate. Since argument structure is determined by thematic content, i.e., agentivity and affectedness, it follows that case assignment is determined in part by thematic content as well. In order to arrive at a framework capable of modelling fine-grained interaction between the parameters of agentivity and affectedness, I begin by employing a set of event-based properties entailed by the verb, inspired by the approach of [5].

I assume a set of properties which refer to modes of participation in events: *instigation, motion, sentience, volition*, and different degrees of *persistence*. *Instigation* entails any argument effecting the event designated by the predicate. *Motion* is entailed just in case the argument is required to be in motion. *Sentience* designates conscious involvement in the event [12] while *volition* designates deliberate engagement in the event. Agents, then, will typically possess one or more of these properties.

*Persistence* is a two-tiered notion, for something can persist existentially, that is, its essence remains the same throughout the event/state, or it can persist qualitatively—i.e., it persists in all its particulars. Either of these can obtain at the beginning and/or the end of the event—in terms of features, we have the following set: *existential persistence (beginning), existential persistence (end), qualitative persistence (beginning)*, and *qualitative persistence (end)*.

Establishing agentivity properties in this manner leads to two diametrically opposed classes in privative opposition, one a full agent possessing all the properties, and the other not entailing any, not even independent existence—e.g., arguments of negative existence statements or incorporated/cognate objects ("sing a song"). Affectedness can be reformulated as a lack of persistence during the event; further, this feature configuration is able to capture the different degrees of affectedness with respect to existence. Totally affected patients, e.g., verbs of destruction/consumption ('destroy', 'eat') entail that their object argument persists existentially at the beginning of the event, but not at the end. Patients which are partially affected (e.g., objects of verbs such as 'damage' or 'move') persist existentially throughout the event, but do not persist qualitatively, i.e., they are changed in some manner. Unaffected entities, most often agents, persist both existentially and qualitatively throughout the event. The opposition between agents and patients falls out from this feature system in that agents will possess total persistence along with a number of other agentivity properties while patients will generally possess no properties save initial persistence and possibly *qualitative persistence (beginning)*.

**Hierarchization of Agentivity Properties.** The above has established a set of properties which make up a predicate's argument structure. Logical entailments among the eight features constrain the combinations possible. For instance, *volition* entails *sentience*, since only sentient beings are capable of volition, and *−existential persistence (end)* entails *−qualitative persistence (end)*, since if an entity does not exist at the end of the event, clearly none of its qualities do either. The remaining combinations can then be given greater structure.

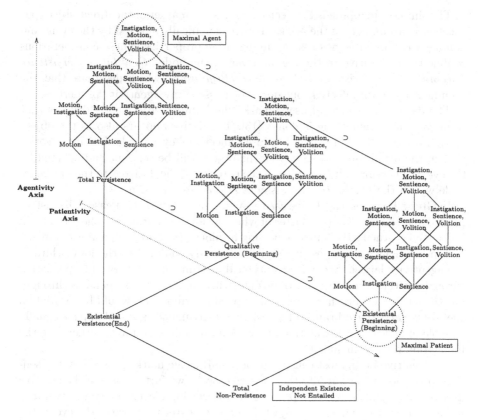

**Fig. 1.** The Agentivity Lattice

The sets of agentivity and persistence properties can be separately ordered by inclusion, giving rise to a lattice structure for each. The Cartesian product of the agentivity and persistence structures results in a larger lattice, shown in figure 1, referred to henceforth as the agentivity lattice. Note that the privative opposition is conspicuous in the structure: the highest node contains all the features (the full agent), the lowest contains none (event internal objects). Further, this lattice exhibits the possible space of argument structure with respect to agentivity.

## 2.1  Mapping the Cases of Ancient Greek

Turning to mapping the cases of Ancient Greek on the lattice, the methodology is rather straight-forward. First, a case's primary function is located on the agentivity lattice, as will be shown in figure 2. Second, the case-marker is identified with the semantic features of its location. It is then incumbent on those features to provide an explanation for the appropriateness of that case for any secondary uses it has accumulated.

The simplest mapping is the accusative. As the marker of the direct object par excellence, arguments in the accusative are canonically affected by the event and non-agentive, i.e., not possessing any agentive properties. These considerations confine the accusative to the region covering the nodes *Qualitative Persistence (Beginning)* and *Existential Persistence (Beginning)*, which designate that the argument has been affected, but does not possess any agentivity properties.

The dative in its central usage marks the indirect object and "denotes that *to* or *for* which something is done" [13]. The dative appears also as the object of such verbs as 'benefit', 'help', 'injure', 'meet', 'obey', 'pardon', 'trust'. Notice that in the usual use of these verbs, the object will be sentient and affected by the event. Therefore, the mapping of the core use of the dative is to the *Sentience* node within the *Qualitative Persistence (Beginning)* branch.

In Greek, however, the dative case is syncretic with two other cases, the instrumental and the locative (the latter of which is not relevant here). The former can be located on the lattice in the following fashion. First, prototypical instruments are not sentient, so the possible region is already confined to the lower-third of the agentivity lattice. Second, prototypical instruments are viewed as persisting throughout the event, i.e., if a tree is cut with an axe, the axe persists throughout the cutting event; therefore, prototypical instrumentals would be located on the *Total Persistence* branch of the lattice. Instrumentals would appear equally capable of at least co-instigation along with an understood agent, therefore the instigation node is included.

The genitive in its most central (adnominal) usage marks possession, the sentient possessor being put into the genitive case.[6] Two further uses of the genitive as a verbal argument reveal a propensity towards high levels of agentivity. First, in most predicates where the object denotes the external cause of the event, the object is put into the genitive, e.g., verbs of emotion and perception ('to hear'). Second, the passive construction in Ancient Greek puts the demoted agent in the genitive case, preceded by the preposition *hupó*. Thus, when appearing as a verbal argument, excepting partitive uses, the genitive is highly agentive, entailing *sentience* and/or *instigation*.

The adnominal genitive primarily denotes static relations, in which neither the head noun nor the genitive-marked noun undergo any change, e.g., inalienable possession, relations of source, of measure, or of quality. When governed by a verb, the genitive also shows a propensity towards total persistence. For instance, as mentioned, 'to hear' takes its object in the genitive. The object heard will persist throughout the hearing event, while the hearer will be affected, and similarly for verbs of emotion. One does not see the genitive marking arguments that are affected or undergo change, unless it falls in with the partitive usage, e.g., 'to touch'. Therefore, the genitive can be mapped, in its possessive uses to the node of the agentivity lattice containing the combination *Sentient* and *Total Persistence* while its agentive uses are mapped to the node containing the combination *Sentient, Instigation* and *Total Persistence*.

---

[6] The genitive also expresses partitivity, yet since I am interested in how the genitive relates to agentivity properties, I leave aside the partitive usages.

The nominative serves to mark subjects and while it ends up most frequently marking agentive arguments, this is only because subjects tend to be agentive. However, the nominative marks subjects of verbs in the passive as well, which are typically patients. Since the nominative can mark any level of agentivity, which is *not* true for the other cases, the nominative is not associated with any particular region of the lattice, i.e., the nominative does not mark agentivity.

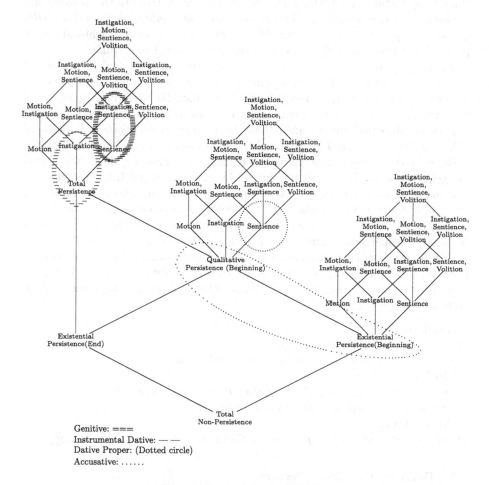

Genitive: ===
Instrumental Dative: — —
Dative Proper: (Dotted circle)
Accusative: ......

**Fig. 2.** Cases of Ancient Greek

**Functional Overlap of the Dative and the Genitive.** The method followed above began with the primary function of a case and derived the semantic properties of the case from that function. In order to ensure that these mappings are valid in general, we must check that secondary uses are in accord with the mappings. An obstacle would appear to arise in that certain functions are designated by more than one case, in particular, the genitive and the dative can both express possessive relations and agents of an event. An examination of the details shows, however, that the properties ascribed to the cases hold, and correspond to the nuances which distinguish the different cases' uses.

Possession marked by the genitive tends towards inalienable possession, designating a static relation which in some sense characterizes the possessor [3]. In contrast, possession marked by the dative tends towards alienable possession, designating "that something is at the disposal of a person or has fallen to his share temporarily" [13, 1480]. These distinctions correspond to the genitive and dative's above mappings onto *Total Persistence* and *Qualitative Persistence (Beginning)*, respectively, since inalienable possession is unchanging, while alienable possession is potentially dynamic, e.g., one has acquired something.

There is a similar division between the genitive of agent and the dative of agent. The genitive with the preposition *hupó* is the default case to mark a demoted agent explicitly connected with the event. The dative of agent, when used with persons, is highly restricted, only appearing when the verb is in the perfect or pluperfect tense, and when the subject of the verb is impersonal [13, 1492]. This usage, although named the 'dative of agent', has much in common with the dative's more principal use of marking beneficiaries, since "the notion of agency does not belong to the dative, but it is a natural inference that the person interested is the agent" [13, 1488]. Therefore, the dative of agent does not diverge from the region of the lattice ascribed to the core usage of the dative. When the dative of agent is a thing, the dative is used whether the subject is personal or impersonal, corresponding to its instrumental use.

The above demonstrates that although the dative shares functions with the genitive, the nuances of these usages are consistent with agentivity properties of its primary uses. In summary, the following mappings have been established, corresponding to figure 2:

**Genitive:**
Possessive uses: *Sentient* and *Total Persistence*
Agentive uses: *Sentient, Instigation* and *Total Persistence*
  **Dative:**
Possessive uses: *Sentient* and *Qualitative Persistence (Beginning)*
Agentive uses: *Instigation* and *Total Persistence*
    **Accusative:**
*Qualitative Persistence (Beginning)* or *Existential Persistence (Beginning)*

## 2.2   Deriving the Case Hierarchy

The above has established mappings of the cases of Greek onto the agentivity lattice. Since the lattice is ordered by inclusion, then the regions associated with the cases are also ordered by inclusion:

$$nominative \subset accusative \subset dative \subset genitive$$

But then, this translates directly into the case hierarchy:

$$nominative < accusative < dative < genitive$$

This result independently motivates the case hierarchy in terms of agentivity rather than resting on claims that some cases are inherently more marked or more oblique than others. Founding the case hierarchy in terms of agentivity gives an explanation for the observed frequency of attraction, viz. genitives are never attracted, datives and nominatives are rarely attracted, and accusatives are regularly attracted. Since the genitive case is the most agentive, there is no other more agentive case to which it could be attracted. Datives can only be attracted by the genitive case and free uses of the dative (e.g., instrumental, dative of agent) were not observed to be attracted. The dative as a direct object, i.e., low in agentivity, is only found with a limited number of verbs, thereupon ensuring that attraction of the dative will be similarly limited. Nominatives are most frequently subjects in active clauses, i.e., agents. Less frequently they are subjects low in agentivity (e.g., passive constructions) and, accordingly, less frequently attracted. Accusatives, however, are standardly patients/themes, i.e., low in agentivity, and therefore they are liable to be attracted to more agentive cases.

That agentivity is the underlying force behind the realization of prominent item's case is reasonable given that an analogous situation holds for subjects, another prominent position. The generalizations behind the various thematic hierarchies have made clear the primacy of agentivity for subject selection, i.e., the most agentive argument is realized as subject. A wider generalization arises: in prominent positions, there is a preference for agentive arguments. Thus, when, say, a relative pronoun is capable of manifesting its relation to its antecedent or its syntactic function, it simply selects whichever is most agentive, highlighting the relation which is most active in the construction.

## 3   An OT Analysis

In section 1, several characteristics of case attraction were isolated. First, two conflicting responsibilities of relative pronouns and antecedents were noted: to designate their syntactic function and to agree. The presence of such competing factors suggests an analysis within the Optimality Theory (OT) framework, which can model such competition.

Second, it was noted that attracted items are low in agentivity and high in discourse prominence. OT permits a method of modelling the interaction between these two factors via the technique of "harmonic alignment". The essential idea is that a prominent element in one category combines most harmoniously with a prominent element in another category.[7]

---

[7] The full definition is given in [9, p.21] : Harmonic Alignment : "Given a binary dimension D1 with a scale X>Y and another dimension D2 with a scale a>b> >z, the harmonic alignment of D1 and D2 is the following pair of harmony scales:
$H_x = X/a \succ X/b \succ ... \succ X/z$
$H_y = Y/z \succ ... \succ Y/b \succ Y/a$
The constraint alignment is the following pair of constraint hierarchies:
$C_x = {}^*X/z >> ... >> {}^*X/b >> {}^*X/a$
$C_y = {}^*Y/a >> {}^*Y/b >> ... >> {}^*Y/z$"

Agentivity and discourse prominence can be put in terms of prominence scales, following [1], where 'X' designates an element high in discourse prominence. By harmonic alignment, the harmonic scales in (5) are derived:

|  | Prominence Scales | Harmonic Alignment |
|---|---|---|
| (5) | Agent>Patient | Agent/X>Patient/X |
|  | X>x | Patient/x>Agent/x |

Case attraction relates to the first of the two harmonic alignment scales in (5), occurring in contexts where the relative pronoun or subject would be marked as "Patient/X". Since this situation is disharmonious, it is sought to be avoided. This is the motivation for case attraction to occur in the first place.

Section 2 established the case hierarchy as an agentivity hierarchy, and so this harmonic alignment scale can be expanded into (6).

(6)   Genitive/X>Dative/X>Accusative/X>Nominative/X

This alignment scale simply states that it if an element is high in discourse prominence, then it is more harmonious to be in the genitive case than in the dative case and so on, which makes the needed bridge between case assignment and the conflict between high discourse prominence and low agentivity.

The competition between designating syntactic function and agreement can be captured by the two following constraints, which compete for assigning case to relative pronouns and their antecedents (see a slightly different take on these constraints in [6]):

FAITH-CASE: lexical items retain the case assigned to them in INPUT (i.e., their structurally assigned case)

AGREE-CASE-Rel.Pronoun-Antecedent: Relative pronouns and their nominal antecedents agree in case

These constraints assume the class of relational structures in INPUT contains information for grammatical and thematic relations. By the principles of OT, these two constraints will be ranked in some order. If FAITH-CASE outranks AGREE-CASE, the case of the relative pronoun will always display the case of its syntactic function within the relative clause. Recalling that attraction is never seen applying to agents, the FAITH-CASE constraint is contextually restricted to agents and non-agents, following the strategy of [14], and FAITH-CASE$_{Agent}$ is ranked highest, ensuring that an agent retains its case-marking. The competition is then seen to be between FAITH-CASE$_{Non-Agent}$ and AGREE-CASE. For Ancient Greek, these two constraints are unordered, so whether the relative pronoun agrees with the antecedent or not is dependent on other factors, and in all cases at least one of the constraints is violated.

These other factors are exactly the case hierarchy in harmonic alignment with the discourse prominence scale, which is ranked below the other constraints. Thus, if an item is disharmonious in that it is low in agentivity and high in discourse prominence, it seeks to become more harmonious by adopting a case with a higher agentivity level, made available by the antecedent in the instance of proper attraction, yet at the cost of violating FAITH-CASE. If the item cannot become more harmonious by agreeing with the case of the antecedent (or relative pronoun for inverse attraction), then it retains its case, since a shift in case would lead to greater disharmony. In this latter scenario, AGREE-CASE is violated, but FAITH-CASE is not. Thus, the winner will be determined by the additional violation marks incurred by way of the case hierarchy. This is shown in tables 2 and 3 which correspond to examples 1 and 4, respectively.

**Table 2.** Proper Attraction Tableau

| Input | F-CASE$_{Agent}$ | F-CASE$_{Non-Agent}$ | AGREE | *Nom/X | *Acc/X | *Dat/X | *Gen/X |
|---|---|---|---|---|---|---|---|
| (i)      tēs eleutherias hē (NOM) | | * | *! | * | | | |
| ☞ (ii)    tēs eleutherias hēs (GEN) | | * | | | | | * |
| (iii)     tēs eleutherias hēi (DAT) | | * | *! | | | * | |
| (iv)     tēs eleutherias hēv (ACC) | | | * | | *! | | |

**Table 3.** Inverse Attraction Tableau

| Input | F-CASE$_{Agent}$ | F-CASE$_{Non-Agent}$ | AGREE | *Nom/X | *Acc/X | *Dat/X | *Gen/X |
|---|---|---|---|---|---|---|---|
| (i)    politeia (NOM) hoian | | | * | *! | | | |
| (ii)    politeias (GEN) hoian | | * | *! | | | | * |
| (iii)   politeiai (DAT) hoian | | * | *! | | | * | |
| ☞ (iv)   politeian (ACC) hoian | | * | | | * | | |

## 4   Conclusion

The above has proposed a solution to the case attraction puzzle by grounding case in agentivity, postulating a preference for agentive arguments in prominent positions, and viewing case attraction as a resolution of that preference, which can then be represented formally within OT by the technique of harmonic alignment. There are several important advantages of this solution. First, proper attraction and inverse attraction are explained by the same mechanism, and the similarity felt to exist between the two phenomena is justified. The technique of harmonic alignment has led to a functional explanation underlying case attraction which makes this solution more satisfactory than merely stating that cases prefer to agree with more oblique cases if possible, which one is forced to conclude if one relies solely upon the case hierarchy. This functional explanation answers why attraction only occurs in this context and why it only affects items which are low in agentivity, in turn, explaining the frequencies of the cases attracted. Third, a theoretical advance has been made by independently deriving the case markedness hierarchy from agentivity properties. No appeal to "greater obliqueness" or similarly vague concepts need be countenanced to make use of the case hierarchy, for it can now be used with the understanding that it is a notational tool, founded on the same semantic principles which underlie argument selection.

**Acknowledgements.** Many thanks to Henk Zeevat under whose supervision this work was carried and also to Andrej Malchukov for discussion. This work was presented at the Sixth International Tbilisi Symposium on Language, Logic and Computation (September 2005) and the NWO-DFG Workshop "Modelling Incremental Interpretation" at Radboud University Nijmegen (November 2005). I would like to thank the audiences for their helpful comments on those occasions, and in particular, those of Helen de Hoop, Barbara Partee, Matthias Schlesewsky and Robert Van Valin.

# References

1. Aissen, J.: Markedness and Subject Choice in Optimality Theory. Natural Language and Linguistic Theory 17, 673–711 (1999)
2. Bianchi, V.: Some Issues in the Syntax of Relative Determiners. In: Alexiadou, A., Law, P., Meinunger, A., Wilder, C. (eds.) The Syntax of Relative Clauses, pp. 53–81. John Benjamins, Amsterdam (2000)
3. Cooper, G.: Attic Greek Prose Syntax, vol. 1. The University of Michigan Press, Ann Arbor, MI (1998)
4. Diggle, J.: Xenophon, Anabasis 3, 1, 6-8 and the Limits of Inverse Attraction. Studi Italiani di filologia classica 20(1-2), 83–86 (2002)
5. Dowty, D.: Thematic Proto-roles and Argument Selection. Language 67, 547–619 (1991)
6. Fanselow, G., Matthias, S., Damir, Ć., Reinhold, K.: Optimal Parsing: Syntactic Parsing Preferences and Optimality Theory. Unpublished Ms (1999)
7. Harbert, W.: Case Attraction and the Hierarchization of Case. In: Proceedings of the Eastern States Conference on Linguistics, vol. 6, pp. 138–149. CLC Publications (1990)
8. Kühner, R., Gerth, B.: Ausführliche Grammatik der griechischen Sprache. Darmstadt (1966)
9. McCarthy, J.: A Thematic Guide to Optimality Theory. Cambridge University Press, Cambridge (2002)
10. Perseus Digital Library: http://www.perseus.tufts.edu/
11. Pittner, K.: The Case of German Relatives. Linguistic Review 12/3, 197–231 (1995)

12. Rozwadowska, B.: Thematic Restrictions on Derived Nominals. In: Wilkins, W. (ed.) Syntax and Semantics, vol. 21, pp. 147–165. Academic Press, London (1988)
13. Smyth, H.W.: Greek Grammar. Harvard University Press, Cambridge (1920)
14. Woolford, E.: Case Patterns. In: Legendre, G., Vikner, S., Grimshaw, J. (eds.) Optimality Theoretic Syntax, pp. 509–543. MIT Press, Cambridge (2001)

# Real World Multi-agent Systems: Information Sharing, Coordination and Planning

Frans C.A. Groen, Matthijs T.J. Spaan, Jelle R. Kok, and Gregor Pavlin

Informatics Institute, University of Amsterdam,
Kruislaan 403, 1098 SJ Amsterdam, The Netherlands

**Abstract.** Applying multi-agent systems in real world scenarios requires several essential research questions to be answered. Agents have to perceive their environment in order to take useful actions. In a multi-agent system this results in a distributed perception of partial information, which has to be fused. Based on the perceived environment the agents have to plan and coordinate their actions. The relation between action and perception, which forms the basis for planning, can be learned by perceiving the result of an action. In this paper we focus these three major research questions.

First, we investigate distributed world models that describe the aspects of the world that are relevant for the problem at hand. Distributed Perception Networks are introduced to fuse observations to obtain robust and efficient situation assessments. Second, we show how coordination graphs can be applied to multi-robot teams to allow for efficient coordination. Third, we present techniques for agent planning in uncertain environments, in which the agent only receives partial information (through its sensors) regarding the true state of environment.

## 1 Introduction

Service robots, transportation systems, exploration of hazardous environments, homeland security and rescue in disaster scenarios [23] are examples where intelligent multi-agent systems could be deployed in real world situations. The societal and economical benefits of making such systems are huge, while at the same time there are still important research questions to be answered before these systems can be applied. Building these systems requires the integration of many technologies such as mechatronics, control theory, computer vision, self-learning systems and cooperative autonomous systems [16]. These agents are "intelligent on-line embedded systems" which are able to operate in dynamic environments inhabited by humans. Local intelligence and mutual communication make systems robust to erroneous perception or malfunctioning of robots.

How to evaluate these complex systems is not an easy question. The current trend to enable comparison of algorithms for parts of the system is to make the data used available on Internet, besides reporting on the algorithms and their results in scientific journals. However, the evaluation of complete real world multi-agent systems is much more complex because it is almost impossible to

B.D. ten Cate and H.W. Zeevat (Eds.): TbiLLC 2005, LNAI 4363, pp. 154–165, 2007.

capture dynamic real-world aspects in static data on the Internet. Simulation is certainly useful in this respect, but these are only an abstraction of reality, and robust comparisons require the deployment of systems in real world scenarios. It has been recognized that international challenges may play an important role in those evaluations. An example is the DARPA Grand Challenge: a race for autonomous ground vehicles through desert-like terrain. A challenge formulated in multi-agent collaboration is the RoboCup challenge [6,15]: to have in 2050 a team of humanoid robots playing a soccer match against a human team.

In section 2 we will discuss challenges for real world multi-agent systems and the research topics involved. To interact with their environment agents have to perceive it. In a multi-agent system this results in a distributed perception of partial information, which has to be fused. Next, Agents have to plan and coordinate their actions, which are based on the perceived environment. The relation between action and perception, forming the basis for planning, can be learned by perceiving the result of an action. In this paper we focus these three research questions, which are addressed in the successive sections in more detail. In section 3 we will discuss distributed world models. Such models form the basis for planning and learning to coordinate the multi-robot team. In robocup these distributed models are shared maps, which form the basis of localization and navigation of the robot-agents. In crisis management scenario's distributed world models facilitate efficient and reliable situation assessment relevant for real world decision making processes. We introduce distributed perception networks [12], that use distributed causal models to interpret large amounts of information. Section 4 explores the framework of coordination graphs for solving multi-agent coordination problems in continuous environments such as RoboCup, as well as how learning can be performed in such settings. Section 5 addresses a second problem, planning under uncertainty, and here we are investigating solution techniques for partially observable Markov decision processes. Finally, section 6 wraps up with conclusions and avenues for future developments.

## 2    Challenges for Real World Multi-agent Systems

In this paper we address some of the challenges of two types of real world multi agent settings: real world robots and distributed situation assessment systems. A challenge should be sufficiently rich so that the different aspects of the problem are well represented. Challenges should not change every year but should have a stable component so that ideas or even best algorithms can be adopted by other competitors, ensuring that a rapid development takes place over the years and incorporating all groups involved.

### 2.1    Real World Robotics

Multi-robot systems in dynamic environments have to cope with several substantial problems. These are summarized in RoboCup which introduces standard challenge settings that allow for an objective comparison of different solutions.

 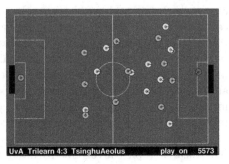

UvA_Trilearn 4:3 TsinghuAeolus          play_on    5573

**Fig. 1.** Two RoboCup leagues: on the left the middle-size robots, on the right the simulated soccer agents

RoboCup's main challenge is to develop a team of humanoid robots playing soccer that is capable of defeating the human world champion in 2050. Competitions in multiple leagues offer the possibility to focus research on different aspects of this challenge.

- In the small-size league each team consists of five small robots of about 15 centimeters in diameter. The ball and the robots are the color coded to facilitate the recognition from the images of a central camera above the field. Since the position of the robots and the ball is known quite accurately, research focuses on robot coordination, team behavior and real time control.
- The robots in the Middle-size league are bigger (about 50 centimeters), see Fig. 1 (left). The objects are again color coded. The main difference with the small-size league is that there is no global vision of the field. Visual information is received from a camera on board of each robot. To enable cooperative team behavior robots have to know where they and the other robots are on the field. So self-localization is a key issue.
- Similar research topics are present in the Sony Legged robot league, where teams of four Sony AIBO's (the well-known robotic toy dogs) compete. These robots walk on four legs. Since every team uses the same robots, the only difference between the teams is in the software.
- In the humanoid league research focuses on the development of robots with a human-like body with the abilities to play soccer against each other. There are two classes: KidSize (30-60cm height) and TeenSize (65-130cm height). Technical challenges involve topics such as penalty kicking, dynamic walking, dribbling and passing.
- The simulation league looks like a standard computer game (see Fig. 1 (right)), but the essential difference is that each player is its own simulated robot, driven by its own program. Each agent has to decide on its own next move. Because simulation frees the researchers from inherent physical limitations these screen players are able to perform on a far more advanced level. This enables the teams to concentrate on cooperative team behavior and tactics.

## 2.2  Multi-agents in Automated Situation Assessment Applications

Situation assessment is indispensable for complex decision making by agents or humans. For example, consider a crisis management scenario, where the decision makers must react to a hazardous situation that takes place after a toxic gas escaped from a chemical plant. Clearly, the crisis managers must be informed about the presence of the gas as quickly as possible. Unfortunately, the gas cannot be observed directly. Instead, situation assessment, i.e. reasoning about the presence of toxic gases, requires interpretation of different types of observations that might result from hidden causes.

In a typical crisis management scenario the presence of a gas could be inferred through interpretation of large quantities of heterogeneous observations obtained through the existing sensory, communication and data storage infrastructure. For example, relevant observations could be obtained from chemical sensors installed in the plant's vicinity and through human reports about smell, haziness, irritation, etc. In addition, Unmanned Aerial Vehicles equipped with sophisticated sensor suites could provide valuable information on the gas concentration in the plant's vicinity.

Such an interpretation of the observations is not trivial, because we often have to deal with a great number of data of different types and often of a low quality. Clearly, the accuracy as well as the efficiency of such interpretation is crucial for adequate decision making where misleading or delayed state estimation can have devastating consequences.

Standardized challenge settings in this area are still being developed. An example is Robot Rescue: the search and rescue for large scale disasters, e.g., searching for survivors after earth quake disasters [12]. This challenge started as a simulation project but now also involves a real environment developed by National Institute of Standards and Technology.

# 3  Distributed World Models

Typical multi-agent systems in real world applications interact with their environment in different ways, which requires knowledge of the relevant states in the world as well as general knowledge about the relevant processes. Such knowledge is captured in appropriate world models which, dependent on the application, make different types of knowledge explicit. To make a multi-agent system robust to failure of an agent or of the communication, world models are distributed throughout the system of communicating agents. Each agent computes a world model by itself from its limited perception and communication with other agents.

## 3.1  Distributed Perception Networks

Distributed world models play a central role in *Distributed Perception Networks*, which are multi-agent systems for the fusion of large amounts of heterogeneous and uncertain information [12]. A Distributed Perception Networks is essentially an organization of agents which support robust and efficient situation assessment through interpretation of information that can be accessed through sensory systems, databases, GSM networks and the world wide web.

The interpretation of the observations is based on causal Bayesian networks, probabilistic models which describe uncertain causal relationships between different phenomena. In a large class of situation assessment problems we can identify sequences of hidden events causing observable events [1]. For example, the presence of a toxic gas will result in a specific conductivity of ionized air which can be measured with sensors, exposed persons will perceive a typical smell and might develop certain health symptoms, which in turn will result in reports. Bayesian networks provide theoretically rigorous and compact mappings between hidden causes of interest and observable effects. By using these networks we can infer hidden causes through backward reasoning, from symptoms to their causes.

Moreover, such causal models are distributed throughout systems of communicating agents. Agents implement local world models encoded through Bayesian networks, which represent basic modeling building blocks. In other words, each agent supports a limited expertise about the domain. Each agent updates its belief over events represented by a single variable. An agent computes a probability distribution over a local variable by using the local causal Bayesian network and a set of inputs. The inputs might be observations (e.g. sensor reports) or probability distributions over certain random variables supplied by other agents.

Belief propagation in a system of agents can be viewed as a combination of several types of algorithms, handling different types of fusion problems [2]. Such belief propagation supports exact inference which (i) is independent of the order of evidence instantiations, (ii) does not require any centralized fusion control and (iii) can efficiently cope with changing network structures at runtime. This is achieved by designing local Bayesian networks in such a way that each agent can compute a probability distribution over its fusion result by processing its local input independently of other agents.

By distributing the world models as well as the inference processes throughout systems of agents, we can often prevent processing and communication bottlenecks as well as a single point of failure.

Also, each Distributed Perception Network is specialized for a particular fusion task, which requires a specific world model that explicitly captures every piece of available evidence and maps it to the hypotheses of interest. Since we deal with applications where the information sources are not known in advance and their constellations can change at runtime, it is impossible to find an adequate causal model prior to the operation. Instead, the information sources are discovered at runtime and the agents assemble local probabilistic world models into adequate distributed Bayesian networks on the fly. In other words, a domain model is assembled out of basic building blocks with clear interfaces on an as needed basis.

---

[1] In this paper an event is synonymous to a realization of a certain situation (i.e. a state).

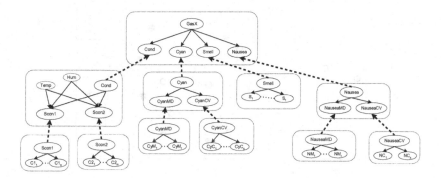

**Fig. 2.** A Distributed Perception Network that fuses information about the existence of high concentration of a toxic gas. Each dotted rectangle represents an agent. Thick dashed lines represent communication between agents, sharing partial fusion results. Each agent makes use of a local Bayesian Network.

In addition, through the modularity of a Distributed Perception Network the design and maintenance of fusion systems are simplified. Simple partial world models can be obtained from different experts or machine learning processes. By complying to few design conventions, simpler models can easily be integrated into complex fusion structures that support very robust belief propagation. Thus, we avoid coordination of many different experts, which would be necessary if the fusion was based on centralized (not distributed) Bayesian networks. In addition, smaller models are easier to generate and fusion systems consisting of Distributed Perception Networks agents can easily be maintained. If the expertise about a certain sub-domain changes, only the local Bayesian networks implementing that expertise need to be replaced. Also, rigorous probabilistic causal models facilitate efficient approaches to distributed resource allocation [10].

Moreover, Distributed Perception Networks support accurate reasoning even if the information sources are very noisy and the modeling parameters deviate significantly from the true distributions between the modeled events. This is very relevant for real world applications, like detecting a high concentration of "Ammonia" (see Fig. 2), where we often cannot obtain precise models and information sources are not perfect. With the help of the Inference Meta Model [13], we show that Distributed Perception Networks can form distributed Bayesian networks which are inherently robust w.r.t. the modeling parameters and facilitate localization of modeling parameters that do not support accurate interpretation in a given situation. Thus, we can estimate the fusion quality and signal potentially misleading results.

The assembly of theoretically sound domain models at runtime is a unique feature of Distributed Perception Networks, which allows efficient fusion of very heterogeneous information obtained from changing information source constellations.

While other recently proposed approaches to distributed information fusion [11,24] support more general domain models than Distributed Perception Networks,

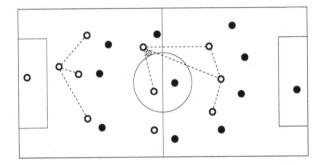

**Fig. 3.** Coordination graph for a typical RoboCup soccer simulation situation. On the left a coordinated defense is shown, and on the right an offense maneuver is planned.

they require a complete knowledge of the available information sources, which makes them unsuitable for certain types of applications, such as detection of critical situations in crisis management processes relying on ad-hoc information source constellations.

## 4    Coordinating a Multi-robot Team

How can intelligent multi-agent systems cooperatively solve a task? The agents interact with each other and coexist in an environment, that they perceive, resulting in a distributed world model. We are interested in fully cooperative multi-robot systems in which all robots have a common goal. Sharing the world model can facilitate the cooperation within such robot teams. We have shown in the past how to coordinate the actions of a multi-robot team by assigning roles to the robots and applying a coordination graph to the problem [7]. Roles are a natural way of introducing domain prior knowledge to a multi-agent problem and provide a flexible solution to the problem of distributing the global task of a team among its members. The role assignment not only reduces the number of actions that have to be considered for each agent, but can also be used to determine which agents depend on each other. In the soccer domain for instance one can easily identify several roles ranging from 'active' or 'passive' depending on whether an agent is in control of the ball or not, to more specialized ones like 'striker', 'defender', 'goalkeeper', etc. Such an assignment of roles provides a natural way to parametrize a coordination structure over a continuous domain. The intuition is that, instead of directly coordinating the agents in a particular situation, we assign roles to the agents based on this situation and subsequently try to 'coordinate' the set of roles.

One approach to efficiently perform this coordination involves the use of a *coordination graph* [3]. In this graph, each node represents an agent, and an edge indicates that the corresponding agents have to coordinate their actions. Payoff functions, defined over the actions of the connected agents, determine the effect of specific local action combinations. In order to reach a jointly (global) optimal action, a variable elimination algorithm is applied that iteratively solves the local coordination problems. For this, messages are propagated through the graph. In a context-specific coordination graph the topology of the graph is first dynamically updated based on the current state of the world before the elimination algorithm is applied [4]. Figure 3 shows such an updated coordination for a typical RoboCup situation, where the defense and offense of the game are automatically separated by conditioning on the context: the location of the ball.

We applied coordination graphs successfully in our RoboCup simulation team by manually specifying both the coordination dependencies and the associated payoff functions [7]. This resulted in the world champion title in the RoboCup-2003 soccer simulation league, illustrating that such a representation can capture very complex and effective policies.

Recently we extended this work by allowing the agents to *learn* the value of the different coordination rules [8]. We have demonstrated how Q-learning, a well known reinforcement learning technique [21], can be efficiently applied to such multi-agent coordination problems. In many problems agents only have to coordinate with a subset of the agents when in a certain state (e.g., two cleaning robots cleaning the same room). We have proposed a multi-agent Q-learning technique, *Sparse Cooperative Q-learning*, that allows a group of agents to learn how to jointly solve a task given the global coordination requirements of the system [9].

## 5   Robotic Planning in Uncertain Environments

Besides coordination agents have to plan their actions. This requires the need for tractable ways of planning under uncertainty. In order for a robot to execute its task well in a real world scenario it has to deal properly with different types of uncertainty: a robot is unsure about the exact consequence of executing a certain action and its sensor observations may be noisy. Robotic planning becomes even harder when different parts of the environment cannot be distinguished by the sensor system of the robot. In these partially observable domains a robot needs to reason with uncertainty explicitly in order to successfully carry out a given task.

As such this planning problem can be seen as a Partially Observable Markov Decision Process (POMDPs) [5], with several applications in operations research [18], artificial intelligence [5], and robotics [17,1,22]. The POMDP defines a sensor model specifying the probability of observing a particular sensor reading in a specific state, and a stochastic transition model which captures the uncertain outcome of executing an action. In many situations a single sensor reading does not provide enough evidence to determine the complete and true state of the system. The framework allows for successfully handling such situations by defining and operating on the *belief state* of a robot. A belief state is a probability distribution over all states of the environment and summarizes all information regarding the past. Solving a POMDP now means computing a policy—i.e., a mapping from belief states to actions—that maximizes the average

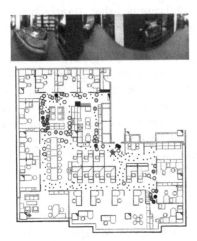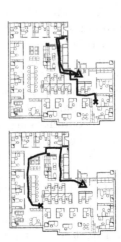

**Fig. 4.** Delivery task in an office environment. On the top left an example observation, below the corresponding observation model, relating observations to states. The darker the dot, the higher the probability. On the right example trajectories computed by Perseus. Start positions are marked with × and the last state of each trajectory is denoted by a △.

collected reward of the robot in the task at hand. Such a policy prescribes for every belief state the action that maximizes the expected reward a robot can obtain in the future. The reward function encodes the robot's task and as such will be provided by the robot's designer.

Unfortunately, solving a POMDP in an exact fashion is an intractable problem. Intuitively speaking, looking one time step deeper into the future requires considering each possible action and each possible observation. A recent line of research on approximate algorithms involves the use of a sampled set of *belief points* on which planning is performed (see e.g., [14]). The idea is that instead of planning over the complete belief space of the robot (which is intractable for large state spaces), planning is carried out only on a limited set of prototype beliefs that have been sampled by letting the robot interact with the environment. We have developed along this line a simple randomized approximate algorithm called *Perseus* that is very competitive to other state-of-the-art methods in terms of computation time and solution quality [20].

We applied this approach to an office delivery task involving a mobile robot with omnidirectional vision in a highly perceptually aliased office environment, where the number of possible robot locations is in the order of hundreds [19]. Figure 4 (left) shows the office environment, together with one of the omnidirectional camera images. We have shown how Perseus can be applied to such robotic planning problems. Robots typically have to deal with large state spaces, high dimensional sensor readings, perceptual aliasing and uncertain actions. We defined a mail delivery task in which a simulated robot has to deliver mail in an office environment. We used principle component analysis to project the omnidirectional camera images the robot observes to a low-dimensional space, in order to able to handle them efficiently. The POMDP requires a discrete observation space, thus we perform clustering in the projected space to extract observation prototypes. We have shown our algorithm can successfully solve the resulting POMDP model. Figure 4 (right) plots two example trajectories. They show the computed policy directs the robot to first move to the pickup states, pick up the mail, and then move to the delivery locations in order to successfully deliver the mail.

## 6   Conclusions and Future Developments

In this paper we have reported on our research on several aspects of real world multi-agent systems.

In this field robot soccer can be seen as a real scientific challenge, which is representative for the application of real world multi-agent systems in practical dynamic situations. Robot soccer competitions is an example of a platform to compare different approaches to these problems and to evaluate them in practice.

We presented our research on coordination within teams of robots which focuses on the use of coordination graphs [7] and extended it by allowing the agents to learn the value of coordination rules [8]. We described our approach to planning in an environment in which a robot is unsure about the exact consequence of executing a certain action and in which its sensor observations are noisy [20].

A multi-agent system result in a distributed perception of partial information, which has to be fused for situation assessment in real world applications [2,12]. We show that the distributed approaches to situation assessment (distributed perception networks), can cope with uncertain domain models and noisy/subjective information sources. In particular, we investigate how distributed causal world models can be used for efficient and reliable interpretation of large quantities of uncertain and heterogeneous information. A strong emphasis is put on the robustness of information fusion using Bayesian networks [13].

## Acknowledgments

This work is supported by PROGRESS and Combined Systems. PROGRESS is the embedded systems research program of the Dutch organization for Scientific Research NWO, the Dutch Ministry of Economic Affairs and the Technology Foundation STW, project AES 5414. Combined Systems is a Senter ICT Breakthrough project, supported by the Dutch Ministry of Economic Affairs, grant number: TSIT2003. We thank the anonymous reviewer for his valuable suggestions and remarks.

## References

1. Cassandra, A.R., Kaelbling, L.P., Kurien, J.A.: Acting under uncertainty: Discrete Bayesian models for mobile robot navigation. In: Proc. of International Conference on Intelligent Robots and Systems (1996)

2. de Oude, P., Ottens, B., Pavlin, G.: Information fusion in distributed probabilistic networks. In: Artificial Intelligence and Applications, pp. 195–201. Innsbruck, Austria (2005)
3. Guestrin, C., Koller, D., Parr, R.: Multiagent planning with factored MDPs. In: Advances in Neural Information Processing Systems 14, The MIT Press, Cambridge (2002)
4. Guestrin, C., Venkataraman, S., Koller, D.: Context-specific multiagent coordination and planning with factored MDPs. In: Proc. of the National Conference on Artificial Intelligence, Edmonton, Canada (July 2002)
5. Kaelbling, L.P., Littman, M.L., Cassandra, A.R.: Planning and acting in partially observable stochastic domains. Artificial Intelligence 101, 99–134 (1998)
6. Kitano, H., Asada, M., Kuniyoshi, Y., Noda, I., Osawa, E.: RoboCup: The robot world cup initiative. In: Johnson, W.L., Hayes-Roth, B. (eds.) Agents'97. Proceedings of the First International Conference on Autonomous Agents, pp. 340–347. ACM Press, New York (1997)
7. Kok, J.R., Spaan, M.T.J., Vlassis, N.: Non-communicative multi-robot coordination in dynamic environments. Robotics and Autonomous Systems 50(2-3), 99–114 (2005)
8. Kok, J.R., Vlassis, N.: Sparse cooperative Q-learning. In: Greiner, R., Schuurmans, D. (eds.) Proc. of the 21st Int. Conf. on Machine Learning, Banff, Canada, July 2004, pp. 481–488. ACM Press, New York (2004)
9. Kok, J.R., Vlassis, N.: Collaborative Multiagent Reinforcement Learning by Payoff Propagation. Journal of Machine Learning Research 7, 1789–1828 (2006)
10. Nunnink, J., Pavlin, G.: A probabilistic approach to resource allocation in distributed fusion systems. In: Proc. Int. Conf. on Autonomous Agents and Multi-Agent Systems, Utrecht, Netherlands, pp. 846–852 (2005)
11. Paskin, M., Guestrin, C.: A robust architecture for distributed inference in sensor networks. Technical Report IRBTR -03-039, Intel Research (2003)
12. Pavlin, G., Maris, M., Nunnink, J.: An agent-based approach to distributed data and information fusion. In: IEEE/WIC/ACM Joint Conference on Intelligent Agent Technology, pp. 466–470. ACM Press, New York (2004)
13. Pavlin, G., Nunnink, J.: Inference meta models: Towards robust information fusion with bayesian networks. In: Proc. Int. Conf. on Information Fusion, Florence, Italy, pp. 846–852 (2003)
14. Pineau, J., Gordon, G., Thrun, S.: Point-based value iteration: An anytime algorithm for POMDPs. In: Proc. Int. Joint Conf. on Artificial Intelligence, Acapulco, Mexico (August 2003)
15. RoboCup official site, http://www.robocup.org
16. Siegwart, R., Nourbakhsh, I.R.: Introduction to Autonomous Mobile Robots. MIT Press, Cambridge (2004)
17. Simmons, R., Koenig, S.: Probabilistic robot navigation in partially observable environments. In: Proc. Int. Joint Conf. on Artificial Intelligence, pp. 1080–1087 (1995)
18. Sondik, E.J.: The optimal control of partially observable Markov processes. PhD thesis, Stanford University (1971)
19. Spaan, M.T.J., Vlassis, N.: A point-based POMDP algorithm for robot planning. In: Proceedings of the IEEE International Conference on Robotics and Automation, New Orleans, Louisiana, pp. 2399–2404. IEEE Computer Society Press, Los Alamitos (2004)
20. Spaan, M.T.J., Vlassis, N.: Perseus: Randomized point-based value iteration for POMDPs. Journal of Artificial Intelligence Research 24, 195–220 (2005)

21. Sutton, R.S., Barto, A.G.: Reinforcement Learning: An Introduction. MIT Press, Cambridge (1998)
22. Theocharous, G., Mahadevan, S.: Approximate planning with hierarchical partially observable Markov decision processes for robot navigation. In: Proceedings of the IEEE International Conference on Robotics and Automation, Washington DC, IEEE Computer Society Press, Los Alamitos (2002)
23. Weiss, G. (ed.): Multiagent Systems: a Modern Approach to Distributed Artificial Intelligence. MIT Press, Cambridge (1999)
24. Xiang, Y.: Probabilistic Reasoning in Multiagent Systems: A Graphical Models Approach. Cambridge University Press, Cambridge (2002)

# Pros and Cons of a Type-Shifting Approach to Russian Genitive of Negation*

Barbara H. Partee and Vladimir Borschev

## 1 Introduction

In our work on the Russian Genitive of Negation (Borschev and Partee 1998a, 1998b, 2002a, 2002b, 2002c, Partee and Borschev 2002, 2004b, In press), we address the semantics of the Genitive of Negation construction and the interplay of lexical, compositional, and contextual factors. In this paper we focus on one interesting semantic proposal that has arisen recently (Kagan 2005, Partee and Borschev 2004b) and arguments both in favor of it and against it. We consider the matter unresolved and worth continued investigation. In this introductory section we review the basic facts of the Genitive of Negation, and some of the key points of existing proposals including our own. In Section 2 we discuss our notion of "Perspective Structure" and the question of where it belongs in the grammar, concluding that it is probably best viewed as a semantic correlate of diathesis shift. In Section 3 we address the principal issue of this paper, the possibility that the relevant diathesis shift in this case involves the demotion of the Genitive-marked NP from a normal referential type e to a property type, <e,t>, raising arguments both for and against such a proposal and pointing to further research which will need to be done.

In many languages, existential sentences have a special syntactic shape, different from regular subject-predicate sentences. But in Russian, with its "freedom" of word order and lack of articles, the difference between existential and "plain" sentences is less obvious in many cases.

(1) a. *V gorode byl        doktor.*
       In town   was-M.SG doctor-NOM.M.SG[1]

---

* We are grateful for valuable discussions and comments to our colleagues Elena Paducheva, Ekaterina Rakhilina, Yakov Testelets, and Igor Yanovich, to audiences at MIT, in Moscow, St. Petersburg, Tbilisi, Prague, Batumi, at SALT 14 and TAG+ 7, to Partee's 2003 semantics class at the Russian State University for the Humanities (RGGU), and to Olga Kagan. This work was supported in part by the National Science Foundation under Grant No. BCS-9905748 to both authors for the collaborative project "Integration of Lexical & Compositional Semantics: Genitives in English and Russian", 1999-2003, and Grant No. BCS-0418311 for the project, "The Russian Genitive of Negation: Integration of Lexical and Compositional Semantics", 2004-07.

[1] In glossing our examples, we use the following abbreviations:

| NOM | nominative | SG | singular |
|-----|------------|-----|----------|
| GEN | genitive | PL | plural |
| ACC | accusative | 1 | first person |
| M | masculine | 2 | second person |
| F | feminine | 3 | third person |
| N | neuter | | |

B.D. ten Cate and H.W. Zeevat (Eds.): TbiLLC 2005, LNAI 4363, pp. 166 – 188, 2007.
© Springer-Verlag Berlin Heidelberg 2007

'There was a doctor in town.'[2]

b. *Doktor*        *byl*       *v*   *gorode.*
doctor-NOM.M.SG     was-M.SG in   town
'The doctor was in town.'

The sentences in (1) seem to differ only in Theme-Rheme structure and word order (and correspondingly in definiteness of the bare NP); but under negation, the well-known "Genitive of Negation" (GenNeg) phenomenon distinguishes the two types sharply[3].

(2)   *Otvet*          *ne*    *prišel.*     –   *Otveta*        *ne*     *prišlo.*
     Answer-**NOM**.M.SG NEG   came-**M.SG** –   Answer-**GEN**.M.SG NEG   came-**N.SG**
     'The answer didn't come.'          'No answer came.'

Intransitive GenNeg sentences are "impersonal": the verb is always **N.SG**. Babby (1980) introduced the terminology "Negated declarative sentences" (NDS), for the sentences with nominative subjects, (3a), and "Negated existential sentences" (NES), for those with genitive "subjects", (4a). The corresponding affirmative sentences (ADS and AES) are in (3b) and (4b).

(3)   NDS   (a) *Otvet*          *iz*     *polka*    *ne*    *prišel.*
               Answer-**NOM**.M.SG from   regiment NEG   arrived-M.SG
               'The answer from the regiment has not arrived.'

      ADS   (b) *Otvet*          *iz*     *polka*     *prišel.*
               Answer-**NOM**.M.SG from   regiment   arrived-M.SG
               'The answer from the regiment has arrived.'

(4)   NES   (a) *Otveta*        *iz*     *polka*    *ne*    *prišlo.*
               Answer-**GEN**.M.SG from   egiment NEG   arrived-**N.SG**
               'There was no answer from the regiment.'

      AES   (b) *Prišel*        *otvet*        *iz*    *polka.*
               Arrived- M.SG    answer-NOM.M.SG from   regiment
               'There was an answer from the regiment.'

An AES obligatorily has a postverbal subject, while in an NES, where the difference is marked by case, the word order can vary. A common view among Russian linguists is that NES's are impersonal, but not AES's[4]: "These sentences are impersonal only when negated. If one removes the negation, they become personal" (Peškovskij 1956, p.334). Examples (5-8) illustrate alternating pairs and cases where either Gen or Nom is obligatory.

---

We use boldface to highlight the relevant occurrences of **NOM** and **GEN** on nouns and **N.SG** on non-agreeing verbs. We do not gloss irrelevant morphology.

[2] Under a marked intonation, this sentence could also be a variant of 'The doctor was in town.' Our examples should be read with neutral intonation.

[3] Most of the examples cited in the first part of the paper come from classic works on the topic such as Ickovič (1974), Apresjan (1985, 1980), Padučeva (1992, 1997), Babby (1980).

[4] Perlmutter and Moore (2002) and Babby (2001) both consider even the affirmative counterparts of these sentences, where the "subject" is necessarily nominative, to be impersonal constructions.

(5) a. NDS: *Stok            talyx vod   ne    nabljudalsja.*
           Runoff-**NOM.M.SG**   melted water NEG  was.observed-M.SG
           'No runoff of thawed snow was observed.'

   b. NES: *Stoka           talyx   vod   ne    nabljudalos'.*
           Runoff-**GEN.M.SG**   melted  water NEG  was.observed-**N.SG**
           'No runoff of thawed snow was observed.' (= There was no runoff.)

(6) a. NDS: *Moroz        ne    čuvstvovalsja.*
           Frost-**NOM.M.SG** NEG be.felt-M.SG
           'The frost was not felt.' (E.g. we were dressed warmly).

   b. NES: *Moroza        ne    čuvstvovalos'.*
           Frost- **GEN.M.SG** NEG be.felt-**N.SG**
           'No frost was felt (there was no frost).'

(7) a. NDS: *(#) *Somnenija     ne    byli.*
           Doubts-**NOM.N.PL**    NEG  were-N.PL

   b. NES: *Somnenij        ne    bylo.*
           Doubts- **GEN.N.PL**   NEG  were-**N.SG**
           'There were no doubts.'

(8) a. NDS: *Lena           ne    pela.*
           Lena-**NOM.F.SG**  NEG  sang-F.SG
           'Lena didn't sing.'

   b. NES: *(#) *Leny      ne    pelo.*
           Lena-**GEN.F.SG**  NEG  sang-**N.SG**

In addition to "subject Gen Neg", there is "object Gen Neg", in which Accusative alternates with Genitive under negation. The semantic effect in that case, if any, is less well understood, although some scholars such as Babyonyshev (1996) believe that is equally a matter of the scope of negation. Chvany (1975), Perlmutter (1978), Pesetsky (1982) and most Western scholars treat the two as a single phenomenon, but without proposing any common semantics other than that Gen Neg happens only under scope of negation. In some Slavic languages, the phenomena diverge (Franks 1995). Russian linguists generally view the two constructions as distinct, with subject Gen Neg having clear semantic motivation and object Gen Neg lacking any systematic semantic effect[5].

Among the generalizations that have been made about the Gen Neg construction(s), some of the most influential are the following.

- A Gen Neg subject is typically indefinite, but not always (Babby 1980, Timberlake 1975).

---

[5] A reviewer wonders why we do not mention other apparent Genitive alternations in Russian. A number of numerals and other quantifiers govern genitive case on their complements but only when the full NP occurs in a position where it otherwise would show nominative or accusative case. And there is the "genitive of animacy", which is really just morphology: the accusative form of masculine animate NPs has the morphological form of the genitive. We do not discuss such constructions because they are more or less fully grammaticized.

- The verb in a Subject Gen Neg sentence is often described as 'semantically empty' (Babby 1980).
- Intransitive Gen Neg sentences are Thetic (Babby 1980). (A number of authors appeal to (Diesing 1992a) for the Nom/Gen alternation as VP-external vs. VP-internal subject.)
- Gen Neg occurs in the scope of sentential negation (just about everyone; but see (Partee and Borschev 2002)).
- A Gen Neg NP (subject or object) has decreased referentiality and tends to be '(existentially) quantificational' (Babby 1980, Bailyn 2004, Jakobson 1971/1936, Neidle 1982, 1988, Pesetsky 1982, Timberlake 1975).
- In the case of Object Gen Neg, many factors contribute to the (probabilistic) choice of Gen vs. Acc: factors favoring Gen include decreased 'individuation' of the NP and decreased transitivity of the verb (Mustajoki 1985, Mustajoki and Heino 1991, Timberlake 1975, Ueda 1993).

Let us focus on "Locative – Existential" pairs like those in (1) and their negations in (9). As discussed by Arutjunova (1976) and Arutjunova and Širjaev (1983), these have parts we will refer to as the "THING" (the doctor), the "LOCation" (the city), and a BE-verb. The BE-verb here is the copula *byt'* 'be', but many verbs can occur in such sentences, as the earlier examples illustrate, and the LOCation may often be implicit rather than explicit.

(9)    a. *V    gorode   ne       bylo       doktora.*
       In    town    NEG     was-**N.SG**   doctor-**GEN.M.SG**
       'There was no doctor in town.'
    b. *Doktor              ne      byl      v      gorode.*
       doctor-**NOM.M.SG**   NEG   was-M.SG   in     town
       'The doctor was not in town.'

We share with many others the intuition that in an existential sentence, the structure is somehow "turned around", to assert of the "LOCation" that it has the "THING" in it. But in what way and at what "level" of structure is the predication "turned around"?

Babby (1980) proposed that the difference is a difference at the level of Theme-Rheme (or Topic-Focus) structure. A number of linguists including Babby (2001) have proposed differences in syntactic structure, without taking a definite stand on the resulting semantics. We proposed in Borschev and Partee (2002a, 2002c) that in addition to topic-focus structure there is a relevant 'Perspectival Structure', relating to the difference in predication in existential vs. predicational sentences.

In the unmarked structure, the THING is chosen as "Perspectival Center"; this is Babby's "Declarative Sentence", a predicational sentence. In an Existential Sentence, the LOC[6] is chosen as "Perspectival Center", and the sentence says of the LOC that it has THING in it. If the LOC is implicit, this is a "thetic judgment".

We have previously described this in terms of a "camera analogy", more specifically an analogy with "what the camera is tracking". A predicational sentence

---

[6] This is oversimplified; the term "LOCation" must be construed broadly, and the sentences are not only about existence but also 'coming into existence', 'being present', occurring, being in one's perceptual field, etc.

keeps the camera fixed on the protagonist (THING as Center); an existential sentence is analogous to the way a security camera is fixed on a scene and records whatever is in that location (LOC as Center).

We also propose what we have called the "Perspectival Center Presupposition", namely that any Perspectival Center must normally be presupposed to exist. From that principle it follows that the nominative subjects in NDS's are normally presupposed to exist, whereas in NES's, only the LOCation is normally presupposed to exist, and the perspectival structure does not provide any existence presupposition for the THING. This is confirmed by examples like (10). There are two ways to say that Petja was not at the concert, and only in (10a), where Petja (nominative) is Perspectival Center, can one felicitously follow up with a denial of the existence of the concert. In (10b) the concert is Perspectival Center, and hence its existence is presupposed, making the subsequent denial of its existence infelicitous.

(10)  (a) *Petja          na koncerte ne     byl.      Koncerta ne   bylo.*
      Petja-**NOM.M.SG** at  concert  NEG  was-**M.SG.** Concert NEG was-**N.SG**
      'Petja was not at the concert . There was no concert.'

   (b) *Peti           na koncerte ne     bylo     #Koncerta ne      bylo.*
      Petja-**GEN.M.SG** at  concert ne   was-**N.SG.** Concert NEG   was-**N.SG**
      'Petja was not at the concert . #There was no concert.'

In the case of quantified NPs, the presupposition of existence becomes rather a presupposition that the domain of quantification is not empty. The nominative subject in (11) presupposes the existence of a non-empty set of students who 'might have been there', whereas the genitive subject in (12) carries no such presupposition.

(11)  *[My nadejalis', čto na seminare budut studenty.] No  ni  odin*
      [We hoped,      that at seminar  will.be students] But NI one-**NOM.M.SG**

      *student            tam  ne   byl*
      student-**NOM.M.SG**   there NEG  was-**M.SG**

      ['We hoped that (some of the) students would be at the seminar.] But not a single one of the students was there.'

(12)  *[My nadejalis',   čto na seminare  budut studenty.] No  ni  odnogo*
      [We hoped,        that at seminar    will.be students] But NI one-**GEN.M.SG**
      *studenta           tam  ne    bylo.*
      student-**GEN.M.SG**   there NEG  was-**N.SG**

      ['We hoped that there would be students at the seminar.] But there was not a single student [or: not a single one of the students] there.'

The semantics of a negated existential sentence (NES) can be summed up as follows: a NES denies the existence of the thing(s) described by the subject NP *in the Perspectival center LOCation* (not necessarily "in the world").

We have seen examples with implicit Perspectival Center locations associated with implicit observers, as in (2) and (6). When the implicit Perspectival Center location is simply "the actual world,", as in (13), the result is a literal denial of existence.

(13)    *Edinorogov           ne       suščestvuet.*

unicorns-GEN.M.PL  NEG  exist-SG
'Unicorns do not exist.'

In Borschev and Partee (1998a), we proposed deriving this semantics from the following construction-specific presupposition:

(14)    **PRESUPPOSED EQUIVALENCE:** An NES presupposes that the following equivalence holds locally in the given context of utterance:

$$V \text{ (THING, \underline{LOC})} \Leftrightarrow BE(\text{THING, \underline{LOC}})$$

In the general case, we assume that verbs have their normal literal meaning, which in most cases is not simply "exist" or "be". If the GenNeg construction is used, the hearer uses contextual information to support an accommodation of the presupposition, perhaps shifting the verb meaning to make it "less agentive". Examples involving the interaction of additional "axioms" deriving from lexical semantics, encyclopedic knowledge, and local contextual information are given in Borschev and Partee (1998b, 2002a).

To summarize: We believe that Perspectival Structure is basically a structuring at the model-theoretic level, like the telic/atelic distinction, or the distinction between Agents and Experiencers. These properties reflect cognitive structuring of the domains that we use language to talk about, and are not simply "given" by the nature of the external world.

A "V(THING, LOC) situation" may be described with the THING as Perspectival Center, or with the LOCation as Perspectival Center, analogous to different choices of "what the camera is tracking."

When the THING is chosen as Perspectival Center, its existence is presupposed, and the sentence speaks of its LOCation and potentially about other properties or states or actions.

When we choose the LOCation as Perspectival Center, the sentence speaks about what THINGs there are (or not) in that situation and/or about what is happening in the situation.

The choice of Perspectival Center, as so described, has much in common with the choice of Theme (Topic) on the one hand, and with the choice of grammatical Subject on the other: all three notions involve structuring something (a situation, a proposition, or a sentence) so that one part is picked out and the rest is in effect predicated of it[7].

## 2   What Is Perspective Structure? Where in the Grammar Is It?

We noted above that Perspectival Structure is metaphorically similar to making a choice of what to track with a video camera: to follow some THING, or to stay fixed on a LOCation. So where in the grammar might such a notion belong?

---

[7] Babby (1980) in fact argued that Gen Neg depends on Theme/Rheme structure; for discussion of what we see as the difference between Theme/Rheme structure and Perspectival Structure, and for arguments that it is Perspectival Structure that is crucial for Gen Neg, see (Borschev and Partee 2002c, Partee and Borschev 2006).

It is not the same as information structure, although it has some similarity with it, and a chosen Perspectival Center may by default also be the Topic: but not always, as we have argued in Borschev and Partee (2002a,c). And it is not directly syntax, although it may well be reflected in the syntax.

It seems primarily to be a choice of what structure we want to impose on some piece of reality that we want to describe. And in this it has something in common with deciding whether to describe a buying or a selling. It is similar in some ways to figure-ground choices, as in choosing whether to say that A is above B or that B is below A. Such choices may involve choosing between distinct lexical items, like *above/below*, or *buy/sell*, or they may involve choosing among different arrangements of argument structure permitted by one and the same predicate, as with *spray/load*, *give/send*, (or they may involve a combination of the two, in languages where argument structure alternations are accompanied by morphological alternations in the verb, additions of particles, etc.)

Our current hypothesis about 'where in the grammar' the choice of Perspective Structure is registered is that it is a "diathesis choice", a choice among two alternative argument structures for verbs that can take both a "THING" and a "LOC" argument, analogous to the argument structure choices (diathetic alternations) for verbs like *spray, load* or like *give, send*. (For *give, send* too there is a debate about whether the diathesis alternation corresponds to differences in semantics (Krifka 1999) or in information structure (Levin and Rappaport Hovav 2002)).

Other recent work on the semantics of diathetic alternations shares our goal of integrating lexical and compositional semantics by exploring which 'axioms' are contributed by lexical semantics and which by the semantics of the constructions (Ackerman and Moore 2001, Bresnan 1994, Dowty 2001, Kiparsky 1997, Krifka 2004). The relevant concept of diathesis originated in the Moscow School[8], and research on the semantics associated with diathetic alternations has a long history in Russian semantics. In Western linguistics, similar concerns are more often addressed under the heading of "argument structure alternations", although the term "diathesis" can also be found in the work of a number of Western scholars, including Babby (1997) and Levin (1989). We believe that research in this area can be greatly advanced if work in these two traditions can be brought together.

What is the semantic difference between *load the truck with hay* and *load the hay on the truck*? There is no systematic truth-conditional difference, but it is often suggested that there are differences in which argument is understood to be 'completely' affected, namely the one chosen as direct object, which is also the one more likely to be a definite NP. Is there a difference in the meaning of *load* when the argument structure shifts in this way? Probably so, since in one version it overlaps in meaning and argument structure with *fill* while in the other it is closer to *put*. We see these questions as similar to our questions about the status of the THING and LOC arguments in the two sentence types.

---

[8] Mel'chuk and Xolodovič (1970) and Xolodovič (1970) were the first to draw a distinction between *voice* and *diathesis*, using *diathesis* as the more general term for syntactic patterns of argument structure realization, reserving the term *voice* for diatheses marked on the verb (e.g. active/passive). The semantics of diathetic alternations continues to figure prominently in Russian lexical semantics (Padučeva 2002).

It is interesting to see that also in the realm of diathesis alternation, the subject of active recent research, there are debates about the relative contribution of lexical semantics, the semantics of the syntactic structures, and the contribution of topic-focus structure. Both Levin and Rappaport Hovav (2002) and a number of Russian linguists (Yanko, Paducheva, and others) are convinced that certain lexical items may select in part for the information-structure roles of certain of their arguments, in ways that may be connected to differences in presuppositional vs. assertional status of parts of their meanings. So while Krifka (1999) and Levin and Rappaport Hovav (2002) are in agreement about many issues concerning the semantics of diathesis alternation, they disagree about the English dative alternation as represented, for instance, by the pair in (15).

(15) a.  Ann threw the ball to Beth.  (V NP PP: the "prepositional object" variant)

      b.  Ann threw Beth the ball.     (V NP NP: the "double object" variant)

Both Krifka and Levin and Rappaport Hovav believe that there is a real semantic difference in the *spray/load* alternation, with the syntactic direct object as the semantically "affected object" in the two diathetic frames. (Fill the truck, or load all the hay.)  But Levin and Rappaport Hovav believe that in the dative alternation, it's a matter of pragmatic implicature rather than semantic entailments. The issue is still open; see Krifka (2004) for a balanced discussion.

In some theories, diathetic changes are all encoded as changes in the verb and its semantics. In other theories, the verb meaning may stay fixed, and there is a change in the semantic contribution of the construction. Russian linguistics is traditionally verb-centered, Western linguistics typically syntax-centered. The current drive in Western theories, tracing in part to the work of Dowty (1978) and of Bresnan (1978), to pack as much of the grammar as possible into the lexicon, should help to decrease the gap between approaches. But there are undoubtedly real differences within a language, or between languages, in 'where' some of these diathetic alternations are located in the grammar. Ackerman and Moore (2001) believe that both kinds of diathetic alternations are possible, and believe that Western theories may be helped by taking a more verb-centered perspective.

A more verb-centered approach may be helpful in the case of Gen Neg, since not only do we often find semantic differences in the senses of the verbs when used with Gen vs. Nom, or (less commonly but sometimes) with Gen vs. Acc, but we also find that Genitive "Subjects" do not score as highly on tests of subject properties as Nominative Subjects, tests which include both the kinds of semantic properties identified by Hopper and Thompson (1981) and Dowty (1991) and syntactic tests proposed by Keenan (1976). Keenan's and similar tests have been discussed with respect to Russian by Babby (1980) and by Testelets (2001).

But the fact that this alternation occurs only in negative sentences makes it different from many familiar diathetic shifts.

It would be tempting to posit a 'negated verb' with its own diathesis shift. There are attested examples of languages with separate negated verbs, especially negations of 'be' or 'have', with their own argument structure, and in many Slavic languages, sentential negation is marked with a preverbal clitic or even a prefix. Bailyn (2004) proposes that sentential Neg, in a relatively high position itself, licenses or checks a Q feature on the verb, and that Q-marked verb may select for a genitive internal argument. That account has some features in common with Pesetsky's original idea (Pesetsky 1982), and also with the idea of Jakobson (1971/1936), modernized in Neidle (1982, 1988), that genitive NPs are in some sense more quantificational than referential.

We conjecture that something along such lines may be semantically interpretable in a compositional way that could do justice to the interplay of compositional and lexical semantics and contextual factors. But that requires further study of the issue of Object Gen Neg, concerning which we are still in the preliminary stages.

## 3  A Possible Type-Shifting Approach to a 'Demotion Diathesis Pattern'

One intriguing hypothesis that goes back to the work of Neidle (1982, 1988) has been raised in recent work of our own (Partee and Borschev 2004a, 2004b) and in Kagan (2005). We articulate it here as the Property-Type Demotion Diathesis Hypothesis.

**The Property-Type Demotion Diathesis Hypothesis:** Wherever there is Nom/Gen or Acc/Gen alternation (both under negation and under intensional verbs), Nom or Acc represents an ordinary e-type argument position ('referential'[9]), whereas a Gen NP is interpreted as property-type: $\langle e,t \rangle$, or $\langle s, \langle e,t \rangle \rangle$.

A stronger variant of the hypothesis could add that with the transitive analog of the existential sentence, and with verbs that have intensional objects ('*ždat'* 'expect, wait for', mentioned earlier), the 'genitive variant' of the verb has a (possibly implicit) *situation argument* which is higher ranked in some sense than the direct object, causing the direct object to be demoted, although it doesn't necessarily stop being object.

When the direct object is 'demoted', the structure does not provide a (situation-relative) existence presupposition, and the Genitive object may get a non-specific or a 'property' reading. In the Acc-taking structure, the (Acc) object is in canonical position, and the argument carries a (situation-relative) existence presupposition. In a Diesing-style (Diesing 1992a) approach (Babyonyshev 1996, Brown 1999), the Gen-object version might be the default, with the option of raising the object out of the VP (for Acc). On the lexical perspective this correlates with a change in verbal valency: When the verb is negated, it takes a 'weaker' kind of object, marked by Genitive, unless that object escapes the scope of the negated verb.

In the case of the intensional verbs like *ždat'* 'expect, wait for' in (16), one might further argue that there is a shift in verb sense correlated with the shift in interpretation of the object. So part of the hypothesis, connecting lexical and structural aspects of diathesis shift, would be that the verb selects for the type of its object.

(16)  a.  *On   ždet   podrugu.*                    (Neidle 1988, p.31)
       He    waits  girlfriend-ACC.F.SG
       'He's waiting for his girlfriend.'

---

[9] Quantified NPs may also end up in e-type positions by any of the commonly posited mechanisms of quantification (different mechanisms in different theoretical frameworks).

b. *On   ždet   otveta                   na vopros.*
He   waits   answer-**GEN.M.SG**   to   question
'He's waiting for an answer to the question.'

Neidle (1988, p. 31) notes that verbs that lexically govern the genitive in Russian, optionally or obligatorily, "tend to be verbs of desire, aim, request, or achievement." When there is a choice, Accusative is used for a specific or generic object, indicating that the object is 'outside the scope' of the semantic action of the verb. The Genitive is normally used when object is indefinite (existentially quantified) and 'within the scope' of the verbal "operator".

As Neidle notes, there can be different ways of characterizing the difference: in terms of relative specificity of the NP object, or in terms of "the specification of the NP either within or outside of the scope of the action of the verb" (Neidle). She would like to say that in either case we are looking at differences in interpretation "associated with differences in the scope of the operation that I will refer to as 'specification'." (p.31)

The idea that such differences may reflect type differences corresponds to the work of Ede Zimmermann (1993), who argued for an alternative to Montague's treatment of intensional verbs. Montague treated verbs like *ždat'* as taking type <s<<e,t>,t>> arguments, i.e. intensions of generalized quantifiers. Zimmermann argued in favor of treating definite and indefinite arguments of intensional verbs, (but not generalized quantifiers) as *properties,* type <s,<e,t>>. [10]

Zimmermann's proposal is that a verb like *seek* on its intensional reading denotes a relation between an individual and a property.

In the case of the potentially intensional verb *ždat'* in (16a-b), we see that its intensional genitive-taking variant in (16b) has all the properties of English *seek*. Its extensional accusative-taking variant, (16a), allows referential NPs and quantificational NPs. We predict that genitive should be disallowed with essentially quantificational NPs such as those formed with *každyj 'each'*: this prediction turns out to be not quite clear-cut[11].

(17)   *? On   ždet   každogo           otveta               na   vopros.*
He   waits   each-**GEN.M.SG**   answer-**GEN.M.SG**   to   question
'He's waiting for each answer to the question.'

In the case of Genitive of Negation, the construction is not intensional. But Russian linguists from Jakobson (1971/1936) to Paducheva (1997, 2004) have argued that Genitive-marked NPs have reduced "referential status", and Western linguists have generally claimed that they must be "indefinite".

Further precedent for the idea of treating 'weakened' NPs as having reduced referentiality comes from the work of de Hoop (1989, 1990, 1992, 1995). She argued

---

[10]BHP defended Montague's analysis for many years because of sentences like "The police were looking for every witness to the crime", which does allow an intensional reading for its clearly quantificational object, but overall Zimmermann's position is strong and we expect that such counterexamples can probably be explained away.

[11]The second author finds this sentence odd but not impossible; some of our informants have rejected it altogether.

for a distinction between "weak case" and "strong case" for direct objects in Germanic languages, with both syntactic and semantic properties. Objects with "strong case" can move to topic position, can escape the scope of various operators, and are interpreted as e-type (or as generalized quantifiers if they are quantified). Objects with "weak case" cannot move far from the verb; they have to stay inside the VP, and consequently they fall under the scope of any operators that affect the VP. And they are interpreted quasi-adverbially: they are of a type to take a transitive verb as argument and give an intransitive verb (phrase) meaning as result. Their adverb-like meaning is just a type-lifted version of an existentially quantified argument-type meaning. But they are thereby restricted to having narrow scope indefinite meanings. This last point relates also to Diesing's work (Diesing 1992a, 1992b, Diesing and Jelinek 1993).

There is a similar connection to the work of van Geenhoven (1995, 1996, 1998a, 1998b), who treats 'weak' object NPs in West Greenlandic as "incorporated to the verb": they are not fully independent objects, but get an existential quantifier from the verb.

There has been a great deal of recent interest in the idea of 'weak NPs' as property-denoting in certain contexts (Farkas and de Swart 2003, Kamp and Bende-Farkas 2001, Landman 2003, Van Geenhoven and McNally 2005), and in the future we can expect to find new kinds of arguments for and against treating particular examples in this way. In this paper we focus on some of the arguments for and against treating Russian Gen Neg NPs as property-denoting.

### 3.1  Non-canonical Objects and Their 'Reduced Referentiality'

Part of our own immediate inspiration in considering this hypothesis is the work of Ackerman and Moore (2001): variation in the semantic type of the object could be a species of diathesis, even if it is considered a direct object in both cases. Ackerman and Moore argue that "diathesis" should not be restricted only to cases where the actual grammatical relation changes, as in shifts from object to oblique, but also extended to cases where a subject or object remains subject or object but is 'weakened', and they cite alternations such as the well-known Accusative/Partitive alternations in Baltic languages among their case studies.

Variation under  Negation is not really *intensional*, but one can argue that there is more than one kind of 'reduced referentiality'.  In the case of intensional NPs, 'reduced referentiality' involves considering existence in alternative possible worlds instead of or in addition to the actual world. In the case of indefinites under negation, if they are non-presuppositional then non-existence may be implied or at least rendered plausible and pragmatically implicated. In the case of predicate NPs and property-type NPs, existence claims generally do not arise except on the abstract level at which properties may be said to exist. So we need to look more closely at all the actual arguments invoked in these various analyses and see which of them have resonance with Russian Gen Neg and Russian objects of intensional verbs.

Sometimes, but not always, we can find an analogue of "existential interpretations" with transitive verbs, with Gen Neg suggesting (although not entailing) non-existence of the denotation of the object NP. With the verb *polučit'* 'receive', we find parallel behavior[12] and interpretation between the object (Gen or Acc) and a passive subject (Gen or Nom), illustrated in (18).

(18)  a.  *On    ne      polučil    pis'ma.*
          he     NEG     received   letter-**GEN**.N.SG
          'He didn't receive any letter.'

      b.  *Pis'ma              ne      bylo         polučeno.*
          letter-**GEN**.N.SG     NEG     was-**N.SG**     received
          'No letter was received.'

      c.  *On    ne      polučil    pis'mo.*
          he     NEG     received   letter-**NOM**.N.SG
          'He didn't receive the letter.'

      d.  *Pis'mo              ne      bylo         polučeno.*
          letter- **NOM**.N.SG     NEG     was-**N.SG**     received
          'The letter was not received.'

All are good, and the interpretations are parallel: Acc/Nom presupposes existence of the letter, Gen suggests no letter exists. But that is not true for all transitive verbs, and accordingly not all negated passive sentences take (Subject) Gen Neg, as seen in (19b).

(19)  a.  *Ja ne    čital (ètix)        knig.*
          I   NEG   read  this-**GEN**.F.PL   book-**GEN**.F.PL
          'I didn't read (these)/the/any books.'

      b.  *\*(Ètix)          knig             ne      bylo         pročitano.*
          this-**GEN**.F.PL   book-**GEN**.F.PL   NEG     was-**N.SG**     read
          (Intended meaning: 'These/the/∅books weren't read.')

We will use these examples as standards for comparison later.

## 3.2  Are Gen Neg NPs Property-Denoting?

### 3.2.1  Evidence in Favor: Parallels to *ždat'*

The initial evidence in favor of the hypothesis comes from parallels to the behavior of Gen Neg with the intensional verb *ždat'*, 'expect, wait for', as observed by Neidle (1982, 1988). Compare the two possible negations of the affirmative extensional sentence (20a) and their parallels to the corresponding use of Acc and Gen with *ždat'* in (16a-b).

(20)  a.  *Petja    našel  otvet.*
          Petja    found  answer-**ACC**.M.SG
          'Petja found the/an answer.'

      b.  *Petja    ne     našel   otvet.*
          Petja    NEG    found   answer-**ACC**.M.SG
          'Petja didn't find the answer.'

---

[12] Thanks to Alexander Letuchiy in my semantics class at RGGU in Moscow in spring 2003 for bringing up this issue and helping to find these examples.

    c. *Petja   ne   našel   otveta.*
       Petja   NEG  found   answer-**GEN.M.SG**
       'Petja didn't find an answer.'

The accusative variant (20b) normally implies actual-world existence of an answer (and says that Petja didn't find it), while the genitive variant (20c) does not.

### 3.2.2  More Evidence: Parallels Between Gen Neg and Subjunctive

Kagan (2005) offers suggestive evidence in favor of the Property-Type Demotion Diathesis Hypothesis based on parallels between Gen Neg and Subjunctive in complements. Variants of her examples[13] below are given in (21): According to Kagan, one can use the negated verb *ne počuvstvovat'* 'not to feel' with either a indicative (21a) or subjunctive (21b) complement, the former carrying the presupposition that it had become better and the latter making no such commitment, parallel to the way in which the same negated verb can take an accusative or genitive NP object (21c-d) with accusative presupposing the existence and the genitive strongly suggesting non-existence.

(21)  a.  *Ivan **ne**  **počuvstvoval,**  **čto**  stalo  lučše*
                                             [variant of Kagan 2005 example (25)]
          Ivan NEG felt         that  became  better
          'Ivan didn't feel that it had become better [which it had].'

      b.  *\*?Ivan **ne**  **počuvstvoval, čtoby**      stalo  lučše*
          Ivan   NEG felt        **that-SUBJUNC**  became  better
          'Ivan didn't feel that it had become better.' i.e., as far as he could tell by feeling, it hadn't.

      c.  *Ivan ne   počuvstvoval xolod.*     [Kagan 2005 example (26)]
          Ivan NEG felt        cold-**ACC.M.SG**
          'Ivan didn't feel the cold.'

      d.  *Ivan ne       počuvstvoval   xoloda.*
          Ivan NEG     felt         cold-**GEN.M.SG**
          'Ivan didn't feel any cold.' i.e., as far as he could feel, there wasn't any coldness.

Such parallels, if more and better examples can be found, would help to support a property-type analysis. The number of verbs which show such parallels may be limited, and almost no two verbs behave exactly the same way, but after initial skepticism, the evidence seems to be that the pattern, if not fully productive, is reasonably robust. Three verbs which clearly work as Kagan has predicted[14] are

---

[13] Thanks to Elena Paducheva, Yakov Testelets, and Igor Yanovich for examples and discussion. Kagan's original examples also used the verb *počuvstvovat'*, but with different complements which struck some as less felicitous than those used here. The second author and most of our consultants find (21b) ill-formed, even with the most plausible choices of lexical items.

[14] Thanks to Igor Yanovich for suggesting the verb *zametit'* 'notice', and to Ljudmila Geist for suggesting the verb *pomnit'* 'remember'.

*zametit'* 'to notice', *videt'* 'to see', and *pomnit'* 'to remember'. We illustrate relevant uses of *zametit'* 'to notice' and *pomnit'* 'to remember'; *videt'* closely follows the pattern of *zametit'*.

(22)  a.  *Ja **ne** **zametil**, čto jubilej      GAI    prazdnovali voditeli.*
      I   NEG  noticed   that anniversary GAI  celebrated  drivers-NOM
      'I did not notice that drivers were celebrating the anniversary of the road police.' (factive)

   b.  *Ja **ne** **zametil**, čtoby        jubilej      GAI prazdnovali voditeli.*
      I   NEG  noticed   **that-SUBJUNC** anniversary GAI celebrated drivers-NOM
      'I did not notice that any drivers were celebrating the anniversary of the road police.' (non-factive) [a headline from svobodanews.org]

   c.  *Ja ne    zametil  vodku     na  stole.*
      I   NEG  noticed   vodka-ACC on   table
      'I didn't notice the vodka on the table.' (presuppositional)

   d.  *Ja ne    zametil  vodki       na stole.*
      I   NEG  noticed  vodka-GEN on table
      'I didn't notice any vodka on the table.' (non-presuppositional)

(23)  a.  *Ja **ne** **pomnila**,   čto  on  byl  s    nami.*
      I   NEG  remembered  that  he was with us
      'I didn't remember that he was with us.' (factive)

   b.  *Ja **ne** **pomnju**[15], čtoby          on byl  s     nami.*
      I   NEG  recall       **that-SUBJUNC** he was  with us
      'I don't recall that he was with us.' (non-factive)

   c.  *Ja ne    pomnila     vodku      na   stole.*
      I   NEG  remembered vodka-ACC  on   table
      'I didn't remember the vodka on the table.' (presuppositional)

   d.  *Ja ne    pomnila  vodki      na  stole.*
      I   NEG  recalled  vodka-GEN on  table
      'I didn't recall any vodka on the table.' (non-presuppositional)

Some verbs seem at first not to work as predicted, but Google searches have overturned most of our skepticism. We list a number of them below, without providing all the examples[16]. When noting the presence or absence of e.g. 'c' forms, we are referring to the pattern of examples (21a-d), (22a-d), and (23a-d).

   (24)(i) *počuvstvovat'* 'to feel': See (21). This verb is disputable, though Kagan cites it as working as predicted. Our informants found (21b) ill-formed, as noted. But a search turned up a number of good examples, such as (25) below.

      (ii) *slyxat'* 'to hear': has three of the four forms easily; but when negated with an NP object, Gen Neg is nearly obligatory and the 'd' forms sound bad. We did eventually find a very few examples on Google with Accusative

---

[15] Past tense is also possible here, but present tense is considerably more natural.

[16] It is all too easy to give 'bad' examples; what is more difficult is to convince oneself that one has exhausted the possibilities of finding suitable 'good' examples.

NP: see (26i,ii); but our consultants do not find those examples perfect. It is a somewhat rare and archaic verb, but it apparently does take all four forms, at least for some speakers.

(iii) *predpolagat'* 'to suppose'– has the first three forms, but when negated, really doesn't like Acc NP object. But again Google turned up a good example: see (27).

(25)  *V xode peregovorov ja **ne počuvstvoval, čtoby** naši partnery nagnetali situaciju*
      'In the course of the talks I did not feel **that-SUBJUNC** our partners forced the situation.'

(26)  (i) *Nikogda **ne slyxal ètu pesnju** v ispolnenii ženščiny.*
          'I never [before] heard that-ACC song-ACC performed by a woman.'

      (ii) *Ty **ne slyxal ètu istoriju**?*

           'Have you not heard that-ACC story-ACC?'

(27)  *Ja dumaju, čto skoree vsego nikto **ne predpologal takoe razvitie** sobytij.*
      'I think that most likely no one supposed/foresaw [such a turn of events]-ACC'

This parallelism between indicative-subjunctive and Acc-Gen, both in distribution and interpretation, gives support to Kagan's arguments in favor of a type-shifting analysis.

### 3.2.3  Evidence Casting Doubt on Property Analysis

We have three arguments against the property analysis for Gen Neg NPs; none of them are absolutely unshakeable, but until a way around them has been found, they seem to cast doubt on the analysis and remove much of its initial attractiveness.

### (i) Proper names

The first argument comes from the fact that proper names, demonstratives, and a number of other prototypically referential NPs participate in Nom-Gen and Acc-Gen alternations under negation. Consider the following pair with negated *videt'* 'see'. As discussed by Chvany (1975) for the Nom-Gen alternation in analogous intransitive sentences, the Accusative choice in (28a) tends to suggest that it was a volitional choice: I didn't get around to seeing Masha (but it can also be neutral with respect to such an implication). The Genitive choice in (28b) often suggests the opposite: I expected to see Masha but she wasn't there (though it can also be neutral).

(28)  a. *Ja    ne     videla   Mašu.*
          I     NEG    see      Masha-ACC.F.SG
          'I didn't see Masha.'

      b. *Ja    ne     videla   Maši.*
          I     NEG    see      Masha-GEN.F.SG
          'I didn't see Masha.'

Examples like (28b) cause problems for all "quantificational" approaches to the Genitive of Negation, unless one can defend imputing to the NP in this case a meaning like "any trace of Masha"[17]. Similar examples with the demonstrative *èto* 'that' are well-known; in fact, Mustajoki and Heino (1991) observe, surprisingly, that bare *èto* is far more likely to occur in the Genitive than in the Accusative under negation.

### (ii) Quantifiers

Further difficulties for the Property-Type Demotion Diathesis Hypothesis come from some of the same kinds of quantificational examples that cause problems for Pesetsky's analysis, examples of the sort illustrated in (29), discussed in Padučeva (1974), Klenin (1978), Neidle (1988), Harves (2002), and Borschev et al (2006).

(29)  a.  *Vanja ne        rešil   vse         zadači.*
          Vanja NEG      solved all-**ACC**   problems-**ACC.F.PL**
          Vanja didn't-solve all-the-problems, i.e. solved none.

     b.  *Vanja ne        rešil   vsex        zadač.*
          Vanja NEG      solved all-**GEN.PL**   problems-**GEN.F.PL**
          Vanja didn't solve all the problems (less than all).

Examples (29a-b) may differ in scope, as in traditional analyses, or perhaps even by having a 'referential (collective) reading' in (a), but they do not differ in intensionality. There is no plausible property-interpretation for (29b).

### (iii) Subjunctive relative clauses

As in Romance languages, objects of *ždat'* may be modified by subjunctive relative clauses when the object is interpreted intensionally, by indicative relative clauses when it is interpreted extensionally. This correlates with Gen/Acc marking on the object. But Gen Neg, on the other hand, never by itself licenses subjunctive relative clauses; relative clauses modifying both Gen-marked and Acc-marked objects are indicative (unless subjunctive is licensed independently by something modal in the sentence.)

### 3.2.4  An alternative Approach: Non-veridicality

Giannakidou (1994, 1998), looking especially at Greek, which shows commonalities in the marking of Negative Polarity Items (NPIs, like English *any, ever*) under negation and of opaque objects of intensional verbs, suggested that some languages take the main semantic property of NPI-licensing constructions not to be "downward monotone" functions as proposed by Ladusaw (1979, 1980), but to be "non-veridicality", defined as follows:

**Definition.** Let *Op* be a monadic propositional operator. Then *Op* is *veridical* just in case *Op p* $\rightarrow p$ is logically valid. Otherwise *Op* is *nonveridical*.

---

[17] Such a suggestion may not be entirely implausible. Compare the English expression, "I looked all around, but no Masha." The ability of a quantifier like *no* to co-occur with a proper noun is as much in need of explanation as the ability of Russian proper nouns to occur with Gen Neg.

The fact that some NPs can occur only in non-veridical contexts (*any student, the slightest sound*) increases the plausibility of the conjecture that some NPs (*a student*) may have a "less referential" meaning in a non-veridical context than they do in a veridical context. See also the explorations of related issues concerning Russian indefinites in Pereltsvaig (2000).

Negation is clearly a non-veridical operator. If intensional contexts are also non-veridical, then this may be the unifying property we are looking for. But although the majority of intensional verbs (as well as modal adverbs and other intensional operators not under discussion here) function as non-veridical operators, not all of them do: *know*, for instance, is intensional but veridical. It is intensional because of the failure of substitutivity of co-extensional NPs in its complement to always preserve truth, but veridical because *John knows that p* entails (or more likely presupposes, but in any case requires) the truth of *p*.

But *know* in fact does not license subjunctive complements in Romance languages (except sometimes under negation!) nor in Russian (at all). So the fact that not all intensional contexts are non-veridical may not be a bad thing: non-veridicality may provide the unifying property that connects negative contexts with an appropriate subset of intensional contexts.

A full exploration of the relevance of non-veridicality to the occurrence of Genitive on NPs in such contexts awaits further work. And such work should also take into account the "quantificational" notions that have played a role in earlier attempts to unify the semantics of Genitive case. There may be more than one way that the 'reduced referentiality' of Gen Neg NPs comes about, licensed by different classes of verbs and by negated verbs. (Cf. multiple kinds of 'Imperfective' meanings.) The property-type idea may be correct for a number of cases, but other 'quantity'-based ideas may be better for other cases.

### 3.3 Speculative Conclusions

We are still optimistic that it will be possible to support traditional claims that Gen NPs are "less referential, less individuated" than Nom/Acc NPs, by combining the diathesis ideas we've been working on together with existing work on Partitive/Accusative alternations in Finnish and existing work on 'weak/strong' NP objects in a number of languages, and together with existing work on existential sentences.

One new ingredient that our work may offer to this line of investigation is an explicit connection between semantics of existential sentences and semantics of weak/strong objects in transitive sentences, and some account of how the verbal diathesis plays a role in both cases. And in the opposite direction, the broader semantic issues discussed here may help shed light on the semantic connection between Subject Gen Neg (the Nom/Gen alternation) and Object Gen Neg (the Acc/Gen alternation).

Given that we have analyzed Subject Gen Neg as always involving existential sentences, we had been having trouble seeing how we could extend a comparable treatment to Object Gen Neg, since only in a small subset of cases does Object Gen Neg involve anything like "existential meanings": it seems to in (18a), but not in (19a), for instance. But if we study the arguments of McNally (1992, 1997, 1998), recent work of Landman (Landman 2003), and ongoing work by Kamp and Bende

Farkas (2001), they all have argued that the NP in an existential sentence in English, German, and possibly in general, does not have normal type e (nor generalized quantifier) meaning, but rather a property type meaning (<e,t> or <s,<e,t>>).

If we could find more support for the arguments that the NP in an existential sentence is interpreted as property type <e,t>[18], whereas the subject position of a Locative or other ordinary sentence is type e, then the parallel between Subject Gen Neg and Object Gen Neg would be at a structural level: in each case the relevant argument is "demoted" from e-type to <e,t>-type, with syntactic and semantic consequences. The extent of the syntactic consequences apparently varies from language to language, and may vary within a language for Subjects vs. Objects; on many views, the Russian Gen Neg subject is no longer subject, but the Gen Neg object is still an object, although a 'weakened' one.

But we are not yet convinced that Gen NPs should all be assigned property type; in Russian in particular proper names occur in sentences that we are inclined to classify as existential, such as (10b) above. Quite possibly the proposed distinction in semantic type is both too rough to capture all the semantic distinctions that really need to be made, and too sharp a distinction to capture the fact that in many pairs of examples a Gen NP and a corresponding Nom- or Acc-marked NP may in fact share readings. Non-veridicality might naturally license decreased existential commitment. Intensionality might rather license decreased specificity. But we may very well not have yet identified the most crucial semantic properties; all of the attempts so far have achieved at best a partial account.

In conclusion, we have not settled the issue of whether the Gen Neg construction always involves a diathesis shift of the Gen Neg NP to property type or not. We have outlined a number of advantages such an approach might offer and a number of problems that argue against it.

As is often the case in linguistics, we find that no two phenomena are completely alike, but linguistic analysis and cross-linguistic comparisons help us, first, to identify generalizations that need to be accounted for, and second, to find formal properties through which we can capture the similarities and differences among the phenomena we observe. The Genitive of Negation and the 'intensional' Genitive in Russian remain a great challenge in part because we still do not have a satisfactory grasp of how broad a generalization their distribution involves. More work on both the empirical generalizations and the identification of explanatorily significant semantic properties still lies ahead.

# References

Ackerman, F., Moore, J.C.: Proto-properties and grammatical encoding: a correspondence theory of argument selection: Stanford monographs in linguistics. CSLI Publications, Stanford, Calif. (2001)

Apresjan, J.D.: Syntaksičeskie priznaki leksem [Syntactic features of lexemes]. Russian Linguistics 9, 289–317 (1985)

---

[18] We will say <e,t> for simplicity even though it may really be <s,<e,t>>.

Apresjan, J.D.: Tipy informacii dlja poverxnostno-semantičeskogo komponenta modeli "Smysl Tekst" [Types of Information for the Surface-Semantic Component of the Model "Meaning Text"]. Wiener Slavistische Almanach/Škola "Jazyki Russkoj Kultury", Vienna/Moscow (1980)

Arutjunova, N.D.: Predloženie i ego smysl [The Sentence and its Meaning]. Nauka, Moscow (1976)

Arutjunova, N.D., Širjaev, E.N.: Russkoe predloženie. Bytijnyj tip (struktura i znacenie). [The Russian Sentence. The Existential Type (Structure and Meaning)]. Russkij jazyk, Moscow (1983)

Babby, L.: Nominalization in Russian. In: Browne, W., Dornisch, E., Kondrashova, N., Zec, D. (eds.) Formal Approaches to Slavic Linguistics: The Cornell Meeting 1995, pp. 54–83. Michigan Slavic Publications, Ann Arbor (1997)

Babby, L.H.: Existential Sentences and Negation in Russian. Karoma Publishers, Ann Arbor, Michigan (1980)

Babby, L.H.: The genitive of negation: a unified analysis. In: Franks, S., King, T.H., Yadroff, M. (eds.) FASL 9. Annual Workshop on Formal Approaches to Slavic Linguistics: The Bloomington Meeting 2000, pp. 39–55. Michigan Slavic Publications, Ann Arbor (2001)

Babyonyshev, M.A.: Structural Connections in Syntax and Processing: Studies in Russian and Japanese. Ph.D. dissertation, MIT (1996)

Bailyn, J.F.: The Case of Q. In: Arnaudova, O., Browne, W., Rivero, M.L., Stojanovic, D.(eds.) FASL 12. Annual Workshop on Formal Approaches to Slavic Languages: The Ottawa Meeting 2003, pp. 1–35. Michigan Slavic Publications, Ann Arbor (2004)

Borschev, V., Partee, B.H.: Bytijnye predloženija i otricanie v russkom jazyke: semantika i kommunikativnaja struktura. [Existential sentences and negation in Russian: semantics and communicative structure]. In: Narin'yani, A.S. (ed.) Dialogue '98: Computational Linguistics and its Applications, pp. 173–182. Xéter, Kazan (1998a)

Borschev, V., Partee, B.H.: Formal and lexical semantics and the genitive in negated existential sentences in Russian. In: Bošković, Ž., Franks, S., Snyder, W. (eds.) Formal Approaches to Slavic Linguistics 6: The Connecticut Meeting 1997, pp. 75–96. Michigan Slavic Publications, Ann Arbor (1998b)

Borschev, V., Partee, B.H.: The Russian genitive of negation in existential sentences: the role of Theme-Rheme structure reconsidered. In: Hajičová, E., Sgall, P., Hana, J., Hoskovec, T. (eds.) Travaux du Cercle Linguistique de Prague (nouvelle série), vol. 4, pp. 185–250. John Benjamins Pub. Co., Amsterdam (2002a)

Borschev, V., Partee, B.H.: O semantike bytijnyx predloženij (On the semantics of existential sentences). Semiotika i Informatika 37, 59–77 (2002b)

Borschev, V., Partee, B.H.: The Russian genitive of negation: Theme-rheme structure or perspective structure? Journal of Slavic Linguistics 10, 105–144 (2002c)

Borschev, V., Paducheva, E.V., Partee, B.H., Testelets, Y.G., Yanovich, I.: Sentential and constituent negation in Russian BE-sentences revisited. In: Lavine, J., Franks, S.L., Tasseva-Kurktchieva, M., Filip, H. (eds.) FASL 14. Formal Approaches to Slavic Linguistics: The Princeton Meeting 2005, pp. 50–65. Michigan Slavic Publications, Ann Arbor (2006)

Bresnan, J.: A realistic transformational grammar. In: Halle, M., Bresnan, J., Miller, G.A. (eds.) Linguistic Theory and Psychological Reality, pp. 1–59. The MIT Press, Cambridge, MA (1978)

Bresnan, J.: Locative inversion and the architecture of Universal Grammar. Language 70, 72–131 (1994)

Brown, S.: The Syntax of Negation in Russian: A Minimalist Approach. CSLI Publications, Stanford (1999)

Chvany, C.V.: On the Syntax of BE-Sentences in Russian. Slavica, Cambridge, MA (1975)

de Hoop, H.: Case assignment and generalized quantifiers. In: Proceedings of NELS 19, pp. 176–190. GLSA, Amherst, MA (1989)

de Hoop, H.: Restrictions on existential sentences and object-scrambling: Some facts from Dutch. In: Halpern, A.L. (ed.) The Proceedings of WCCFL 9, Stanford, Calif., pp. 277–288 (1990)

de Hoop, H.: Case configuration and noun phrase interpretation. University of Groningen, Ph.D. Dissertation (1992)

de Hoop, H.: On the characterization of the weak-strong distinction. In: Bach, E., Jelinek, E., Kratzer, A., Partee, B.H. (eds.) Quantification in Natural Languages, pp. 421–450. Kluwer, Dordrecht (1995)

Diesing, M.: Indefinites. MIT Press, Cambridge, MA (1992a)

Diesing, M.: Bare Plural Subjects and the Derivation of Logical Representations. Linguistic Inquiry 22, 353–380 (1992b)

Diesing, M., Jelinek, E.: The Syntax and Semantics of Object Shift. Working Papers in Scandinavian Syntax 51 (1993)

Dowty, D.: Governed transformations as lexical rules in a Montague Grammar. Linguistic Inquiry 9, 393–426 (1978)

Dowty, D.: Thematic proto-roles and argument selection. Language 67, 547–619 (1991)

Dowty, D.: The semantic asymmetry of 'argument alternations' (and why it matters). In: van der Meer, G., ter Meulen, A.G.B. (eds.) Groninger Arbeiten zur germanistischen Linguistik, vol. 44, Center for Language and Cognition, Groningen (2001)

Farkas, D.F., de Swart, H.: The Semantics of Incorporation: From Argument Structure to Discourse Transparency: Stanford Monographs in Linguistics. CSLI Publications, Stanford, CA (2003)

Franks, S.: Parameters of Slavic Morphosyntax. Oxford University Press, Oxford (1995)

Giannakidou, A.: The Semantic Licensing of NPIs and the Modern Greek Subjunctive. Language and Cognition 4, 55–68 (1994)

Giannakidou, A.: Polarity Sensitivity as (Non)Veridical Dependency. John Benjamins, Amsterdam (1998)

Harves, S.A.: Unaccusative Syntax in Russian. Ph.D. dissertation, Princeton University (2002)

Hopper, P., Thompson, S.: Transitivity in grammar and discourse. Language 56, 251–299 (1981)

Ickovič, V.A.: Očerki sintaksičeskoj normy [Remarks on the syntactic norm]. In: Zolotova, G.A. (ed.) Sintaksis i norma, Moscow, Nauka, pp. 43–106 (1974)

Jakobson, R.: Beitrag zur allgemeinen Kasuslehre: Gesamtbedeutungen der russische Kasus. In: Selected Writings II, pp. 23–71. Mouton, The Hague (originally published in 1936) (1971)

Kagan, O.: A modal analysis of genitive case in Russian. Ms. Jerusalem (2005)

Kamp, H., Bende-Farkas, A.: Indefinites and binding: From specificity to incorporation. Lecture notes from the 13th ESSLLI summer school in Helsinki, Ms. Stuttgart (2001)

Keenan, E.: Towards a Universal Definition of "Subject". In: Li, C. (ed.) Subject and Topic, pp. 303–333. Academic Press, New York (1976)

Kiparsky, P.: Remarks on denominal verbs. In: Alsina, A., Bresnan, J., Sells, P. (eds.) Complex Predicates, pp. 473–500. CSLI Publications, Stanford (1997)

Klenin, E.: Quantification, partitivity, and the genitive of negation in Russian. In: Comrie, B. (ed.) Classification of Grammatical Categories, pp. 163–182. Linguistic Research, Inc., Edmonton (1978)

Krifka, M.: Manner in dative alternation. In: Bird, S., Carnie, A., Haugen, J.D., Norquest, P. (eds.) WCCFL 18. Proceedings of the Eighteenth West Coast Conference on Formal Linguistics, pp. 1–14. Cascadilla Press, Somerville/Medford, MA (1999)

Krifka, M.: Semantic and pragmatic conditions for the Dative Alternation. Korean Journal of English Language and Linguistics 4, 1–32 (2004)

Ladusaw, W.: Polarity Sensitivity as Inherent Scope Relations. Ph.D. dissertation, University of Texas at Austin (1979)

Ladusaw, W.: On the notion "affective" in the analysis of negative polarity items. Journal of Linguistic Research 1, 1–16 (1980)

Landman, F.: Indefinites and the Type of Sets: Explorations in Semantics. Blackwell Publishing, Oxford (2003)

Levin, B.: English Verbal Diathesis: Lexicon Project Working Papers \#32 MIT, Cambridge, MA

Levin, B., Rappaport Hovav, M.: Handout Spain: What Alternates in the Dative Alternation? In: The 2002 Conference on Role and Reference Grammar: New Topics in Functional Linguistics: The Cognitive and Discoursive Dimension of Morphology, Syntax and Semantics, July 27-28, 2002, Universidad de La Rioja, Logrono, Spain (2002)

McNally, L.: An interpretation for the English Existential Construction. Ph.D. dissertation, University of California at Santa Cruz (1992)

McNally, L.: A semantics for the English existential construction: Outstanding Dissertations in Linguistics. Garland, New York (1997)

McNally, L.: Existential sentences without existential quantification. Linguistics and Philosophy 21, 353–392 (1998)

Mel'chuk, I.A., Xolodovič, A.A.: K teorii grammatičeskogo zaloga 'Towards a theory of grammatical voice'. Narody Azii i Afriki 4, 111–124 (1970)

Mustajoki, A.: Padež dopolnenija v russkix otricatel'nyx predloženijax 1: Izyskanija novyx metodov v izučenii staroj problemy: Slavica Helsingiensia 2. Helsinki University Press, Helsinki (1985)

Mustajoki, A., Heino, H.: Case selection for the direct object in Russian negative clauses. Part II: Report on a Statistical Analysis: Slavica Helsingiensia 9. Department of Slavonic Languages, University of Helsinki, Helsinki (1991)

Neidle, C.: The Role of Case in Russian Syntax. Linguistics and Philosophy, Ph.D. dissertation, MIT (1982)

Neidle, C.: The Role of Case in Russian Syntax: Studies in Natural Language and Linguistic Theory 10. Kluwer, Dordrecht (1988)

Padučeva, E.V.: O semantike sintaksisa: materialy k transformacionnoj grammatike russkogo jazyka [On the Semantics of Syntax: Materials toward the Transformational Grammar of Russian]. Nauka, Moscow (1974)

Padučeva, E.V.: O semantičeskom podxode k sintaksisu i genitivnom sub"ekte glagola BYT' [On the semantic approach to syntax and the genitive subject of the verb BYT' 'BE']. Russian Linguistics 16, 53–63 (1992)

Padučeva, E.V.: Roditel'nyj sub"ekta v otricatel'nom predloženii: sintaksis ili semantika? [Genitive subject in a negative sentence: syntax or semantics?]. Voprosy Jazykoznanija 2, 101–116 (1997)

Padučeva, E.V.: Diateza i diatetičeskij sdvig ('Diathesis and diathesis shift'). Russian Linguistics 26, 179–215 (2002)

Padučeva, E.V.: Dinamičeskie modeli v semantike leksiki [Dynamic models in lexical sem-
antics]. Jazyki slavjanskoj kultury, Moscow (2004)

Partee, B.H., Borschev, V.: Genitive of negation and scope of negation in Russian existential
sentences. In: Toman, J. (ed.) FASL 10. Annual Workshop on Formal Approaches to Slavic
Linguistics: the Second Ann Arbor Meeting 2001, pp. 181–200. Michigan Slavic Publications, Ann Arbor (2002)

Partee, B.H., Borschev, V.: The Russian genitive of negation and diathesis alternation:
interaction of lexical and compositional semantics. In: Handout for TAG+7: 7th International Workshop on Tree Adjoining Grammars and Related Formalisms, May 20-22, 2004,
Simon Fraser University, Vancouver (2004a)

Partee, B.H., Borschev, V.: The semantics of Russian Genitive of Negation: The nature and role
of Perspectival Structure. In: Watanabe, K., Young, R.B. (eds.) Proceedings of Semantics
and Linguistic Theory (SALT) 14, pp. 212–234. CLC Publications, Ithaca, NY (2004b)

Partee, B.H., Borschev, V.: Information structure, Perspectival Structure, diathesis alternation,
and the Russian Genitive of Negation. In: Gyuris, B., Kálmán, L., Piñón, C., Varasdi, K.
(eds.) LoLa 9. Proceedings of Ninth Symposium on Logic and Language, Besenyötelek,
Hungary, August 24-26, 2006, pp. 120–129. Research Institute for Linguistics, Hungarian
Academy of Sciences, Theoretical Linguistics Programme, Eötvös Loránd University,
Budapest (2006)

Partee, B.H., Borschev, V.: Existential sentences, BE, and the Genitive of Negation in Russian.
In: Comorovski, I., von Heusinger, K. (eds.) Existence: Semantics and Syntax, Kluwer/
Springer, Dordrecht (in press)

Pereltsvaig, A.: Monotonicity-based vs. veridicality-based approaches to negative polarity:
evidence from Russian. In: King, T.H., Sekerina, I.A. (eds.) Formal Approaches to Slavic
Linguistics: The Philadelphia Meeting 1999, pp. 328–346. Michigan Slavic Publications,
Ann Arbor (2000)

Perlmutter, D.: Impersonal passives and the unaccusative hypothesis. In: BLS 4. Proceedings of
the Fourth Annual Meeting of the Berkeley Linguistics Society, pp. 157–189. Berkeley
Linguistics Society, Berkeley, CA (1978)

Perlmutter, D., Moore, J.: Language-internal explanation: The distribution of Russian imper-
sonals. Language 78, 619–650 (2002)

Pesetsky, D.: Paths and Categories. Ph.D. dissertation, MIT (1982)

Peškovskij, A.M.: Russkij sintaksis v naučnom osveščenii [Russian syntax in a scientific light],
7th edn. Gosučpedgiz, Moscow (1956) (3rd edn. 1928)

Testelets, Y.G.: Vvedenie v obščij sintaksis [Introduction to General Syntax]. Rossijskij
Gosudarstvennyj Gumanitarnyj Universitet (RGGU), Moscow (2001)

Timberlake, A.: Hierarchies in the Genitive of Negation. Slavic and East European Journal 19,
123–138 (1975)

Ueda, M.: Set-membership interpretations and the genitive of negation. Russian Linguistics 17,
237–261 (1993)

van Geenhoven, V.: Semantic incorporation: a uniform semantics for West Greenlandic noun
incorporation and West Germanic bare plural configurations. In: CLS 31: Papers from the
Thirty First Meeting of the Chicago Linguistic Society, Chicago Linguistic Society, Chicago
(1995)

van Geenhoven, V.: Semantic Incorporation and Indefinite Descriptions: Semantic and Syntactic Aspects of Noun Incorporation in West Greenlandic. Ph.D. Dissertation, University of Tübingen (1996)

van Geenhoven, V.: On the argument structure of some noun incorporating verbs in West Greenlandic. In: Butt, M., Geuder, W. (eds.) The projection of arguments: Lexical and compositional factors, pp. 225–263. CSLI Publications, Stanford (1998a)

Van Geenhoven, V.: Semantic Incorporation and Indefinite Descriptions: Semantic and Syntactic Aspects of Noun Incorporation in West Greenlandic: Dissertations in linguistics. CSLI Publications, Stanford, Calif. (1998b)

Van Geenhoven, V., McNally, L.: On the property analysis of opaque complements. Lingua 115, 885–914 (2005)

Xolodovič, A.A.: Zalog I: Opredelenie. Isčislenie [Voice I: Definition and Calculus]. In: Kategorija zaloga. Materialy konferencii [The Category of Voice. Conference Materials], Leningrad, pp. 2–26 (1970)

Zimmermann, T.E.: On the proper treatment of opacity in certain verbs. Natural Language Semantics 1, 148–171 (1993)

# A Whether Forecast

Kjell Johan Sæbø

University of Oslo
Department of European Languages
k.j.sabo@ilos.uio.no

**Abstract.** It is a well-known fact that only factive propositional attitude predicates are felicitous with *wh-* (indirect question) complements.
It has also been noted that so-called emotive factive predicates are only
felicitous with some, not all, indirect question complements. But the
reasons for these two constraints have remained unclear. I propose a
competition-based explanation in terms of optimality theoretic pragmatics: Due to the competition with factive predicates, predicates like *believe*
are infelicitous with complements automatically verifying the factive
presupposition; and emotive factive predicates are infelicitous with *wh-*
complements to the extent that these complements compete with more
informative *that* complements. To arrive at these results, it is necessary
to assume an analysis of questions on which they denote propositions
and to be more careful than has been customary about the formulation
of the presuppositions of factive and what I call super-factive predicates.

## 1   Introduction: Two Problems

1. Since Boër (1978) and Lewis (1982), it has been a mystery why not *believe*
but only *know* (or generally, as it seems, only factive predicates) are felicitous
with *wh-* (indirect question) complements:

(1)     Nani knows how high Mt. Shkhara is.

(2)     #Nani believes how high Mt. Shkhara is.

(3)     Nani knows that Mt. Shkhara is 5068 m high.

(4)     Nani believes that Mt. Shkhara is 5068 m high.

On a standard view, the view taken, i.a., by Kiparsky and Kiparsky (1970),
*know* and *believe* only differ semantically in the factive presupposition that only
*know* has, and, *wh-* and *that* complement clauses uniformly denote propositions
(the former denoting world-dependent propositions, the intension a nonconstant
function from worlds; the latter denoting world-independent propositions, the
intension a constant function from worlds). I will refer to this view as the **simple
semantics**.

It should thus be possible to interpret (2) as saying that however high Mount
Shkhara is, Nani believes that it is that high – that is, the same as (1) (minus the
factive presupposition). But in fact, (2) does not seem to have any interpretation.

B.D. ten Cate and H.W. Zeevat (Eds.): TbiLLC 2005, LNAI 4363, pp. 189–199, 2007.
© Springer-Verlag Berlin Heidelberg 2007

There have been various attempts at accounting for this (see Egré (2005) for a recent survey). The simple semantics has been challenged, e.g., by Ginzburg (1995: 582ff.), who suggests that a verb like *know* takes facts in its denotation, while a verb like *believe* takes only propositions, and a question cannot be coerced to a proposition. This account has been criticized for being essentially stipulative (Egré 2005). It would certainly be nice if we could maintain that both *know* and *believe* embed propositions. I will adhere to the simple semantics – the theory of Groenendijk and Stokhof (1982), opting for a pragmatic, competition-based account vindicating suggestions made by Boër (1978: 333):

> It is the inherent factivity of 'who'-clauses which makes them bad company for nonfactive verbs of propositional attitude. Usually, the pragmatic point of using a nonfactive is to leave open the question of the truth-value of the proposition which is the object of that attitude, and this point is frustrated by the semantics of 'who'-clauses.

I will base this account on Bidirectional Optimality Theory (BOT) and on the ideas developed by Blutner (1998, 2000, 2002, 2004, 2006).

2. Elliott(1982) and Grimshaw (1977) noted that emotive predicates like *incredible* are only felicitous with some *wh-* complements:

(5)    I agree it's amazing what sounds they can make.

(6)    ?It's amazing which team won the Champions League.

(7)    It's amazing that Valencia won the Champions League.

(8)    #It is amazing whether Real won the Champions League.

Their conclusion was that these predicates do not embed interrogatives but exclamatives, and, in particular, *whether* clauses can only be interrogatives. This view has met with criticism more recently (Huddleston 1993, Lahiri 2000, d'Avis 2002, Abels 2005). At any rate, as long as the semantic difference between interrogatives and exclamatives or that between *know* and *amazing* is not clear, it is not explanative. Again, my account will be based on BOT, centering on the competition between *wh-* and *that*.

## 2    The Semantics of *Savoir Si* and *Croire Que*

Groenendijk and Stokhof (e.g. 1982) work with two-sorted type theory (Gallin 1975), and so will I. Here, world variables are in the semantic representations and can be abstracted over, and there is a designated variable $(i)$ for the actual world.

The semantics of some salient words can be represented as follows:

$$that'_i = \lambda\phi_{<s,t>}\ \phi$$
$$whether'_i = \lambda\phi_{<s,t>}\ \lambda j\ (\phi_j = \phi_i)$$
$$know'_i = \lambda\psi_{<s,t>}\ \lambda x\ \mathcal{B}_i(\psi)(x)_< \lambda i(\psi_i) >$$
$$believe'_i = \lambda\psi_{<s,t>}\ \lambda x\ \mathcal{B}_i(\psi)(x)$$

The subjunction *that* simply denotes the identity function on propositions. Normally, neither that nor the subjunction *whether* will meet a type $< s, t >$, proposition denoting expression but a type $t$, truth value denoting expression; however, a composition rule enables the function to apply to the sister's intension:

**Intensional Functional Application**

$$f_{<<s,a>,b>} + \xi_{<a>} = f(\lambda i \xi)$$

The angled brackets in the representation of *know* enclose the presupposition of factivity. This subscript notation has become customary (cf. Beaver 1997). I assume a standard, general formulation of presupposition verification (CG = Common Ground):

**Presupposition Verification**

$\phi_{i< \pi >}$ is only defined if $\pi$ follows from the Common Ground at $i$ $(CG_i \subseteq \pi)$.

Note that the factive presupposition cannot simply be $\psi$. When $\psi$ is a *whether* clause, the sentence would presuppose that $\phi$ has the same truth value as in the actual world. That is, the sentence would presuppose what the subject of *know* is claimed to know, and that is obviously too strong. The presupposition of (1) would only be verified if the hearer and the speaker, conscious of the Common Ground, were to know how high Mt. Shkhara is. Presupposed is instead that which in the *whether* case is a tautology but in the *that* case reduces to $\psi$, the complement proposition. I will call this, the **diagonal** (cf. e.g. Zimmermann 1991), the *rectified complement proposition* (the RCP).

With these components in place, we can represent the meaning of the sentence (9) compositionally in the tree below. The presupposition of factivity emerges as the tautology.

(9)    Elle sait    s'        il pleut.
       She knows whether it' s raining.

$$\mathcal{B}_i(\lambda j \ (il \ pleut_j = il \ pleut_i))(elle)_{< \lambda i(il \ pleut_i = il \ pleut_i) >}$$
$$= \mathcal{B}_i(\lambda j \ (il \ pleut_j = il \ pleut_i))(elle)_{< \mathcal{T} >}$$

$elle \quad \lambda x \ \mathcal{B}_i(\lambda j \ (il \ pleut_j = il \ pleut_i))(x)_{< \lambda i(\lambda j(il \ pleut_j = il \ pleut_i)_i) >}$

$sait \qquad \lambda j \ (il \ pleut_j = il \ pleut_i)$

$s \ ' \qquad\qquad il \ pleut_i$

# 3   Blocked Content, Blocked Form

I would like to propose that (2) (or any case of *believe wh-*) is systematically (and thus in a sense conventionally) dispreferred because of the competition it gets from (1) (or any case of *know wh-*), which due to its factive presupposition is only compatible with the situation that the Rectified Complement Proposition (RCP) follows from the Common Ground (CG) – a necessity when the complement is a question; while (2) is left with the implicature that it does not – an impossibility.

## 3.1   Contingent Case: Partial Blocking

Let us first consider the case of *know that* versus *believe that*.

A particular interpretation of a given expression can be blocked if it can be expressed more precisely by an alternative expression. Bidirectional Optimality Theory (BOT) (Blutner 1998, ..., 2006) can account for such blocking effects. Consider the minimal pair (10) and (11), where the factive presupposition is in both cases verified but the factive *know* is preferred over the nonfactive *believe*:

(10)   Hi Polly. Love your column. I have a difficult question. I am married. But I recently met a woman who I really like and am attracted to. When I met her, we really hit it off and talked for hours. I was very tempted to, as they say, "come on" to her, but I did not. She is unmarried. I did not know how she would react – she knows I am married.

(11)   Hi Polly. Love your column. I have a difficult question. I am married. But I recently met a woman who I really like and am attracted to. When I met her, we really hit it off and talked for hours. I was very tempted to, as they say, "come on" to her, but I did not. She is unmarried. I did not know how she would react – ?? she believes I am married.

Note that the oddity of (11) does not follow from the semantics of *believe*. The absence of factivity is just as compatible with the situation where factivity is verified as with the situation where factivity is not verified. In BOT, however, the pairing of the nonfactive *believe* with the situation that factivity is verified can emerge as suboptimal and be blocked. It is a partial blocking, since pairing *believe* with the situation that factivity is not verified will emerge as optimal. Partial blocking is mostly accounted for in terms of the notion of weak optimality, but here it is sufficient to use the notion of strong (bidirectional) optimality, for a pair of an interpretation (or "content") and an expression (or "form").

### Strong Bidirectional Optimality

A form-content pair $< f, c >$ is strongly optimal iff
$f$ is at least as good for $c$ as any candidate form $f'$ and
$c$ is at least as good for $f$ as any candidate content $c'$.

Goodness can be defined in terms of a variety of constraints; here it suffices to use the measure of the probability of the content given the meaning of the form, and only this; the two competing forms are in themselves equally harmonic.

## Goodness

$< f, c >$ is at least as good as $< f', c' >$ iff $P(c/[\![f]\!]) \geq P(c'/[\![f']\!])$

Consider, in the abstract, the four form-content pairs $< f_1, c_1 >$, $< f_1, c_2 >$, $< f_2, c_1 >$, $< f_2, c_2 >$, where $c_1$ and $c_2$ are mutually exclusive and jointly exhaustive specifications of the meaning of $f_1$ or $f_2$. If $c_1$ is more probable given $f_1$ than given $f_2$, this means that $f_1$ is more informative than $f_2$ in relation to $c_1$, reflecting the Gricean Maxim of Quantity in the speaker's, production perspective; and if $c_2$ is no less probable than $c_1$ given $f_2$, $c_2$ is a Quantity-based conversational implicature of $f_2$ in the hearer's, interpretation perspective.

Let us now pair the forms ($f_1$) *Jane knows* $\psi$ and ($f_2$) *Jane believes* $\psi$ with the pair of contents ($\mathcal{B}_i(\psi)(Jane)$, i.e. Jane believes $\psi$, the common denominator for the two more specific interpretations, and) ($c_1$) $CG_i \subseteq \lambda i(\psi_i)$ (i.e. the RCP follows from the Common Ground, factivity is verified) and $\neg(CG_i \subseteq \lambda i(\psi_i))$ (i.e. the RCP fails to follow from the Common Ground, factivity is falsified) (see **Table 1**).

**Table 1.** Probability of factivity $\pm$ verified given $\pm$ factivity

| $P(\cdot/[\![\cdot]\!])$ | $CG_i \subseteq \lambda i(\psi_i)$ | $\neg(CG_i \subseteq \lambda i(\psi_i))$ |
|---|---|---|
| *Jane knows* $\psi$ | $\Rightarrow 1$ | $0$ |
| *Jane believes* $\psi$ | $\frac{1}{2}$ | $\Rightarrow \frac{1}{2}$ |

The cells in the tableau represent the conditional probability values of the contents ($c_1$ and $c_2$) given the semantics of the forms ($f_1$ and $f_2$). These values should be as high as possible. We see that the conditional probability of ($c_1/[\![f_1]\!]$) is maximal – the best situation – while that of ($c_2/[\![f_1]\!]$) is (due to the presupposition) minimal – the worst situation. The upper left 1 compares favourably to the lower left $\frac{1}{2}$ as well, reflecting the Gricean Maxim of Quantity: The form $f_1$, but not the form $f_2$, is maximally informative with regard to the content $c_1$, and the latter form is blocked for this content.

Basically, ($c_2/[\![f_2]\!]$) has the same conditional probability value as ($c_1/[\![f_2]\!]$), however, because its value is higher than that of ($c_2/[\![f_1]\!]$), the content $c_1$ is blocked for the form $f_2$, reflecting a Gricean conversational implicature. Hence the oddness of (11). "She believes I am married" is forced to convey that the RCP (here that I am married) does not follow from the CG. If it does follow, the speaker should choose (10); (11) with its implicature clashes with CG reality.

This clash is a mild one, as it is a contingent, a conversational matter. The speaker may have reason to ignore the prior "cancellation" of the implicature, creating a shift in perspective, a suspension of belief in the Common Ground. What is blocked is a certain interpretation for a certain form, and vice versa;

and deblocking is possible. So although the oddity of (11) is distinct enough, it does not border on ungrammaticality.

## 3.2  A Priori Case: Total Blocking

But in addition to this contingent *that* case, there is the apriori *wh-* case.

(12)    #She believes whether I am married.

Here the RCP follows from the – any – CG by virtue of the meaning of *whether*. The reason the last sentence in (11) is not out *per se* is that it *can* make sense – it depends on the CG; whereas the reason (12) *is* out *per se* is that it *cannot* make sense – irrespectively of the CG. Before the sentence is finished, the signal that the RCP does not follow from the CG clashes with the signal that it does.

Recall from Section 3.1 that *Jane believes* $\psi$ implicates $\neg(\mathrm{CG}_i \subseteq \lambda i(\psi_i))$; for $\psi = \lambda j\ (\phi_j = \phi_i)$ this implicature amounts to saying that the tautology fails to follow from the Common Ground, which is impossible, since a (the) tautology follows from any set of propositions.

More generally, whenever $\psi$ comes from a *wh-* clause, we necessarily have that $\mathrm{CG}_i \subseteq \lambda i(\psi_i)$. Only one content is thus possible, and the form *Jane believes* $\psi$ is blocked for that content because the $\neg(\mathrm{CG}_i \subseteq \lambda i(\psi_i))$ implicature persists.

As long as only the truth conditions of a sentence like (12) are considered, there is nothing to distinguish it from the corresponding *know* sentence:

**Table 2.** Probability of factivity verified given ±factivity; $\psi = $ *whether* $\phi$

| $P(\cdot/[\![\cdot]\!])$ | $\mathrm{CG}_i \subseteq \lambda i(\psi_i)$ | $\neg(\mathrm{CG}_i \subseteq \lambda i(\psi_i))$ |
|---|---|---|
| *Jane knows* $\psi$ | 1 | 0 |
| *Jane believes* $\psi$ | 1 | 0 |

Once the implicature is taken into account, however, this changes:

*Jane believes* $\psi$ implicates $\neg(\mathrm{CG}_i \subseteq \lambda i(\psi_i))$. For $\psi = $ *whether* $\phi$, this is

$$\neg(\mathrm{CG}_i \subseteq \lambda i(\lambda j\ (\phi_j = \phi_i)_i)) =$$
$$\neg(\mathrm{CG}_i \subseteq \lambda i(\phi_i = \phi_i)) =$$
$$\neg(\mathrm{CG}_i \subseteq \top) = \bot$$

In words, the *believe* sentence conversationally implicates the contradiction. This causes what amounts to a "total blocking", accounting for its infelicity, bordering on ungrammaticality, while anchoring it in pragmatics.

Note that what might save cases like (11) – the speaker may have reason to disregard the prior "cancellation" of the implicature – could not apply to (12); a simultaneous "cancellation" cannot be disregarded.

On this account, then, the inappropriateness of a form is attributed to its neurotic content. Zimmermann (2006) offers an account of the infelicity of (the German version of) *Jane wants to know that* $\phi$ along similar lines.

There are some uses of *believe* where the missing factivity is not the only distinctive feature vis-à-vis *know*, so that there is no minimal competition in this regard. One such use can be paraphrased by *accept*. When *believe* is used in this sense, *Jane believes* $\psi$ presupposes that someone tries to convince her of $\psi$, and the blocking with regard to *wh-* complements is to a certain extent lifted. This provides indirect evidence in support of the competition-based account.

(13)    No one believes how old I am.

(14)    I think he actually believes how serious this is now.

(15)    The American 1st Marine Division answered but their operator refused to believe who our operator was speaking for.

It is true that we still do not find *whether* complements. The reason, it can be argued, lies in a competition between *whether* and *that* – a phenomenon which plays a major role in the next section.

## 4  Surprise Predicates and the *wh-* / *that* Competition

It has often been noted that "surprise predicates", like *surprised* or *surprising*, do not embed polar interrogatives (cf. e.g. Abels 2005). Thus:

(16)   #I'm surprised (at) whether he was found guilty.

This has been contrasted with other *wh-* clauses which such predicates do embed:

(17)    We will be surprised who goes to Heaven.

So in much of the relevant literature, the common notion has been that there is something special about *whether* clauses. Elliott (1982) and Grimshaw (1977) held that surprise predicates do not embed interrogatives but exclamatives and that *whether* clauses can only be interrogatives, not exclamatives.

Abels (2005) assumes that these clauses denote singleton sets of propositions, contradicting presuppositions carried by surprise predicates. However, first, there is scarce evidence for this assumption. Indeed, in the theory of Groenendijk and Stokhof (1982), any *wh-* clause has the same type of denotation – a proposition. The *who* clause in (17), say, denotes the set of worlds where the set of people going to Heaven equals the set of people going to Heaven in the actual world. Second, the proposed presupposition would seem to be more reasonable as an entailment.

Moreover and more importantly, more thorough investigations, some made by Lahiri (2002), suggest that the facts are really not as clear-cut as previous work has made them appear. Rather, we can observe that

– some *wh-* clauses, beyond *whether* clauses, are easier than others,

– some surprise predicates are stricter than others,

– there are cases where surprise predicates do embed polar interrogatives.

The total picture suggests a gradience in several dimensions and an account in terms of a competition with *that* clauses. The "easy" *wh-* clauses, the "sloppy" emotive predicates, and the cases where polar interrogatives are possible all serve to, in various ways, weaken the competition with corresponding *that* clauses; this is what makes them relatively felicitous.

The "strict" predicates, like *(it's) amazing, incredible*, seem to presuppose the embedded proposition (and not just, like *know*, the RCP):

(18)    "It's incredible what he has done today," said Armstrong's team coach,
        . . .
        It's incredible what he has done today $\Rightarrow$
        I (we) know what he has done today

At least, they presuppose that the speaker knows the embedded proposition. I will call these predicates **super-factive**. The more liberal predicates do not strictly presuppose (that the speaker knows) the embedded proposition, but there is in any case a tendency for the speaker to know:

(19)    Paul was surprised what had happened to the Galatians.

Now when the *wh-* proposition does follow from the CG or the speaker's beliefs, there is in principle a competition with a corresponding *that* clause, – only, there can be a variety of reasons that the competition is not as strong as, say, in (20): There may be a need to withhold information, cf. (21), where a *that* clause would ruin the hearer's suspense; it may be that a certain information structure can only be conveyed with the *wh-* clause, cf. (22), where, say, *Dumbledore died* instead of *who died* would preclude the sole focus on the verb.

(20)    ??"It's incredible who won," said Italy's coach, Arrigo Sacchi.[1]

(21)    I was disappointed at who did it.

(22)    I was surprised who died, weren't you?

Or – importantly – a corresponding *that* clause may in some way or other be indeterminate or radically uneconomical, as in the case of (23).

(23)    It's incredible who you meet on the train.

While (20) invites the reaction 'if you know that Italy or Brazil won, why don't you say so?', although the speaker of (23) will know the embedded proposition, he will be unable to spell it out in terms of values for *who* in a *that* clause. The only realistic *that* clause alternative would be something like *that you meet the people you meet* – a clause with the same meaning as the *who* clause. This is a

---

[1] Google returns one hit for "amazing who won"; there Amazing is the name of a race horse.

case of an essentially world-dependent proposition. Such cases are not rare; *how* (+ adj.) clause propositions are usually impossible to express by *that* clauses.

These properties of the utterance situation and the content of the *wh-* word facilitate *wh-* complements by rendering competing *that* complements less appropriate and thus less competitive. This leaves us with the following generalization.

### Generalization

The stronger the competition with a *that* clause, the worse the *wh-* clause.

To account for the limiting case of *whether* complements, it is useful to observe the following.

### Observation

The competition is at its strongest when a "strict" – super-factive – predicate combines with a *whether* clause.

Simplifying a bit (the presupposition is probably not simply $\phi$ but $\phi[i/v]$ for some $v$ and verifiable not with respect to the Common Ground but to the speaker's beliefs), we can define a super-factive predicate like *amazing* as follows:

$$amazing'_i = \lambda\psi_{<s,t>}\ \mathcal{A}_i(\psi)<\psi>$$

Due to this presupposition there are in the case of *whether* only two cases: Either (the speaker believes that) $\phi$ follows from the Common Ground or (she believes that) $\neg\phi$ follows from the Common Ground, – and *whether* loses in both cases; cf. **Table 3**. Whether the "content" is one or the other, its probability value given the semantics of the *whether* form is lower than its value given the semantics of this or the other *that* form.

**Table 3.** Probability of $\phi$ or $\neg\phi$ in CG wrt. super-factivity with *that* $\phi$ or *whether* $\phi$

| $inf(\cdot/[\![\cdot]\!])$ | $\mathrm{CG}_i \subseteq \phi$ | $\mathrm{CG}_i \subseteq \neg\phi$ |
|:---:|:---:|:---:|
| *it's amazing that* $\phi$ | $\Rightarrow 1$ | $0$ |
| *it's amazing whether* $\phi$ | $\frac{1}{2}$ | $\frac{1}{2}$ |
| *it's amazing that* $\neg\phi$ | $0$ | $\Rightarrow 1$ |

With a predicate like *surprised*, however, we do find *whether* clauses embedded when a corresponding *that* clause is for some reason indeterminate. This is a strong indication that the relevant constraint has nothing to do with syntax or semantics as such but everything to do with competition and pragmatics.

The reasons that a corresponding *that* clause is indeterminate is, to be sure, in part semantic: In (24), there is, in effect, a quantification (through *seldom*, binding *a person*) over several *whether* clauses, some corresponding to one *that* clause, some to the other; in (25), there is a need to withhold information from the reader; in (26), there is a real lack of information on the part of the speaker.

(24)     Not that I was a boffin at psychometric testing, but we were seldom surprised at whether a person went to an Officer company or an NCO company.

(25)     Don't read this installment before seeing the episode if you want to be surprised at whether or not Hercules makes it.

(26)     I think we both feel this one will be a boy. But, we would rather be surprised whether it is a boy or not.

The common denominator, however, is this: The situation depicted in Table 3 fails to obtain because the premiss that $\phi$ or $\neg\phi$ follows from the common ground fails – be it that one must consider several instances, some where $\phi$, some where $\neg\phi$ follows from the common ground, that $\phi$ or $\neg\phi$ follows from the speaker's ground but not from the hearer's ground (and this should remain so), or, finally, that $\phi$ or $\neg\phi$ fails to follow even from the speaker's ground – and this should remain so as well.

# 5   Conclusions

I have sketched pragmatic, optimality theoretic solutions to two problems which have seemed to require semantic stipulations: The fact that *believe*, unlike *know*, cannot embed *wh-* clauses would seem to force the conclusion (Ginzburg 1995) that *wh-* clauses and *that* clauses do not both denote propositions; and the fact that emotive predicates cannot embed *whether* clauses would seem to call for a special semantics for this type of *wh-* clause (Abels 2005). But of course, both courses of action carry a certain theoretical cost.

By contrast, the account I have proposed, appealing to a competition with *know* and with *that*, is free of extra semantic assumptions; indeed, it rests on the premiss that *know* and *believe*, and *that* and *whether*, are of the same type, differing minimally. In addition, certain observations attesting to a gradience in acceptability support the competition-based analysis: As it appears, when the competitor – *know* and *that* clauses – is less competitive, differing more than minimally from *believe* and *wh-* clauses, the constraints soften. In sum, although the analysis I have suggested may not be the final formulation, an explanation based on optimality theoretic pragmatics does seem basically correct.

# References

Abels, K.: Remarks on Grimshaw's clausal typology. In: Maier, E., Bary, C., Huitink, J. (eds.) Proceedings of SuB9, Nijmegen, pp. 1–15 (2005)

Beaver, D.: Presuppositions. In: van Benthem, J., ter Meulen, A. (eds.) The Handbook of Logic and Language, pp. 939–1008. North-Holland, Elsevier, Amsterdam (1997)

Blutner, R.: Lexical Pragmatics. Journal of Semantics 15, 115–162 (1998)

Blutner, R.: Some Aspects of Optimality in Natural Language Interpretation. Journal of Semantics 17, 189–216 (2000)

Blutner, R.: Lexical Semantics and Pragmatics. In: Hamm, F., Zimmermann, E. (eds.) Semantics (= Linguistische Berichte Sonderheft 10), pp. 27–58 (2002)

Blutner, R.: Pragmatics and the lexicon. In: Horn, L., Ward, G. (eds.) Handbook of Pragmatics, pp. 488–514. Blackwell, Oxford (2004)

Blutner, R.: Embedded Implicatures and Optimality Theoretic Pragmatics. In: Solstad, T., Grønn, A., Haug, D. (eds.) A Festschrift for Kjell Johan Sæbø, Oslo, pp. 11–29 (2006)

Blutner, R., Zeevat, H.: Optimality Theory and Pragmatics. Palgrave MacMillan, London (2003)

Boër, S.: Towards a Theory of Indirect Question Clauses. Linguistics and Philosophy 2, 307–345 (1978)

d'Avis, F.: On the interpretation of wh- clauses in exclamative environments. Theoretical Linguistics 28, 5–32 (2002)

Egré, P.: Question-Embedding and Factivity. Presentation at the 3iéme Journée de Sémantique et Modélisation, ENS, Paris (2005)

Elliott, D.: The Grammar of Emotive and Exclamative Sentences in English. Doctoral dissertation, Ohio State University (1971)

Gallin, D.: Intensional and higher-order modal logic, Amsterdam (1975)

Ginzburg, J.: Resolving Questions, II. Linguistics and Philosophy 18, 567–609 (1995)

Grimshaw, J.: English Wh-Constructions and the Theory of Grammar. Doctoral dissertation, University of Massachusetts, Amherst (1977)

Grimshaw, J.: Complement selection and the lexicon. Linguistic Inquiry 10, 279–326 (1979)

Groenendijk, J., Stokhof, M.: Semantic analysis of Wh-complements. Linguistics and Philosophy 5, 175–233 (1982)

Huddleston, R.: Remarks on the Construction. You won't believe who Ed has married. Lingua 91, 175–184 (1993)

Kiparsky, P., Kiparsky, C.: Fact. In: Bierwisch, M., Heidolph, K.E. (eds.) Progress in Linguistics, pp. 143–173. Mouton, The Hague (1970)

Lahiri, U.: Lexical Selection and Quantificational Variability in Embedded Interrogatives. Linguistics and Philosophy 23, 325–389 (2000)

Lahiri, U.: Questions and Answers in Embedded Contexts. OUP, New York (2002)

Lewis, D.: Whether Report. In: Pauli, T. (ed.) Philosophical Essays Dedicated to Lennart Åqvist on his Fiftieth Birthday, Uppsala, pp. 194–206 (1982)

Zimmermann, E.: Kontextabhängigkeit. In: Stechow, A., Wunderlich, D. (eds.) Semantics. An International Handbook of Contemporary Research, Berlin, pp. 156–229 (1991)

Zimmermann, E.: Knowledge and Desire, from a German Perspective. In: Solstad, T., Grønn, A., Haug, D. (eds.) A Festschrift for Kjell Johan Sæbø, Oslo, pp. 211–223 (2006)

# Participants in Action: The Interplay of Aspectual Meanings and Thematic Relations in the Semantics of Semitic Morphology

Reut Tsarfaty

Institute for Logic Language and Computation, University of Amsterdam
Plantage Muidergracht 24, 1018 TV Amsterdam, The Netherlands
rtsarfat@science.uva.nl

**Abstract.** This work aims to demonstrate that event structure and thematic relations are closely intertwined. Specifically, we show that in Modern Hebrew the choice of a morphological template has profound effects on the event structure of derived verbs. These effects are correlated with the thematic features marked by the templates, and are mediated by the aspectual classification of the lexical material provided by roots.

## 1 Background

Verbs, nouns, and adjectives in Semitic languages are derived from (tri-) consonantal roots plugged into templates of consonant/vowel skeletons. The lexical items in (1), for example, are all derived from the same root, $[y][l][d]$.

(1) The root $[y][l][d]$ (birth, child)[1]

| Nouns | Verbs | Adjectives |
|---|---|---|
| $[y]i[l]o[d]$ beget | $[y]a[l]a[d]$ give birth | $mu[][l]a[d]$ innate |
| $[y]e[l]e[d]$ child | $[y]i[l](l)e[d]$ deliver a child | |
| $[y]a[l]i[d]$ native | | |

In Modern Hebrew (MH), verbs are derived using a set of seven templates termed 'binyanim'. The MH verbal templates are typically arranged in a two-dimensional grid, as shown in (2) together with their traditional names.

(2) The Verbal Templates

| | Simple | Intensive | Causative |
|---|---|---|---|
| Active | Pa'al | Pi'el | Hiph'il |
| Passive | — | Pu'al | Huph'al |
| Middle | Niph'al | Hitpa'el | — |

---

[1] In the transliteration I use here [C] marks a consonantal slot, (C) marks an obligatory doubled consonant, and [] indicates omission of a consonant due phonological reasons.

B.D. ten Cate and H.W. Zeevat (Eds.): TbiLLC 2005, LNAI 4363, pp. 200–215, 2007.
© Springer-Verlag Berlin Heidelberg 2007

Putting a root through different templates results in different lexical items which correspond to different verbs in English, as exemplified in (3).

(3)   The root $[x][l][k]$ (a part, share, smooth)

|  | Simple | Intensive | Causative |
|---|---|---|---|
| Active | $[x]a[l]a[k]$ to share | $[x]i[l](l)e[k]$ to divide | $he[x]e[l]i[k]$ make smooth |
| Passive | — | $[x]u[l](l)a[k]$ be divided | $hu[x][l]a[k]$ smoothed out |
| Middle | $ne[x][l]a[k]$ to differ | $hit[x]a[l](l)e[k]$ to glide | — |

These templates differ significantly from typical 'grammatical operators' as they are not fully productive, and equi-root verbs in different templates show surprising idiosyncrasies. For example, the verbs in (4) are all derived from the same root, [k][b][l], yet their meanings seem unrelated. Further, putting the same root through the middle template, Niph'al, is ungrammatical, as shown in (5).

(4)   a.  $[k][b][l]$ + Pa'al = *kaḅal* (complain)
      b.  $[k][b][l]$ + Pi'el = *kibel* (receive)
      c.  $[k][b][l]$ + Hiph'il = *hikbil* (parallel)

(5)   a.  $[k][b][l]$ + Niph'al = *∗nikbal*

This has led some linguists to conclude that the templates are arbitrary, that root/template combinations are inherent in the lexicon, and that the templates are irrelevant for making semantic predictions. [Doron(2003)] was the first to demonstrate that the Semitic templates have systematic semantic contribution, albeit restricted to the thematic domain. Here we propose that the templates contribute aspectual meanings as well. The key idea is that participants are elements in the temporal extension of an event, and therefore marked thematic relations affect the verbs' aspectual content. Thus, treating events and participants in the same theoretical framework allows us to investigate aspectual meanings in languages that do not grammaticalize aspect, yet mark thematic relations with formal means.

The remainder of this paper is organized as follows. In section 2 we pose our research question, and elaborate on the theoretical preliminaries required to answer this question. In section 3 we spell out our hypothesis about thematic relations and aspectual meanings, followed by the methodological guidelines we adopt in section 4. Section 5 provides a brief introduction to Event Calculus, an axiomatic system we use to formalize our theoretical findings in section 6, and in section 7 we apply our theory to three of the MH templates, the so-called *active* templates, Pa'al, Pi'el and Hiph'il. Then, section 8 describes the experimental setup and preliminary results of an empirical investigation we conducted to support our theoretical findings and in section 9 we summarize and conclude.

## 2   Research Questions

MH has a three-way tense system that grammaticalizes past, present and future, and no aspectual inflectional morphology as it is in some Indo-European

Languages. To illustrate, the MH simple verb "avad' (to work) can be interpreted in various ways (e.g., complete, ongoing or completed) as demonstrated in (6).

(6)   a.   hu 'avad          maher
          he work.Past.MS3 fast

          He worked/was working/had worked/had been working fast

      b.   hu 'oved          maher
          he work.Pres.MS3 fast

          He works/is working/has been working fast

      c.   hu ya'avod        maher
          he work.Fut.MS3 fast

          He will work/will be working fast

The lack of grammatical aspect in the MH tense system raises the question whether means to denote aspect can be found 'elsewhere' in the language, for instance, in its derivational morphology. Specifically, we investigate whether the MH verbal morphological templates carry aspectual meanings. However, such theoretical investigation requires addressing several related questions:

(7)   a.   Are MH verbs formed at the level of syntax or listed in the lexicon?

      b.   Do the MH templates systematically contribute to verbs' meanings?

      c.   Do the MH templates systematically contribute aspectual meanings?

A response to (7a) follows from principles of Distributed Morphology (DM) [Halle and Marantz(1993)]. According to DM, a model for Semitic languages is assumed to have a 'narrow lexicon' consisting of the basic units on which the syntax operates. In the case of MH, the 'narrow lexicon' contains coarse-grained consonantal roots and the morphemes realized in the templates. Verbs are constructed in the syntax (formally, 'fusing') by the same processes that construct phrases and sentences (formally, 'merging'). These processes are relevant for making semantic predictions, yet they allow for idiosyncrasies relative to context (as it is the case, for instance, with the meanings of idioms).

Using principles of DM, [Doron(2003)] answers the question posed in (7b). Doron argues that the contribution of the templates is not transparent yet systematic, and that it is reflected in the *thematic* domain. In Doron's account, the templates realize functional heads that alter or modify the thematic relations of the arguments projected/licensed by the root. The contribution is therefore, systematic, however mediated by an underlying thematic classification, and should be examined relative to the lexical material provided by the root.

However, in Doron's account thematic and aspectual operators are orthogonal, as their presupposed classification systems are disjoint. So our question remains (7c) — do the templates make a systematic aspectual contribution?

## 3   The Hypothesis

The term *thematic roles* refers to semantic distinctions between NP complements of verbs, which conceptually represent participants in situations. Linguists traditionally referred to a closed set of roles (e.g. agent, theme, location, goal and source) and tried to uniquely assign them to surface forms.

[Dowty(1991)] surveyed difficulties with this traditional view and proposed that thematic relations are not discrete, but belong to fuzzy categories ranging from a Proto-agent to a Proto-patient. Further, [Dowty(1991)] established that thematic relations are selected in accord with the event denoted by the verb at hand.[2] Here we hypothesize that the converse also holds, i.e., that *the event structure of derived verbs changes to accord with altered thematic relations.*

We assume that roots carry basic meanings that induce a preliminary event classification à la [Vendler(1967)]. According to Doron, the templates alter thematic relations projected by the root. We claim that the event structure of the verb at hand changes to accommodate the altered thematic relations, thus affecting the event structure of derived verbs (henceforth, their *aspectual meaning*) in a predictable way.

## 4   The Methodology

In analyzing aspectual meanings of derived verbs we appeal to theories of *markedness*, a move inspired by [Smith(1991)]. Markedness is concerned with the relations among members of a closed system. The underlying assumption is that a choice is made between *available* alternatives, and thus the contrast between the alternatives is an inherent part of users' choice. [Comrie(1976)] pointed out that marked aspectual choices are typically morphologically marked. So, we start out by examining the morphological material the templates attach to roots, as demonstrated in (8).

(8)   Morphological Patterns of the Modern Hebrew Templates

|  | Simple | Intensive | Causative |  |
|---|---|---|---|---|
| Active | $[C]a[C]a[C]$ | $[C]i[C](C)e[C]$ | $Hi[C][C]i[C]$ |  |
| Passive | — | $[C]u[C](C)a[C]$ | $Hu[C][C]a[C]$ | u-a |
| Middle | $Ni[C][C]a[C]$ | $HiT[C]a[C](C)e[C]$ | — | i-a(-e) |
|  |  | doubled (C) | prefixed H |  |

The templates implement two dimensions of morphological marking. The vertical dimension, which is marked consonantally, and the horizontal, which is marked by vocalization [Doron(2003)]. The *Simple-Active* template is morphologically unmarked, and thus we use it to approximate the aspectual meaning of the root. Next we consider aspectual pairs that consist of the unmarked template (Pa'al) and the available oppositions of templates that are morphologically marked with respect to it. We contrast the meanings of such pairs, and examine whether

---

[2] This view is also implicit in Doron's account, as her thematic classification is relative to the lexical material of the root, and therefore to the event denoted by it.

the aspectual meaning of a marked form changes relative to the aspectual meaning of the unmarked form with the same root.[3]

# 5   Formal Setting

The departure point for our semantic account is Smith's two-component theory of aspect, in which a speaker chooses a constellation of *lexical* and *grammatical* morphemes to express her aspectual choice of *situation type* and *viewpoint*, respectively [Smith(1991)]. To formalize such notions as 'situation type' and 'viewpoint' we use Event Calculus, a formalism to reason about time and change.

**Event Calculus (EC).** Event Calculus [van Lambalgen and Hamm(2005)] is a formalism based on the notion of 'planning', where a 'plan' requires that an agent desires to achieve a goal and sets a sequence of actions in order to achieve that goal. It has been empirically shown that knowledge of goals/plans plays a crucial role in humans' structuring and relating of events in narratives [Trabasso and Stein(1994)] and in children's acquisition of linguistic means to denote temporal and aspectual distinctions [Berman and Slobin(1994)]. Thus, the representation format of EC is assumed to fit the way we construct our conscious experience of time. Furthermore, a plan involves "reasoning about events, both actions of agents and events in the environment, and about properties of the agent and the environment", and thus it naturally extends to accommodate notions of a thematic nature, e.g., an agent, a goal, and a changing theme. Finally, a plan can be shown to be provably correct, and the actions necessary to achieve one's goal can be computed, which makes the EC also logically and computationally adequate as a semantic tool for capturing aspectual distinctions.

Formally, EC requires (at least) events ($e, e'..$), time instants ($t_1, t_2..$), and time dependent properties called *fluents* ($f_1, f_2..$). The time is represented by the real numbers ($\mathbb{R}, <, +, \times, 0, 1$), which serve as the raw material from which we construct our conscious experience of time.

**EC Situation Types.** Informally, verbs refer to events which are a conceptualization of a certain portion of time. EC hypothesizes that human conceptualization of events is driven by goals, and formalizes 'eventualities' as follows.[4]

**Definition 1.** *An* eventuality $E$ *is a structure* $\langle f_1, f_2, e, f_3 \rangle$ *where:*

1. $f_1$ *represents an activity which exerts a force*
2. $f_2$ *represents a changing object/state driven by the force of $f_1$*
3. $e$ *represents a canonical goal (a culminating event)*
4. $f_3$ *represents a state (of having achieved the goal)*

---

[3] Note that we do not suggest here that marked verbal forms are *derived* from unmarked one. All forms are derived from *roots*, and we use the unmarked template merely to provide a preliminary aspectual classification of roots' lexical material.

[4] We drop the term 'event', in order not to confuse it with formal event-types/tokens.

An eventuality in EC is an abbreviation for a fully specified scenario: a sequence of general statements universally quantified with respect to time. Together with the EC axioms, the scenario defines a micro-theory of the temporal/causal relations in the event.[5] Using the eventuality quadruples, EC represents different *Aktionsarten*, or *situation types*.

For MH we assume a four-way classification to aspectual classes as proposed in [Yitzhaki(2003)] and represent it as follows, where '+' indicates the presence of the corresponding event/fluent in the scenario and '−' indicates its absence.[6]

**Definition 2.** Aktionsarten

1. States *(e.g. love, know)* $\langle -, -, -, + \rangle$
2. Achievements *(e.g. fall, break)* $\langle -, -, +, + \rangle$
3. Activities (wide) *(e.g. walk, push)* $\langle +, +, -, - \rangle$
4. Accomplishments *(e.g. build, create)* $\langle +, +, +, + \rangle$

**EC Viewpoints.** The lexical material (described by the eventuality quadruples) can be looked at from different viewpoints, and this distinction lies at the heart of important aspectual notions, e.g., the progressive. EC formalizes *viewpoints* using integrity constraints that associate the *reference time* (cf. [Reichenbach(1947)]) with specific components in the quadruple. Since MH does not have inflectional morphology that manifests such distinctions, we use integrity constraints to define a *default* viewpoint for each of the situation types, marked here with $[+]$.[7]

**Definition 3.** Viewpoints

1. States *(e.g. love, know)* $\langle -, -, -, [+] \rangle$
2. Achievement *(e.g. fall, break)* $\langle -, -, [+], + \rangle$
3. Activities (wide) *(e.g. walk, push)* $\langle [+], +, -, - \rangle$
4. Accomplishments *(e.g. build, create)* $\langle [+], +, +, + \rangle$

**EC Thematic roles.** EC allows fluents to be associated with entities in the real world that possess the property they mark. Therefore we can extend the formal description of the fluents in the eventuality quadruple with the participants associated with them. We use Dowty's *Proto-roles* lists to determine the kind of participant a fluent should be associated with, using a simple voting mechanism based on the counts of properties in the lists (cf. his argument selection principle).

---

[5] See [van Lambalgen and Hamm(2005)] for a complete technical exposition.

[6] [Yitzhaki(2003)] investigates lexical aspect in MH, and based on various linguistic tests she develops she proposes a four-way classification of MH verbs to aspectual classes induced by the presence or absence of two semantic features. In this account, her 'interval' feature corresponds to the existence of a dynamic component $\langle f_1, f_2, -, - \rangle$ in the quadruple, and the 'telic' feature corresponds to the presence of a canonical goal $\langle -, -, e, - \rangle$.

[7] The full formalization of viewpoints in EC bears the forms ?HoldsAt$(f, R), R \gtrless now$ *succeeds* and ?Happens$(e, R), R \gtrless now$ *succeeds* where $R$ is the reference time. However, for the purpose of the current exposition these abbreviations will suffice.

**Definition 4.** Thematic Relations

1. $f_1$ *is associated with a* Proto-agent
2. $f_2$ *is associated with a* Proto-patient *(an incremental theme)*
3. $f_3$ *is associated with a* Proto-agent *(an experiencer) or a* Proto-patient *(a theme), relative to the situation type.*

This brief formal exposition serves to show that the extended theory of EC allows us to formalize situation types, viewpoints, and thematic relations in a single framework. This, in turn, enables us to pinpoint how an eventuality structure is affected when a certain thematic relation is modified.

# 6    An Account of Aspect in Modern Hebrew

**Syntax.** A model for Semitic languages in DM assumes a 'narrow lexicon' that contains the units on which the syntax operates, listed in (9).

(9)    a.  Roots: $\{R : R = [C][C][C], [C]$ *is a consonant*$\}$
       b.  Templates: $\{$Pa'al, Pi'el, Hiph'il, Pu'al, Huph'al, Niph'al, Hitpa'el$\}$

The following definitions recapitulate formally the derivation of MH verbs.

**Definition 5.** *Let* R *be a consonantal root and let* T *be a morphological template. Then* $R + T = V$ *is a verbal form in MH.*

**Definition 6.** *Let* R *be a consonantal root,* T *be a morphological template, and let* V *be the result form of* $R + T$*. The verbal form* V *is grammatical if it has a listed phonological form in the 'vocabulary*[8] *and ungrammatical otherwise.*

**Definition 7.** *Let* V *be a verbal form in MH,* $R_V$ *be its consonantal root, and* $T_V$ *be its template.*[9] *If* $T_V =$ Pa'al, *then* V *is* simple, *otherwise it is* non-simple.

**Semantics.** In our account, aspectual meanings are derived from the meaning of roots and the morphemes realized in the templates. Roots provide the verb with a preliminary situation type, and the templates mark thematic features. According to [Doron(2003)], the templates mark two dimensions of thematic features, namely *Agency* and *Voice*, as described in (10).

(10)      *Agency:* $\iota$ (intensive), $\gamma$ (causative)

         *Voice:* $\pi$ (passive), $\mu$ (middle)

The morphemes realized in the templates correspond to the two dimensions of morphological marking, as shown in (11).

---

[8] A 'vocabulary' is a presupposed component of the DM framework [Halle and Marantz(1993)].

[9] MH grammar guarantees that each verbal form in MH has a unique root and a unique template, and thus $R_V$ and $T_V$ are, in fact, functions.

(11)    Thematic Features Marked by the Modern Hebrew Templates

| | *Simple* | *Intensive* | *Causative* | |
|---|---|---|---|---|
| *Active* | [ ] | $[+\iota]$ | $[+\gamma]$ | |
| *Passive* | — | $[+\iota, +\pi]$ | $[+\gamma, +\pi]$ | $[+\pi]$ |
| *Middle* | $[+\mu]$ | $[+\iota, +\mu]$ | — | $[+\mu]$ |
| | | $[+\iota]$ | $[+\gamma]$ | |

The derivation of aspectual meanings proceeds as follows. The root provides the verb with a preliminary eventuality scenario, which is the eventuality associated with the root put through the unmarked template Pa'al. The template defines *criteria*, which are additional general statements and integrity constraints. The additional statements guarantee the existence of the fluents/events required by the marked thematic feature, and the integrity constraints relate those with the reference point of the eventuality. The result scenario is thus given by the *sum* of the eventuality scenario and the criteria. This sum operation goes beyond mere addition and takes the existing micro-theory into account; repeated statements are eliminated (*union*), unknown parameters (fluents/events) identify with existing ones (*unification*), remaining parameters are instantiated based on context (*instantiation*) and specific integrity constraints override default ones. The event structure of the resulting verb can then be simply read off from the result scenario with its newly specified viewpoint. This process is schematically presented in (12), where $PSCEN$ is the preliminary scenario, $C_\mathsf{T}$ is the criteria defined by the template, and $RSCEN$ is the result scenario.[10]

(12)
| | | | | |
|---|---|---|---|---|
| Syntax: | R | + | T | $=$ V |
| Semantics: | $E_\mathsf{R}$ | $+ (\iota\|\gamma + \pi\|\mu) =$ | | $E_V$ |
| Aspectual Meaning: | $PSCEN_\mathsf{R} +$ | $C_\mathsf{T}$ | $= RSCEN_V$ | |

# 7    Applications

**The Simple Template Pa'al**

The simple template, Pa'al, is morphologically unmarked and semantically unmodified. Thus, the aspectual meaning of the verb is determined solely by the lexical material of the root. Pa'al verbs may be of any situation type, as in (13).

(13)    a.    States
        1.  $[a][h][\breve{b}]$ + Pa'al = *ahab* (love)
        2.  $[y][d][']$ + Pa'al = *yada* (know)
    b.    Achievements
        1.  $[x][\breve{b}][r]$ + Pa'al = *xabar* (join)

---

[10] For further details concerning the 'sum' operation and the derivation process refer to [Tsarfaty(2005a)], e.g., section 6.2.3.

    2. $[n][\breve{p}][l]$ + Pa'al = $na\breve{p}al$ (fall)

  c. Activities

    1. $[h][l][\breve{k}]$ + Pa'al = $hala\breve{k}$ (walk)

    2. $[d][x][\breve{p}]$ + Pa'al = $daxa\breve{p}$ (push)

  d. Accomplishments

    1. $[b][n][h]$ + Pa'al = $bana$ (build)

    2. $[y][c][r]$ + Pa'al = $yacar$ (create)

## The Intensive Template Pi'el

The intensive template, Pi'el, is morphologically marked with a double middle consonant and semantically marked with the thematic feature $[+\iota]$. Representative examples for Pa'al/Pi'el alternations are illustrated in (14).

(14)   a.  1. $[y][d][']$ + Pa'al = $yada'$ (know)

        2. $[y][d][']$ + Pi'el = $yidde'a$ (inform)

    b.  1. $[x][b][r]$ + Pa'al = $xa\breve{b}ar$ (join)

        2. $[x][b][r]$ + Pi'el = $xibber$ (connect)

    c.  1. $[h][l][\breve{k}]$ + Pa'al = $hala\breve{k}$ (walk)

        2. $[h][l][\breve{k}]$ + Pi'el = $hille\breve{k}$ (walk intensively, walk around)

    d.  1. $[y][c][r]$ + Pa'al = $yacar$ (create)

        2. $[y][c][r]$ + Pi'el = $yiccer$ (manufacture)

According to [Doron(2003)], the $[+\iota]$ feature reclassifies the agent in the situation as an *actor*, where an *actor* is an entity capable of exerting force. In our account, this requires the eventuality quadruple to include (at least) an activity exerting force, and possibly a changing fluent driven by this force. So, the result scenario for intensive verbs must minimally encompass the statements for $\langle f_1, f_2, -, - \rangle$ (formally defined in EC as a *dynamics*). Further, the marked thematic feature fixes the actor as the marked reference point for the event, i.e., $\langle [f_1], f_2, -, - \rangle$.

To illustrate the effect of this requirement on the derivation of aspectual meanings, consider first intensive verbs with achievement roots. An achievement root plugged into the simple template results in a simple verb denoting an achievement, which presents the preliminary scenario $\langle -, -, [e], f \rangle$. The marked thematic feature $[+\iota]$ requires the eventuality scenario to contain, at least, the following components, with a newly specified viewpoint $\langle [f_1], f_2, -, - \rangle$. Summing the scenario and the $[+\iota]$ criteria results in the following result scenario and sets a new reference point for the entire scenario. The new situation type and viewpoint of the derived verb can now be read off of the result scenario.

$$\langle -, -, [e], f \rangle + \langle [f_1], f_2, -, - \rangle \rightsquigarrow \langle [f_1], f_2, e, f \rangle$$

More generally, we claim that plugging an achievement root through the intensive template has the effect of adding a preparatory phase, in which an actor exerts a force which brings about the canonical goal. The resulting eventuality structure then mirrors the structure of an accomplishment and the viewpoint is fixed on the 'preparation' fluent.[11]

Repeating the same procedure for roots from different aspectual classes gives us different predictions. The resulting scenarios are provided in (15).[12]

(15)    a.   State ............... $\langle -, -, -, [+] \rangle + \langle [+], +, -, - \rangle \rightsquigarrow \langle [+], +, +, + \rangle$

       b.   Achievement .... $\langle -, -, [+], + \rangle + \langle [+], +, -, - \rangle \rightsquigarrow \langle [+], +, +, + \rangle$

       c.   Activity ............ $\langle [+], +, -, - \rangle + \langle [+], +, -, - \rangle \rightsquigarrow \langle [+], +, -, - \rangle$

       d.   Accomplishment $\langle [+], +, +, + \rangle + \langle [+], +, -, - \rangle \rightsquigarrow \langle [+], +, +, + \rangle$

We exemplify the resulting aspectual shifts with our representative examples in (16). Activities and accomplishments in the intensive form (16a–b) maintain the same event structure as simple ones, since the additional fluents simply unify with existing ones. Achievements and states (16c–d) are extended with a dynamic component which proceeds, and brings about, the (change of) state.

(16)    a.   *State* $\langle -, -, -, [+] \rangle \rightsquigarrow$ *Accomplishment* $\langle [+], +, +, + \rangle$

         i.   $[y][d]['] + \text{Pa'al} = yada'$ (know)

        ii.   $[y][d]['] + \text{Pi'el} = yidde'a$ (inform)

       b.   *Achievement* $\langle -, -, [+], + \rangle \rightsquigarrow$ *Accomplishment* $\langle [+], +, +, + \rangle$

         i.   $[x][b][r] + \text{Pa'al} = xa\breve{b}ar$ (join)

        ii.   $[x][b][r] + \text{Pi'el} = xibber$ (connect)

       c.   *Activity* $\langle [+], +, -, - \rangle \rightsquigarrow$ *Activity* $\langle [+], +, -, - \rangle$

         i.   $[h][l][\breve{k}] + \text{Pa'al} = hala\breve{k}$ (walk)

        ii.   $[h][l][\breve{k}] + \text{Pi'el} = hille\breve{k}$ (walk around)

       d.   *Accomplishment* $\langle [+], +, +, + \rangle \rightsquigarrow$ *Accomplishment* $\langle [+], +, +, + \rangle$

         i.   $[y][c][r] + \text{Pa'al} = yacar$ (produce)

        ii.   $[y][c][r] + \text{Pi'el} = yiccer$ (manufacture)

**A note on transitivity alternations.** Many intensive verbs, but not all of them, show increased valence.[13] The present proposal allows us to predict how to delineate the valency increasing alternations as precisely the ones in which the added fluents cannot unify with the ones in the preliminary scenario. As a result, activities and accomplishments maintain the same number of participants in the result scenario, while stative roots show increased valence that follows from the addition of fluents associated with an actor $f_1$ and an incremental theme $f_2$.

---

[11] Similar, but not identical, effects appear when putting English achievement verbs in the progressive, cf. 'progressive achievements' in [Rothstein(2004)].

[12] Stative intensive verbs illustrate how 'instantiation' takes place. It has been observed for both Biblical Hebrew [Creason(1995)] and MH [Doron(2003)] that stative verbs are ambiguous between a stative and an inchoative reading. So, the latter change of state fills in the slot $e$ required by the EC axioms relating a state to a dynamics.

[13] [Creason(1995)] classifies Pi'el verbs as the transitive counterpart of the Pa'al, yet accounts for intransitive Pi'els by stipulating a sub-categorization of the Pi'el verbs.

**A note on denominal Pi'els.** Not all intensive verbs have a simple verb counterpart. Some intensive verbs are derived from so-called *denominal* roots. The meaning of denominal roots can be approximated by the noun denoted by it. The noun predicate can be associated with a parametrized fluent $f_2(x)$ (denoting, roughly, 'the amount of $x$') as lexical material for the preliminary scenario filling in the second slot in the quadruple (i.e., the incremental theme). The preliminary scenario then specifies the following quadruple $\langle -, +, -, - \rangle$, and the contribution of the intensive template fills in the activity slot as usual. The resulting scenario gives rise to a wide variety of denominal intensive verbs already identified by [Doron(2003)], e.g., (17), using the same derivation process.

(17)   $\langle -, [+], -, - \rangle + \langle [+], +, -, - \rangle \rightsquigarrow \langle [+], +, -, - \rangle$

    a.  1.  $[s][m][n] + noun = \check{s}emen$ (oil)

         2.  $[s][m][n] + $ Pi'el $= \check{s}immen$ (lubricate)

    b.  1.  $[a][b][k] + noun = a\check{b}ak$ (dust)

         2.  $[a][b][k] + $ Pi'el $= ibbek$ (remove dust)

Note that the contribution of the intensive template remains neutral with respect to telicity. In many cases, a telic point may be provided by context. Such effects are also available with similar verbs in English in which the quantity/measure of the incremental theme remains underspecified (contrast, e.g. (17b) the activity 'dust' and the accomplishment 'dust the table', cf. [Levin and Hovav(1991)]).

## The Causative Template Hiph'il

Morphological causatives in MH are derived by fusing consonantal roots with the so-called causative template Hiph'il. The causative template is morphologically marked with a prefixed H and semantically marked with the $[+\gamma]$ thematic feature. Morphological causatives in MH give rise to a wide range of meanings that does not necessarily coincide with causation in its strict sense. For example, it is debatable whether the meaning of feed ought to be 'cause to eat' (18d).

(18)   a.  1.  $[p][x][d] + $ Pa'al $= paxad$ (fear)

         2.  $[p][x][d] + $ Hiph'il $= hi\check{p}xid$ (frighten)

    b.  1.  $[n][\check{p}][l] + $ Pa'al $= na\check{p}al$ (fall)

         2.  $[n][\check{p}][l] + $ Hiph'il $= hippil$ (fell, made fall, cause to fall)

    c.  1.  $[r][k][d] + $ Pa'al $= rakad$ (dance)

         2.  $[r][k][d] + $ Hiph'il $= hirkid$ (made dance, cause to dance)

    d.  1.  $[a][\check{k}][l] + $ Pa'al $= a\check{k}al$ (eat)

         2.  $[a][\check{k}][l] + $ Hiph'il $= he'e\check{k}il$ (feed)

As of yet, research into lexical semantics has not shown a systematic correlation between causative constructions and aspectual meanings. In particular, [Levin(2000)] shows that causatives cannot be reduced to any one kind of Aktionsart. However, causatives are valency increasing operations, thereby encoding speakers' choice to incorporate an additional element (a cause) into the event description. According to our hypothesis, this would make them aspectually marked as well.

[Tsarfaty(2005b)] sets out to make the desired link between causative constructions and aspectual meanings using a revised version of Smith's causal chain [Smith(1991)]. The crucial observation is that causative constructions contribute a 'cause' element which is distinct from elements already existing in the representation of a given situation. Since not all situations map onto the same span of the causal chain, the addition of a preceding 'cause' element gives rise to new event interpretations. Further, marking an explicit 'cause' focuses the linguistic description on the forces behind the initiation and development of the event, thus altering its aspectual viewpoint.

This is in accord with the thematic account proposed by [Doron(2003)]. Doron shows that the causative template contributes an external participant that serves as the cause to the event at hand. We claim that the addition of an external participant alters the eventuality structure by filling in the immediately preceding slots. The new viewpoint is focused on this newly added element(s). (19) illustrates schematically the effect of this process on different roots.

(19)   a.  State .............. $\langle -, -, -, [+] \rangle + [+\gamma] \rightsquigarrow \langle -, -, [+], + \rangle$

   b.  Achievement .... $\langle -, -, [+], + \rangle + [+\gamma] \rightsquigarrow \langle [+], +, +, + \rangle$

   c.  Activity ........... $\langle [+], +, -, - \rangle + [+\gamma] \rightsquigarrow \langle [+], +, [+], +, -, - \rangle$

   d.  Accomplishment $\langle [+], +, +, + \rangle + [+\gamma] \rightsquigarrow \langle [+], +, [+], +, +, + \rangle$

The resulting scenarios are illustrated in (20a–d). Note that durative events require hexatuples of the form $\langle f_1^0, f_2^0, f_1, f_2, e, f_3 \rangle$ where fluents $f_1^0, f_2^0$ stimulate the dynamics $\langle f_1, f_2, -, - \rangle$, and the reference point $[f_1]$ coincides with $[f_1^0]$.[14]

(20)   a.  *State* $\langle -, -, -, [+] \rangle \rightsquigarrow$ *Inchoative state* $\langle -, -, [+], + \rangle$
   1.  $[d][a][g]$ + Pa'al = *da'ag* (be worried)
   2.  $[d][a][g]$ + Hiph'il = *hid'id* (make worry)

   b.  *Achievement* $\langle -, -, [+], + \rangle \rightsquigarrow$ *Progressive achievement* $\langle [+], +, +, + \rangle$
   1.  $[n][\check{p}][l]$ + Pa'al = *napal* (fall)
   2.  $[n][\check{p}][l]$ + Hiph'il = *hippil* (fell, made fall, cause to fall)

   c.  *Activity* $\langle [+], +, -, - \rangle \rightsquigarrow$ *Ingressive activity* $\langle [+], +, [+], +, -, - \rangle$
   1.  $[r][k][d]$ + Pa'al = *rakad* (dance)
   2.  $[r][k][d]$ + Hiph'il = *hirkid* (cause to dance, made dance)

   d.  *Accomplish.* $\langle [+], +, +, + \rangle \rightsquigarrow$ *Ingressive accomplish.* $\langle [+], +, [+], +, +, + \rangle$
   1.  $[a][\check{k}][l]$ + Pa'al = *akal* (eat)
   2.  $[a][\check{k}][l]$ + Hiph'il = *he'ekil* (feed)

---

[14] Formally, one integrity constraint defines the reference point for the eventuality as the activity fluent $?\mathsf{HoldsAt}(f_1, R), R \gtrless now$ *succeeds* and another one conditions the activity on a dynamic cause: $?\mathsf{HoldsAt}(f_1, R), \neg\mathsf{HoldsAt}(f_1^0, R)$ *fails*. Note that the latter constraint also determines the directionality of the causal relation.

In (20a), the state of 'being worried' comes about due to a certain cause, which gives the event an inchoative interpretation. In (20b), the event 'fall' is extended to include a preparatory phase that precedes and causes it, giving it the interpretation of a progressive achievement (which mirrors an accomplishment). In (20c) and (20d), the durative events are extended to include a preceding dynamics that continuously stimulates the 'caused' event and provides it with an ingressive interpretation. In (20c) for instance, the stimulus for the dancing event must span over the interval in which the dancing event takes place, and the 'dancing' fluent is dependent on it. In (20d) similarly the 'eating' fluent is stimulated by an activity of 'feeding', and both must hold at the reference time.

**Denominal Hiph'ils.** The same proposal accounts for the aspectual meanings of *denominal* causatives, i.e. causative verbs that are derived from nouns. Again we can associate the object denoted by the noun with $f_2$, the template fills in $f_1$ with the essential 'cause', and the result gives rise to a variety of wide activities, including the emission verbs mentioned in [Doron(2003)], e.g., (21).

(21)   $noun \langle -, [+], -, - \rangle \rightsquigarrow activity \langle [+], +, -, - \rangle$

    a.   1.  $[r]['][š] + noun = ra'aš$ (noise)

          2.  $[r]['][š] + $ Hiph'il $= hir'iš$ (emit noise)

    b.   1.  $[y][z]['] + noun = ze'a$ (sweat)

          2.  $[y][z]['] + $ Hiph'il $= hizi'a$ (to sweat)

The analysis of denominal verbs in MH serves to demonstrate the two core components of our theory. First, that the addition of a new participant adds also the aspectual context in which it operates, and second, that Semitic derivational morphology has an indispensable aspectual contribution.

## 8   Empirical Investigation

Following our goal/plan hypothesis we expect children and adults to be sensitive to various aspectual distinctions and mark them using the linguistic means provided by their language. Here we are specifically interested in examining whether templates' alternation is employed by MH native speakers to mark aspectual distinctions. In order to find empirical evidence for such aspectual choices in MH and for the developmental trends in the usage of different verbal forms in different ages, we used an experimental setup inspired by [Berman and Slobin(1994)]. We asked 22 native MH speakers (ages 3–30) to narrate a story based on a wordless picture book from two different viewpoints. Once while walking through the pictures ('Part I') and once in retrospect, after the successful resolution of the plot ('Part II').[15] Grounding the different narratives in the same pictures allows us to examine how different speakers describe the same situation, and the twofold structure of the experiment allows us to compare different descriptions of the same situation from different viewpoints.

---

[15] For 3–4-year old children the task was limited to Part I only.

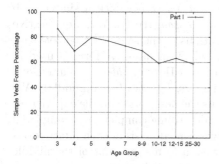

**Fig. 1.** Percentage of simple verb forms used in Part I (avg. per age group)

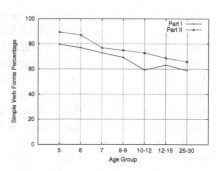

**Fig. 2.** Percentage of simple verb forms used in Parts I, II (avg. per age group)

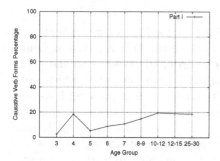

**Fig. 3.** Percentage of causative verbs used in Part I (avg. per age group)

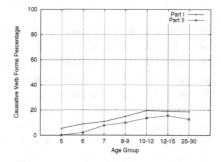

**Fig. 4.** Percentage of causative verbs used in Parts I, II (avg. per age group)

Figures 1 and 2 summarize the use of simple verb forms in the narratives. Figure 1 shows decreasing use of simple verb forms with age, thus a respective increase in the use of non-simple forms. This indicates that adult-like use of the morphological templates requires a longer acquisition phase than, e.g., mastering the grammatical tenses (already achieved by age 3, [Berman and Slobin(1994)]).[16] Figure 2 shows for all age groups a persistent increase in simple verb forms in 'Part II' relative to 'Part I'. This shows a preference for simple verbs when describing complete/completed events in retrospect to drive the story time-line forward. The distribution of causative verbs, demonstrated in figures 3 and 4, shows the exact opposite trend. Figure 3 shows an increasing use of causative verb forms with age, whereas figure 4 shows a consistent decrease in the use of causative verb forms, for all ages, in 'Part II' relative to 'Part I'. This indicates a clear preference for causative verbs when describing incomplete events as they happen, and for focusing the description on the initiation and development, rather than on the completion, of the event.

As of yet we have not found a consistent trend in the usage of intensive verbs per age or a consistent difference between viewpoints. This is possibly due to

---

[16] Note that tense marking is obligatory while marked choices of the kind discussed here are voluntary.

the fact that many intensive verbs used in the narratives lack a simple verb counterpart (e.g. *xippes* (searched, looked for), *nissah* (tried)). Yet, a qualitative analysis shows that middle/intensive alternations in the same root behave similarly to simple/causative alternations, i.e., when an intensive form is used in 'Part I' the respective middle form is used in 'Part II' (e.g. *'ibbed* (lose.intensive) vs. *ne'ebad* (lost.middle), *yibbeš* (dry.intensive) vs. *hitaybeš* (dried.middle)). We conjecture here that middle verbs, which focus the description on the experiencer of a resulting state, are more appropriate for describing complete and completed events, more so than intensive verbs. However, the analysis of such alternations will only be complete when accompanied with a formal account of the middle templates' contribution, which is beyond the scope of this paper.

## 9    Conclusion

We presented a two-dimensional theory of aspect for MH, in which both lexical and grammatical morphemes are taken into account. The lexical morphemes are roots which are classified to preliminary aspectual classes, and the grammatical morphemes are the morphemes realized in the templates, which mark thematic features that affect the eventuality structure in a principled fashion. [Dowty(1991)] has already shown that a proper treatment of thematic roles cannot be complete without taking event structure into account. The Semitic templates, formerly associated with phenomena of the thematic domain (voice and agency, transitivity alternations [Doron(2003)]) provided us with an example in the opposite direction: a formal treatment of the event structure cannot be complete without taking thematic classification into account.

Treating aspectual content and thematic relations within the same theoretical framework allows one to make precise predictions concerning subtle aspectual distinctions in languages that mark the kind of participants involved rather than strictly aspectual notions such as perfectivity or the progressive. In the future we hope to treat voice alternations within the same theoretical and empirical framework. By this we hope to provide further evidence for the interplay between aspectual content of events and thematic description of their participants, and to establish further the indispensable aspectual contribution of Semitic derivational morphology.

## Acknowledgments

I am grateful to Prof. Michiel van Lambalgen for supervising this work and to Darrin Hindsill for much discussion throughout. I thank Prof. Susan Rothstein for discussion and comments on earlier notes. Parts of this work were presented at the tenth Batumi symposium, the Fifteenth Amsterdam Colloquium and at the linguistics seminar of the Hebrew University of Jerusalem. I'd like to thank the audience of these meetings, in particular Edit Doron, Nissim Francez, Anita Mittwoch, Barbara Partee and Malka Rappaport-Hovav for comments and feedback. As of 2005 my work is funded by the Netherlands Organization for Scientific Research (NWO) grant number 017.001.271 which is gratefully acknowledged.

# References

[Berman and Slobin(1994)] Berman, R.A., Slobin, D.I.: Relating Events in Narrative: A Crosslinguistic Developmental Study. Lawrence Erlbaum, New Jersey (1994)

[Comrie(1976)] Comrie, B.: Aspect: An Introduction to the Study of Verbal Aspect and Related Problems. Cambridge University Press, Cambridge (1976)

[Creason(1995)] Creason, S.A.: Semantic Classes of Hebrew Verbs: A Study of Aktionsart in the Hebrew Verbal System. PhD thesis, The University of Chicago (1995)

[Doron(2003)] Doron, E.: Agency and Voice: The Semantics of the Semitic Templates. Natural Language Semantics (11), 1–67 (2003)

[Dowty(1991)] Dowty, D.R.: Thematic Proto-roles and Argument Selection. Language 67(3), 547–619 (1991)

[Halle and Marantz(1993)] Halle, M., Marantz, A.: Distributed Morphology. In: Hale, K., Keyser, S.J. (eds.) The View from Building 20, pp. 111–176. MIT Press, Cambridge, Mass (1993)

[Levin(2000)] Levin, B.: Aspect, Lexical Semantic Representation, and Argument Expression. In: Proceedings of the 26th meeting, Berkeley Linguistics Society (2000)

[Levin and Hovav(1991)] Levin, B., Hovav, M.R.: Wiping the Slate Clean: A Lexical Semantic Exploration. In: Levin, B., Pinker, S. (eds.) Lexical and Conceptual Semantics, ch. 5, pp. 123–152. Blackwell, Oxford (1991)

[Reichenbach(1947)] Reichenbach, H.: Elements of Symbolic Logic. Macmillan, London (1947)

[Rothstein(2004)] Rothstein, S.: Structuring Events: A Study in the Semantics of Lexical Aspect. Blackwell, Oxford (2004)

[Smith(1991)] Smith, C.S.: The Parameter of Aspect. Kluwer, Dordrecht (1991)

[Trabasso and Stein(1994)] Trabasso, T., Stein, N.L.: Using Goal/plan Knowledge to Merge the Past with the Present and the Future in Narrating Events On-line. In: Roberts, R.J., Haith, M., Benson, J.B., Pennington, B.F. (eds.) Future Oriented Processes, ch. 10, The University of Chicago Press, Chicago (1994)

[Tsarfaty(2005a)] Tsarfaty, R.: 'binyanim ba'avir': An Investigation of Aspect Semantics in Modern Hebrew. Master's thesis, ILLC, University of Amsterdam (2005)

[Tsarfaty(2005b)] Tsarfaty, R.: Connecting Causative Constructions and Aspectual Meanings: A Case Study from Semitic Derivational Morphology. In: Proceedings of the Fifteenth Amsterdam Colloquium (2005)

[van Lambalgen and Hamm(2005)] van Lambalgen, M., Hamm, F.: The Proper Treatment of Events. Blackwell, Oxford (2005)

[Vendler(1967)] Vendler, Z.: Linguistics in Philosophy. In: Chapter 4, pp. 97–121. Cornell University Press, Ithaca, New York (1967)

[Yitzhaki(2003)] Yitzhaki, D.: The Semantics of Lexical Aspect in Modern Hebrew. Master's thesis, Bar-Ilan University, Ramat Gan, Israel (2003)

# Natural Logic for Natural Language

Jan van Eijck

CWI, Amsterdam and Uil-OTS, Utrecht University
jve@cwi.nl
http://www.cwi.nl/~jve

**Abstract.** For a cognitive account of reasoning it is useful to factor out the syntactic aspect — the aspect that has to do with pattern matching and simple substitution — from the rest. The calculus of monotonicity, alias the calculus of natural logic, does precisely this, for it is a calculus of appropriate substitutions at marked positions in syntactic structures. We first introduce the semantic and the syntactic sides of monotonicity reasoning or 'natural logic', and propose an improvement to the syntactic monotonicity calculus, in the form of an improved algorithm for monotonicity marking. Next, we focus on the role of monotonicity in syllogistic reasoning. In particular, we show how the syllogistic inference rules (for traditional syllogistics, but also for a broader class of quantifiers) can be decomposed in a monotonicity component, an argument swap component, and an existential import component. Finally, we connect the decomposition of syllogistics to the doctrine of distribution.

## 1  Introduction

To develop a cognitive account of reasoning, a promising approach is to factor out the syntactic aspect — the aspect that has to do with pattern matching on syntactic structures — from the rest. An obvious candidate for this that has been around for some time now is the so-called calculus of monotonicity. This calculus has a semantic side and a syntactic side. The semantic foundation of monotonicity reasoning is a generalization of the notion of logical consequence to arbitrary types, by defining partial orderings $\Longrightarrow$ on all types (not just the type of sentences, but also those of verb phrases, predicates, adjectives, quantifiers, and so on). In terms of this, one can define what it means to be an order-preserving or an order reversing function from type $\alpha$ to type $\beta$. Order preserving functions are the functions $f$ that are such that if $x \Longrightarrow y$ then $f(x) \Longrightarrow f(y)$. Order reversing functions are the functions $f$ that are such that if $x \Longrightarrow y$ then $f(y) \Longrightarrow f(x)$.

The syntactic side of the calculus of monotonicity is the marking of monotonicity of syntactic components in a syntactic structure. Let $S$ be a syntactic structure, and let $A$ be a component of that structure. Suppose that $A$ has type $\alpha$ and $S$ has type $\beta$. Consider the syntactic function $F$ that consists of replacing component $A$ by other suitable components of type $\alpha$. In other words, consider the function $F = \lambda Y.S[Y/A]$. Then the semantic counterpart of $F$ is a function $f$ of type $\alpha \to \beta$. Soundness and completeness of a monotonicity calculus have to do with the relation between $F$ and $f$.

B.D. ten Cate and H.W. Zeevat (Eds.): TbiLLC 2005, LNAI 4363, pp. 216–230, 2007.

A monotonicity marking algorithm is *sound* if the following holds: if $A$ is marked $+$ in $S$, then the function that interprets $\lambda Y.S[Y/A]$ is monotonicity preserving, and if $A$ is marked $-$ in $S$, then the function that interprets $\lambda Y.S[Y/A]$ is monotonicity reversing.

A monotonicity marking algorithm is *complete* if the following holds: if the function that interprets $\lambda Y.S[Y/A]$ is monotonicity preserving then $A$ is marked $+$ in $S$, and if the function that interprets $\lambda Y.S[Y/A]$ is monotonicity reversing, then $A$ is marked $-$ in $S$.

Explanations of aspects of the human reasoning faculty must be based on hypotheses about calculating mechanisms. Monotonicity calculi have been proposed time and again in the literature as candidates for such mechanisms, by philosophers [23,11], logicians [5,22], computer scientists [21], linguists [8], and most recently by cognitive scientists [15], with less or more explicit suggestions to use them as a basis for generating hypotheses about processing load in human reasoning. The catch phrases for this enterprise used to be 'natural logic' or 'logic for natural language', for the logic that was meant to provide an account of the way human reasoners actually reason.

The structure of the paper is as follows. First we review the semantic side of monotonicity reasoning. Next, we look at the syntactic side, and propose an improvement of existing algorithms for monotonicity marking. Then, as a first step in developing a cognitive perspective on reasoning, we look at syllogistic reasoning and slight extensions of it, under the aspect of monotonicity. We show how the syllogistic reasoning rules can be decomposed in a monotonicity component (a monotonicity rule), a rule for argument swapping in symmetric quantifiers (a symmetry rule), and a rule for invoking the existential force of the syllogistic quantifiers (an existential import rule). The paper winds up by linking the monotonicity part of syllogistics to the doctrine of distribution.

## 2    Semantics of Monotonicity

Just as we can say that 'Gaia is smiling' logically implies 'Gaia is smiling or Gaia is crying', we would like to say that 'smiling' logically involves 'smiling or crying', or that 'dancing' logically implies 'moving', but also that 'at least three' logically implies 'at least two', and so on.

'Gaia is smiling' is a sentence, 'smiling' is a predicate, 'at least three' is a quantifier. We know what entailment means for sentences. One sentence entails another if whenever the first one is true the second one is. The obvious way to lift this notion to predicates is by stipulating that one predicate entails another if it holds for every subject that the sentence one gets by combining that subject with the first predicate entails the sentence one gets by combining the subject with the second predicate. Similarly for quantifiers. To get a sentence from 'at least three', one has to combine the quantifier with a noun and a verb. Since indeed it holds for every noun N and verb V that 'at least three N V' entails 'at least two N V', we can say that 'at least three' entails 'at least two'.

This idea of lifting entailment from the category of sentences to arbitrary categories was made fully precise by Van Benthem in [5]. The semantics of monotonicity from [5], given in terms of partial orders on arbitrary semantic domains (supposed to correspond to various syntactic categories), effectively extends the notion of logical entailment from the level of sentences to that of verb phrases, quantifiers, noun phrases, adjectives, and so on.

Van Benthem starts out from the basic types $t$ (truth values, the type of sentences), and $e$ (entities, the type of proper names). Complex types are defined by recursion, as follows: (i) $e$ and $t$ are types. (ii) if $\alpha$ and $\beta$ are types, then $\alpha \to \beta$ is a type. The entailment relation is defined as follows (we use $E :: \alpha$ for "syntactic expression $E$ has semantic type $\alpha$):

- If $E, E' :: e$ then $I(E) \Longrightarrow I(E') := I(E) = I(E')$.
- If $E, E' :: t$ then $I(E) \Longrightarrow I(E') := I(E) \leq I(E')$.
- If $E, E' :: \alpha \to \beta$ then $I(E) \Longrightarrow I(E')$ iff

$$\text{for all } x \in D_\alpha, I(E)(x) \Longrightarrow I(E')(x).$$

Here $I(E)$ denotes the interpretation of $E$, and $D_\alpha$ is used for the domain of objects of type $\alpha$. If $E :: \alpha$ then $I(E) \in D_\alpha$, i.e., the interpretation of $E$ is an object in $D_\alpha$, the domain of objects of type $\alpha$.

This definition yields results like the following:

$$\text{beautiful and intelligent} \Longrightarrow \text{beautiful}$$

$$\text{cry} \Longrightarrow \text{cry or sulk}$$

$$\text{Mary} \Longrightarrow \text{some woman}$$

$$\text{at most 1} \Longrightarrow \text{at most 2}$$

The 'order calculus' implied by this definition got reinvented in [13].

**Theorem 1.** *If the domain $D_e$ is finite, then for any type $\alpha$ the relation $\Longrightarrow_\alpha$ is decidable, and the monotonicity properties of any $F : \alpha \to \beta$ are decidable.*

*Proof.* If $D_e$ is finite, then $D_\alpha$ will be finite for any type $\alpha$.

To decide whether $f : D_\alpha \to D_\beta$ is order preserving (monotone increasing), check whether $f(x) \Longrightarrow f(y)$ for the finite number of pairs $(x, y)$ with $x \Longrightarrow y$.

To decide whether $f$ is order reversing (monotone decreasing), check whether $f(y) \Longrightarrow f(x)$ for the finite number of pairs $(x, y)$ with $x \Longrightarrow y$.     □

The decidability result was for fixed finite sizes of the domain. But note that the result still holds if you put an arbitrary finite treshold on the domain size:

**Theorem 2.** *For any finite threshold $k$ on the domain size, and for any type $\alpha$ the relation $\Longrightarrow_\alpha^{\leq k}$ ($\Longrightarrow_\alpha$ for all domains up to size $k$) is decidable, and the monotonicity properties of any $F : \alpha \to \beta$ are decidable.*

*Proof.* Just check the $\Longrightarrow_\alpha^0, \ldots, \Longrightarrow_\alpha^k$ in turn.     □

Below we will study the generalized syllogistic quantifiers based on 'At most $K$'. If we evaluate these in universes up to some fixed size, all inferences expressed in terms of them are decidable.

# 3    General Structure of Rules for Monotonicity Reasoning

A monotonicity preserving function $F$ can be represented as a kind of 'mental model' [17], as follows:

$$\frac{X \Longrightarrow Y}{F(X) \Longrightarrow F(Y)} \; F \uparrow$$

Here it is assumed that $X, Y$ are expressions of a logical type $\alpha$ that is partially ordered by $\Longrightarrow$, that $F(X), F(Y)$ are expressions of logical type $\beta$ that is partially ordered by $\Longrightarrow$, and that $F$ is an order-preserving function of type $\alpha \to \beta$. One way of reading the rule is as an explication of the fact that $F$ is order preserving (or monotone increasing). Another way of reading the rule is as an inference rule triggered by a function $F$ that is known to be order preserving. $F \uparrow$ expresses that $F$ is order preserving.

The mental model somehow represents the 'transfer' by $F$ of the growth of $X$ to the growth of $F(X)$, with details largely irrelevant. Indeed, the lack of formal detail of the publications in the mental models school seems to indicate that mental models are meant to provide a suggestive *metaphor* of cognitive processing rather than a formal mechanism. The metaphor suggests that when the mental picture of 'uniform growth' is put in reverse, processing load increases:

$$\frac{X \Longrightarrow Y}{F(X) \Longleftarrow F(Y)} \; F \downarrow$$

Again, there are various ways to read this rule. $F \downarrow$ expresses that $F$ is order reversing (or: monotone decreasing).

For an appreciation of the generality of the monotonicity rule, it is illuminating to look at some special cases. If $X, Y, F(X), F(Y)$ all have type $t$, then $\Longrightarrow$ is logical consequence (or logical implication), and $F(X)$, $F(Y)$ are statements, and we get:

$$\frac{X \Longrightarrow Y \quad F(X)}{F(Y)} \; F \uparrow$$

An example of this would be: infer from 'Mary dances implies Mary moves' (with 'Mary dances' for $X$ and 'Mary moves' for $Y$), and 'Mary dances gracefully' (with 'gracefully' for $F$) that 'Mary moves gracefully'.

$$\frac{X \Longrightarrow Y \quad F(Y)}{F(X)} \; F \downarrow$$

Reading $X$ and $Y$ as above, and reading $F$ as negation, we get the following example of this rule: infer from An example of this would be: infer from 'Mary dances implies Mary moves' and 'Mary does not move' (with 'does not' for $F$) that 'Mary does not dance'.

In the case where $X, Y$ are sets (type $e \to t$) and $F(X), (F(Y)$ are truth values, $F$ has type $(e \to t) \to t$ (the type of quantifiers), and we get:

$$\frac{Q(X) \quad X \subseteq Y}{Q(Y)} \; Q\uparrow$$

For an example, let $X$ stand for 'dancing', $Y$ for 'moving', and $Q$ for 'everyone'. Then the rule says that one may conclude from 'everyone is dancing' and 'dancing involves moving' that 'everyone is moving'.

$$\frac{Q(Y) \quad X \subseteq Y}{Q(X)} \; Q\downarrow$$

To get an example of this, read $X$ and $Y$ as above, and interpret $Q$ as 'nobody'.

In fact, $F$ may have further internal structure, i.e., $F(X)$ may have the form of binary generalized quantifier $\mathrm{Quant}(X, P)$ or $\mathrm{Quant}(P, X)$. This gives us four possible monotonicity rules for binary quantifiers. Examples of binary quantifiers are *all*, with monotonicity properties $(\downarrow, \uparrow)$, *some*, with $(\uparrow, \uparrow)$, *no*, with $(\downarrow, \downarrow)$, and *most*, with $(\_, \uparrow)$.

$$\frac{\mathrm{Quant}(X, P) \quad X \subseteq Y}{\mathrm{Quant}(Y, P)} \; \mathrm{Quant}(\uparrow, \_)$$

Example: infer from 'some philosophers are mortal' and 'philosophers are humans' that 'some humans are mortal'.

$$\frac{\mathrm{Quant}(P, X) \quad X \subseteq Y}{\mathrm{Quant}(P, Y)} \; \mathrm{Quant}(\_, \uparrow)$$

Example: infer from 'most philosophers are human' and 'humans are mortal' that 'most philosophers are mortal'.

$$\frac{\mathrm{Quant}(Y, P) \quad X \subseteq Y}{\mathrm{Quant}(X, P)} \; \mathrm{Quant}(\downarrow, \_)$$

Example: infer from 'all humans are mortal' and 'philosophers are human' that 'all philosophers are mortal'.

$$\frac{\mathrm{Quant}(P, Y) \quad X \subseteq Y}{\mathrm{Quant}(P, X)} \; \mathrm{Quant}(\_, \downarrow)$$

Example: infer from 'no philosophers are mortal' and 'humans are mortal' that 'no philosophers are human'.

## 4    Polarity Marking Revisited

If we can manage to parse a syntactic structure $S$ in some way or other as a monotonicity preserving function $F$ taking an argument $A$, we can make an inference step, given a suitable trigger. If we can parse $S$ as a monotonicity reversing function $F$ taking an argument $A$, we can make an inference step, given a suitable trigger. In an application of a monotonicity rule, one of the premisses is of the form $X \Rightarrow Y$, for some $X, Y$ of the same type. We call this premisse the trigger of the rule. In fact, polarity marking is an enrichment of syntax that can be viewed as a 'shallow' alternative for a translation into logical form.

Existing polarity marking calculi [22,8,6] are all based in one way or another on Sanchez's [22] bottom-up algorithm for polarity marking, which needs a separate pass for determining polarity in context. We propose to replace this by a top-down polarity marking algorithm, with the advantage that it takes context into account and computes polarity in a single pass. Here are some comparisons:

- Our approach assigns marking maps as part of the (bottom-up) syntax structure building process and next computes markings top-down.
- Sanchez' algorithm [22] works bottom-up and has three stages: (i) marking argument positions in lexical entries, (ii) propagating the markings to other categories, and (iii) polarity determination of nodes $C$ by counting the number of plusses and minuses on a path from the root to $C$.
- The approach of Dowty [8] is constraint-based and bottom up. This necessitates multiplication of syntactic categories for items that can occur in both positive and negative positions.
- The approach of [6] is also bottom up. It uses the machinery of multimodal categorial grammar, for which the issue of parsing complexity is still open (no polynomial parsing algorithm is known). Our approach to monotonicity marking avoids the machinery of multimodal categorial grammar.
- The 'order calculus' of [13] is a proof system for $\Longrightarrow$ for a particular natural language fragment. The system does not separate out polarity marking from $\Longrightarrow$ calculation. Because of the fact that for all but the simplest natural language fragments the $\Longrightarrow$ relation has much higher complexity than polarity marking (which can always be done in polynomial time), this is a design flaw.

The three maps on polarity markings that our algorithm employs are (i) preservation, (ii) reversal, and (iii) breaking of polarity. Polarity marking is fully determined by the polarity preserving and reversing properties of the semantic functions involved. Let polarity markings $m$ range over $\{+, -, 0\}$. Instead of explicitly giving the function, in a monotonicity calculus it is enough to give the mappings on polarity markings: preservation (the mapping $i$), reversal (the mapping $r$), or breaking of monotonicity (the mapping $b$), with $i$ the identity map, $r$ the map given by $r(+) = -, r(-) = +, r(0) = r(0)$, and $b$ given by $b(x) = 0$. Using $m$ for the domain $\{+, -, 0\}$, we see that maps on polarity markings have the type $m \to m$.

---

*Polarity Map Assignment*

**Leaf Marking** Functional lexical categories have all their result categories labelled with marker transformers. Lexical argument categories get an unlabelled basic category.

**Tree Marking** If C consists of a function $C_f/A$ and an argument A, where $f$ is a marker transformer, (or of an argument A and a function $A\backslash C_f$, or of an argument A, a function $A\backslash C_f/B$ and an argument B), then C gets marker transformer $f$.

In this algorithm, polarity maps are annotations on result categories, as in the following example lexicon.

$$C(\text{every}) = (S_i/\text{VP})_r/\text{CN} \qquad C(\text{did}) \quad = \text{VP}_i/\text{INF}$$
$$C(\text{some}) = (S_i/\text{VP})_i/\text{CN} \qquad C(\text{didn't}) = \text{VP}_r/\text{INF}$$
$$C(\text{no}) \quad = (S_r/\text{VP})_r/\text{CN} \qquad C(\text{man}) \quad = \text{CN}$$
$$C(\text{any}) \quad = (S_i/\text{VP})_i/\text{CN} \qquad C(\text{that}) \quad = \text{CN}\backslash\text{CN}_i/\text{VP}$$
$$C(\text{the}) \quad = (S_i/\text{VP})_b/\text{CN} \qquad C(\text{laugh}) \quad = \text{INF}$$
$$C(\text{most}) = (S_i/\text{VP})_b/\text{CN} \qquad C(\text{laughed}) = \text{VP}$$
$$C(\text{Ann}) \quad = S_i/\text{VP} \qquad\qquad C(\text{kissed}) \quad = \text{VP}_i/(S/\text{VP})$$

The category $(S_i/\text{VP})_r/\text{CN}$ for 'every' reflects the fact that the semantic function for this quantifier reverses monotonicity direction for its first argument, and keeps the monotonicity direction the same for its second argument.

Syntax trees are built using the familiar categorial grammar construction process, where $A/B$ combines with $B$ to form $[_A A/B\ B]$, $B\backslash A$ combines with $B$ to form $[_A B\ B\backslash A]$, and $B\backslash A/C$ combines with $B$ and $C$ to form $[_A B\ B\backslash A/C\ C]$. An example is in Figure 1.

The polarity marking algorithm works top-down, using the polarity marking maps at the nodes as guidance for determining the polarity markings of the argument nodes (the function nodes always inherit the marking of their parents, for reasons explained in [5]).

---

*Polarity Marking Algorithm*

**Root Marking** The main structure C to be marked has positive polarity, so it is marked with +.

**Component Marking** If a structure C has polarity marking $k$, then:

  **Leaf Marking** If C is a leaf, then done.

  **Composite Marking** If C consists of a function (C/A) and argument A (or an argument A and a function A\C, or an argument A, a function A\C/B and an argument B), then the function gets polarity marking $k$, and the argument(s) get polarity marking $f(k)$, where $f$ is the polarity marking map at node C.

---

This algorithm in fact defines a function from syntax trees with polarity marking maps to syntax trees with polarity marking maps and markings. The result of running the algorithm on the example tree is in Figure 2.

A monotonicity calculus can be based on the polarity marking algorithm plus information about the mappings on polarity markings of functional lexical elements and information about the $\Longrightarrow$ ordering, by means of the following rules:

$$\frac{[_S \cdots X^+ \cdots] \quad X \Longrightarrow Y}{[_S \cdots Y^+ \cdots]}$$

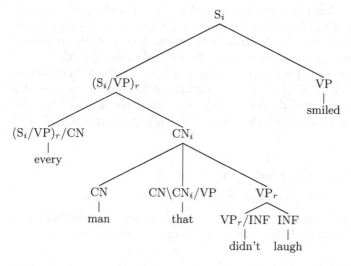

**Fig. 1.** 'Every man that didn't laugh smiled'

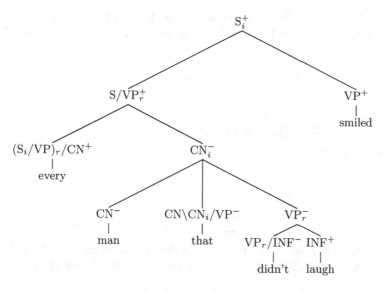

**Fig. 2.** Marked version of Figure 1

$$\frac{[_S \cdots X^- \cdots] \quad Y \Longrightarrow X}{[_S \cdots Y^- \cdots]}$$

Determination of $[_S \cdots X^+ \cdots]$ and $[_S \cdots X^- \cdots]$ is done by an algorithm for parsing plus monotonicity marking; for any reasonable grammar formalism it may be assumed that this can be done in polynomial time. Determination of $\Longrightarrow$ for the category of $X$ and $Y$ is another manner. As is explained in [19], this relation may have a high complexity, even for fairly simple fragments.

But even if $\implies$ is hard to compute, partial information about this relation (say, for basic categories), is enough for drawing interesting sound conclusions. Information about the $\implies$ ordering for basic categories is supposedly available as basic semantic knowledge of language users. In an implementation, this kind of knowledge can be extracted from semantic databases like Wordnet. The Wordnet [12] *hyperonym* relation encodes the $\implies$ relation on the logical type $e \to t$ of nouns. If Wordnet gives the information that 'cat' has hyperonym 'feline', that 'feline' has hyperonym 'mammal', that 'mammal' has hyperonym 'animal', then we can translate this as:

$$\text{cat} \implies \text{feline}$$

$$\text{feline} \implies \text{mammal}$$

$$\text{mammal} \implies \text{animal}$$

This combined with shallow text processing and monotonicity marking allows us to use Wordnet to draw shallow inferences from texts about cats.

## 5   Monotonicity in Syllogistics

Monotonicity calculi can be viewed as the logical mechanics of syllogistic theory [11,4,9]. The cornerstone of syllogistics is the following well-known Square of Opposition:

$$\text{All}(\downarrow, \uparrow) \quad \rule[0.5ex]{1em}{0.4pt}\rule[0.5ex]{1em}{0.4pt} \quad \text{No}(\downarrow, \downarrow)$$
$$\downarrow \qquad\qquad\qquad \downarrow$$
$$\text{Some}(\uparrow, \uparrow) \quad \rule[0.5ex]{1em}{0.4pt}\rule[0.5ex]{1em}{0.4pt} \quad \text{NotAll}(\uparrow, \downarrow)$$

In set-theoretic notation:

$$P \subseteq Q \quad \rule[0.5ex]{1em}{0.4pt}\rule[0.5ex]{1em}{0.4pt} \quad P \subseteq \overline{Q}$$
$$\downarrow \qquad\qquad \downarrow$$
$$P \not\subseteq \overline{Q} \quad \rule[0.5ex]{1em}{0.4pt}\rule[0.5ex]{1em}{0.4pt} \quad P \not\subseteq Q$$

The inferencing that goes on in syllogistics reduces to applications of SYM, EI, and MON, where MON is the monotonicity rule, while SYM and EI are the following rules:

- **SYM or Symmetry** is the rule that infers $\text{Quant}(Q, P)$ from $\text{Quant}(P, Q)$ for symmetric quantifiers. *Some* and *No* are symmetric.
- **EI or Existential Import** is the principle that every term has a non-empty extension.

$P \subseteq Q$ together with $P \neq \emptyset$ yields $P \cap Q \neq \emptyset$, i.e.: From *All P are Q* it follows by EI that *Some P are Q* $P \subseteq \overline{Q}$ together with $P \neq \emptyset$ yields $P \cap \overline{Q} \neq \emptyset$, i.e.: From *No P are Q* it follows by EI that *Not all P are Q*.

In the context of syllogistics, the **Monotonicity triggers** are the following quantifiers:

- All P Q: $P \subseteq Q$,
- No P Q: $P \subseteq \overline{Q}, Q \subseteq \overline{P}$.

Since there is only a finite number of valid syllogistic patterns, completeness of the rules MON, SYM, EI for syllogistics can be proved by checking that every valid syllogistic pattern can be 'decomposed' into applications of MON, SYM and EI (see Section 6 below for examples). A computer program for this is given in [10]. Modulo the correctness of the program, this establishes:

**Theorem 3.** *The calculus consisting of the rules MON, SYM and EI is complete for syllogistics.*

It is well-known that a generalization of syllogistics can be based on the following parametrized version of Square of Opposition ([4,9]):

$$\text{AllExceptAtMost } N \ (\downarrow, \uparrow) =\!=\!=\!= \text{AtMost } N \ (\downarrow, \downarrow)$$

$$\downarrow \qquad\qquad\qquad \downarrow$$

$$\text{AtLeast } (N+1) \ (\uparrow, \uparrow) =\!=\!=\!= \text{AtLeast } (N+1) \text{ Not } (\uparrow, \downarrow)$$

The traditional square is the special case of this with $N$ set to 0.
Using $P \subseteq_n Q$ for

$$\exists P' \subseteq P(|P - P'| \le n \wedge P' \subseteq Q),$$

we see that generalized monotonicity triggers now appear in the following guises:

- AllExceptAtMost n P Q: $P \subseteq_n Q$,
- AtMost n P Q: $P \subseteq_n \overline{Q}, Q \subseteq_n \overline{P}$.

Here is the generalized square in set-theoretic notation:

$$P \subseteq_n Q =\!=\!=\!= P \subseteq_n \overline{Q}$$

$$\downarrow \qquad\qquad \downarrow$$

$$P \not\subseteq_n \overline{Q} =\!=\!=\!= P \not\subseteq_n Q$$

Applications of monotonicity reasoning in this generalized setting look like this:

$$\frac{P \subseteq_n Q \quad Q \subseteq_m R}{P \subseteq_{n+m} R}$$

Using $P \cap_n Q$ for $|P \cap Q| \ge n$, we see that $P \cap_{n+1} Q$ is equivalent to $P \not\subseteq_n \overline{Q}$. We get:

$$\frac{P \cap_n Q \quad Q \subseteq_m R}{P \cap_{n \dot- m} R}$$

where $n \dot- m$ denotes cut-off subtraction (if $n \le m$ then $n \dot- m = 0$).

Note that existential import yields nothing new for the new quantifiers. For let $n \geq 1$. Then from $P \neq \emptyset$ and $P \subseteq_n Q$ it does *not follow* that $P \cap Q \neq \emptyset$.

The situation changes when we adopt the following natural generalization of existential import, to keep in step with the new situation:

> Generalized existential import (GEI) for predicate $P$ is the requirement that $|P| > n$.

Existential import for standard syllogistics is the special case of this where $n = 0$. Note that GEI does have an effect: from $|P| > n$ and $P \subseteq_n Q$ it *does follow* that $P \cap Q \neq \emptyset$.

Again, by a careful case by case analysis, we can establish:

**Theorem 4.** *The calculus consisting of the rules MON, SYM and GEI is complete for generalized syllogistics.*

The monotonicity behaviour of the function $\lambda n \lambda P \lambda Q.P \subseteq_n Q$ is given by:

$$\frac{P \subseteq_n Q \quad n \leq m}{P \subseteq_m Q}$$

This yields the monotonicity marker map $((S_i/VP)_r/CN)_i/NUM$ for 'all except at most'. To build natural language fragments for generalized syllogistics, one can use a lexicon that has entries like the following:

| | | | | | |
|---|---|---|---|---|---|
| $C(\text{all})$ | $=$ | $(S_i/VP)_r/CN$ | $C(\text{Greeks})$ | $=$ | CN |
| $C(\text{some})$ | $=$ | $(S_i/VP)_i/CN$ | $C(\text{Atheneans})$ | $=$ | CN |
| $C(\text{no})$ | $=$ | $(S_r/VP)_r/CN$ | $C(\text{barbarians})$ | $=$ | CN |
| $C(\text{not all})$ | $=$ | $(S_r/VP)_i/CN$ | $C(\text{philosophers})$ | $=$ | CN |
| $C(1), C(2), \ldots$ | $=$ | NUM | $C(\text{sophists})$ | $=$ | CN |
| $C(\text{all except at most})$ | $=$ | $((S_i/VP)_r/CN)_i/NUM$ | $C(\text{cynics})$ | $=$ | CN |
| $C(\text{at least})$ | $=$ | $((S_i/VP)_r/CN)_r/NUM$ | $C(\text{are})$ | $=$ | $VP_i/CN$ |
| $C(\text{at most})$ | $=$ | $((S_i/VP)_r/CN)_i/NUM$ | $C(\text{are not})$ | $=$ | $VP_r/CN$ |

For such fragments, one can state and prove completeness results for monotonicity reasoning, by comparing the calculus with rules MON, SYM and GEI to the semantic consequence relation for first order models that result from interpreting the fragment: domains of discourse, plus interpretations for the common nouns. [19] gives an assessment of the complexity of the satisfiability problem for a variety of fragments starting from syllogistic theory. Syllogistic satisfiability is decidable in polynomial time. If relative clauses are added the complexity becomes NP, further addition of transitive verbs moves the complexity to EXPTIME, and so on. One can look at these findings in various ways. In [19] the conclusion is drawn that the programme of natural logic is hopeless:

> [...] from a complexity-theoretic point of view, there is every reason to believe that, for all but the most impoverished fragments, reasoning using schemata based on the syntax of natural language will confer no advantage whatever.

One may also draw the conclusion that natural logic is perhaps more complex and more interesting and more challenging than people used to believe.

## 6     Fine Structure of Syllogisms

Every valid syllogism involves exactly one application of the monotonicity rule, either triggered by 'All' or by 'No' (or in the generalized case, by 'All except at most $N$' or by 'At most $N$'). Arguably, the syllogisms that just involve monotonicity are the simplest ones. A syllogism may or may not involve an application of the following rules:

1. symmetry of a premise,
2. symmetry of the conclusion,
3. existential import of a premise
4. existential import of the conclusion.

As an example of decomposition of a syllogism in terms of the rules MON, SYM and EI, here are two possible decompositions of the syllogism *fesapo*:

$$\cfrac{\cfrac{\text{No } C \ B}{\text{No } B \ C} \text{ Sn} \quad \cfrac{\cfrac{\cfrac{\text{All } B \ A}{\text{Some } B \ A} \text{ Ea}}{\text{Some } A \ B} \text{ Ss}}{}\text{ Mn}}{\text{Some } A \ \overline{C}}$$

$$\cfrac{\cfrac{\cfrac{\text{No } C \ B}{\text{No } B \ C} \text{ Sn} \quad \cfrac{\text{All } B \ A}{\text{Some } B \ A} \text{ Ea}}{\text{Some } \overline{C} \ A} \text{ Mn}}{\text{Some } A \ \overline{C}} \text{ Ss}$$

Here $Mn$ denotes an application of MON with *No* as trigger, $Ea$ denotes EI for *All*, $Ss$ denotes SYM for *Some*, and so on.

Measured in terms of decomposition complexity, *fesapo* is the most complex valid syllogism. In an empirical set-up of [7], the inference from 'No B C, All B A' to 'NotAll A C' (the *fesapo* pattern) is only recognized as valid in 8 percent of the cases, while in a staggering 61 percent of the cases, subjects think, erroneously, that the conclusion *No A C* follows from the premises. The only cases where the scores are still lower for endorsement of a valid conclusion are cases where the conclusion follows by existential import from a universal negative conclusion that is *also* valid, and that is recognized in a majority of cases as being valid.

## 7     Monotonicity and Distribution

An important heuristics in traditional logic is the doctrine of distribution, consisting of the following two rules:

1. the middle term of a valid syllogism has to be distributed in at least one of the premises,

2. if a term of a valid syllogism is distributed in the conclusion it has to be distributed in one of the premises.

Prior [20] gives the following explanation of what 'distributed' means in these rules:

> It is often said [...] that a distibuted term refers to all, and an undistributed term to only a part, of its extension. But in what way does "Some men are mortal", for example, refer to only a part of the class of men? Any man whatever will do to verify it: if any man whatever turns out to be mortal, "Some men are mortal" is true. What the traditional writers were trying to express seems to be something of the following sort: a term $t$ is distributed in a proposition $f(t)$ if and only if it is replaceable in $f(t)$, without loss of truth, by any term "falling under it" in the way that a species falls under a genus.

Interpreting 'being distributed' like this, we can see that

From 'All A B' and 'All B C' infer 'All A C'

has the middle term $B$ distributed in 'All B C', in agreement with the first rule of distribution, while $B$ violates the first rule of distribution in the following invalid pattern:

From 'All A B' and 'Some B C' infer 'All A C'.

An invalid pattern that violates the second rule of distribution is:

From 'Some A B' and 'All B C' infer 'All A C'.

Here $A$ is distributed in the conclusion, but not in the premise where it occurs.

Prior's suggestion of a modern version of the doctrine of distribution is taken up in Van Benthem [4]. In Van Eijck [9] the relations between traditional logic (syllogistic theory) and generalized quantifier theory [18,1,3] are worked out further, with due attention to the role of monotonicity in syllogistic reasoning, and with the observation that the square of opposition generalizes to quantifiers defined from *At least n*.

Hodges [16] relates the doctrine of distribution to monotonicity (just as [20,4,9] had done before), and gives a semantic argument to show that the correctness of the two rules of distribution follows from the interpretation of 'distributed term' as 'term in a downward monotone position'. The doctrine of distribution also follows from our completeness result. Consider the first rule of distribution, saying that the middle term has to be distributed in at least one of the premises. If the trigger of the monotonicity rule is 'No P Q', then this condition is always fulfilled, for both P and Q are in downward position. If the trigger of the monotonicity rule is 'All P Q', then the condition is fulfilled if P is the middle term, for P is in a downward position in 'All P Q', and it is also fulfilled if Q is the middle term, for the monotonicity rule allows substitution of Q by P in the other premise only if Q is in downward position in that premise. Hodges shows that the second rule of distribution follows from the first rule, as follows. Let $\phi$ and $\psi$ be the two premises, and assume P is in downward position in $\chi(P)$, where

$\phi$, $\psi$, therefore $\chi(P)$

is a valid syllogism. Assume, without loss of generality, that P is a term in $\phi$, and suppose that P is in upward position in $\phi(P)$. Then

$\phi(P)$, $\overline{\chi}(P)$, therefore $\overline{\psi}$

is also a valid syllogism. But in this syllogism P is the middle term. Moreover, the effect of wide scope negation is that P is in upward position in $\overline{\chi}(P)$, and we have a contradiction with the first rule of distribution.

# 8    Related and Future Work

Sanchez [22] is an extensive study of the role of monotonicity in 'natural reasoning', with as main contribution an algorithm for monotonicity marking, and a system for monotonicity reasoning in terms of monotonicity markings. This work is based on [5], and is in turn the basis of almost all later proposals for monotonicity calculi.

In Geurts [14] a monotonicity based system of reasoning for syllogistics is sketched, in terms of Sanchez-style monotonicity markings. The claim is made that monotonicity, symmetry and existential import account for all syllogistic inference, but the presentation of the rules is too informal to admit a proof of this. Geurts' intention is to explain empirical findings about accomplishment in syllogistic reasoning tasks in terms of complexity of inference in his reasoning system. It seems clear that the interest of syllogistics for cognitive science lies in the mechanism of monotonicity. Connecting the logical exploration of this mechanism with empirical findings in the psychology of reasoning is an obvious next goal. The hypothesis of [15] that reversal of monotonicity increases human processing load can be linked to the mental models metaphor. Interestingly, from a logical point of view the reversed monotonicity pattern is no more complex than the pattern of preserved monotonicity.

Monotonicity calculi can be specified in a fully precise manner, by presenting them as proof calculi, consisting of axioms and inference rules. Such calculi are meant to capture standard notions of logical consequence: they are not calculi of logical falsehoods. If they can be used to explain where human reasoners err, it should be in an indirect manner, by making clear what the added complexity of a particular task is in comparison with tasks where human reasoners tend not to err. This suggests that, given a suitably precise version of a monotonicity calculus, it should be possible to flesh out the mental models metaphor as a formally precise extension of the monotonicity calculus, a kind of add-on tool that allows us to classify reasoning tasks with respect to their claims on the human processing faculty [2].

*Acknowledgement.* Thanks to Fabian Battaglini for getting me interested in the topic of natural logic again, and for inspiring discussions. Thanks to Ian Pratt and two anonymous referees for spotting errors in and providing illuminating comments to an earlier version of this paper. All remaining errors are my own.

# References

1. Barwise, J., Cooper, R.: Generalized quantifiers and natural language. Linguistics and Philosophy 4, 159–219 (1981)
2. Battaglini, F.: Monotonicity and cognition. Manuscript, Uil-OTS, Utrecht (2006)
3. van Benthem, J.: Questions about quantifiers. Journal of Symbolic Logic 49, 443–466 (1984)
4. van Benthem, J.: Essays in Logical Semantics. Reidel, Dordrecht (1986)
5. van Benthem, J.: Language in Action: categories, lambdas and dynamic logic. Studies in Logic 130. Elsevier, Amsterdam (1991)
6. Bernardi, R.: Reasoning with Polarity in Categorial Type Logic. PhD thesis, Uil-OTS, Utrecht University (2002)
7. Chater, N., Oaksford, M.: The probability heuristics model of syllogistic reasoning. Cognitive Psychology 38, 191–258 (1999)
8. Dowty, D.: Negative polarity and concord marking in natural language reasoning. In: SALT Proceedings (1994)
9. van Eijck, J.: Generalized quantifiers and traditional logic. In: van Benthem, J., ter Meulen, A. (eds.) Generalized Quantifiers, Theory and Applications, Foris, Dordrecht (1985)
10. van Eijck, J.: Syllogistics = monotonicity + symmetry + existential import. Technical Report SEN-R0512, CWI, Amsterdam (July 2005), available from http://db.cwi.nl/rapporten/
11. Englebretsen, G.: Notes on the new syllogistic. Logique et Analyse 85–86, 111–120 (1979)
12. Fellbaum, C.: Wordnet, an electronic lexical database. MIT Press, Cambridge (1998)
13. Fyodorov, Y., Winter, Y., Francez, N.: Order-based inference in natural logic. Logic Journal of the IGPL 11, 385–416 (2003)
14. Geurts, B.: Reasoning with quantifiers. Cognition 86, 223–251 (2003)
15. Geurts, B., van der Slik, F.: Monotonicity and processing load. Journal of Semantics 22, 97–117 (2005)
16. Hodges, W.: The laws of distribution for syllogisms. Notre Dame Journal of Formal Logic 39, 221–230 (1998)
17. Johnson-Laird, P.N.: Mental Models; towards a cognitive science of language, inference and consciousness. Cambridge University Press, Cambridge (1983)
18. Mostowski, A.: On a generalization of quantifiers. Fundamenta Mathematica 44, 12–36 (1957)
19. Pratt-Hartmann, I.: Fragments of language. Journal of Logic, Language and Information 13(2), 207–223 (2004)
20. Prior, A.N.: Traditional logic. In: Edwards, P. (ed.) The Encyclopedia of Philosophy, vol. 5, pp. 34–45. Macmillan, NYC (1967)
21. Purdy, W.C.: A logic for natural language. Notre Dame Journal of Formal Logic 32, 409–425 (1991)
22. Sánchez, V.: Studies on Natural Logic and Categorial Grammar. PhD thesis, University of Amsterdam (1991)
23. Sommers, F.: The Logic of Natural Language. Cambridge University Press, Cambridge (1982)

# Georgian as the Testing-Ground for Theories of Tense and Aspect

UiLOTS, Utrecht University
verkuyl@let.uu.nl
http://www.let.uu.nl/~henk.verkuyl/personal

**Abstract.** The aim of the present paper is to investigate the possibility
for Western tense theories to be applied successfully to the description of
the Georgian tense system. Georgian tense is extremely complex because
the Georgian language is agglutinative which means that semantic information which is scattered over the sentence in Germanic and Romance
languages is expressed by a morphologically very complex verbal form
that has many other duties to fulfill apart from expressing temporal information. It will be argued that the binary tense system as developed
in [8] and modernized in [9] is indeed applicable and, after an extension,
may even explain in a sufficient degree of depth why Georgian tense
is expressed as it is, especially as far as the aorist is concerned. The
description of the Georgian tenses—both the analytic ones and the synthetic ones—in terms of binary oppositions seems more adequate than
a description in terms of the standard ternary make up of the Reichenbachian framework.

## 1  Georgian Tense

In Georgian a verbal form has many duties to fulfill because verbal forms are
very complex units of information by the agglutinative nature of the language.
Its synthetic verbal forms present the problem of determining the way in which
temporal information is encoded among other sorts of information such as transitivity, aspect and mood, the encoding of thematic roles in the form of case
marking, directionality, among other things. The complexity of the verb forms
led Georgian grammarians (e.g. [7], [2], [1]) into rejecting the notion of tense.
They rather prefer to speak about screeves, because some verb forms mix plain
time reference with information such as evidentiality, desire, possible completion, etc. making it impossible for them to isolate strictly temporal information
from other sorts of information expressed by these forms.

Although there are several verb classes that are distinguished on the basis of
their morphological properties such as the affixes taken by their stem, the tense
system will be discussed here with the help of just one verb, the transitive verb
*c'era* (write) which will be given without arguments and in the 3rd singular
person. This is because this oversimplification does not harm the main point of
the present paper that is going to be made. Following the numbering of screeves

B.D. ten Cate and H.W. Zeevat (Eds.): TbiLLC 2005, LNAI 4363, pp. 231–246, 2007.
© Springer-Verlag Berlin Heidelberg 2007

**Table 1.** The indicative tense forms of *c'era* (write) in Georgian

| Tense | IMPERFECTIVE | PERFECTIVE |
|---|---|---|
| 1 Present | c'er-s | |
| 2 Imperfect | c'er-d-a | |
| 4 Future | | da-c'er-s |
| 5 Conditional Past | | da-c'er-d-a |
| 7 Aorist | c'er-a | da-c'er-a |
| 9 Perfect | u-c'er-ia | da-u-c'er-i-a |
| 10 Pluperfect | e-c'er-a | da-e-c'er-a |

and three analytic tenses:

| | | |
|---|---|---|
| 12 Analytic Perfect | | da-c'er-il-i a-kv-s |
| 13 Analytic PluPerfect | | da-c'er-il-i h-kon-d-a |
| 14 Analytic Future | | da-c'er-il-i e-kn-eb-a |

as used by [7] and [2], there are seven synthetic indicative tense forms presented
in Table 1. The numbering is based on a scheme from [1] in which the missing
numbers (3, 6, 8, 11) cover subjunctive forms. Hillery's numbering will be used
here to be able to refer to a certain tense form both by its name and by the
corresponding fixed number, the latter in some of the diagrams below.

A short characterization of the semantics of the tenses is necessary. The list
of tenses in Table 1 shows the opposition between imperfective and perfective
forms: the presence of the *da*-morpheme indicates completion. The Present and
Imperfect lack a perfective form. The Present 1 deviates from its English counterpart in that *c'ers* may express both that he is writing and that he writes,
dependent, of course, on the context. The Imperfect 2 *c'erda* (wrote) may per-
tain to a situation in which he was writing but also to situations in which he used
to write. Hillery states that the Future 4 corresponds to the English Future but
it is important to see that only a perfective form can be used: *dac'ers* expresses
something like 'he will write and complete his writing', where *da-* is a preverb
expressing completion. However, not all verb classes need a preverb to express
this. Moreover, the English *He will write* will be translated as *dac'ers*, without
necessarily invoking the perfective preverb meaning. Yet if compared with the
Analytic Future 14, the Future 4 has some perfective flavor. The Conditional
Past 5 is used to report about repeated actions that have been completed in
the past: *Giorgi c'erils dac'erda holme* means 'George used to write a letter and
complete it (each time)', completion being a feature of each of the writings making up the series that formed the habit. In conditional sentences the sense of a
habit disappears.

The Aorist 7 and the Perfect tenses 9 and 10 have imperfective forms alongside
the perfective ones. According to Hillery, the imperfective forms are extremely
rare so he leaves them out of his treatment of the screeves. Kakhi Sakhltkhutsishvili (pers. comm.) raises some doubts about that by saying that they do occur
though not as frequently as their perfective counterparts, but if they occur, they

have their own specific meanings. For example, the Imperfective Perfect in *c'erili uc'eria* expresses that there is evidence for his writing on a letter but the evidence includes also the information that the letter was half-finished. I will leave the three imperfective forms in 7, 9 and 10 out for the rest of the paper until it becomes necessary, at the very end, to include them in the discussion again.

The Aorist 7 *dac'era* is used to speak about a single completed event in the past. The Perfect 9 *dauc'eria* also pertains to a single completed event in the past but crucial for its use is the fact that the result of what took place in the past is evident in the present. It is therefore often called the first evidential Perfect. It is essential for the proper use of *dauc'eria* that at the point of speech there is sufficient evidence for the fact that he has written (something). It is perfectly possible to say *gus'in c'erili uc'eria* (lit: he has written a letter yesterday). The Pluperfect 10 *daec'era* is the same as the Perfect except for the fact that the completed past event is related to some point of reference in the past. In this respect it has the same features as the English Pluperfect.

As to the remaining three analytic forms, it must be established that these contain the passive participle *dac'erili* accompanied by an auxiliary. The three meanings involved express what their English counterparts express. They are not treated as genuine tenses on the ground that the auxiliary forms *akvs*, *ekneba* and *hkonda* are considered to have their own tense which is absent in the infinitival form of the main verb. The analytic Perfects do not express evidentiality at all. It is interesting to observe that *\*gus'in c'erili dac'erili akvs* (lit: he has written a letter yesterday) is absolutely not allowed in Georgian.

Most Georgian grammarians distinguish just two tenses: Present and Past. By so doing they first exclude the analytic tenses from the synthetic ones by arguing that the Perfect Participle *da-c'er-il-i* does not express tense and then they take Present and Future (1, 4) in the synthetic forms together as opposed to the Past-forms (2, 5, 7, 9 and 10). As far as the exclusion of the analytic forms is concerned, I will not follow that line of thought: on the same ground one could argue that English and Dutch have just two tenses by excluding auxilaries as carriers of temporal information. We are interested, however, in which way temporal information is encoded in a language and have to abstract from the choice between analytic forms and synthetic forms. In short, one should be able to characterize the correspondences and differences between 9 and 12 and between 10 and 13 in terms of the same semantic tools.

Returning to the restriction of presenting only the tense forms of one verb *c'era*, which might be misleading due to aspectual properties of the stem which could be absent in other stems, it should be underlined that it is hardly possible, not to say impossible, to give a conjugation pattern that is representative for all Georgian verbs. But we are specifically interested in the temporal semantics of the tense forms. The Georgian equivalents of English verbs like *love* (Vendler's Statives) and *die* (Vendler's Achievements), *si-q'var-ul-i* and *kvd-om-a* respectively, do not give a picture that differs from the semantics of the tense forms in Table 1, although the lexical semantics of the verb involved, of course, plays a role in the resulting interpretation. For example, the Analytic Perfect form *s'e-q'var-eb-ul-i ari-s* (he is in love/he has fallen in love with somebody) expresses a sense of resultativeness or completedness due to the Perfective or Past Participle form of the verb, on the basis of an inference due to the stative nature of its stem. Something similar applies to *mkvd-ar-i i-q'-o* (he was dead/he had died), although in this case *mkvd-ar-i* is considered an Active or Present Participle which also expresses a state resulting from a transition. Finally, what is expressed by the two corresponding Aorist forms *s'e-u-q'var-d-a* (he fell in love with) and *mo-k'vd-a* (he died) does not deviate from the *da-c'er-a*-form discussed above in terms of locating the eventuality in question. In view of considerations like these, the data demonstrated with the help of the verb *c'era* may be taken to be representative for the system that underlies Georgian verbs as far as the temporal structure they express is concerned.

## 2   Reichenbach's Matrix

The most popular Western tense theory is without doubt the one proposed in [5]. In the past sixty years it has brought about a family of tense theories, one could say, because most of the proposals extending or modifying Reichenbach's tense system consider themselves Reichenbachian. By this, one should understand two things: (a) the system is based on two tripartitions: the first one is Past-Present-Future, the second one is Anterior-Synchronous-Posterior; (b) apart from the traditional points E (the point representing the event E) and the point S (the point of speech S) the system introduces an auxiliary point of reference, called R, which together with E and S form the by now well-known Reichenbachian tense configurations. Table 2 presents English, French, Russian and Georgian tense forms. I assume sufficient familiarity with the way in which tense configurations are construed on the basis of the three points S, R and E, so that there is no problem in "reading" the matrix. As pointed out in [9], going through it one yields a number of problems that turn out to be decisive for a choice between the $3 \times 3$-make up of the Reichenbachian system and the $2 \times 2 \times 2$-approach that will be discussed below.

To begin with it is obvious that the matrix cannot harbour one English tense form: *would have written*. This means that it does not fulfill the requirement that each tense form be accounted for. A second problem is that in English the tense form *will write* is connected with three different configurations in the cells 6,8 and 9. In French the form *écrira* occurs only in two cells (6,8) and *va écrire* only in cell 8. In Russian *napishet* cannot occur in cell 8. There is (still) no principled account for these differences. Moreover, the cells 3 and 7 are configurationally overfull. This means that R relates to S and E in a way that is not completely satisfactory, because one would like to have one configuration per cell.

The system can also not explain why the distinction between the Present Perfect in 1 and the Past Perfect in 4 is blurred in Russian and why the Present Perfect, the Imparfait and the Passé Simple in French differ as they do. At first

**Table 2.** Reichenbach's matrix for English (8 forms), French (14 forms), Russian (5 forms) and Georgian (10 forms)

| | Past   R–S | Present   R,S | Future   S–R |
|---|---|---|---|
| Anterior<br><br>E–R | 1. Anterior Past<br>E–R–S<br><br>*had written*<br>*avait écrit, écrivit*<br>*napisál*<br>**daec'era** (10)<br>**dac'erili hkonda** (13) | 2. Anterior Present<br>E–R,S<br><br>*has written*<br>*a écrit, écrivit*<br>*napisál*<br>**dauc'eria** (9)<br>**dac'erili akvs** (12) | 3. Anterior Future<br>E,S–R , E–S–R, S–E–R<br><br>*will have written*<br>*aura écrit*<br><br>**dac'ers** (4)<br>**dac'erili ekneba** (14) |
| Simple<br><br>E,R | 4. Simple Past<br>E,R–S<br><br>*wrote*<br>*écrivit, écrivait*<br>*pisál*<br>**c'erda** (2)<br>**dac'era** (7)<br>**dauc'eria** (9) | 5. Simple Present<br>E,R,S<br><br>*writes*<br>*écrit*<br>*pishet*<br>**c'ers** (1) | 6. Simple Future<br>S – R,E<br><br>*will write*<br>*écrira*<br>*napishet*<br>**dac'ers** (4) |
| Posterior<br><br>R–E | 7. Posterior Past<br>**R–E–S**, R– S,E, R–S–E<br><br>*would write*<br>*écrirait, allait écrire*<br><br>**dac'erda** (5) | 8. Posterior Present<br>S,R – E<br><br>*will write*<br>*écrira, va écrire*<br>*budet pisat'* | 9. Posterior Future<br>S – R – E<br><br>*will write*<br>\**écrira, ira écrire* |

sight it looks as if this problem carries over to Georgian because here the Aorist forms can be located both in the cells 1 and 2, there being no way to restrict them to just one cell. Moreover, there is no way to separate the analytic forms from the synthetic forms.

Although these problems are well-known and attempts have been made to improve on Reichenbach's original proposal, the tendency in the literature is to maintain the 3 × 3-approach (cf. [3], [4], [10] among many others). Te Winkel's 2 × 2 × 2-approach is crucially different, so it would not help for me to solve problems for Georgian met by Reichenbachian 3 × 3-systems that have been improved on the problems just enumerated. If Te Winkel's approach turns out to be fruitful for the treatment of Georgian tense, this implies that a 3 × 3-approach cannot be considered equally successful. It is not so much the fact that in a binary approach Future is no longer directly related to the point of speech S by taking posteriority as 'later than any point', it is rather the binary nature of the tense oppositions that turns out to be dramatically involved in getting a grip on the complexity of Georgian tense.

## 3  Te Winkel's Binary System

For Dutch, [8] offers a tense system in which the eight tense forms are described by three binary oppositions: (i) Present - Past; (ii) Synchronous - Posterior; and (iii) Imperfect - Perfect. Te Winkel's system has been compared with Reichenbach's approach in [9] and modernized in [12]. Its syntactic base is given in Figure 1. Type-logically both POST and PERF are of type $\langle\langle i,t\rangle,\langle i,t\rangle\rangle$: they take

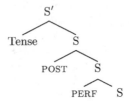

**Fig. 1.** Tense structure

a tenseless S of type $\langle i,t\rangle$ yielding a tenseless S.[1] The two Tense-operators PRES and PAST are of type $\langle\langle i,t\rangle,t\rangle$. They take a tenseless S of type $\langle i,t\rangle$ and yield a tensed S' of type $t$.

### 3.1  Present-Past

The first opposition is crucially connected to the point of speech, which I will call **n**: PRES positions a point of reference or, as I would like to say, an index i in **n**, whereas PAST positions i anterior to **n**. In terms of Te Winkel:

> In thinking one starts from one of two points in time: either from the present or from the past. In the former case everything is seen as it appears at the moment at which one is thinking; in the latter case as it appeared at the moment at which one is thinking (in the past). (1866:68; translation)

Suppose that one represents the tenseless sentence (1a) as in (1b):

(1)  a. Mary write the letter
     b. $\lambda i'.\mathrm{Write}(i')(b)(m)$

The index $i'$ represents the event-information connected with the predication. Te Winkel's intention can be captured by the two tense operators defined as:

(2)  a. PRES := $\lambda\phi\exists!i[\phi[i] \wedge i \simeq n]$
     b. PAST := $\lambda\phi\exists!i[\phi[i] \wedge i < n]$

---

[1] A tenseless S is taken as pertaining to a set of $i$-entities, which roughly can be taken as corresponding to a set of events. An index $i$ represents a numerical value (a natural number) standing for the temporal information expressed by the predication (compare the use of 18 in September 18, where 18 represents a stretch defined in the Real numbers). This avoids the (naive-physics) approach of mereologically based analyses (cf. [11]).

**Fig. 2.** Past and Present

They introduce an index i which is located in the present or in the past. The symbol $\simeq$ in the definition of PRES stands for the binary relation of being synchronous. More than the popular symbol $\circ$ for overlap, $\simeq$ signifies the sense of occurring at the same time. And that is what we need: by (2a) **n** and i are in the same stretch of time which we call the present, **n** being contained by i or identical to i or (possibly) containing i. What $\simeq$ is intended to express is that both i and **n** are part of a present rather than being the present itself. Thus it is assumed that the interpretation of what counts as **n** is contextually determined. The PAST-operator applied to the tenseless (1b) yields:

(3)   PAST(Mary write the letter) $\leadsto$
$\quad \lambda\phi\exists!i[\phi[i] \wedge i < n](\lambda i'.\text{Write}(i')(b)(m))$
$\quad = \exists!i[\lambda i'.\text{Write}(i')(m)(m)[i] \wedge i < n]$
$\quad = \exists!i[\text{Write}(i)(b)(m) \wedge i < n]$

This says that there is a contextually definite index preceding the point of speech at which Mary is writing the letter appeared. Because the index precedes **n**, the event in question is in the past. The two configurations that occur on the basis of (2) are given in Figure 2. It is easy to recognize Reichenbachian points in these configurations. However, the two remaining oppositions introduce more complex configurations of indices

## 3.2   Synchronous-Posterior

The second opposition introduces an index, say j, which does not relate directly to **n** because it is positioned with respect to the index i: either synchronous or posterior to it. In Dutch the opposition can be made visible by the opposition between the absence or presence of the auxiliary *zullen* (shall, will)).

> An action is either synchronous or posterior with respect to each of the two points in time mentioned. The forms of the verb indicate these different relations: *Hij belooft* (he promises)[synchr.] *dat hij het doen zal* (that he will do it)[posterior with respect to a present point in time]; *Hij beloofde* (he promised)[past] *dat hij het doen zou* (that he would do it)[posterior with respect to a point of time in the past]. (tranlated from 1866:68-9)

The appropriate two operators can be defined as:

(4)   a. SYN   $:= \lambda\phi\lambda i'\exists!j[\phi[j] \wedge i' \simeq j]$
$\quad$ b. POST $:= \lambda\phi\lambda i'\exists!j[\phi[j] \wedge i' < j]$

a: Posterior Past        b: Simple Future

**Fig. 3.** Posterior Past and Present Posteriority

As said earlier, the two operators in (4) take a (tenseless) $\phi$ of type $\langle i,t \rangle$ in order to yield a formula of type $\langle i,t \rangle$. So, in fact, the system describes here the contribution of the auxiliary *zullen* (shall) to the tense information in the case of posteriority, whereas the covert operator SYN accounts for the absence of it. The Simple Future is present due to the presence of i at **n**, and future because the index j is posterior to i, as is made visible in Figure 3b. Note the structural similarity between the two configurations. In general, posteriority is defined here as not necessarily bound to the point of speech, but as a general way to express the relation 'later than'. This makes it unnecessary to have three configurations for the Posterior Past as in Reichenbach's cell 7 in Figure 2 because what counts is the relation between i and j. Reichenbach's three configurations for the Future in the cells 6, 8 and 9 are restricted to the one in cell 6. As in French, Dutch has a form that fits into cell 9: *Marie zal de brief gaan schrijven* (lit. Mary will go to write the letter) but it will have a far more complex configuration than Reichenbach suggests.

### 3.3   Imperfect-Perfect

The third opposition introduces an index k representing the information connected with the event E and positioned in j or anterior to j. Here the opposition can be made concrete by the absence or presence of the auxiliary *hebben*(have). Te Winkel defines it as:

> An action expressed by a verb is thought of as going on as an *action in progress*, or as having been done, as a *completed action* ... (1866:69; translation)

This can be translated into:

(5) a. IMP   := $\lambda\phi\lambda i'\exists!k[\phi[k] \wedge k' \preceq i']$
    b. PERF := $\lambda\phi\lambda i'\exists!k[\phi(k) \wedge k \prec i']$

$\preceq$ is to be taken as expressing indeterminacy, i.e. as 'not yet $\prec$'. This makes i' in (5a) the (virtual) present of the ongoing k. At this stage it is perhaps illuminating to point out that the full configuration of a Present Perfect looks like Figure 4b, where i can be taken as having the same present as (or perhaps: being the present of) the point of speech **n** and j as the present of the ongoing event. In other words, the richness of indices provides for two sorts of embedding of the crucial elements **n** and E. The point of speech **n** is embedded in something ongoing of which **n** is a part whereas the index k associated with the event E

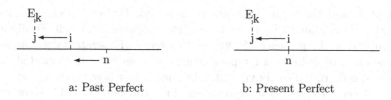

a: Past Perfect                    b: Present Perfect

**Fig. 4.** Past and Present Perfect

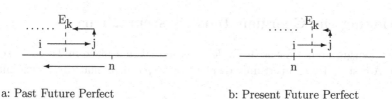

a: Past Future Perfect                    b: Present Future Perfect

**Fig. 5.** Posteriority and Anteriority

of the predication is also embedded in its own 'present'. The tense relates these two sorts of present in a way that will be elucidated below in more detail. The configurations of the remaining two tenses are given in Figure 5.

The tense system is organized in such a way that a structural parallelism between the tense forms is clearly visible. One can easily check the parallelism by looking at Figures 2–5 and by observing that in each of them the two diagrams are identical except for the relations between i and n. The following two lines also show that the Present-subsystem and the Past-subsystem are built up in the same way:

PRES(SYN)(IMP), PRES(POST)(IMP), PRES(SYN)(PERF), PRES(POST)(PERF)
PAST(SYN)(IMP), PAST(POST)(IMP), PAST(SYN)(PERF), PAST(POST)(PERF).

For Dutch and English the $2 \times 2 \times 2$-approach works satisfactorily: all eight tenses are covered. But there are many languages not having eight tenses. For languages with more than eight forms, such as Bulgarian, French but also Georgian, the problem that arises turns out to concern the aorist forms. Questions that are to be posed in those cases are whether one of the three oppositions above is recursive, a candidate for such a solution being the (still existing but quite rare) French form *Marie avait eu écrit la lettre* (lit. Marie had had written the letter) or whether a different sort of opposition is in play. The latter solution will be proposed for Georgian and is to be considered seriously for the Bulgarian aorist and the French Passé Simple. For languages having less than eight forms, such as Russian, the solution of the problem of having too many oppositions will be to find a way to reduce them on the basis of convincing evidence. It will be suggested that here also the aorist plays a role.

A final point should be added with respect to the third opposition. Verbal forms in Dutch and English are not perfective in the aspectual sense of that term. For the Present Perfect tense form defined by PRES(SYN)(PERF), for example,

Te Winkel used the term 'Voltooid' (Completed, Perfect) to characterize its semantics. The point to be made here with a view on what will be discussed later on is that the presence of PRES in this series of operators determines the interpretation of PERF in a temporal sense, because PERF is connected to the point of speech **n**, indirectly via PRES. In languages where this is not the case, PERF will need a different interpretation. This will be argued for some of the Georgian tenses as well as for Russian.

## 4   Making the Georgian Tense System Binary

All the Georgian tense forms in Table 1 can be given a place in Table 3 except for the Aorist 7. Table 3 certainly displays some parallels that can be explained

**Table 3.** Georgian tenses as defined by operators

| Operators | Tense forms | Correspondent | Name |
|---|---|---|---|
| PRES(SYN)(IMP) | 1 *c'ers* | (writes) | Present |
| PRES(POST)(IMP) | | (will write) | |
| PRES(SYN)(PERF) | 9 *dauc'eria* | (has written) | Present Perfect |
| | 12 *dac'erili akvs* | (has written) | Analytic Perfect |
| PRES(POST)(PERF) | 4 *dac'ers* | (will [have] wri[t]te[n]) | Future |
| | 14 *dac'erili ekneba* | (will have written) | Analytic Future |
| | | | |
| PAST(SYN)(IMP) | 2 *c'erda* | (wrote) | Imperfect |
| PAST(POST)(IMP) | | (would write) | |
| PAST(SYN)(PERF) | 10 *daec'era* | (had written) | PluPerfect |
| | 13 *dac'erili hkonda* | (had written) | Analytic PluPerfect |
| PAST(POST)(PERF) | 5 *dac'erda* | (would [have] wri[t]te[n]) | Conditional Past |

on the basis of the binary oppositions that make up the system: 1 - 2, 4 - 5, 9 -10 and 12 - 13. These four pairs concern the Pres/Past-opposition. On the basis of the presence of the preverb *da-* in the PERF-forms 4 and 5 and its absence in the IMP-forms 1 and 2 one could argue that the IMP- vs. PERF-opposition is morphologically visible. The evident problem connected with it is that *dac'ers* does not correspond to the English *He will have written* unless this is interpreted as 'He will write and complete his writing'. In the case of *dac'erda* one has to interpret the English *He would have written* as 'He would write (as a habit) and complete his writings'. The important thing here is to see that PERF plays a role in an opposition if we are prepared to think in terms of a non-temporal counterpart of the Germanic perf in (5b).

The SYN vs. POST-opposition is present in Table 3 in the opposition between 9/12 + 10/13 on the one hand and 4/14 + 5 on the other hand. This means that it is possible to take the tense forms marked by the presence of POST as expressing posteriority rather than as a now-bound future. In respect to 5 *dac'erda* this can be made concrete by assuming that it positions the index i in the series of writings (each of which is completed) but the series itself is not

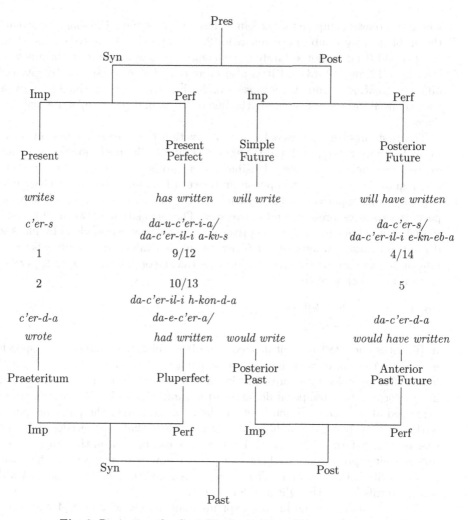

**Fig. 6.** Projecting the Georgian forms into a binary structure

completed. It may have continued, which gives the tense form its posterior flavor as in the English temporal interpretation of *She would send a letter every day telling all the details of what they were doing.*

The non-occurrence of the Aorist in Table 3 turns out to be of importance. We should have been worried if it found a place in the system of oppositions. Before embarking on the question of how to give a position to the Aorist in the system as a whole, let me first pay attention to some problems with respect to Table 3 that clearly should be solved first. The problems become more transparent if we add to Table 3 a diagram in Figure 6 on page 241. It reveals the structural parallelism between the tenses in a binary system by showing that nine tenses can be given a place in the system on the basis of the same three oppositions that characterize the Germanic and Romance languages, but it also clearly shows where two tenses compete for the same place in the system. The diagram reveals the problem of the double occurrences 9/12, 4/14 and 10/13: the system based on (2), (4) and (5) does not separate the evidential perfect forms from the analytic ones in 9/12 and 10/13 and it is also clear that 4 *dac'ers* should be given a different treatment from 14 *dac'erili ekneba*. Finally, *dac'erda* should be given an evidential interpretation along the line of 'He would (used to) write and has done it'.

The first problem is raised by the observation that Georgian has no tense forms for PRES(POST)(IMP) and for PAST(POST)(IMP): its posterior forms do not express incompleteness. One plausible way to go is to find a solution to this problem in the nature of the opposition between Past and Present. In Germanic languages this opposition is clearly equipollent: if a tense form does not express past, it expresses present, and conversely. The opposition between PRES and PAST in Georgian turns out to be privative: the information provided by PRES is default, unmarked, whereas PAST invokes a marked value, so that PRES is to be interpreted as 'non-past'. This would mean that Georgian takes in PRES/PAST-opposition in (2) as in (6).

(6)  a. PAST := $\lambda\phi\exists!i[\phi[i] \wedge i \leq c_n]$
     b. PRES := $\lambda\phi\exists!i[\phi[i] \wedge i \not\leq c_n]$

In (6) PRES and PAST are not defined in a direct relation to the point of speech **n**. The PAST-operator is anchored in some point $c_n$ that serves as the contextual 'now', often provided by an adverbial in such a way that the eventuality described in $\phi$ is located in a temporal domain in the same way as in the binary system explained above. The relation between the eventuality and the point of speech is thus left unspecified but it is contextually clear that $c_n$ precedes **n** in the case of a PAST-form.[2] The French Passé Simple can be seen in this way: it does not explicitly presume that there is a present now with respect to which the $\phi$-eventuality is to be located. There is a different anchorage: the point $c_n$. I will return to this line of thought in the last section.

The definition of PRES in (6a) explains immediately why both 4 and 5 are (POST)(PERF) rather than (POST)(IMP). The use of PRES as the default unmarked tense presumes that $c_n$ is or contains the point **n** or follows **n** but PRES does not give **n** the configurational position that it occupies in Figures 2 - 5. The SYN-forms 1 *c'ers* and 2 *c'erda* cover a larger part of the i-related future than the corresponding forms *writes* or *wrote* do in English. So the presence of the perfective *da-* in 4 *dac'ers* and 5 *dac'erda* can be used to express completion with respect to an index i which is synchronous to or follows **n** in the case of *dac'ers* or to express completion with respect to an i in the past in the case of *dac'erda*.

The second problem is the analytic-synthetic doubling. The analytic forms 12, 13 and 14 not only occupy the place of their English counterparts, there is also a close translational correspondence in meaning. This does not hold for the perfective synthetic forms in 9 and 10: they cannot be simply translated into

---

[2] This is why '$\leq$' is taken as the relation between i and $c_n$ in (6) rather than '$<$'.

the English *He has written* and *He had written,* because the English forms are not used on the basis of evidence. One may explain the difference between the analytic and synthetic forms by arguing that for the former the Present/Past-opposition is equipollent and for the synthetic forms privative. This is because the difference between 12 and 13 is clearly based on a difference between the present tense form and a past tense form of the auxiliary, whereas the form *kneba* is a present analogously to the present form *will* in *He will write.*

An interesting line of thought becomes visible now. The analytic Georgian forms are younger than the synthetic ones; they have emerged hundreds of years ago whereas the synthetic ones have existed for thousands of years. If the analytic forms are indeed equipollent, one may explain their arrival by the need to relate eventualities directly to the point of speech $n$ as in (2) rather than indirectly as in (6). This means that different 'forces' have been working on the Present/Past-opposition, so that the current system reveals a struggle between two tendencies each of which is defined in (2) and (6), respectively: one in which the Present is formally marked and relates the eventuality to the point of speech $n$—the newer one—in (2), and the older one in which the Present is the "garbage can" for all that is not Past in (6). In the last section, this point will be taken up again.

The third problem that should be solved concerns the Perfect imperfective form *u-c'er-ia* in 9 and the Pluperfect form *e-c'er-a* in 10. The apparent paradox between their status as a perfect tense expressing imperfectivity can be explained by the fact that they express the resultative imperfectivity meaning 'for a while'. They are comparable with Russian aspectual modifiers like *po-* operating on the time stretch rather than on the eventuality. So the problem can be solved by assuming that tense forms tend to specialize.

More in general, some remarks about the interaction between the pairs Imperfect/Perfect and Imperfective/Perfective are in order here. The PERF-operator in (5b) is defined in terms of the atemporal relation $\prec$. For an equipollent PRES/PAST-opposition as in Dutch and English and given in (2) it can be argued that the IMP/PERF-opposition receives a temporal interpretation due to the fact that the index i in the system is directly related to $n$ and so $\prec$ is, in fact, temporalised into a $<$-relation. In the privative counterpart (6), the PRES- and PAST-operators are not tied up to $n$ in this way. That is, there is no opposition between i $\simeq$ $n$ and i $<$ $n$, because there is no need to accommodate $n$ in the system: one can do with the i-index with respect to some contextually determined point $c_n$ which is not $n$. This means that perfectivity in a system built up on the basis of (6) is bound to express completedness in a different way from what the PERF-operator does in Germanic languages like Dutch and English. The following section has this in mind.

## 5   The Aorist

In Georgian, the Aorist is used as a narrative tense expressing no tie with the speaker's position in time: it's just past in the form of blunt anteriority, not as a means to connect the eventuality to the now-point $n$ as is the case of all tenses

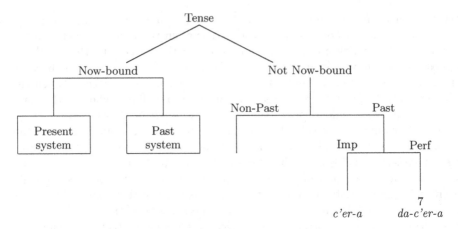

**Fig. 7.** Positioning the Aorist

in Figure 6. In that sense, it is predicted by the binary approach that the Aorist cannot be given a place in the system of the three oppositions under discussion if it is based on a Present/Past-opposition as defined in (2). The Aorist 7 falls outside such a system in a way resembling the Passé Simple in French and the Aorist in Bulgarian. This poses a problem, namely to explain the important place that the Aorist has in the Georgian tense system.

The solution is—maintaining a binary approach—to assume that in the older stages of Georgian in which the Aorist was formed, the primary opposition was not Present vs. Past but rather a more fundamental opposition which I shall call Now-bound vs. Not-Now-bound. In other words, Georgian opted for being a Not-Now-bound language by using an opposition between Past and non-Past without having an index i that ties up to **n**, such as defined in (6). This results into an opposition in which Past simply expresses anteriority with respect to any available value, predominantly of an adverbial nature.

From the technical point of view, this makes the Synchronous/Posterior-distinction in (4) superfluous, or at least quite different from the opposition defined in (4), because SYN and POST are typically dependent on the equipollent nature of the Present/Past-opposition. It does not make sense to define an index j in terms of the complementary value of the past: there is no well-defined point i for j to relate to.

Such a line of thought would explain the position of 7 in Figure 7 outside the system in Figure 6. It gives the Aorist its present place as a remnant of an older phase in which the opposition Now-bound/Not-Now-bound was actualized as the primary opposition of the system.The imperfective aorist form *c'era* is still available. Its position in the system reveals that the Imperfective/Perfective-opposition was already available at the time that the Aorist was still reigning supreme as the expression of a not-Now-bound tense.

Times have changed and so the analytic forms have appeared in the language as relatively new forms at the cost of the Aorist, contributing to the development of the Now-bound tense system that occupies the left-hand place in Figure 7. It is attractive to assume that the arrival of the new analytic forms has to do with a change in the nature of the opposition. Two of the three analytic perfect forms are present forms because in the binary system 12 is formed by (PRES)(SYN) and 14 by (PRES)(POST), whereas the third analytic perfect 13 is a past form due to (PAST)(SYN). All three are to be interpreted as being related to the point of speech n just like their Western counterparts. So, the analytic forms may result from the need or the wish to have a Now-bound system. In this way, it can be understood why the Synthetic Perfect can occur with *gus'in* (yesterday) and why it is not allowed to use this adverbial in the Analytic Perfect, as in English. Some forms, such as 1 *c'ers*(writes) and 2 *c'erda* (wrote) can easily "live" both in a not-Now-bound system and a Now-bound system. For some forms such as *dauc'eria* and *daec'era*, however, it seems to be more difficult to get into a newly developed system, also because they have to defend a position with respect to the newcomers. Like the Aorist they have specialized in certain meanings that are not expressed by the analytic forms.

These remarks concerning the Georgian aorist seem to carry over to Russian and other languages having aorist tense tradition, such as Bulgarian. Russian tense has typically features of a not-now-bound system, which also explains why so many aspects of verbal information are aspectual rather than temporal. The present paper may have indicated a systematic way of dealing with choices made by languages in terms of binary oppositions.

*Acknowledgement.* This paper reports about the scientific framework underlying the dissertation project [6] on Georgian tense and aspect by Kakhi Sakhltkhut-sishvili at the UILOTS. One of its goals is to apply the binary system described here in order to see whether it is useful in unraveling the mysteries of the extremely complex Georgian verbal system. In this paper, the binary approach follows from my earlier work on tense, but the Georgian data as well as the empirical basis for the ideas developed here are, of course, completely due to Kakhi. I thank him for this very nice cooperation and I hope that the results may contribute to his grasp on the complexity of the Georgian tense system by convincing him that a binary approach may reveal certain hidden regularities in the seeming disorder. I also thank two anonymous reviewers for their careful remarks that have led to important improvements.

# References

1. Hewitt, B.G. (ed.): Georgian; a Structural Reference Grammar. John Benjamins Publishing Company, Amsterdam, Philadelphia (1995)
2. Hillery, P.J. (ed.): The Georgian Language. An Outline Grammatical Summary. Internet Publication (1996), Internet Publisher Armazi.com www.armazi.com/georgian
3. Kamp, H., Reyle, U.: From Discourse to Logic. Introduction to Modeltheoretic Semantics of Natural Language, Formal Logic and Discourse Representation Theory. Studies in Linguistics and Philosophy, vol. 42. Kluwer Academic Publishers, Dordrecht (1993)

4. Rathert, M.: Textures of Time. The Interplay of the Perfect, Durative Adverbs, and Extended-Now-Adverbs in German and English. PhD thesis, Tuebingen, Tuebingen (2003)
5. Reichenbach, H.: Elements of Symbolic Logic. The Macmillan Company, New York (first free press paperback edition 1966 edn.) (1947)
6. Sakhltkhutsishvili, K.: Semantics of Georgian tense and aspect systems. PhD thesis, UILOTS Utrecht University, Utrecht (in preparation 2007)
7. Shanidze, A. (ed.): Basics of the Grammar of the Georgian Language. Tbilisi University Press, Tbilisi (written in Georgian) (1980)
8. Te Winkel, L.A.: Over de wijzen en tijden der werkwoorden. De Taalgids 8, 66–75 (1866)
9. Verkuyl, H.J., Le Loux-Schuringa, J.A.: Once upon a tense. Linguistics and Philosophy 8, 237–261 (1985)
10. Verkuyl, H., Vet, C., Borillo, A., Bras, M., Le Draoulec, A., Molendijk, A., de Swart, H., Vetters, C., Vieu, L.: Tense and aspect in sentences. In: Corblin, F., de Swart, H. (eds.) Handbook of French Semantics, pp. 233–270. CSLI Publications, Stanford, CA (2004)
11. Verkuyl, H.J.: Events or indices. In: Gerbrandy, J., Marx, M., de Rijke, M., Venema, Y. (eds.) JFAK. Essays dedicated to Johan van Benthem on the Occasion of his 50th Birthday, pages 25. Vossiuspers AUP, Amsterdam (1999), Internet publication: via http://www.let.uu.nl/~Henk.Verkuyl/personal/tense/eoi.pdf
12. Verkuyl, H.J.: On the compositionality of tense: merging Reichenbach and Prior, http://www.let.uu.nl/~Henk.Verkuyl/personal/tense/prtw.pdf

# Some Criteria of Decidability for Axiomatic Systems in Three-Valued Logic

I.D. Zaslavsky

Institute for Informatics and Automation Problems,
Armenian National Academy of Sciences,
Yerevan, Armenia

**Abstract.** Two criteria of decidability for axiomatic systems based on J.Lukasiewicz's three-valued logic are established.

**Keywords:** three-valued predicate, Luk-theory, Luk-consistent theory, Luk-complete theory, Luk-decidable theory.

**1. Introduction.** This article may be considered as continuation of the articles [7] to [10], where axiomatic systems based on J.Lukasiewicz's three-valued logic were investigated. First, we shall briefly describe a number of notions used in the papers [7] to [10]. Axiomatic system represents a set of predicate formulas, where the logical operations $\&, \vee, \supset, \rceil, \forall, \exists$ are interpreted according to J.Lukasiewicz's truth tables ([1], [4], [5]), and predicate symbols are interpreted as logical functions having the values "true", "false", and "undefined" (precise definitions will be given below). The following notions are considered in the articles [7] to [10]: (1) a Luk-model of an axiomatic system; (2) a Luk-theory based on an axiomatic system; (3) a Luk-consistent Luk-theory; (4) a Luk-complete Luk-theory (the prefix "Luk" denotes here that the corresponding notion is considered in the framework of J.Lukasiewicz's logic; the prefix will be suppressed in some cases, if it doesn't cause any ambiguity). Definitions of these notions are mostly similar to corresponding definitions in the classical logic (for example, an interpretation of predicate and functional symbols is said to be a Luk-model of a given axiomatic Luk-theory if all the axioms of the theory have the value «true" concerning this interpretation). However the notion of Luk-completeness is essentially different from the corresponding classical one, namely: a Luk-consistent Luk-theory is said to be Luk-complete if the following statement holds for every closed formula A in the language of the theory: either A, or $\rceil$A, or $(A \supset \rceil A)$ & $(\rceil A \supset A)$ belongs to the theory. The mentioned notions and their relations with the corresponding classical notions are investigated in the papers [7] to [10]. Particularly, for every Luk-theory $\Omega$ its *classical image* $\Omega^+$ is defined which gives some description of $\Omega$ by means of the classical logic. Similarly, for every classical formal theory $\Omega$ its Luk-image Luk $(\Omega)$ is defined. The relations between $\Omega$ and $\Omega^+$, as well as the relations between $\Omega$ and Luk $(\Omega)$ are investigated in [10]. Note that no isomorphism exists between the classical formal theories and the Luk-theories. For example, Luk $(\Omega^+)$ is in general not equivalent to $\Omega$, and Luk $(\Omega)^+$ is in general not equivalent to $\Omega$ (see [10]).

B.D. ten Cate and H.W. Zeevat (Eds.): TbiLLC 2005, LNAI 4363, pp. 247–259, 2007.
© Springer-Verlag Berlin Heidelberg 2007

Below the investigation of the mentioned concepts will be continued. The notion of Luk-decidable Luk-theory will be introduced. A necessary and sufficient condition of the Luk-decidability of a Luk-theory will be established (Theorem 1); the formulation of this condition is similar to the corresponding theorem in classical logic [3], although the content of this statement is different from the classical case. It will be proved (Theorem 2) that a Luk-theory $\Omega$ is Luk-decidable if and only if $\Omega^+$ is decidable in the classical sense. The formulations of Theorems 1 and 2 were published in [11].

**2.** Let us recall some definitions given in [7], [8] and [9]. Logical values in J.Lukasiewicz's three-valued logic are expressed as in [7] – [11] by their numerical codes: 2 ("true"), 1 ("undefined"), 0 ("false"). The language of first order predicate calculus with enumerable sets of predicate and functional symbols $p_1, p_2, \ldots, f_1, f_2, \ldots$ is considered; we assume that every symbol $p_i$ and $f_i$ have a fixed dimension ([2], [3], [4]). The symbols of logical constants $T$ ("true"), $F$ ("false"), $U$ ("undefined") are included in this language as elementary formulas. By LP ( or by $L^*P$) we denote the set of all predicate formulas (or respectively the set of all predicate formulas not containing the symbols $T, F, U$).

*Three-valued n-dimensional predicate* on a non-empty set M is defined as a mapping of the $n$-th Cartesian degree $M^n$ of M into the set $\{0,1,2\}$ (so, if p is a three-valued n-dimensional predicate on M, then for every $n$-tuple $(x_1, x_2,\ldots, x_n)$, where $x_i \in$ M, $1 \le i \le n$, the value $p(x_1, x_2,\ldots, x_n)$ is either 0, or 1, or 2). Logical connectives &, $\vee$, $\supset$, $\neg$ are interpreted according to the truth-tables of J.Lukasiewicz's logic ([1], [4], [5]), namely, if $x$ and $y$ are logical values of formulas respectively $A$ and $B$, then $\min(x,y)$, $\max(x,y)$, $2 - \max(0, x - y)$, and $2 - x$ are the values respectively of formulas $(A \& B)$, $(A \vee B)$, $(A \supset B)$, $\neg A$. The quantifiers $\forall$ and $\exists$ are interpreted respectively as infinite conjunction and infinite disjunction; namely, if $p(y, x_1, x_2,\ldots, x_{n-1})$ is an $n$-dimensional three-valued predicate on M, then $\forall y p(y, x_1, x_2,\ldots, x_{n-1})$ (respectively $\exists y p(y, x_1, x_2,\ldots, x_{n-1})$) is an $(n$-1)-dimensional predicate on M, such that its logical value in any point $(x_1, x_2,\ldots, x_{n-1})$ is the minimum (respectively maximum) of the values $p(y, x_1, x_2,\ldots, x_{n-1})$ for $y \in$ M.

*Weak implication* $(A \supseteq B)$, *weak negation* $\neg^\circ A$ and *equivalence* $(A \sim B)$ are defined respectively as $(A \supset (A \supset B))$, $(A \supset \neg A)$, and $(A \supset B) \& (B \supset A)$.

A *signature* Z is any set of predicate and functional symbols; we considered only such signatures where the sets of indices $i$ and $j$, such that $p_i \in$ Z and $f_j \in$ Z, are recursive. By L(Z) (or by $L^*(Z)$), where Z is a signature, we denote the set of predicate formulas belonging to LP (or respectively to $L^*P$) and containing no predicate and functional symbols out of Z.

By *Subst(A, x, s)*, where $A$ is a formula, $x$ is a variable and $s$ is a term, we denote the formula obtained from A by substitution of $s$ for all free occurences of $x$ in A; we consider only admissible substitutions (in the usual sense; this notion is equivalent, for example, to the notion: "s is substitutable for x in A" (see [2])). By $(\forall\forall)$ (or by $(\exists\exists)$) we denote any group of universal (respectively of existential) quantifiers; by

$(\forall\forall\forall)(A)$ (or by $(\exists\exists\exists)(A)$), where $A$ is a formula, we denote the closure of $A$ by universal (respectively by existential) quantifiers.

A *Luk-assignment* on a non-empty set M for a signature Z is defined as a set of interpretations of predicate and functional symbols when every $n$-dimensional predicate symbol belonging to Z is interpreted as an $n$-dimensional predicate on M, and every $n$-dimensional functional symbol belonging to Z is interpreted as a mapping of $M^n$ into M. The *interpretation* of a formula $A$ in a signature Z concerning a Luk-assignment $\delta$ on M for Z is defined as a three-valued predicate on M obtained when every predicate and functional symbol in $A$ is replaced by its interpretation given in $\delta$.

*Axiomatic system* in the given signature Z is defined as an enumerable set (possibly finite or empty) of closed formulas $(A_0, A_1, ...)$ in the language L(Z). A Luk-assignment $\delta$ on Z is said to be *Luk-model* of an axiomatic system $(A_0, A_1, ...)$ in Z if the interpretations of all $A_i$ concerning $\delta$ are equal to 2 ("true"). An axiomatic system is said to be *Luk-consistent* if it has a Luk-model; otherwise it is said to be *Luk-inconsistent*. A formula $B$ in a signature Z is said to be *Luk-corollary* of a given axiomatic system $\Omega$ in Z if interpretation of $B$ concerning every Luk-model of $\Omega$ represents a three-valued predicate such that its value in any point is equal to 2 ("true"). The *Luk-theory* based on $\Omega$ is the set of all closed Luk-corollaries of $\Omega$. A formula $B$ in Z is said to be *identically Luk-true* if its interpretation concerning every Luk-assignment on Z is a three-valued predicate everywhere equal to 2 ("true"). If $\theta$ is a Luk-theory based on some axiomatic system $\Omega$ in a signature Z, and $B_0, B_1, ..., B_m$ are closed formulas in Z, then by $\theta \cup \{B_0, B_1, ..., B_m\}$ we denote a Luk-theory based on the axiomatic system $\Omega \cup \{B_0, B_1, ...B_m\}$ obtained from $\Omega$ by adding $B_0, B_1, ..., B_m$ as new axioms.

A Luk-theory based on an axiomatic system $\Omega$ is said to be Luk-consistent if $\Omega$ is Luk-consistent.

Sometimes we shall consider the Luk-theories without introducing special notations for the axiomatic systems generating them. In such cases all formulas belonging to a given Luk-theory $\theta$ are considered as axioms in the axiomatic system generating $\theta$.

A Luk-consistent axiomatic system $\Omega$ in a signature Z is said to be *Luk-complete* (as well as the Luk-theory based on $\Omega$) if every closed formula $B$ in L(Z) possesses the following property: either $B$, or $\neg B$, or $(B \supset \neg B)\,\&\,(\neg B \supset B)$ is a Luk-corollary of $\Omega$.

*Gödel numbering* of formulas in LP is defined in the usual way (for example, similarly to definitions in [2]). A set $\Sigma$ of formulas is said to be *recursively enumerable* (or *recursive*) if the set of Gödel numbers of formulas belonging to $\Sigma$ is recursively enumerable (or respectively recursive). We assume that the introduced Gödel numbering has the following property: if Z is any signature, such that the set of indices of predicate and functional symbols belonging to Z is recursive (recall that only such signatures are considered in this article), then the languages L(Z) and $L^*(Z)$ are recursive. Clearly, the usually considered Gödel numberings (for example, Gödel numberings introduced in [2], [3], [4]) possess this property.

Let $\Omega$ be an axiomatic system in a signature Z, and $\theta$ be a Luk-theory based on $\Omega$. We say that $\Omega$ and $\theta$ are *Luk-decidable* if the set of formulas belonging to $\theta$ is recursive.

Let $\theta_0, \theta_1, \theta_2, \ldots$ be a sequence of Luk-theories in a signature Z. We say that the sequence $\theta_0, \theta_1, \theta_2, \ldots$ is *effectively generated* if there exists a two-dimensional recursively enumerable predicate $\pi(i, j)$ on natural numbers, such that $\pi(i, j)$ is true for $i$ and $j$ if and only if $i$ is a Gödel number of a formula belonging to $\theta_j$.

**Theorem 1.** *A Luk-theory in a signature Z is decidable if and only if it is recursively enumerable and can be represented as intersection of an effectively generated sequence of Luk-complete theories in Z.*

As mentioned above, this theorem is similar to the corresponding theorem in the classical logic (see [3], Theorem 1 in Chapter 5, p. 269). The proof of the Theorem 1 will be given in the Section 3; it is similar to the proof of the mentioned theorem in [3], however it has peculiarities connected with the properties of J.Lukasiewicz's logic.

Recall now some definitions given in [7], [9] and [10] that are necessary for formulation of the Theorem 2. We introduce a correspondence between the predicate symbols $p$ and pairs of the predicate symbols $(p^+, p^-)$ in such a way that the following conditions are satisfied: (1) for every predicate symbol $p$ there exists a single pair $(p^+, p^-)$ corresponding to $p$; (2) in every pair $(p^+, p^-)$ the symbols $p^+$ and $p^-$ are different; (3) the dimensions of $p^+$ and $p^-$ are equal to the dimension of $p$; (4) the pairs $(p^+, p^-)$ corresponding to different $p$ have no common elements; (5) axiomatic systems considered in the framework of J.Lukasiewicz's logic (as well as their signatures) contain no predicate symbol having the form $p^+$ or $p^-$; (6) the introduced correspondence is effective, i.e. there exists an effective procedure making possible the construction of a pair $(p^+, p^-)$ corresponding to the given symbol $p$. Clearly, such a correspondence can be constructed. (For example, if $p_0, p_1, p_2, \ldots$ are all predicate symbols having the given dimension, then $p_i^+$ may be defined as $p_{4i+1}$, and $p_i^-$ as $p_{4i+3}$, in this case we use only predicate symbols $p_j$ having even indices $j$ in axiomatic systems considered in the framework of J.Lukasiewicz's logic).

Let us describe, on intuitive level, the use of predicate symbols $p^+$ and $p^-$. They will denote classical predicates giving a description of a three-valued predicate $p$. Namely, $p^+$ is true in such points (and only in such points) where $p$ is true; $p^-$ is true in such points (and only in such points) where $p$ is false. So both $p^+$ and $p^-$ are false in the points where $p$ is undefined. The formulas $A^+$ and $A^-$ described below give on the same way a classical description of a formula $A$.

Let us define the operations $^+$ and $^-$ as follows. For every given formula $A \in LP$ the formulas $A^+$ and $A^-$ are defined inductively by the following rules (where $D_0$ is some fixed closed predicate formula in $L^*P$):

1)    If $A$ is an elementary formula having the form $p(s_1, s_2, ..., s_n)$ (where $s_1, s_2, ..., s_n$ are any terms), then $A^+$ is $p^+(s_1, s_2, ..., s_n)$, $A^-$ is $p^-(s_1, s_2, ..., s_n)$.

2)    $(B \& C)^+$ is $(B^+ \& C^+)$; $(B \& C)^-$ is $(B^- \lor C^-)$.

3)    $(B \lor C)^+$ is $(B^+ \lor C^+)$; $(B \lor C)^-$ is $(B^- \& C^-)$.

4)    $(\neg B)^+$ is $B^-$; $(\neg B)^-$ is $B^+$.

5)    $(B \supset C)^+$ is $((B^+ \supset C^+) \& (C^- \supset B^-))$; $(B \supset C)^-$ is $(B^+ \& C^-)$.

6)    $(\forall x(B))^+$ is $\forall x(B^+)$; $(\forall x(B))^-$ is $\exists x(B^-)$.

7)    $(\exists x(B))^+$ is $\exists x(B^+)$; $(\exists x(B))^-$ is $\forall x(B^-)$.

8)    $T^+$ is $(D_0 \supset D_0)$; $T^-$ is $\neg(D_0 \supset D_0)$.

9)    $F^+$ is $\neg(D_0 \supset D_0)$; $F^-$ is $(D_0 \supset D_0)$.

10)    $U^+$ is $\neg(D_0 \supset D_0)$; $U^-$ is $\neg(D_0 \supset D_0)$.

Clearly $A^+ \in L^*P$, $A^- \in L^*P$ for every $A \in LP$; the formulas $A^+$ and $A^-$ can be effectively constructed for every given $A \in LP$.

If $p$ is any $n$-dimensional predicate symbol, then the formula

$$\forall x_1 \forall x_2 ... \forall x_n \neg(p^+(x_1, x_2, ..., x_n) \& p^-(x_1, x_2, ..., x_n))$$

will be denoted below by $Dis(p)$.

Let $Z$ be any signature. By $Z^+$ we denote a signature containing the symbols $p^+$ and $p^-$ for all $p \in Z$ and all functional symbols $f \in Z$ (and no other symbol).

Let $\Omega = (A_0, A_1, A_2, ...)$ be an axiomatic system in a signature $Z$. The *classical image* $\Omega^+$ of $\Omega$ is defined as an axiomatic system in $Z^+$ (and in the language $L^*(Z^+)$) containing the axioms $A_i^+$ for all $A_i \in \Omega$, and $Dis(p)$ for all $p \in Z$ (and no other axiom). Axiomatic system having the form $\Omega^+$ will be considered in the framework of the classical predicate logic. If $\theta$ is a Luk-theory based on an axiomatic system $\Omega$, then its classical image $\theta^+$ is defined as a classical formal theory based on the axiomatic system $\Omega^+$ in the language $L^*(Z^+)$.

**Theorem 2.** *A Luk-theory $\theta$ based on an axiomatic system $\Omega$ is Luk-decidable if and only if the classical image $\theta^+$ of $\theta$ is decidable in the classical sense.*

**3.** In this section the proofs of the Theorems 1 and 2 will be given; they will be based on the Lemmas 1 – 7 to be proved below.

Let us recall the definition of HLU calculus in the language LP given in [7], [9] and [10] (in [7] the calculus is denoted as HLE). This calculus is defined by the single rule of inference *modus ponens*

$$\frac{A \quad (A \supset B)}{B}$$

and by the following axiom schemes HLU$_1$-HLU$_{21}$ and axioms HLU$_{22}$-HLU$_{25}$ (where $A$, $B$, $C$ are any formulas in LP; $x$ is any variable; $D$ is any formula in LP not containing free occurrences of $x$; $s$ is any term):

(HLU$_1$)    $(\forall\forall)(A \supset (B \supset A))$ ;

(HLU$_2$)    $(\forall\forall)((A \supset (B \supset C)) \supset (B \supset (A \supset C)))$ ;

(HLU$_3$)    $(\forall\forall)((A \supset B) \supset ((B \supset C) \supset (A \supset C)))$ ;

(HLU$_4$)    $(\forall\forall)((A \supset (A \supset B)) \supset ((\neg B \supset (\neg B \supset \neg A)) \supset (A \supset B)))$ ;

(HLU$_5$)    $(\forall\forall)((A \supset B) \supset (\neg B \supset \neg A))$ ;

(HLU$_6$)    $(\forall\forall)(A \supset \neg\neg A)$ ;

(HLU$_7$)    $(\forall\forall)(\neg\neg A \supset A)$ ;

(HLU$_8$)    $(\forall\forall)((A \,\&\, B) \supset A)$ ;

(HLU$_9$)    $(\forall\forall)((A \,\&\, B) \supset B)$ ;

(HLU$_{10}$)   $(\forall\forall)((C \supset A) \supset ((C \supset B) \supset (C \supset (A \,\&\, B))))$ ;

(HLU$_{11}$)   $(\forall\forall)(A \supset (A \vee B))$ ;

(HLU$_{12}$)   $(\forall\forall)(B \supset (A \vee B))$ ;

(HLU$_{13}$)   $(\forall\forall)((A \supset C) \supset ((B \supset C) \supset ((A \vee B) \supset C)))$ ;

(HLU$_{14}$)   $(\forall\forall)(\forall x(A) \supset Subst(A, x, s))$ ;

(HLU$_{15}$)   $(\forall\forall)(D \supset \forall x(D))$ ;

(HLU$_{16}$)   $(\forall\forall)(\forall x(A \supset B) \supset (\forall x(A) \supset \forall x(B)))$ ;

(HLU$_{17}$)   $(\forall\forall)(Subst(A, x, s) \supset \exists x(A))$ ;

(HLU$_{18}$)   $(\forall\forall)(\exists x(D) \supset D)$ ;

(HLU$_{19}$)   $(\forall\forall)(\forall x(A \supset B) \supset (\exists x(A) \supset \exists x(B)))$ ;

(HLU$_{20}$)   $(\forall\forall)(\forall x(A \supset (A \supset B)) \supset (\exists x(A) \supset (\exists x(A) \supset \exists x(B))))$ ;

(HLU$_{21}$)   $(\forall\forall)(((A \supset \neg A) \supset \neg(A \supset \neg A)) \supset A)$ ;

(HLU$_{22}$)   $T$ ;

(HLU$_{23}$)   $\neg F$ ;

(HLU$_{24}$)   $(U \supset \neg U)$ ;

(HLU$_{25}$)   $(\neg U \supset U)$ .

Deducibility of the formula $B$ from presumptions $A_1, A_2, ..., A_n$ in HLU is defined in the usual way; it will be denoted by $A_1, A_2, ..., A_n \vdash B$. Sometimes we shall write $\Sigma \vdash B$, where $\Sigma$ is an infinite set of formulas; such a notation will mean that $B$ is deducible in HLU from some finite subset of $\Sigma$.

The following properties of HLU are established in [9] (cf. also [6], [7] and [10]):

(1) ("First theorem of completeness for HLU"). A formula $A \in$ LP is deducible in HLU from the empty list of presumptions if and only if it is identically Luk-true. (see [7], theorem 2.2, p. 312; [9], lemma 6.7, p. 52).

(2)   ("Second theorem of completeness for HLU"). If $\Omega$ is an axiomatic system in a signature Z, B is a formula in L(Z), then $\Omega \vdash B$ if and only if B is a Luk-corollary of $\Omega$.

(see [9]), theorems 3.1 and 3.2, pp. 29-30).

(3)   An axiomatic system $\Omega$ is Luk-inconsistent if and only if $\Omega \vdash B$ for every $B \in$ LP.

(This statement is easily obtained from (2); let us note that every formula having the form $\neg A \supset (A \supset B)$ is identically Luk-true, hence it is deducible in HLU; so, if $\Sigma \vdash A$ and $\Sigma \vdash \neg A$, then $\Sigma \vdash B$ for every $B \in$ LP).

(4)   ("First form of deduction theorem for HLU"). If $\Sigma$ is a set of formulas, A and B are formulas such that $\Sigma, A \vdash B$, then $\Sigma \vdash A \supseteq B$.

(see [6], p. 106; [9], p. 40).

(5)   ("Second form of deduction theorem for HLU"). If $\Sigma$ is a set of formulas, A and B are formulas such that $\Sigma, A \vdash B$ and $\Sigma, \neg A \vdash \neg B$, then $\Sigma \vdash A \supset B$.

(see [6], p. 106; [9], p. 40).

Let us note that the classical form of deduction theorem (If $\Sigma, A \vdash B$, then $\Sigma \vdash A \supset B$ ) is in general not valid for HLU.

**Lemma 1.** *Let $\Omega$ be a recursively enumerable axiomatic system in a signature Z, and $\theta$ be a Luk-theory based on $\Omega$. Then $\theta$ is recursively enumerable.*

The proof is easily obtained using the definition of the HLU calculus and the second theorem of completeness for HLU.

**Note.** The reverse statement is trivial: if a Luk-theory $\theta$ is recursively enumerable then it is based on some recursively enumerable axiomatic system (for example, coinciding with $\theta$).

**Lemma 2.** *Let $\theta$ be a recursively enumerable and Luk-complete Luk-theory in a signature Z. Then $\theta$ is Luk-decidable.*

**Proof.** Let $\Sigma_1, \Sigma_2, \Sigma_3$ be sets of formulas A in the language L(Z) such that, respectively, $A \in \theta$, $\neg A \in \theta$, $(A \supset \neg A) \& (\neg A \supset A) \in \theta$. Clearly, these sets are recursively enumerable and disjoint (because $\theta$ is Luk-consistent). The union $\Sigma_1 \cup \Sigma_2 \cup \Sigma_3$ is the set of all closed formulas in L(Z) (because $\theta$ is Luk-complete), hence it is recursive. The intersection of sets $\Sigma_1$ and $\Sigma_2 \cup \Sigma_3$ is empty. Using the well-known E. Post's theorem, we conclude that $\Sigma_1$ is recursive. This completes the proof.

Let $\Omega$ be a Luk-consistent axiomatic system in a signature Z and $\theta$ be a Luk-theory based on $\Omega$. By $[\theta]$ we denote a set of closed formulas $A \in L(Z)$ such that the Luk-theory based on the axiomatic system $\Omega \cup \{A\}$ is Luk-consistent.

**Note.** If $\theta$ is Luk-consistent, then, obviously, $\theta \subseteq [\theta]$.

**Lemma 3.** *Let $\Omega$ be a Luk-consistent axiomatic system in a signature Z; $\theta$ be a Luk-theory based on $\Omega$. Then a formula $A \in L(Z)$ belongs to $[\theta]$ if and only if the formula $A \supset \neg A$ does not belong to $\theta$.*

**Proof.** Assume that a formula $A \in L(Z)$ belongs to $[\theta]$. Then the Luk-theory based on $\Omega \cup \{A\}$ is Luk-consistent. If $A \supset \neg A$ belongs to $\theta$, then $\Omega \vdash A \supset \neg A$, hence $\Omega \cup \{A\} \vdash A$, $\Omega \cup \{A\} \vdash \neg A$, and therefore $\Omega \cup \{A\}$ shall be Luk-inconsistent, but it is not so.

Now assume that $A \supset \neg A$ does not belong to $\theta$, then $A \in [\theta]$. Indeed, if $A \notin [\theta]$, then $\Omega \cup \{A\}$ is Luk-inconsistent, hence $\Omega \cup \{A\} \vdash B$ for every formula $B \in L(Z)$. In particular, $\Omega \cup \{A\} \vdash \neg A$, and $\Omega \cup \{\neg\neg A\} \vdash \neg A$ (we use here the scheme HLU$_7$). Using the second form of deduction theorem for HLU we obtain that $\Omega \vdash A \supset \neg A$, hence $A \supset \neg A \in \theta$, but it is not so. This completes the proof.

**Lemma 4.** *Let $\Omega$ be a Luk-consistent axiomatic system in a signature Z; $\theta$ be a Luk-theory based on $\Omega$; $\theta_0, \theta_1, \theta_2, \ldots$ be an effectively generated sequence of Luk-complete Luk-theories in Z such that $\theta$ is the intersection of $\theta_i$ for all i. Then $[\theta]$ is recursively enumerable.*

**Proof.** Clearly that $\theta \subseteq \theta_i$ for all $i$, but all $\theta_i$ are Luk-consistent (because they are Luk-complete), hence, if $A \in \theta_i$ for some $i$ then $A \in [\theta]$. Let $\Gamma$ be the union of $\theta_i$ for all $i$. Clearly, $\Gamma$ is recursively enumerable, because it is the union of effectively generated sequence of recursively enumerable sets. We shall prove that $\Gamma = [\theta]$.

Indeed, let $A$ be a closed formula, $A \in \Gamma$. Then $A \in \theta_i$ for some $i$, and $A \in [\theta]$, as it is established above. Now let us assume that $A \in [\theta]$. Using Lemma 3 we conclude that the formula $A \supset \neg A$ does not belong to $\theta$. But $\theta$ is the intersection of $\theta_i$, hence $A \supset \neg A$ does not belong to $\theta_i$ for some $i$. We can conclude that the formulas $\neg A$ and $(A \supset \neg A) \& (\neg A \supset A)$ do not belong to $\theta_i$ also. Indeed, if $\neg A$ belongs to $\theta_i$, then, using the axiom scheme HLU$_1$, we conclude that $A \supset \neg A$ belongs to $\theta_i$, but it is not so. Similarly, if $(A \supset \neg A) \& (\neg A \supset A)$ belongs to $\theta_i$, then using the axiom scheme HLU$_8$, we conclude that $A \supset \neg A$ belongs to $\theta_i$, but it is not so. The Luk-theory $\theta_i$ is Luk-complete, hence either $A$, or $A \supset \neg A$, or $(A \supset \neg A) \& (\neg A \supset A)$ belong to $\theta_i$. We conclude that $A \in \theta_i$, hence $A \in \Gamma$, and the equality $\Gamma = [\theta]$ is proved. So, $[\theta]$ is recursively enumerable, because $\Gamma$ is recursively enumerable. This completes the proof.

**Lemma 5.** *Let $\Omega$ be an axiomatic system in a signature Z; $\theta$ be a Luk-theory based on $\Omega$; A be a closed formula in L(Z). Then $\neg^\circ\neg^\circ A \in \theta$ if and only if $A \in \theta$.*

**Proof.** The axiom scheme $HLU_{21}$ may be represented as $(\forall\forall)(\neg^\circ\neg^\circ A \supset A)$, hence $\neg^\circ\neg^\circ A \supset A$ is deducible in HLU , so, if $\neg^\circ\neg^\circ A \in \theta$ then $A \in \theta$. It is easily seen that the formula $A \supseteq \neg^\circ\neg^\circ A$ is identically Luk-true, hence it is deducible in HLU. So, if $A \in \theta$ then $\neg^\circ\neg^\circ A \in \theta$. This completes the proof.

**Note.** It is easily seen that $A \supset \neg^\circ\neg^\circ A$ is in general not deducible in HLU.

**Lemma 6.** *Let $\Omega$ be an axiomatic system in a signature Z; B be a formula in the language L(Z). Then B is a Luk-corollary of $\Omega$ if and only if $B^+$ is deducible from $\Omega^+$ in the classical predicate logic.*

This statement is proved in [10] (see [10], Lemma 4.6) and in [9] (see [9], Lemma 6.3).

**Lemma 7.** *Let $\Omega$ be an axiomatic system in a signature Z. Then for any formula $A \in L^*(Z^+)$ there exists a formula $B \in L^*(Z)$ containing the same free variables as A and such that the formula $(B^+ \sim A)$ is deducible from $\Omega^+$ in the classical predicate logic.*

This statement is proved in [10] (see [10], Lemma 4.4).

**Note.** We shall use below the construction of the formula $B^+$; let us recall this construction as it is given in [10], Lemma 4.4. If $A$ is an elementary formula $p^+(s_1, s_2, ..., s_n)$ or $p^-(s_1, s_2, ..., s_n)$ then $B$ is, respectively, $p(s_1, s_2, ..., s_n)$ or $\neg p(s_1, s_2, ..., s_n)$. If $A$ is $(A_1 \& A_2)$, $(A_1 \vee A_2)$, $(A_1 \supset A_2)$, $\neg A_1$, $\forall x(A_1)$, $\exists x(A_1)$, then $B$ is, respectively, $(B_1 \& B_2)$, $(B_1 \vee B_2)$, $(B_1 \supseteq B_2)$, $\neg^\circ B_1$, $\forall x(B_1)$, $\exists x(B_1)$, where $B_1$ and $B_2$ are formulas obtained by induction and satisfying the conditions of Lemma for $A_1$ and $A_2$.

**Proof of Theorem 1.** Let $\Omega$ be a recursively enumerable axiomatic system in a signature Z; $\theta$ be a Luk-theory based on $\Omega$; $\theta_0, \theta_1, \theta_2, ...$ be an effectively generated sequence of Luk-complete theories in Z, such that $\theta$ is the intersection of all $\theta_i$. We shall prove that in this case $\theta$ is Luk-decidable.

Indeed, $\theta$ is obviously Luk-consistent. Let $\Sigma$ be a set of formulas in the language L(Z) having the form $A \supset \neg A$; $\Sigma_1$ be $\Sigma \cap \theta$, and $\Sigma_2$ be a set of formulas belonging to $\Sigma$ and not belonging to $\theta$. Clearly, $\Sigma$ is recursive, $\Sigma = \Sigma_1 \cup \Sigma_2$, $\Sigma_1$ and $\Sigma_2$ are disjoint, $\Sigma_1$ is recursively enumerable. But $\Sigma_2$ is the set of formulas having the form $A \supset \neg A$ and not belonging to $\theta$; using Lemma 3 we conclude that a closed formula $A \in L(Z)$ belongs to $[\theta]$, if and only if $A \supset \neg A \in \Sigma_2$. Using Lemma 4 we obtain that $[\theta]$ is recursively enumerable, hence $\Sigma_2$ is recursively enumerable. Now using the earlier mentioned E. Post's theorem, we conclude that $\Sigma_1$ and $\Sigma_2$ are recursive.

The set $\Sigma_1$ is the set of formulas in $\theta$ having the form $A \supset \neg A$ (that is, $\neg^{\circ} A_1$). Let us consider the set $\Sigma_3$ of closed formulas in $L(Z)$ having the form $\neg^{\circ} \neg^{\circ} A$. Obviously, $\Sigma_3$ is recursive, hence $\Sigma_1 \cap \Sigma_3$ is also recursive. The set $\Sigma_1 \cap \Sigma_3$ is the set of formulas having the form $\neg^{\circ} \neg^{\circ} A$ and belonging to $\theta$. Using Lemma 5 we conclude that $\neg^{\circ} \neg^{\circ} A \in \Sigma_1 \cap \Sigma_3$, if and only if $A \in \theta$. Hence $\theta$ is recursive. So, we have proved that $\theta$ is Luk-decidable.

Now let us assume that $\theta$ is Luk-decidable, that is, $\theta$ is recursive. Using Lemma 3 we obtain that $[\theta]$ is also recursive. Let us introduce the recursive sequences of formulas $A_0, A_1, \ldots$ and $B_0, B_1, \ldots$ such that the sequence $A_0, A_1, \ldots$ consists of all closed formulas belonging to $L(Z)$, and the sequence $B_0, B_1, \ldots$ consists of all closed formulas belonging to $[\theta]$. For every natural number $i$ we construct now an axiomatic system $\Omega_i = (C_{i,0}, C_{i,1}, \ldots)$ which is recursively generated by the following rules:

(1)  $C_{i,0}$ is $B_i$.

(2)  If the formulas $C_{i,0}, C_{i,1}, \ldots, C_{i,m}$ are already constructed, then we try to find an index $k$ such that the formula $B_k$ would have one of three following forms:

$$(C_{i,0} \,\&\, C_{i,1} \,\&\, \ldots \,\&\, C_{i,m}) \,\&\, A_m \text{, or}$$
$$(C_{i,0} \,\&\, C_{i,1} \,\&\, \ldots \,\&\, C_{i,m}) \,\&\, \neg A_m \text{, or}$$
$$(C_{i,0} \,\&\, C_{i,1} \,\&\, \ldots \,\&\, C_{i,m}) \,\&\, (A_m \supset \neg A_m) \,\&\, (\neg A_m \supset A_m).$$

If no such $k$ exists, then the process of generating $\Omega_i$ is stopped. If there exists such $k$, then we take a minimal $k$ satisfying the mentioned condition and construct the formula $C_{i,m+1}$ as respectively $A_m$, or $\neg A_m$, or $(A_m \supset \neg A_m) \,\&\, (\neg A_m \supset A_m)$, in the cases when $B_k$ has a form $(C_{i,0} \,\&\, C_{i,1} \,\&\, \ldots \,\&\, C_{i,m}) \,\&\, A_m$, or $(C_{i,0} \,\&\, C_{i,1} \,\&\, \ldots \,\&\, C_{i,m}) \,\&\, \neg A_m$, or $(C_{i,0} \,\&\, C_{i,1} \,\&\, \ldots \,\&\, C_{i,m}) \,\&$ $\&\, ((A_m \supset \neg A_m) \,\&\, (\neg A_m \supset A_m))$. So the sequence of axiomatic systems $\Omega_0, \Omega_1, \ldots$, as well as the sequence of corresponding Luk-theories $\theta_0, \theta_1, \ldots$ is constructed. Clearly, the sequence $\theta_0, \theta_1, \ldots$ is effectively generated.

Now we shall prove by induction on $m$ that for every $\Omega_i$ the following conditions are satisfied on every $m$-th step of the construction:

(A)  The formula $C_{i,0} \,\&\, C_{i,1} \,\&\, \ldots \,\&\, C_{i,m}$ belongs to $[\theta]$.

(B)  There exists an index $k$ such that $B_k$ has one of three forms mentioned above.

(So, the process of construction for every $\Omega_i$ cannot be stopped).

Indeed, let $m$ be equal to 0. Clearly, $C_{i,0} \in [\theta]$. Let us prove that there exists $k$ such that $B_k$ is either $C_{i,0} \& A_0$, or $C_{i,0} \& \neg A_0$, or $C_{i,0} \& ((A_0 \supset \neg A_0) \& (\neg A_0 \supset A_0))$. If there is no such $k$ that the formula $B_k$ is $C_{i,0} \& A_0$, then $C_{i,0} \& A_0$ does not belong to $[\theta]$; so the Luk-theory $\theta \cup \{C_{i,0} \& A_0\}$ is Luk-inconsistent. Similarly to the proof of Lemma 3 we conclude that $\theta \cup \{C_{i,0}\} \vdash A_0 \supset \neg A_0$. Further, if there is no $k$ such that the formula $B_k$ is $C_{i,0} \& \neg A_0$, then $C_{i,0} \& \neg A_0$ does not belong to $[\theta]$; so the Luk-theory $\theta \cup \{C_{i,0} \& \neg A_0\}$ is Luk-inconsistent. Similarly to the preceding case we conclude that $\theta \cup \{C_{i,0}\} \vdash \neg A_0 \supset \neg \neg A_0$, hence $\theta \cup \{C_{i,0}\} \vdash \neg A_0 \supset A_0$. We obtain that if an index $k$ does not exist in two preceding cases, then

$$\theta \cup \{C_{i,0}\} \vdash ((A_0 \supset \neg A_0) \& (\neg A_0 \supset A_0)).$$

But the theory $\theta \cup \{C_{i,0}\}$ is Luk-consistent, hence the theory $\theta \cup \{C_{i,0} \& ((A_0 \supset \neg A_0) \& (\neg A_0 \supset A_0))\}$ is also Luk-consistent.

So, we obtain that $C_{i,0} \& ((A_0 \supset \neg A_0) \& (\neg A_0 \supset A_0)) \in [\theta]$, and there exists an index $k$ such that $B_k$ is $C_{i,0} \& ((A_0 \supset \neg A_0) \& (\neg A_0 \supset A_0))$. It is proved that there exists a required index $k$ in one of three considered cases. Taking $C_{i,1}$ as it is described in the rules given above, we obtain obviously, that the formula $C_{i,0} \& C_{i,1}$ belongs to $[\theta]$.

The proof in the general case is similar to the case when $m = 0$. Indeed, let us assume that the formulas $C_{i,0}, C_{i,1}, ..., C_{i,m}$ are already constructed. If there is no $k$ such that $B_k$ is $(C_{i,0} \& C_{i,1} \& ... \& C_{i,m}) \& A_m$, then similarly to the considerations for $m = 0$ we conclude that the theory

$$\theta \cup \{(C_{i,0} \& C_{i,1} \& ... \& C_{i,m}) \& A_m\}$$

is Luk-inconsistent, hence

$$\theta \cup \{(C_{i,0} \& C_{i,1} \& ... \& C_{i,m})\} \vdash A_m \supset \neg A_m.$$

If there is no $k$ such that $B_k$ is $(C_{i,0} \& C_{i,1} \& ... \& C_{i,m}) \& \neg A_m$ then the theory

$$\theta \cup \{(C_{i,0} \& C_{i,1} \& ... \& C_{i,m}) \& \neg A_m\}$$

is Luk-inconsistent, hence

$$\theta \cup \{(C_{i,0} \& C_{i,1} \& ... \& C_{i,m})\} \vdash \neg A_m \supset A_m.$$

If a required index $k$ does not exist in two mentioned cases, then

$$\theta \cup \{(C_{i,0} \& C_{i,1} \& ... \& C_{i,m})\} \vdash ((A_m \supset \neg A_m) \& (\neg A_m \supset A_m)).$$

But we have by induction that the theory $\theta \cup \{(C_{i,0} \mathbin{\&} C_{i,1} \mathbin{\&} ... \mathbin{\&} C_{i,m})\}$ is Luk-consistent,                    hence                    the                    theory $\theta \cup \{(C_{i,0} \mathbin{\&} C_{i,1} \mathbin{\&} ... \mathbin{\&} C_{i,m}) \mathbin{\&} ((A_m \supset \neg A_m) \mathbin{\&} (\neg A_m \supset A_m))\}$    is    also    Luk-consistent, so that the formula

$$(C_{i,0} \mathbin{\&} C_{i,1} \mathbin{\&} ... \mathbin{\&} C_{i,m}) \mathbin{\&} ((A_m \supset \neg A_m) \mathbin{\&} (\neg A_m \supset A_m))$$

belongs to $[\theta]$, and there exists a required index $k$ in the third case. Hence, there exists a required index $k$ in one of the mentioned cases. Taking $C_{i,m+1}$ as it is described in the rules given above we obtain that the formula

$$(C_{i,0} \mathbin{\&} C_{i,1} \mathbin{\&} ... \mathbin{\&} C_{i,m}) \mathbin{\&} C_{i,m+1}$$

belongs to $[\theta]$. So the statements (A) and (B) are proved.

Clearly, all the Luk-theories $\theta_i$ based on $\Omega_i$ are Luk-complete because for every closed formula $A_m \in L(Z)$ either $A_m$, or $\neg A_m$, or $(A_m \supset \neg A_m) \mathbin{\&} (\neg A_m \supset A_m)$ belongs to $\theta_i$. All $\theta_i$ are Luk-consistent, because every finite part of every $\Omega_i$ is Luk-consistent.

If for some $m$, in process of construction of a system $\Omega_i$, the formula $A_m$ belongs to    $\theta$,    then    the    theories    $\theta \cup \{(C_{i,0} \mathbin{\&} C_{i,1} \mathbin{\&} ... \mathbin{\&} C_{i,m}) \mathbin{\&} \neg A_m\}$    and $\theta \cup \{(C_{i,0} \mathbin{\&} C_{i,1} \mathbin{\&} ... \mathbin{\&} C_{i,m}) \mathbin{\&} \quad \mathbin{\&} ((A_m \supset \neg A_m) \mathbin{\&} (\neg A_m \supset A_m))\}$    are    Luk-inconsistent, so that $C_{i,m+1} = A_m$. Hence $\theta \subseteq \theta_i$ for every $i$, and $\theta$ is contained in the intersection of $\theta_i$. Let us prove that $\theta$ coincides with this intersection.

Indeed, assume that a closed formula $A \in L(Z)$ does not belong to $\theta$. Then $\neg^\circ \neg^\circ A$ also does not belong to $\theta$ (by Lemma 5). Using Lemma 3, we conclude that $\neg^\circ A$ belongs to $[\theta]$. Hence $\neg^\circ A$ (that is $A \supset \neg A$) is equal to $B_k$ for some $k$, so $A \supset \neg A \in \Omega_k$. But in this case $A$ cannot belong to $\theta_k$, otherwise $\Omega_k$ would be Luk-inconsistent. Hence $A$ does not belong to the intersection of $\theta_i$. This completes the proof of Theorem 1.

**Proof of Theorem 2.** Let $\Omega$ be an axiomatic system in a signature Z; $\theta$ be a Luk-theory based on $\Omega$; $\Omega^+$ be the classical image of $\Omega$ in the signature $Z^+$; $\theta^+$ be the classical formal theory in the language $L^*(Z^+)$ based on $\Omega^+$. Let us assume that $\theta^+$ is decidable in the classical sense. Then $\theta^+$ is recursive. It follows immediately from the definitions of $A^+$ and $A^-$ that there exists an algorithm $\alpha$ which gives for every closed formula $B \in L(Z)$ the formula $\alpha(B) = B^+$. Using Lemma 6, we conclude that $B \in \theta$ if and only if $\alpha(B) \in \theta^+$. Hence the set $\theta$ is $m$-reducible to a recursive set $\theta^+$, so it is also recursive, and $\theta$ is Luk-decidable.

Now assume that $\theta$ is Luk-decidable, meaning that $\theta$ is recursive. Using Lemma 7 (and the note following this Lemma) we conclude that there exists an algorithm $\beta$ which gives for every closed formula $A \in L^*(Z^+)$ the formula $\beta(A) = B \in L(Z)$, such that the formula $(B^+ \sim A)$ is deducible from $\Omega^+$ in the classical predicate calculus. Hence $A \in \theta^+$ if and only if $B^+ \in \theta^+$, or equivalently $B \in \theta$. So $\theta^+$ is $m$-reducible to $\theta$, hence $\theta^+$ is recursive, and $\theta^+$ is decidable in the classical sense. This completes the proof of Theorem 2.

## Acknowledgements

The author is grateful to Henk Zeevat, to Balder ten Cate and to Leonid P. Murza for the help in the formulation of the final version of this article.

## References

[1] Bols, L., Borowik, P.: Many-valued Logics1: Theoretical Foundations. Springer, Heidelberg (1992)

[2] Enderton, H.B.: A Mathematical Introduction to Logic, 2nd edn. Academic Press, San Diego, Harcourt (2001)

[3] Ershov, Y.L.: Problems of Decidability and Constructive Models (in Russian). Nauka, Moskow (1980)

[4] Kleene, S.C.: Introduction to Metamathematics. D.van Nostrand Comp., Inc., New York - Toronto (1952)

[5] Lukasiewicz, J.: O logice trojwartosciowej (in Polish). Ruch filozoficzny (Lwow) N5, 168–171 (1920)

[6] Zaslavsky, I.D.: Symmetric Constructive Logic (in Russian). Publ. House of Acad. Sci. Arm. SSR (1978)

[7] Zaslavsky, I.D.: On a logically but not functionally complete calculus in three-valued logic. In: The Tbilisi Symposium on Logic, Language and Computation, selected papers, pp. 309–313. CSLI publications, Stanford, California (1998)

[8] Zaslavsky, I.D.: On the Completeness Properties of the Systems of Symmetric Constructive and Three-valued Logic. In: International Conference 21st Days of Weak Arithmetics, St.Petersburg, Russia, June 7-9, 2002, pp. 17–18. Abstracts, St.Petersburg (2002), URL: http://at.yorku.ca/cgi-bin/amca/cail-01

[9] Zaslavsky, I.D.: Formal axiomatic theories on the base of three-valued logic (in Russian). In: Zapiski nauchnykh seminarov POMI. Proceedings of Scientific Seminars in St.Petersburg Department of Steklov Institute of Mathematics, Russian Acad. Sci, St.Petersburg. Theory of Complexity of Computations VIII, vol. 304, pp. 19–74 (2003)

[10] Zaslavsky, I.D.: Some criteria of completeness for axiomatic systems in three-valued logic. Transactions of the Institute for Informatics and Automation Problems of National Acad. Sci. Armenia. Mathematical Problems of Computer Science, vol. 27, pp. 174–202 (2006)

[11] Zaslavsky, I.D.: On decidable axiomatic theories in three-valued logic. In: The Batumi Symposium on Logic, Language and Computation, Abstracts of Reports, Batumi (2005)

# Doubling: The Semantic Driving Force Behind Functional Categories

Hedde Zeijlstra

University of Amsterdam, Spuistraat 13 (lsg NTK)
1019 VB Amsterdam, The Netherlands
zeijlstra@uva.nl
http://home.medewerker.uva.nl/h.h.zeijlstra

**Abstract.** In this paper I argue that the set of formal features that can head a functional projection is not predetermined by UG but derived through L1 acquisition. I formulate a hypothesis that says that every functional category F is realised as a semantic feature [F] unless there are overt doubling effects in the L1 input with respect to F; this feature is then analysed as a formal feature [i/uF]. In the first part of the paper I provide a theoretical motivation for this hypothesis, in the second part I test this proposal with a case study, namely the cross-linguistic distribution of Negative Concord (NC). I demonstrate that in NC languages negation must be analysed as a formal feature [i/uNEG], whereas in Double Negation languages this feature remains a semantic feature [NEG] (always interpreted as a negative operator), thus paving the way for an explanation of NC in terms of syntactic agreement. In the third part I argue that the application of the hypothesis to the phenomenon of negation yields two predictions that can be tested empirically. First I demonstrate how this hypothesis predicts negative markers Neg° can be available only in NC languages; second, independent change of the syntactic status of negative markers, can invoke a change with respect to the exhibition of NC in a particular language. Both predictions are proven to be correct. I finally argue what the consequences of the proposal presented in this paper are for both the syntactic structure of the clause and second for the way parameters are associated to lexical items.

**Keywords:** Diachronic syntax, Doubling, Flexible syntax, Formal features, Functional projections, Learnability, Negation, Negative Concord.

## 1  Introduction

A central topic in the study of the syntax-semantics interface concerns the question what exactly constitutes the set of functional projections, or more precisely, what constitutes the set of formal features that are able to project. Since [34]'s work on the split-IP hypothesis many analyses have assumed a rich functional structure, consisting of a UG-based set of functional heads that are present in each clausal domain ([1] for quantifier positions, [37] for the CP domain, [45], [46] for negation or [9] for the IP domain). This approach has become known as the *cartographic* approach (cf. [10],

B.D. ten Cate and H.W. Zeevat (Eds.): TbiLLC 2005, LNAI 4363, pp. 260–280, 2007.

[22], [38] for an overview of recent papers). Under this approach the set of functional projections is not taken to result from other grammatical properties, but is rather taken as a starting point for grammatical analyses.

An alternative view on grammar, standardly referred to as *building block grammars* or the *what you see is what you get (wysiwyg)*[1] approach (cf. [3], [17], [22], [25], [30]), takes syntactic trees to be as small as possible. Apparently, in many cases there is empirical evidence for the presence of a functional projection in a particular clause, e.g. due to the presence of an overt functional head. The main difference, however, between the building block grammar approach and the cartographic approach (in its most radical sense) is that in the first approach the presence of a particular functional projection in a particular sentence in a particular language does not imply its presence in all clauses, or all languages, whereas this is the basic line of reasoning under the latter approach (cf. [9], [40]). However, the question what exactly determines the amount and distribution of functional projections remains open.

An intermediate approach between *cartography* and *building block / wysiwyg grammars* is [16]'s *feature scattering approach*. [16] argue that the set of formal features is universal and hierarchically ordered. All formal features may in principle project a head. Cross-linguistic differences are then accounted for by allowing different features to syncretise on one formal head, as long as their hierarchical ordering is kept intact. Under this approach, a universal set of formal features is reconciled with cross-linguistic differences in the clausal architecture. It should however be acknowledged that the differences between the approach and cartographic approach are not as clear as it seems. Only in the most radical cartographic analyses ([9], [40]) each formal feature corresponds to a separate functional projection. [37] also allows feature scattering, e.g. in the case of English [Force] and [Fin(iteness)] when there is no morphosyntactic argument to assume that they must host different head positions.

Ultimately, both the cartographic and [16]'s approach take the set of formal features to be determined by UG. In the present paper I propose a radically different perspective on the set of formal features, namely that UG does not contain any formal feature at all, but that the set of formal features (and consequently, the set of functional projections) is created during language acquisition. This paper thus breaks with the idea that the set of formal features represents the set of substantive universals or the set of semantic operators. Such an has been attractive since it links cross-linguistic variation to ways of realising these semantic operators, but, as I propose in the present paper, such a connection does not have to depend on the stipulated uniformity of the set of formal features. In this paper I also argue that these operators form the basis for the set of formal features, but I argue that formal features are derived from them, and I provide empirical and theoretical motivations for this claim. As a result it remains possible to connect cross-linguistic variation to the different ways of expressing particular semantic operators without stipulating a set of formal features that is uniform across languages.

The question of what constitutes functional projections and thus the set of formal features that are able to project is not only important for a better understanding of the syntax-semantics-interface, but is also of acute interest to the study of parameters.

---

[1] The term *wysiwyg* is adopted from [39]; the term *building block grammars* from Ad Neeleman (p.c.).

This is due to [4]'s assumption that parametric values are associated with properties of functional heads, a view on parametric variation that has been adopted in the Minimalist Program (cf. [6], [7]). For instance, the *Wh (fronting / in situ)* parameter follows from the presence of a [WH] feature on C° that either triggers movement of *Wh* terms to a sentence-initial position or allows them to remain in situ. However, once it is assumed that the pool of formal features in a language is not cross-linguistically identical, it becomes questionable whether parametric variation can still be tied down to properties of functional heads. Under a flexible approach the fact that in *Wh* languages *Wh* terms do not move to sentence-initial position can be said to result from a lack of a formal [Wh] feature that would trigger such movement. Under such an analysis the *Wh* parameter can no longer be reduced to properties of C° (note that the availability of C° is also subject to cross-linguistic variation; languages may lack a CP at all, if there is no proper trigger/cue for it during L1 acquisition). Hence a flexible approach to the question whether the set of formal features is uniform across languages may have strong consequences for the status of theories of parametric variation.

In the following section I provide some theoretical backgrounds and present my proposal, the Flexible Formal Feature Hypothesis (FFFH), arguing that a particular feature [F] can only be analysed as a formal feature able to create a functional projection FP if and only if there are (substantial) instances of doubling effects (multiple morphosyntactic manifestations of a single semantic operator) with respect to F present in language input during first language acquisition. After that, in section 3, I illustrate how the FFFH works by discussing a case-study: negation and Negative Concord. In this section I demonstrate that negation is a syntactically flexible functional category: in Negative Concord languages negation is realised as a formal feature, in Double Negation languages it is not. This calls for an explanation of Negative Concord in terms of syntactic agreement. In section 4, two more consequences of the application of the FFFH to negation are discussed: (i) the syntax of (negative) markers and (ii) patterns of diachronic change. Here I show that the FFFH makes correct predictions, thus providing empirical evidence for it. Section 5 concludes.

## 2  Formal Features Result from Doubling Effects

In the Minimalist Program ([6], [7], [8]) Lexical Items (LIs) are assumed to be bundles of three kinds of features: phonological features, semantic features and formal features. In the present paper the distinction between formal features and semantic features is of particular interest. First, I focus on the question as to what exactly the differences are between formal and semantic features. Second, the question rises of how these differences can be acquired during L1 acquisition.

### 2.1  Formal Features

As LIs consist of three different kinds of features, three different sets of features can be distinguished: the set of phonological features, the set of formal features and the set of semantic features. Following standard minimalist assumptions on the architecture of grammar, the set of formal features and the set of semantic features intersect, whereas the set of phonological features does not intersect with any of the two other sets. The relations between the sets are illustrated in in Fig.1.

As the sets of formal and semantic features intersect, formal features come in two kinds: formal features that have semantic content and formal features that do not. Therefore every formal feature (i.e. every formal feature on a lexical element) has a value ±interpretable: interpretable formal features can be interpreted at LF, the interface between grammar and the (semantic) Conceptual-Intentional system; uninterpretable features do not carry any semantic content and should therefore be deleted in the derivation before reaching LF in order not to violate the Principle of Full Interpretation ([6]). Uninterpretable features ([uF]'s) can be deleted by means of establishing a checking relation with a corresponding interpretable feature [iF].

Phonological features    Formal features    Semantic features

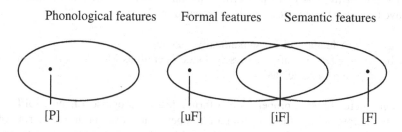

[P]    [uF]    [iF]    [F]

**Fig. 1.** Venn diagram of the sets of grammatical features with examples of each kind of features

A good example of a formal feature is the person feature (a so-called φ-feature). It is interpretable on DP's, but uninterpretable on verbs. Therefore finite verbs must enter a relation with a subject, so that the uninterpretable person feature on the verb is checked against the interpretable feature on the subject and is deleted. An example of a proper semantic feature is *sex* (as opposed to *gender*), which does not trigger any syntactic operation. No feature has to be deleted, as sex can always be interpreted.

Now the following question arises: how can one distinguish an interpretable formal feature [iF] from a semantic feature [F]? From a semantic perspective the two are indistinguishable, as they have identical semantic content:

(1)    $\|X_{[iF]}\| = \|X_{[F]}\|$

Syntactically, there is however a major distinction between an element carrying [iF] and an element carrying [F]. The first, but not the latter is able to check uninterpretable features ([uF]'s). Checking of uninterpretable features thus forms a diagnostic test to distinguish interpretable formal features from purely semantic features. Suppose that a sentence containing a Lexical Item Y carries a feature [uF] is grammatical. Due to the Principle of Full Interpretation ([6]) this feature must have been checked against a feature carrying [iF]. Now suppose that a lexical Item Z is the only element in the proper licensing domain of Y that has an interpretation such that its feature must be either [iF] or [F]. In this case it must be that Z carries [iF] and not [F], since otherwise the sentence could not have been grammatical. In other words, if a Lexical Item A is able to check a feature [uF] on B, A must carry [iF].[2]

Hence, the occurrence of elements carrying uninterpretable features in grammatical sentences, forms the only diagnostic to distinguish elements carrying interpretable formal features from elements carrying purely semantic features. However, this immediately raises the question how it can be determined whether a particular Lexical Item carries an uninterpretable formal feature.

## 2.2  Uninterpretable Features and Doubling Effects

So, the question how to determine whether an LI carries a formal feature [iF] or a semantic feature [F] reduces to the question how to determine whether there is an LI visible that carries a feature [uF]. This question is much easier to address: LIs carrying [uF]'s exhibit (at least) two properties that can easily be recognised (which already have been mentioned above) and are repeated in (2).

(2)    a.    A feature [uF] is semantically vacuous.
       b.    A feature [uF] triggers syntactic operations Move and Agree in order to be deleted.

At first sight there are three properties that form a test to recognise a feature [uF]: its semantic uninterpretability, the triggering of an operation Move and the triggering of an operation Agree. Below I argue that all of these three properties reduce to one single property: doubling.

First, although a feature [uF] is meaningless, it must establish a syntactic relationship with an element that carries [iF] and that therefore must have semantic content. This is illustrated in the following example with the person feature [i/u2SG]:

(3)    a.    Du      komm-st                          German
             You     come
       b.    [$_{TP}$ Du$_{[i2SG]}$ kommst$_{[u2SG]}$ ]
                    └_____┘

In (3) it is shown that the information that the subject is a 2$^{nd}$ person singular pronoun is encoded twice in the morphosyntax: first by the choice of the subject *du*, second by the person marker –*st* on the verbal stem. Since there is only one 2$^{nd}$ person singular subject in the semantics of the sentence, the subject marker on the verb is meaningless.

At this stage the question emerges why a certain morpheme is semantically vacuous. In cases of overt doubling, such as (3), the fact that the presence of one semantic operator is manifested twice in the morpho-syntax forms evidence that at least one of the two elements must carry no semantic content. But how to analyse cases in which

---

[2] *Visible* means that the presence of this LI must be clear. This does not mean that this element must have phonological contents. It suffices that its presence must be evident. This evidence can be provided by overtness, but also by triggering of syntactic operations or changing the grammatical status of a sentence.

an inflectional morpheme is the only overt marker of a semantic operator? This is for instance the case with pro-drop:

(4)     Canta                                        Italian
        sings.3SG.SING
        'He/she sings'

According to [36] among many others, sentences such as (4) are considered to contain an abstract subject whose presence is marked by the subject marking on the verb. Following this line of reasoning the subject marking on the verb is then no longer the carrier of the semantics of the 3rd person singular subject.

Now, let us discuss the expression of English past tense:

(5)     You walked

In (5) it is unclear whether the morpheme *–ed* on *walk* is the phonological realisation of the past tense operator. Although this may look like a natural assumption, nothing a priori forbids an analysis where the inflectional morpheme is semantically vacuous and the past tense operator is an abstract adverbial operator (whose presence is marked by the tense marker on the verb). This latter option is available since nothing requires that a Lexical Item that carries an interpretable formal feature must be phonologically realised. In the previous section it has only been argued for that [iF] is carried by a visible Lexical Item. If for instance the dependent (the element carrying a [uF]) is phonologically realised (and the sentence is grammatical) the presence of the element carrying [iF] has already been made visible and therefore does not necessarily have to contain phonological material.

Here I Follow [32] and [41], who on the bases of their analyses of sequence-of-tense effects and the interaction between tense and (distributive) quantifiers have convincingly shown that it is imposible to analyse the past tense morpheme as the past tense operator. The first option, in which *-ed* is the relisation of a semantic past tense operator, is ruled out. Hence *-ed* must be considered to carry a [uPAST] rather than an [iPAST] feature. Consequently, (5) contains a covert past tense adverbial.

The examples in (3)-(4) are already an example of the syntactic operation Agree. In (3) at some point in the derivation the verb's [u2SG] feature is checked against a corresponding [i2SG] feature. Without an Agree relation between *du* and *kommst*, the sentence would be ungrammatical; if *kommst* did not have any uninterpretable person features at all, it could not have triggered an Agree relation in the first place. The same holds *mutatis mutandis* for the relation between the abstract subject and the finite verb in (4) and the relation between the past tense operator and the tensed verb in (5). In (3) the semantic operator is overtly manifested more than once, a phenomenon that is known as *doubling*. In (4) and (5) there is only one overt marker of the subject pronoun or the past tense respectively, but there are again multiple elements in the morpho-syntax visible that correspond to a single semantic operator. Therefore, although in (4) and (5) only one marker has been realised phonologically, these sentences also exhibit *doubling*. Agree is always a result of a doubling effect.

Such an Agree relation is not restricted to two elements (one [iF], one [uF]), also multiple [uF]'s can establish a relation with a single [iF]. [19], [20] and [43] refer to this phenomenon as *multiple Agree*. This is illustrated in (6) below for Spanish, where the gender and number features on the noun are also manifested on the determiner and the adjective.[3,4]

(6)      Las                chicas              guapas                    Spanish
         The[uFEM][uPL]  girls[iFEM][iPL]  pretty[uFEM][uPL]
         'The pretty girls'

Now, let us have a look at the operation Move. Checking requirements of uninterpretable features always trigger movement. It follows immediately that Move should follow from doubling properties, since Move is a superfunction of Agree (Move = Agree + Pied-piping + Merge). It has been argued that *Wh* fronting is triggered by an uninterpretable *Wh* feature [uWH] on C.[5] By moving the *Wh* word, which carries an [iWH] feature, to Spec,CP, the [uWH] feature in C° can be checked against this [iWH]. This is illustrated in (7).

(7)

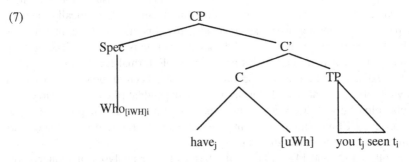

In (7) the *Wh* feature is present three times in total in the structure: as [iWH] on the Wh word, as [uWH] on C° and as a deleted [iWH] on the trace. Given that the *Wh* term had to be fronted, it can be determined that C° must contain an uninterpretable feature [uWH]. In other words, Move makes the presence of an uninterpretable feature [uWH] visible although this feature itself has not been spelled-out. Hence Move, too, results from a double manifestation of the Wh feature in the sentence.

---

[3] In this example I analyse *chicas* as carrying [iPL]. However, I want to keep the option open that the plural morphology on the noun is also uninterpretable and that an abstract operator is responsible for the plural semantics.

[4] The example may yield some questions about the semantics of numerals. In an example like *las dos chicas guapas* (the two girls pretty) the numeral *dos* requires a semantically plural complement. Informally speaking, I suggest, without commiting myself, that its semantics must be something like 'taking two of ...' Under such an approach *dos* itself has not a plural (semantic or formal) feature. Number mismatches in those cases simply follow from mismatches between the lexical semantics of *dos* and the plural operator (regardless whether it ishosted on the noun or left abstract).

[5] The question is of course why [uWH] on C° cannot be checked under Agree. This requires an additional explanation. Either one assumes the presence of an [EPP] feature on C° that requires C°'s Spec position to be filled, or one assumes that Agree is in fact always an instance of Move (feature movement or other movement). Nothing in this paper relies crucially on what motivates Move in this example.

It remains of course an open question why in (7) the checking relation cannot be established by Agree as well. Much debate is going on about this question. In some recent minimalist versions it is assumed that in English $C°$ has an additional EPP feature that is responsible for the movement. For the moment I will not engage in this discussion. It suffices to say that Move is a superfunction of Agree and since doubling is a triggering force behind Agree, it is behind Move too. Consequently, Move cannot take place without being triggered by uninterpretable features.

As we have seen, doubling is the driving force behind the existence of uninterpretable features. Without any doubling in natural language no uninterpretable formal features would exist, and thus no formal features. This immediately rises the question why there should be doubling in natural language in the first place? In this paper I do not address this issue, since this question would require a paper on itself, but ultimately the existence of doubling should follow from interface conditions, as (ideally) every grammatical property. Since there does not seem to be any semantic advantage to doubling, the question calls for a phonological explanation. In [49] I analyse doubling as a result of a phonological desideratum to spell-out as many functional markers on one Lexical Element. For a survey of the arguments and explanation, the reader is referred to that paper.

A second question that waits to be answered is why doubling should lead uninterpretable material. After all, could there not be some semantic device that is responsible for the proper readings if very morpho-syntactic marker did have semantic content? Take as example the minimal pair in (8).

(8)    a.    John walked

       b.    Yesterday John walked

I have argued that –*ed* on walked does not contain an interpretable past tense feature, and that past tense in (9a) is induced by an abstract adverbial operator, call it $Op_{PAST}$. Is past tense also induced by $Op_{PAST}$ in (9b)? The answer to this question depends on the featural make-up of *yesterday*. Does it contain a feature [iF] or not? Arguably not, since yesterday is perfectly compatible with present perfect constructions, as shown below. Thus if yesterday were the element responsible for the checking of the uninterpretable tense feature in (9b), (9a) would lead to a feature checking mismatch and be ruled out.

(9)    Yesterday John has walked

Hence it makes more sense to adopt common analyses on these semantics of *yesterday* and say that it somehow relates to the topic time. This implies that in (9b) $Op_{PAST}$ is also part of the sentence. But $Op_{PAST}$ and yesterday do not give rise to an iterative past tense reading. Why is this not a case of doubling either? This is due to the fact that *yesterday* modifies on $Op_{PAST}$ and that for instance in neo-Davidsonian event semantics a conjunction of *yesterday* operating on an event variable and past tense doing the same thing also leads to the correct interpretation of (9b).

(10)    ...$\exists$e.[**yesterday'**(e) & **past'**(e) & ...]

As there are two semantic operators (yesterday and Op$_{PAST}$) available in the interpretation of (9b), there is no doubling. Doubling is only the case if a morpho-syntactic marker expressing the presence of a semantic operator cannot have the lexical semantics of this operator as well. In the literature this has been proposed for many instances of marking, such as tense marking, perfect marking, modality marking, person marking, etc. (cf. [42] for an exhaustive overview of this literature, see also [49] for an argument why all inflectional morphology must involve redundant material).

Markers of a semantic operator Op$_F$ that cannot be the realisation of this semantic operation must carry [uF]. Thus, whenever there is 'real' doubling with respect to F, there is a [uF] present, and whenever a [uF] feature is present in a syntactic structure, there is doubling with respect to F.

Before continuing the discussion, a few words need to be said about the following problem: the fact that [uF] is semantically vacuous seems to be at odds with the fact that it contains the information that it must be checked with a feature ([iF]) that encodes particular *semantic* information. This problem (an instance of Look Ahead, since apparently the properties that are visible on LF already play a role during the derivation) has been accounted for in terms of feature valuation (cf. [8]). The difference between interpretable and uninterpretable features would be rephrased in terms of lexically valued versus unvalued features. Valued features are then interpretable at LF, whereas unvalued features are not. Under Agree, unvalued features are valued (without proper valuation the derivation would crash at LF). After valuation they are deleted, deletion being a by-effect of Agree. However, the idea that features that are valued during syntax are uninterpretable at LF as opposed to the idea that features that are valued in the lexicion are LF interpretable is pure stipulation, and therefore it does not really solve the problem.

I argue that the problem disappears under a closer look to what counts as syntax and what counts as semantics. In order to keep [uF] semantically vacuous, [uF] may contain only syntactic information. This information encodes that a lexical item carrying [uF] must stand in an Agree relation to an element that carries a feature [iF]. Although [iF] has semantic content, it also has syntactic content. This follows immediately from the architecture of grammar: if [iF] would lack any syntactic content, it could not have been a formal feature in the first place and it would be a purely semantic feature [F]. It is this syntactic content of [iF] that checks [uF] and causes its deletion. Since [iF] is not only a syntactic feature, but also a semantic feature (it is an element of the intersection of the two sets of features), its syntactic part does not have to be deleted: [iF] has semantic content as well and therefore it does not violate the principle of Full Interpretation at LF.

Finally, a word on purely semantic features. Although I adopt the architecture in 0, I am not strongly committed to the existence of semantic features in the model of grammar. A particular element is asigned a particular semantic feaature [F], if it contains a semantic operator Op$_F$ in its lexical semantics and it does not get formalised (i.e. it cannot be analysed as [iF]). A negative quantifier (in a Double Negation language) is said to carry a feature [NEG] since its lexical semantics carries a logical negation ($\lambda P \lambda Q \neg \exists x [P(x) \& Q(x)]$ for English *no*, for instance). Under a strong lexical feature approach, the Lexical Item *no* is composed out of a semantic feature [NEG] and many other features, such as quantificational features. A more model-theoretical semantics approach would take [NEG] to count as a label encoding that the Lexical

Item is semantically negative. Under such an approach purely semantic features do not have an ontological status anymore. Interpretable formal features would then be purely syntactic features that also label the presence of a particular semantic operator. In this paper I will restrict myself to the feature approach, but the analysis can be perfectly implemented in theories without semantic features.

Now we can reformulate the answer to the question asked in the beginning of this subsection: how can an [iF] be distinguished from a [F]? The answer is that whenever there is doubling with respect to F, there are (only) formal features ([iF]/[uF]). Two features [iF] or two features [F] would result in an iterative reading that contains two semantic operators $Op_F$.[6] Following this line of reasoning, if there is no doubling with respect to F, there is no reason to assume that F is a formal feature. In those cases, every instance of F always corresponds to a semantic feature [F]. Therefore I put forward the following hypothesis:

(11)    *Flexible Formal Feature Hypothesis (FFFH)*
    a.      If and only if there are doubling effects with respect to a semantic operator $OP_F$ in the language input, all features of F are formal feature [i/uF].
    b.      If there are no doubling effects with respect to a semantic operator $OP_F$ in the language input, all features of F are semantic features ([F]).

This hypothesis, if correct, has consequences for the architecture of grammar. It rejects the idea that the set of formal features is fixed by UG, and states that every semantic operator[7] in principle can be part of the syntactic vocabulary (i.e. the set of formal features) or remains within the realm of semantics. Before elaborating the proposal and its consequences in abstract terms, I first provide a case study, which shows that this hypothesis based on the idea that the set of formal features is not predetermined by UG makes correct predictions when applied to a particular empirical phenomenon.

# 3 Case Study: Negation and Negative Concord

The case study to test the FFFH presented above concerns negation. Doubling with respect to negation is clearly detectable, since two semantic negations always cancel

---

[6] The reason why one semantic opertor cannot correspond to multiple features [(i)F] is that this leads to a violation of compositionality. Each feature [(i)F] corresponds to a semantic operotor OpF, and two elements carrying [(i)F] must give rise to an iterative reading. In order to avoid uninterpretable features, some scholars ([11], [18]) have introduced absorption rules for multiple *Wh* words or negative quantifiers. However, these mechanisms introduce non-compositionality in the model, a step which should only be taken if it is absolutely unavoidable. This is however not the case, since one still finds lots of instances of uninterpretability in natural languages, such as subject marking on verbs. Hence adopting mechanism does not lead to abolishing uninterpretable material.

[7] For a discussion about what exactly constitutes the class of semantic operators the reader is referred to [12], [24] and [39].

each other out. If two negative elements do not cancel each other out, but yield one semantic negation, at least one of the two negative elements must be uninterpretable. This phenomenon is well described and known as Negative Concord (NC).[8]

One can distinguish three different types of languages with respect to multiple negation: (i) Double Negation (DN) languages, in which two negative elements always cancel each other out; (ii) Strict NC languages, in which multiple (clause-internal) negative elements (both negative markers and n-words[9]) yield only one semantic negation; and (iii) Non-strict NC languages, where either a preverbal n-word or a preverbal negative marker establishes an NC relation with a postverbal n-word. However, a negative marker in this type of language may not follow preverbal n-words. An example of a DN language is Dutch, an example of a Strict NC language is Czech and an example of a Non-strict NC language is Italian, as is illustrated in (12)-(14) below.

(12)  a.  Jan  ziet  *niemand*                         Dutch
          Jan  sees  n-body
          'Jan doesn't see anybody'
      b.  *Niemand* zegt *niets*
          N-body    says n-thing
          'Nobody says nothing'

(13)  a.  Milan *(ne-)*vidi  *nikoho*                   Czech
          Milan  NEG.saw  n-body
          'Milan doesn't see anybody'
      b.  Dnes  *(ne-)*volá  *nikdo*
          Today  NEG.calls  n-body
          'Today nobody calls'
      c.  Dnes  *nikdo*   *(ne-)*volá
          Today  n-body     NEG.calls
          'Today nobody calls'

(14)  a.  Gianni *(non)* ha telefonato a *nessuno*   Italian
          Gianni NEG      has called    to n-body
          'Gianni didn't call anybody'
      b.  Ieri           *(non)* ha telefonato *nessuno*
          Yesterday  NEG  has called       n-body
          'Yesterday nobody called'
      c.  Ieri           *nessuno* (**non*) ha telefonato (a *nessuno*)
          Yesterday  n-body  NEG   has called       to n-body
          'Yesterday nobody called (anybody)'

In Dutch, two negations cancel each other out, and thus the sentences in (12) contain only one negative element. This is either the negative marker *niet* or a negative

---

[8] For a more detailed decription of NC effects see [48].

[9] The term *n-word* is due to [28] and defined in [15] as elements that seem to exhibit semantically negative behaviour in some contexts, but semantically non-negative behaviour in other contexts.

quantifier, as illustrated below in (15)-(17). Note that the locus of the negative operator at LF does not coincide with its relative position at surface structure, but this is due to quantifier raising (independent from negation) in (15) or V2 in (17). Hence there are no doubling effects with respect to negation. As a result from the FFFH it follows that negation in Dutch is not formalised (or grammaticalised): the only negative feature [NEG] in Dutch is a semantic feature.

(15)    Jan doet *niets*              $\neg\exists x.[\textbf{thing'}(x) \& \textbf{do'}(j, x)]$[10]
            [NEG]
        Jan does n-thing

(16)    *Niemand* komt               $\neg\exists x.[\textbf{person'}(x) \& \textbf{come'}(x)]$
            [NEG]
        N-body comes

(17)    Jan loopt *niet*             $\neg\textbf{walk'}(j)$
            [NEG]
        Jan walks NEG

Things are different, however, in NC languages. Let us start by discussing the Non-strict NC language Italian. In Italian postverbal n-words obligatorily need to be accompanied by the negative marker *non* or a preverbal n-word. This means that a large part of negative sentences in the L1 input consists of sentences such as (18).

(18)    Gianni *non*  ha visto *nessuno*     $\neg\exists x.[\textbf{person'}(x) \& \textbf{see'}(g, x)]$
            [iNEG]         [uNEG]
        Gianni NEG has seen n-body

Since (18) contains more than one negative element, but only one negation in its semantics, only one of the negative elements can be semantically negative and the other one must be semantically non-negative. The latter element must therefore carry an uninterpretable formal negative feature [uNEG], and, negation being formalised in this language, the negative operator carries [iNEG] and not [NEG]. Negation scopes from the position occupied by *non*.[11] *Non* thus carries [iNEG] and *nessuno* carries [uNEG]. This distribution cannot be reversed, since otherwise a sentence such as (19) is expected to be grammatical, contra fact.

(19)    *Gianni ha visto  *nessuno*
        Gianni has seen   n-body
        'Gianni hasn't seen anybody'

*Non*'s [iNEG] feature also enables it to express sentential negation. This is shown in (20) where *non* functions as the negative operator.

---

[10] For reasons of readability tense is neglected in all these readings.
[11] Following Aristotle/Horn that negation is not a propositional but a predicative operator.

(20)    *Non* ha telefonato Gianni                $\neg$**call'(g)**
        [iNEG]

The fact that *non* is the carrier of [iNEG] and n-words carry [uNEG] seems to be problematic in one respect, namely that Italian also allows sentences such as (21). Here *non* is absent (and may not even be included). Hence, all overt negative elements carry [uNEG].

(21)    *Nessuno* ha telefonato a *nessuno*       $\neg\exists x\exists y[$**person'**$(x)$ & **person'**$(y)$
        [uNEG]              [uNEG]                      & **call'**$(x, y)]$

However, given the grammaticality and the semantics of the sentence, one element must carry the feature [iNEG]. Basically, there are two ways out. One possibility is to analyse n-words as being lexically ambiguous between negative quantifiers and non-negative indefinites (cf. [21]), but this would render (19) grammatical. The other way is to assume that negation is induced by a (phonologically) abstract negative operator ($Op_\neg$), whose presence is marked by the overt n-words. Then (21) would be analysed as follows:

(22)    $Op_\neg$    *nessuno* ha telefonato a *nessuno*
        [iNEG]    [uNEG]                   [uNEG]

This analysis is supported by the fact that if the subject n-word is focussed and the negative marker *non* is included, the sentences achieves a DN reading. Hence, apart from the presence of *non*, a second negative operator must be at work.

(23)    $Op_\neg$    *nessuno non* ha telefonato a  *nessuno*
        [iNEG]    [uNEG] [iNEG]                 [uNEG]

Consequently, given the fact that in Italian not every instance of negation is semantically negative, negation is formalised and every negative element carries a formal negative feature: n-words carry [uNEG] and the negative marker *non* and $Op_\neg$ carry [iNEG].

In Czech, the application of the FFFH leads to slightly different results. First, since Czech is an NC language, negation must be formalised and n-words are attributed a feature [uNEG]. However the (default) assumption that the negative marker carries [iNEG] cannot be drawn on this basis yet. The negative operator could also be left abstract. Hence, the value of the formal feature of the negative marker in (24) cannot be determined on the basis of this example.

(24)    Milan    *ne*-vidi *nikoho*             $\neg\exists x.[$**person'**$(x)$ & **see'**$(m, x)]$
                 [?NEG] [uNEG]

In Italian we saw that *non* must be the negative operator, since negation takes scope from the position that it occupies. Consequently, no n-word is allowed to surface left of this marker (with the exception of constructions like (23)). However, in Czech n-words are allowed to occur both to the left and to the right of the negative marker.

This means that negation cannot scope from the surface position of *ne*, since otherwise the negative operator would be (asymmetrically) c-commanded by the semantically non-negative n-word, and, contrary to fact, yield a reading in which the indefinite outscopes negation. The only way to analyse *ne* then, is as a negative marker that carries [uNEG] and which establishes a feature checking relation (along with the n-words) with a higher abstract negative operator:

(25)    $Op_\neg$    *Nikdo*    *ne*-volá              $\neg\exists x.[\textbf{person'}(x) \ \& \ \textbf{call'}(x)]$
        [iNEG]  [uNEG]   [uNEG]

As a final consequence, single occurrences of *ne* cannot be taken to be realisations of the negative operator, but markings of such an operator. In (26) the negative marker indicates the presence of $Op_\neg$, which in its turn is responsible for the negative semantics of the sentence.

(26)    Milan    $Op_\neg$    *ne*-volá              $\neg\textbf{call'}(m)$
                 [iNEG]  [uNEG]

Hence, in Czech even the negative marker is semantically non-negative. Czech and Italian thus differ with respect to the formalisation of negation to the extent that the negative marker in Italian carries [iNEG], whereas the negative marker in Czech carries [uNEG]. Note that this corresponds to the phonological status of the two markers: in Czech the negative marker exhibits prefixal behaviour, thus suggesting that it should be treated on a par with tense/agreement morphology. Italian *non* is a (phonologically stronger) particle that can be semantically active by itself.

The application of the FFFH calls for an analysis of NC as a form of syntactic agreement. Such an approach has been initiated by [26] and adopted by [5] and [48]. It should be noted however that these are not the only accounts for NC. Other accounts treat NC as a form of polyadic quantification ([11]), [18], [44]) or treat n-words as Negative Polarity Items (cf. [13], [14], [28]). Space limits prevent me from doing justices to these theories by evaluating them and argue why they do not solve several off the problems that can be solved under the syntactic agreement approach. The reader is referred to [48] for an evaluation of different theories of NC.

## 4   Consequences

The FFFH and the exact analysis of NC in terms of syntactic agreement make several predictions that I discuss in this section. First, I argue that the status of the negative feature (formal or semantic) has some consequences regarding the appearance and distribution of the negative projection (NegP after [34]). Second, I show that the FFFH makes correct predictions about the consequences of diachronic change with respect to the obligatoriness or optional occurrence of the negative marker.

### 4.1  Negative Features and Projections

Now let us have a look at the relation between the formal status of negative features and the syntactic status of negative markers. Negative markers come about in different forms. In some languages (e.g. Turkish) the negative marker is part of the verbal inflectional morphology; in other examples the negative marker is a bit stronger. Italian *non* is a (phonological) strong particle, and the Czech particle *ne* is (phonologically) weak.[12] German *nicht* on the other hand is even too strong to be a particle and is standardly analysed as an adverb. Examples are in (27)-(29).

(27)    John elmalari ser-*me*-di[13]                           Turkish
        John apples like.NEG.PAST.3SG                          (affixal)
        'John doesn't like apples'

(28)    a.    Milan *ne*-volá                                   Czech
              Milan NEG.calls                                  (weak particle)
              'Milan doesn't call'
        b.    Gianni *non* ha telefonato                       Italian
              Gianni NEG has called                            (strong particle)
              'Gianni didn't call'

(29)    Hans kommt *nicht*                                     German
        Hans comes NEG                                         (adverbial)
        'Hans doesn't come'

Note also that it is not mandatory that a language has only one negative marker. Catalan has a strong negative particle *no* and an additional optional negative adverbial marker (*pas*) whereas in West Flemish the weak negative particle *en* is only optionally present, next to the standard adverbial negative marker *nie*. Standard French even has two obligatory negative markers (*ne ... pas*), as demonstrated in (30).

(30)    a.    *No* serà (*pas*) facil                          Catalan
              NEG be.FUT.3SG NEG easy
              'It won't be easy'
        b.    Valère (*en*) klaapt *nie*                       West Flemish
              Valère NEG talks NEG
              'Valère doesn't talk'
        c.    Jean *ne* mange *pas*                            French
              Jean NEG eats NEG
              'Jean doesn't eat'

I adopt the standard analysis that negative affixes and weak and strong negative particles should be assigned syntactic head ($X°$) status, whereas negative adverbials are specifiers/adjuncts, thus exhibiting XP status (cf. [29], [35], [45], [46], [47], [48]).

The difference between $X°$ and XP markers has influence on functional structure. $X°$ negative markers must (by definition) be able to project themselves, yielding a

---

[12] I refrain from the discussion whether Czech *ne* should be analysed as a clitical, prefixal or as a real particle. It will become clear from the following discussion that the outcome would not be relevant for the final analysis in terms of $X°$/XP status.

[13] Example from [33], also cited in [47].

clausal position Neg°. On the other hand, XP negative markers may occupy the speci-
fier position of a projection that is projected by a (possibly abstract) negative head
Neg°, Spec,NegP (as is the standard analysis for most adverbial negative markers),
but this is not necessarily the case. It could also be an adverbial negative marker that
occupies an adjunct/specifier position of another projection, for instance a $v$P adjunct
position. In that case it is not necessary that there is a special functional projection
NegP present in the clausal structure (it is not excluded either).

Now the question follows: when is a negative feature able to project? [16] addressed this problem in terms of their feature scattering principle, arguing that each
feature can project a head. However, given the modular view of grammar in which
features are divided into different classes, the question emerges which kind of features
can head a projection. One would not argue that every lexical semantic feature or
every phonological feature might have its own projection. Feature projection is a
syntactic operation, and should thus only apply to material that is visible to syntax.
Hence, the most straightforward hypothesis is that only formal features can project.
This means that a feature can only head a projection if it is a formal feature [i/uF].

Consequently, it follows immediately that the availability of a negative projection
NegP in a particular language depends on the question whether negation has been a
formal feature [i/uNEG] in this language. This leads to the following prediction: only
in languages that exhibit doubling effects with respect to negation (i.e. only in NC
languages) may NegP be available. This prediction can easily be tested, as it has been
argued above that X° negative markers occupy a Neg° position, whereas adverbial
negative markers do not have to occupy a Spec,NegP position. Therefore we expect
that only in the set of NC languages can one find negative markers X° (see (31)).

(31)    a.    NC:   [u/iNEG]/[X]              b.    Non-NC:    [X]

              [u/iNEG]     X                        [NEG]      [X]

In [48] this prediction has been tested for a threefold of empirical domains (a sample
of 267 Dutch dialectal varieties, a sample of 25 historical texts, and a set of 25 other
languages from different families) and been shown to be correct.[14] Thus empirical
evidence for the FFFH has been provided.

## 4.2  Negation and Diachronic Change

Since [23] it is known that a large majority of languages has developed with respect to
the expression of negation. These changes concern both the syntax of the negative

---

[14] Two kinds of exceptions have been found. First, Standard English, being a non-NC language,
allows for the negative marker *n't* ,which behaves like a negative head. Possibly this is related to the fact English is on its way to transforming itself into an NC language (cf. [48]).
English negation can be said to exhibit doubling effects, as it may trigger movement (negative inversion). Alternatively, [50] have suggested that the combination of an auxiliary + *n't*
is lexicalised. Then *n't* does not behave like a syntactic head (thanks to an anonymous reviewer for pointing this out to me).

Second, a number of Southeast Asian languages lack n-words. In those languages however,
it can be shown that negative markers trigger Move, thus exhibiting a doubling effect as well.

marker and the occurrence of NC. As follows from the previous subsection, these two phenomena are not unrelated. In this subsection, I first discuss how the FFFH predicts the change from Dutch from an NC language into a DN language as a result of so-called *en*-deletion.

Middle Dutch was a language that used two negative markers *en/ne ... niet* to express sentential negation, as shown in (32). However, in most cases which contained an n-word only the preverbal negative marker *en/ne* was present, as in (33).

(32)    Dat si *niet en* sach dat si sochte[15]                    Middle Dutch
        That she NEG NEG saw that she looked.for
        'That she didn't see what she looked for'

(33)    Ic *en* sag *niemen*                                       Middle Dutch
        NEG saw n-body
        'I didn't see anybody'

As in most languages exhibiting two negative markers, one of them disappears in the course of time. 16th and 17th century Holland Dutch in most cases left out the preverbal negative marker *en/ne*, and only exhibited *niet*. As a consequence of this development, the presence of *en/ne* also lost ground in constructions with n-words, resulting in expressions like (34).

(34)    Ic sag *niemen*                                           17th Cent. Dutch
        I saw n-body
        'I didn't see anybody'

Hence, the language input contained fewer and fewer constructions like the ones in (35) and more and more expressions in which an n-word was the only negative element in the sentence. As the cue to assign n-words a [uNEG] feature gradually disappeared, n-words were no longer analysed as carrying [uNEG], but got reanalysed as carrying [NEG] (36).[16]

(35)    a.      *Op¬*     en       niemen
                [iNEG]   [uNEG]   [uNEG]
        b.      *Op¬*     niemen   en
                [iNEG]   [uNEG]   [uNEG]

(36)    Ic sag *niemen*
               [NEG]

To conclude, the two developments described above show exactly how a change in the syntax of negative markers leads to a change in the interpretation of multiple negative expressions. Note that these latter changes follow directly from the FFFH and no other additional account has to be adopted.

---

[15] [27: 20042].
[16] Similarly, the negative marker *niet* also got analysed as having a [NEG] feature.

## 5 Conclusions

In this paper I first argued on theoretical grounds that the set of formal features, i.e. the set of features that can head a functional projection, is not provided by UG, but is a result of L1 acquisition. Only those semantic features that exhibit visible doubling effects are formalised (or grammaticalised). This has been formulated in the FFFH. Consequently, as only formal features can project, the number of functional projections FP that a particular grammar has at its disposal is limited by the FFFH. Each grammar, based on the language input during L1 acquisition, makes a particular choice of semantic operators that can be realised as FP's. Thus clausal structure is subject to cross-linguistic variation and not a uniform UG-based template.

In the second part of this paper I applied the FFFH to the domain of negation. Negation is a semantic operator that differs cross-linguistically in the way it surfaces in morphosyntax. Languages differ with respect to whether they exhibit doubling effects (known as NC) and thus the result of this application is that only in NC languages is negation formalised. In DN languages negation is not realised as a formal feature.

The consequences of the flexible formal status of negation are empirically testable. Not only do they call for an analysis of NC in terms of syntactic agreement (cf. [48] where I show that such an analysis solves many problems that other analyses have been facing). They also make correct predictions about the syntactic status of negative markers and the diachronic relation between the syntax of negative marker(s) and the occurrence of NC. First, it is shown that only NC languages may exhibit a negative marker Neg°. Second, it follows that if the (optional) negative marker for independent reasons ceases to occur in particular contexts, this may influence the visible doubling effects and therefore alter the status of the language as a (Strict) NC language.

Furthermore, the proposal presented above allows formulating predictions in terms of typological implications, which can be tested empirically. This is an interesting result, as it has been questioned whether typological implications count as linguistic evidence.[17] I hope to have shown in this paper that typological implications can be used as a testing mechanism for different proposal concerning the status of formal features.

Finally, as mentioned in the introduction, the adoption of hypotheses such as the FFFH has serious consequences for the conjecture that parametric variation can be reduced to different properties of (functional) heads. In the sections above, strong evidence has been put forward that the negative feature is only formal in a number of languages. DN languages lack such a formal feature [i/uNEG] and therefore can never produce a negative head Neg°. Consequently the NC parameter (±NC) can never be tied down to a value of the formal feature [NEG] associated to Neg°. The parametric variation with respect to multiple negation lies one level higher, namely whether or not the semantic operator *negation* is formalised. Hence, the NC parameter can be reduced to a semantic feature, but not to a syntactic feature. The NC parameter is thus a result of the fact that negation may but does not have to be formalised, a result of the FFFH. Note that not all parameters follow directly from the FFFH. The Strict vs.

---

[17] See [31] who recently reopened the debate.

Non-strict NC parameter can still be reduced to the i/u value of the formal feature [i/uNEG] on Neg°. However, the very existence of such a 'subparameter' again follows from the FFFH (without its application no Neg° is available in the first place). If this line of reasoning turns out to be correct many parameters can be derived from the FFFH, removing these out of UG, much in the same way as the set of formal features. Obviously such a prediction needs to be evaluated for a large number of parameters, but even if it turns out to be incorrect for a number of parameters, it still holds for the NC parameter that it can be derived from L1 acquisition and thus should not be thought of as a linguistic primitive.

Of course, the FFFH is still programmatic in nature. It seems to make correct predictions for negation, but it should be evaluated for a number of other functional categories in order to determine its full strength. I think that the evidence provided in this paper sheds more light on how the syntactic vocabulary is created.

**Acknowledgements.** For discussion and helpful comments I want to thank Arnim von Stechow, Doris Penka, Maren Pannemann, Walter Schweikert, Wolfgang Sternefeldt, and the audiences the 6th Tbilisi Symposium on Logic, language and Computation and the Workshop on the Structure of Parametric Variation.

# References

1. Beghelli, F., Stowell, T.: Distributivity and Negation. The syntax of each and every. In: Szabolcsi, A.A. (ed.) Ways of scope taking, pp. 71–107. Kluwer Academic Publishers, Dordrecht (1997)
2. Belletti, A. (ed.): Structures and Beyond. The cartography of Syntactic Structures, vol. 3. Oxford University Press, Oxford (2004)
3. Bobaljik, J., Thrainsson, H.: Two heads aren't always better than one. Syntax 1, 37–71 (1998)
4. Borer, H.: Parametric Syntax: Case Studies in Semitic and Romance Languages. Foris, Dordrecht (1984)
5. Brown, S.: The Syntax of Negation in Russian. CSLI Publications, Stanford (1999)
6. Chomsky, N.: The minimalist program. The MIT Press, Cambridge, MA (1995)
7. Chomsky, N.: Minimalist Inquiries: the Framework. In: Martin, R., Michael, D., Uriagereka, J. (eds.) Step by Step. Essays in Honor of Howard Lasnik, pp. 89–155. The MIT Press, Cambridge, MA (2000)
8. Chomsky, N.: Derivation by Phase. In: Kenstowicz, M. (ed.) Ken Hale: a Life in Language, pp. 1–52. The MIT Press, Cambridge, MA (2001)
9. Cinqe, G.: Adverbs and functional heads. Oxford University Press, Oxford (1999)
10. Cinque, G. (ed.): Functional structure in DP and IP. The cartography of Syntactic Structures, vol. 1. Oxford University Press, Oxford (2002)
11. De Swart, H., Sag, I.: Negative Concord in Romance. Linguistics & Philosophy 25, 373–417 (2002)
12. von Fintel, K.: The formal semantics of grammaticalization. NELS 25, 175–189 (1995)
13. Giannakidou, A.: The landscape of polarity items. PhD Dissertation, University of Groningen (1997)
14. Giannakidou, A.: Negative ... Concord? Natural Language and Linguistic Theory 18, 457–523 (2000)

15. Giannakidou, A.: N-words and Negative Concord. In: Everaert, M., Goedeman, R., Van Riemsdijk, H. (eds.) The Syntax Companion, vol. III, Blackwell, London (2006)
16. Giorgi, A., Pianesi, F.: Tense and aspect: from semantics to morphosyntax. Oxford University Press, Oxford (1997)
17. Grimshaw, K.: Projections, heads and optimality. Linguistic Inquiry 28(1997), 373–442 (1997)
18. Haegeman, L., Zanuttini, R.: Negative Concord in West Flemish. In: Belletti, A., Rizzi, L. (eds.) Parameters and Functional Heads. Essays in Comparative Syntax, pp. 117–179. Oxford University Press, Oxford (1996)
19. Hiraiwa, K.: Multiple Agreement and the Defective Interventione Effect. Ms. MIT Press, Cambridge (2001)
20. Hiraiwa, K.: Dimensions in Syntax. Ms. University of Tokyo (2005)
21. Herburger, E.: The negative concord puzzle revisited. Natural Language Semantics 9, 289–333 (2001)
22. Iatridou, S.: About AgrP. Linguistic Inquiry 21, 421–459 (1990)
23. Jespersen, O.: Negation in English. Host, Copenhagen (1917)
24. Keenan, E., Stabler, E.: Bare Grammar, lectures on linguistic invariants. CSLI Publications, Stanford (2003)
25. Koeneman, O.: The Flexible Nature of Verb Movement. PhD. Dissertation Utrecht University (2000)
26. Ladusaw, W.A.: Expressing negation. In: Barker, C., Dowty, D. (eds.) SALT II, Cornell Linguistic Circle, Cornell (1992)
27. Jonckbloet, W.J.A. (ed.): Roman van Lancelot (XIIIe eeuw). Naar het (eenig-bekende) handschrift der Koninklijke Bibliotheek, op gezag van het gouvernement uitgegeven. 's-Gravenhage (1846-1849). In: Van Oostrom, F. (ed.) Middelnederlands. SDU, Den Haag (1998), CD-ROM
28. Laka, I.: Negation in Syntax: on the Nature of Functional Categories and Projections. PhD dissertation, MIT (1990)
29. Merchant, J.: Why no(t). Ms. University of Chicago (2001)
30. Neeleman, A., Van der Koot, H.: The Configurational Matrix. Linguistic Inquiry 33, 529–574 (2002)
31. Newmeyer, F.: Typological Evidence and Universal Grammar. Studies in language 28, 527–548 (2004)
32. Ogihara, T.: The Semantics of Tense in Embedded Clauses. Linguistic Inquiry 26, 663–679 (1995)
33. Ouhalla, J.: Functional categories and parametric variation. Routledge, London, New York (1991)
34. Pollock, J.-Y.: Verb Movement, Universal Grammar, and the Structure of IP. Linguistic Inquiry 20, 365–424 (1989)
35. Rowlett, P.: Sentential Negation in French. Oxford University Press, Oxford (1998)
36. Rizzi, L.: Null Objects in Italian and the Theory of pro. Linguistic Inquiry 17, 501–557 (1986)
37. Rizzi, L.: The fine structure of the left periphery. In: Haegeman, L. (ed.) Elements of grammar: Handbook in generative syntax, pp. 281–337. Kluwer, Dordrecht (1997)
38. Rizzi, L. (ed.): The structure of CP and IP, The cartography of Syntactic Structures, vol. 2. Oxford University Press, Oxford (2002)
39. Roberts, I., Roussou, A.: Syntactic Change. A Minimalist Approach to Grammaticalisation. Cambridge University Press, Cambridge (2003)

40. Starke, M.: On the Inexistence of Specifiers and the Nature of Heads. In: Belletti, A. (ed.) Structures and Beyond. The cartography of Syntactic Structures, vol. 3, pp. 252–268. Oxford University Press, Oxford (2004)

41. von Stechow, A.: Semantisches und morhologisches Tempus: Zur temoralen Orientierung vonm Einstellungen und Modalen. Neue Beiträge zur Germanistik 4, 3–6 (2005)

42. von Stechow, A.: Types of iF/uF agreement. Ms. University of Tuebingen (2006)

43. Ura, H.: Multiple Feature-Checking: A Theory of Grammatical Function Splitting. PhD Dissertation, MIT (1996)

44. Zanuttini, R.: Syntactic Properties of Sentential Negation. PhD Dissertation, University of Pennsylvania (1991)

45. Zanuttini, R.: Negation and clausal structure. A Comparative Study of Romance languages, Oxford studies in comparative syntax. Oxford University Press, Oxford (1997a)

46. Zanuttini, R.: Negation and verb movement. In: Haegeman, L. (ed.) Elements of grammar: Handbook in generative syntax, pp. 214–245. Kluwer, Dordrecht (1997b)

47. Zanuttini, R.: Sentential Negation. In: Baltin, M., Collins, C. (eds.) The Handbook of Contemporary Syntactic Theory, pp. 511–535. Blackwell, London (2001)

48. Zeijlstra, H.: Sentential Negation and Negative Concord. LOT Publications, Utrecht (2004)

49. Zeijlstra, H.: Functional structure, formal features and parametric variation: consequences of conflicting interface condition. Ms. University of Tuebingen (2006)

50. Zwicky, A., Pullum, G.: Clitisazition vs. Inflection: English n't. Language 59, 502–513 (1983)

# Author Index

# Lecture Notes in Artificial Intelligence (LNAI)

Vol. 4562: D. Harris (Ed.), Engineering Psychology and Cognitive Ergonomics. XXIII, 879 pages. 2007.

Vol. 4548: N. Olivetti (Ed.), Automated Reasoning with Analytic Tableaux and Related Methods. X, 245 pages. 2007.

Vol. 4539: N.H. Bshouty, C. Gentile (Eds.), Learning Theory. XII, 634 pages. 2007.

Vol. 4529: P. Melin, O. Castillo, L.T. Aguilar, J. Kacprzyk, W. Pedrycz (Eds.), Foundations of Fuzzy Logic and Soft Computing. XIX, 830 pages. 2007.

Vol. 4520: M.V. Butz, O. Sigaud, G. Pezzulo, G. Baldassarre (Eds.), Anticipatory Behavior in Adaptive Learning Systems. X, 379 pages. 2007.

Vol. 4511: C. Conati, K. McCoy, G. Paliouras (Eds.), User Modeling 2007. XVI, 487 pages. 2007.

Vol. 4509: Z. Kobti, D. Wu (Eds.), Advances in Artificial Intelligence. XII, 552 pages. 2007.

Vol. 4496: N.T. Nguyen, A. Grzech, R.J. Howlett, L.C. Jain (Eds.), Agent and Multi-Agent Systems: Technologies and Applications. XXI, 1046 pages. 2007.

Vol. 4483: C. Baral, G. Brewka, J. Schlipf (Eds.), Logic Programming and Nonmonotonic Reasoning. IX, 327 pages. 2007.

Vol. 4482: A. An, J. Stefanowski, S. Ramanna, C.J. Butz, W. Pedrycz, G. Wang (Eds.), Rough Sets, Fuzzy Sets, Data Mining and Granular Computing. XIV, 585 pages. 2007.

Vol. 4481: J. Yao, P. Lingras, W.-Z. Wu, M. Szczuka, N.J. Cercone, D. Ślęzak (Eds.), Rough Sets and Knowledge Technology. XIV, 576 pages. 2007.

Vol. 4476: V. Gorodetsky, C. Zhang, V.A. Skormin, L. Cao (Eds.), Autonomous Intelligent Systems: Multi-Agents and Data Mining. XIII, 323 pages. 2007.

Vol. 4456: Y. Wang, Y.-m. Cheung, H. Liu (Eds.), Computational Intelligence and Security. XXIII, 1118 pages. 2007.

Vol. 4455: S. Muggleton, R. Otero, A. Tamaddoni-Nezhad (Eds.), Inductive Logic Programming. XII, 456 pages. 2007.

Vol. 4452: M. Fasli, O. Shehory (Eds.), Agent-Mediated Electronic Commerce. VIII, 249 pages. 2007.

Vol. 4451: T.S. Huang, A. Nijholt, M. Pantic, A. Pentland (Eds.), Artifical Intelligence for Human Computing. XVI, 359 pages. 2007.

Vol. 4441: C. Müller (Ed.), Speaker Classification. X, 309 pages. 2007.

Vol. 4438: L. Maicher, A. Sigel, L.M. Garshol (Eds.), Leveraging the Semantics of Topic Maps. X, 257 pages. 2007.

Vol. 4434: G. Lakemeyer, E. Sklar, D.G. Sorrenti, T. Takahashi (Eds.), RoboCup 2006: Robot Soccer World Cup X. XIII, 566 pages. 2007.

Vol. 4429: R. Lu, J.H. Siekmann, C. Ullrich (Eds.), Cognitive Systems. X, 161 pages. 2007.

Vol. 4428: S. Edelkamp, A. Lomuscio (Eds.), Model Checking and Artificial Intelligence. IX, 185 pages. 2007.

Vol. 4426: Z.-H. Zhou, H. Li, Q. Yang (Eds.), Advances in Knowledge Discovery and Data Mining. XXV, 1161 pages. 2007.

Vol. 4411: R.H. Bordini, M. Dastani, J. Dix, A.E.F. Seghrouchni (Eds.), Programming Multi-Agent Systems. XIV, 249 pages. 2007.

Vol. 4410: A. Branco (Ed.), Anaphora: Analysis, Algorithms and Applications. X, 191 pages. 2007.

Vol. 4399: T. Kovacs, X. Llorà, K. Takadama, P.L. Lanzi, W. Stolzmann, S.W. Wilson (Eds.), Learning Classifier Systems. XII, 345 pages. 2007.

Vol. 4390: S.O. Kuznetsov, S. Schmidt (Eds.), Formal Concept Analysis. X, 329 pages. 2007.

Vol. 4389: D. Weyns, H. Van Dyke Parunak, F. Michel (Eds.), Environments for Multi-Agent Systems III. X, 273 pages. 2007.

Vol. 4386: P. Noriega, J. Vázquez-Salceda, G. Boella, O. Boissier, V. Dignum, N. Fornara, E. Matson (Eds.), Coordination, Organizations, Institutions, and Norms in Agent Systems II. XI, 373 pages. 2007.

Vol. 4384: T. Washio, K. Satoh, H. Takeda, A. Inokuchi (Eds.), New Frontiers in Artificial Intelligence. IX, 401 pages. 2007.

Vol. 4371: K. Inoue, K. Satoh, F. Toni (Eds.), Computational Logic in Multi-Agent Systems. X, 315 pages. 2007.

Vol. 4369: M. Umeda, A. Wolf, O. Bartenstein, U. Geske, D. Seipel, O. Takata (Eds.), Declarative Programming for Knowledge Management. X, 229 pages. 2006.

Vol. 4363: B.D. ten Cate, H.W. Zeevat (Eds.), Logic, Language, and Computation. XII, 281 pages. 2007.

Vol. 4343: C. Müller (Ed.), Speaker Classification I. X, 355 pages. 2007.

Vol. 4342: H. de Swart, E. Orłowska, G. Schmidt, M. Roubens (Eds.), Theory and Applications of Relational Structures as Knowledge Instruments II. X, 373 pages. 2006.

Vol. 4335: S.A. Brueckner, S. Hassas, M. Jelasity, D. Yamins (Eds.), Engineering Self-Organising Systems. XII, 212 pages. 2007.

Vol. 4334: B. Beckert, R. Hähnle, P.H. Schmitt (Eds.), Verification of Object-Oriented Software. XXIX, 658 pages. 2007.

Vol. 4333: U. Reimer, D. Karagiannis (Eds.), Practical Aspects of Knowledge Management. XII, 338 pages. 2006.

Vol. 4327: M. Baldoni, U. Endriss (Eds.), Declarative Agent Languages and Technologies IV. VIII, 257 pages. 2006.

Vol. 4314: C. Freksa, M. Kohlhase, K. Schill (Eds.), KI 2006: Advances in Artificial Intelligence. XII, 458 pages. 2007.

Vol. 4304: A. Sattar, B.-h. Kang (Eds.), AI 2006: Advances in Artificial Intelligence. XXVII, 1303 pages. 2006.

Vol. 4303: A. Hoffmann, B.-h. Kang, D. Richards, S. Tsumoto (Eds.), Advances in Knowledge Acquisition and Management. XI, 259 pages. 2006.